Boston's Immigrants

1790–1880

Boston's Immigrants

A STUDY IN ACCULTURATION

Revised and Enlarged Edition

OSCAR HANDLIN

THE BELKNAP PRESS OF

HARVARD UNIVERSITY PRESS

Cambridge, Massachusetts

London, England

Copyright © *1941, 1959, 1979, by the President and*
Fellows of Harvard College
Copyright © *1969 by Oscar Handlin*

10   9   8   7   6   5

Library of Congress Catalog Card Number 59-7653
ISBN 0-674-07985-x (paper)
ISBN 0-674-07980-9 (cloth)
Printed in the United States of America

TO

MY MOTHER AND FATHER

Preface to the 1979 Edition

IN 1959 when the second edition of this book appeared, urbanism was not yet a discrete field of historical inquiry; nor was ethnicity. Nor had historians defined distinct modes of relating politics or religion to the city and to immigration. In 1941 when the first edition appeared those developments were even farther away.

Since then, progress and the social sciences have freed historians from traditional notions about cities, politics, religion, and ethnicity. Yet the attentive reader who compares the contents of this book with the claims for advance in the promotional essays of the 1970s will discover disconcerting evidence of similarity.*

How was it that back in those primitive days before liberation at the hands of anthropologists, sociologists, and statisticians one historian was able to treat the precise subjects which in 1978 seemed to have an entirely novel aspect? A work which finds more readers and sells more copies almost forty years after publication than it did in its entire first printing must have some durable quality about it.

*See for example Timothy L. Smith, "New Approaches to the Study of Immigration in Twentieth-Century America," *American Historical Review*, 71 (1965–66), 1265 ff., and "Religion and Ethnicity in America," *ibid.*, 83 (December 1978), 155 ff.

Preface to the 1979 Edition

Boston's Immigrants was volume 50 of the Harvard Historical Studies. Volume 48 was the *Reign of King Pym* by J. H. Hexter. Volume 49 was *A Wavering Friendship: Russia and Austria, 1876–1878* by George Hoover Rupp. Volume 51 was *Public Opinion Propaganda and Politics in Eighteenth Century England* by Thomas W. Perry. Volume 52 was *The Revolutionary Committees in the Departments of France* by J. B. Sirich. In other words, *Boston's Immigrants* was not written or published with regard to immediate criteria of social relevance or of its relationship to the social sciences. It was a work of history, of a piece with the other distinguished volumes in the series within which it appeared. That it was later to be taken up and read by a wider public had nothing to do with the mode of its composition. But the mode of its composition did have something to do with its durability. The fact that it was written as a monograph based on the documentary evidence, freed it of pressure from the fads and fashions of 1941 and permits it still to speak in 1979.

O. H.
March 1979
Cambridge

Foreword

Not of the mighty! not of the world's friends
Have I aspired to speak within these leaves;
These best befit their joyful kindred pens —
My path lies where a broken people grieves. . . .[1]

THE origins of a social process of any importance must be sought "in the internal constitution of the social *milieu.*"[2] The character of the environment — the community in its broadest sense — is particularly important in the study of the contact of dissimilar cultures. It is the field where unfamiliar groups meet, discover each other, and join in a hard relationship that results in either acculturation or conflict. As such, the qualities of the environment subtly condition all the forces involved and often exercise a determining influence upon their evolution.

Only by considering immigrant adjustment on the local scale can the influence of the *milieu* be given full weight. Comprehending that, the practical sociologists heretofore most directly concerned with these matters have produced a number of excellent community studies. But since restrictive legislation has pushed the immigration problem into his sphere, the historian now faces the primary obligation of analyzing it. In the study of the community, however, he meets peculiar difficulties. Lacking the sociologist's or anthropologist's direct access to the subject by questionnaires or observation, he must piece together his story from widely diversified sources, and, tethered within the limits of that which is known, impale upon a rigid page the intimate lives and deepest feelings of humble men and women who leave behind few formal records.

Between 1790 and 1880, thousands of these humble men and women transferred their residences to Boston. This study describes historically their settlement in the community. From a consideration of the society the immigrants * found on arrival and the society they left behind, it attempts to explore the basic factors influencing their economic, physical, and intellectual adjustment, and seeks in the character of that adjustment the forces promoting or discouraging group consciousness and group conflict.

This work thus extends into a "relatively unformulated field of social science." Working in a poorly charted field, I was fortunate to be able to draw upon the friendly guidance and stimulating advice of Arthur Meier Schlesinger, who has in his own work done much to widen the scope of the historical discipline and to break down the parochial boundaries between the various social sciences. Mr. Schlesinger suggested the subject of the doctoral dissertation of which this study is an outgrowth and carefully criticized each step of its progress. Only those who have profited similarly from his guidance can truly appreciate the impelling drive that comes from his conscientious teaching and from the stimulus of his vigorous scholarship. More important, contact with a deeply

* "Immigrant" refers, in this study, to persons of whatever nationality who transferred their residence to Boston from outside it, though primary attention is directed to newcomers from Europe.

human personality revealed the realm of history that transcends immediate questions of techniques and the accumulation of material, and lies in the sphere of the understanding.

At the close of a long task it is good to remember the assistance from many sources that lightened the inevitable drudgeries of research. Much of this work was carried on under scholarships and fellowships offered by the Department of History and the Graduate School of Arts and Sciences at Harvard University for which I am deeply grateful. The criticisms of many kind friends clarified a host of problems. Paul H. Buck read the entire manuscript twice, and Hans Rosenberg, David V. Glass, and Samuel J. Hurwitz let me profit from their opinions on various sections. The late Marcus L. Hansen was free with his advice in a field of which he was master. Robert D. White assisted me with the drawings. George O'Brien helped me find my way in the Irish materials; Father Thomas T. McAvoy allowed me to use the Brownson papers; Father John Sexton made available the files of the *Pilot* in St. John's Ecclesiastical Seminary before those were microfilmed; and the custodians of all the libraries mentioned on page 266 cheerfully allowed me to use their collections.

And I owe a particular debt to Mary Flug Handlin for devoted collaboration.

O. H.

Cambridge, Massachusetts
September, 1941

Contents

ILLUSTRATIONS

Illustrations

TABLES

xvi

Tables

∽ I ∽

Social Boston

1790–1845

There is a city in our world upon which the light of the sun of righteousness has risen. There is a sun which beams in its full meridian splendour upon it. Its influences are quickening and invigorating the souls which dwell within it. It is the same from which every pure stream of thought and purpose and perform-ance emanates. It is the city that is set on high. "It cannot be hid." It is Boston. The morality of Boston is more pure than that of any other city in America.[1]

THE Boston merchants who with their allies masqueraded as Indians and flavored the waters about Griffin's Wharf with the fine strong tea of the East India Company were scarcely aware that in protecting their immediate interests they were destroying the foundations of their prosperity. Few realized that the impending breach between the Crown and its colonies was to widen steadily in the following two years, and lead inevitably to separation; and even fewer foresaw the full economic implications of separation. There was a blustering bravado about these men, a feeling of self-confidence, engendered by years of smuggling in defiance of royal officials, which enabled them to speak bravely enough of independence. But all too soon, they understood that they themselves would suffer most thereby.

For normally, before 1763, Boston functioned as an integral part of the British imperial system, subsisting largely by reason of her position as purveyor of rum to Africa and of slaves to the West Indies in the great triangular traffic. This had been the keystone of her economy ever since John Winthrop had warned her to "look out to the West Indies for a trade." [2] All her commerce was concentrated in it; she had not even the "bread trade" with which a fertile back country had endowed New York and Philadelphia. Even Boston's industry, consisting either in the conversion of West Indian sugar into rum or, to a considerable extent, in the manufacture of naval stores to outfit ships, was involved directly or indirectly in this commerce. With the possible exception of fishing, there was but one other important source where the Boston merchants might seek profits — in the evasion of duties accepted elsewhere. That smuggling was an activity of long standing in the Bay Colony finds ample confirmation in the plaintive reports of John Randolph. [3] But after 1763 the attempts to introduce the "new colonial system" inordinately stimulated such enterprises; as Boston's position in the trade with the islands weakened, merchants shifted to the principal alternative open to them. [4]

Reforms in the collection of revenue and revision of duties downward, however, rendered even illicit profits precarious, and drove the traders into the hazardous course of revolution. [5] The independence that followed destroyed the city's principal occupations. Commerce languished under

2

hostile British legislation, while sharply curtailed imports and an efficient customs service rendered smuggling both unprofitable and impracticable. By a series of acts culminating in that of 1788, the English reserved the trade of their colonies for their own bottoms. The rejection by Congress of Article XII of Jay's Treaty nullified the few British concessions and completely eliminated the possibility of reviving trade with the West Indies. For some time vestiges of commerce with the French and Spanish islands persisted, but, because of the turmoil of the war years 1791–1815, always sporadically and uncertainly. The prohibition of the slave trade and, finally, the abolition of slavery in the British possessions, removed an essential commodity and ended any hopes that might have remained for the restoration of the triangular traffic.[6]

Independence also destroyed Boston's share in the direct trade between England and the North American continent. The Orders in Council of 1783 limited imports from America to naval stores and a few other commodities. The government of Massachusetts retaliated with prohibitive duties on English shipping. But since no other state did likewise, commerce merely shifted to other American ports. As a result, the English could boast that "the 600,000 tonnage of shipping usually employed in that trade are now entirely English bottoms whereas before they were nearly one-half American."[7]

The resultant decrease in Boston's business threatened to continue indefinitely.[8] But there were providential turnings in the ways of commerce; and eventually the merchants recouped their losses in new markets. Profits from privateering and from neutral trading tided them over while they vigorously pursued the quest for unknown trade routes. Venturesome Boston skippers, pushing their boats down the South Atlantic and through the Straits, traced the first of these and founded the great China trade. Although New York and Salem had made contact with the Orient in the 1780's, trade had been handicapped at first by the absence of a commodity for which there was a demand in China. But on August 9, 1790, the *Columbia,* captained by Robert Gray, returned from a three-year voyage in which she had circumnavigated the globe, with the news that furs, which brought so high a price in the river marts of Canton, could be acquired for trifling trinkets along the coast of Oregon. This discovery effected a revolution in Boston's economic prospects; by 1792 a new triangular traffic was well established. Carrying cargoes of copper, cloth, iron, and clothes, ships left the city each autumn, arriving at the Columbia River the following spring. There they remained from eighteen to twenty months, bargaining their wares for furs. Then they were off across the Pacific, generally stopping at the Sandwich Islands (Hawaii) for sandalwood, or at California to make illicit deals with the Spaniards. In Canton, they disposed of their stock, and, by way of the Cape of Good Hope, returned with Chinese teas, textiles and porcelain. Bostonians rushed into this enormously profitable trade so quickly that among the Chinooks and other West Coast Indians "Boston-men" soon became synonymous with Americans.[9]

At about the same time, the foundations were laid for a new triangular trade with Russia in which Bostonians exchanged West Indian sugar for linens and iron. This business developed such proportions during the troubled period of the continental blockade, when the Czar permitted "the free admission of nankin in Russian ports," that Bostonians declared John Quincy Adams' mission to Saint Petersburg "of the utmost importance to the commerce of the United States, and the most honorable appointment abroad that is in the gift of our government. . . ." [10]

Although commerce with China and Russia lasted throughout this period, it encountered serious obstacles arising out of the fact that Boston was never more than an entrepôt. All the essential commodities of this trade were drawn from far-off ports as accessible to other cities as to Boston. Based upon the enterprise and initiative of Boston merchants rather than upon the city's advantageous position or natural resources, this commerce had no permanent or durable roots. The prosperity arising from it was superficial and temporary, confined largely to those immediately engaged in it. Its uncertainty became especially apparent in the 1820's when Chinese exports shifted almost exclusively to tea, for which New York was a better market than Boston, and in the 1830's when the supply of northwest furs began to fall off.[11] To some extent, cheap textiles from the Merrimac replaced otter skins from the Columbia, but Lowell and Lawrence could not compete with Manchester and Birmingham. Thereafter Boston's position declined steadily and only the extension of the ice trade to the Far East in the same decade saved the Boston merchants from complete collapse.[12]

A staple product for export, or a wide New England market for imports, alone could firmly ground the roots of trade in Boston's economic life; and both depended upon the back country. But while the hinterland of the other great ports —

New York, Philadelphia, Baltimore, and New Orleans — constantly expanded, Boston's was contracting. Trade with the backwoods of Connecticut and Massachusetts whence had come a limited number of agricultural staples, and, to a certain extent, with the Maine and New Hampshire forests from which were drawn the timber and naval stores for old and New England, had never been important as compared with the triangular traffic, and had declined after 1790.[13] The completion of the Erie Canal in 1825 immediately diverted the produce of large sections of western Massachusetts to New York and ultimately established a link between that city and the fertile plains of the trans-Allegheny west which all the subsequent efforts of commercial Boston proved incapable of breaking.[14] Geographically, Boston could not profit by the use of canals. The only rivers in Massachusetts that might be used advantageously were the Connecticut, the Blackstone, and the Merrimac. But the first two would benefit Hartford or Providence, and, indirectly New York; the third, Portsmouth.[15] Even the advent of the railroads, despite Boston's pioneer role, brought no solution. Contemporaries soon pointed out that *"Boston* is not a thriving, that is, not an increasing town. It wants a fertile back country, and it is too far removed from the western states to be engaged in the supply of that new and vast emporium. . . ." [16]

Bostonians had not failed to realize that "the city is derived from the country" and ever since 1791, when they projected a canal to Worcester, Massachusetts legislators had sought to extend the back country.[17] The Erie Canal forced upon the state the realization that "some decisive measures are *necessary* to facilitate the intercourse between Boston and . . .

6

Albany," and a railroad was recommended.[18] But not until 1831 was the first line chartered in Massachusetts, and not until 1835 was the first ready for traffic. Although the Western Railroad opened in December, 1841, Bostonians proved singularly inept in the management of their own affairs, and not until after the Civil War was there a direct connection between the Boston wharves and Chicago. By that time the other great ports had already effected permanent contact with the west and had preëmpted its trade.[19]

For a time, tremendous expansion in the industrial hinterland compensated for Boston's shrinking agricultural environs. The period directly following the War of 1812 witnessed the amazing growth of textile centers at Lowell, Fall River, and the mill towns of the Merrimac. For these factories and for the shoe industries about Lynn, Boston became the entrepôt through which goods flowed to all quarters of the continent. On the basis of these enterprises, a flourishing coasting business in which shoes and cotton goods were exchanged for corn and cotton developed with the south.[20] Ultimately, this trade too acquired triangular features. The excess cotton from the slave-tilled fields of the south which New England mills could not absorb found a ready market in Liverpool, and the transatlantic leg of the process tended to become increasingly important.[21] Eventually, however, Boston's failure to develop links to the hinterland undermined her position as carrier even for New England manufacturers. These found it more profitable to exchange their products in New York for the wheat of the west and the cotton of the south already being brought there. Following the trend, many Boston merchants like the Tappans set up

7

branches in New York, and many more sent their ships to swell the commerce that flowed up the Hudson.[22] In this trade, as elsewhere, Boston's commerce rested upon an extremely uncertain base, though it grew steadily if not sensationally.[23]

Nevertheless, the resultant prosperity, though impermanent and derived from external sources, had an important effect upon the city's integral economic life; it made Boston a powerful financial center and the greatest money market in America in these years, its "available capital . . . being even greater than that of New York." [24] Previously, some surplus funds had accrued from land, particularly from real estate within the city limits, and some, from amassment started in the colonial period — though on a rather small scale. But, essentially, Boston capital blossomed forth in the federal period in the fortunes of the China princes whose risky ventures yielded large profits in lump unsteady sums which could not be immediately reinvested.[25]

This surplus led to a phenomenal development in banking which continued to the Civil War in spite of successive depressions. In 1790 Boston had only one bank. By 1800 she had three — a branch of the Bank of the United States, the Union Bank, and the Massachusetts Bank — with a combined capital of less than $2,000,000. The last named had been uniformly successful since its foundation in 1784, often paying as much as 16 per cent interest on its capital of $300,000.[26] After the War of 1812 growth was sensational: in the decade 1810–20 six new banks were incorporated with a combined capital of $8,500,000. Thereafter, in a startling spurt, there were six new incorporations in 1822, three in 1825, two in

1826, one in 1827, six in 1828, six in 1831, six in 1832, five in 1833, and sixteen new incorporations or expansions in 1836 alone. By 1830 Boston was second only to New York in financial strength and resources, and, when the panic of 1837 intervened, was ready to surpass her rival. Progress in the following years, while not as extraordinary, continued steadily until the panic of 1857 and the Civil War upset the money market.[27]

These huge resources, seeking an outlet, promoted the development of industry and transportation in the interior of Massachusetts in the decades following the War of 1812. Between 1780 and 1840, some 2,254 corporations were founded in the state with an aggregate capital of $238,139,222.66, largely raised in Boston. Of these, by far the most important were those devoted to manufacturing. The power of $100,-000,000 of Boston money gave Boston capitalists a solid grip upon the factories of Haverhill, of Waltham, of Lowell, and of Fall River, from which they drew a steady stream of dividends.[28] Their money also sponsored great railroads, first across Massachusetts and New England, and finally across the whole continent.[29]

However, while Boston capital built great industries outside of Boston, it failed to develop them at home. In 1790 Boston was a village of small artisans and handicraftsmen, its industry centered in the need for satisfying the home market. Tailors and cobblers, butchers and grocers, went about the business of feeding and clothing the Bostonians much as they had a hundred years earlier. Whatever other enterprise there was, grew out of and was subsidiary to the commercial activities of the city. Chandlers and ropemakers, duck weav-

9

ers and sparmakers there were, but of autonomous industrial activity there was no sign.[30] A boom in shipbuilding in the 1790's soon collapsed, and Boston was replaced by the towns of the lower Merrimac and the North River, not regaining her position as the shipbuilder for Massachusetts until well into the 1840's when Donald McKay began to mold the trim figures of his clipper ships in the East Boston yards of Enoch Train.[31]

Even in 1845, whatever industry existed in the city was small in scale and local in character. By far the majority of those engaged in industry at that date were employed either in establishments of ten or less or were unclassifiable, that is, worked in their homes.[32] In 1845, the whole number of industrial workers, including the last group, was less than 10,-000 in a population of 165,000.[33] Only the manufacture of glass and of iron, which needed considerable labor and lacked the inventions which made possible a mechanized factory system located in the suburbs of Boston.[34]

Two factors caused Boston capitalists to invest their money not in Boston, but in the new towns around it. In the first place, in at least two major industries inventions had not yet enabled the factory system to replace the domestic or putting-out system which operated most economically in rural districts. Thus Miss Martineau found that "shoe-making at Lynn is carried on almost entirely in private dwellings, from the circumstance that the people who do it are almost all farmers or fishermen likewise. . . . The whole family works . . . during the winter; and in the summer the father and sons turn out into the fields, or go fishing." [35] The towns near Boston "attracted masons, carpenters and other workmen, in the winter season, when their own professions were dull, to pursue shoemaking. . . ." [36] This system also characterized the manufacture of ready-made clothing and shirts, in which the sewing was given out in all parts of New England to women who worked for pin-money in spare moments.[37]

Even industries in which the factory system prevailed did not flourish in Boston. Machines depended upon water power, for the fee simple of a good site "would not cost the annual expense of a steam engine." [38] Yet despite the efforts of Uriah Cotting and other Bostonians to harness the Mill Dam for manufacturing, the swift waters of the Merrimac and the upper Charles offered superior attractions. Furthermore, Boston offered no advantages as to labor supply. Within the city there were no appreciable numbers of men ready and willing to work at wages low enough to foster the establishment of profitable new enterprises. But in the country areas, farm girls whose families found it increasingly difficult to eke a living out of the hard New England soil, gladly spent a few years in the mills before marriage in order to help out financially at home, and to gather a dowry as well. More tractable, more exploitable, and more plentiful than any labor source then in Boston, they stimulated the diversion of capital away from the city.

Except for fishing, which fluctuated in significance and never in this period became as important as elsewhere in Massachusetts, there was no other economic activity of any proportions.[39] Boston remained in 1845 a town of small traders, of petty artisans and handicraftsmen, and of great merchant princes who built fortunes out of their "enterprise, intelligence, and frugality," and used the city as a base for their far-flung activities.⁴⁰ Commercially, Boston's foundations were unstable, and the eastern trade which constituted the whole of its glittering superstructure had already slipped into a decline. Industrially, there seemed little to look forward to, for large-scale ventures failed to locate there. The field of handicrafts was limited and the prospects of the agricultural environs of Boston were meager indeed.⁴¹

As against the promise of the broad fields and the new cities of the west and south, Boston offered few opportunities to those who lacked the twin advantages of birth and capital. Enterprising young men who made no headway chose to depart, and led a steady stream of emigration from the city. Although to observers it seemed the most homogeneous American community, throughout this period the proportion of native Bostonians was actually dwindling. By 1850, only half the descendants of the Bostonians of 1820 still lived there. Consequently, Boston receded steadily from its third place in 1790 on the roster of American cities. Although its absolute numbers increased slowly, its rate of growth was small compared to that of its rivals. And that its population did not decline absolutely was due in fact, not to the maintenance of its native stock, or to migrations from abroad, but to incursions in the 1820's and 1830's from the depressed rural areas of New England.⁴²

Though wealth stimulated only finance and banking in Boston, it nevertheless was put to interest there in many other ways. The merchant's contact with the world exerted a profound influence upon the whole social character of the city, transforming it from John Hancock's theaterless town of 1790 to the gracious cosmopolitan Hub of Ticknor and

Bancroft in 1845. Absence of business activity and of heavy industries requiring a large proletariat obviated the development of slums and blighted areas. And windfall money fortuitously acquired was benevolently parted with for urban improvements. The enhancement of the city accentuated Bostonians' civic consciousness and pride. They seriously accepted their responsibilities as citizens and actively concerned themselves with solving municipal problems.

In 1790 Bulfinch's Pillar replaced the old Beacon Hill light, blown down the preceding year, initiating a process which levelled the three heights of Beacon Hill, nibbled at the fastness of Fort Hill, filled in the old Mill Pond with their sands, threw the famous Mill Dam across the sluggish waters of the Back Bay, doubled the town's area by filling in flats along its waterfront, and united it with its neighbors by a row of sturdy bridges. Levelling the hills was primarily a matter of real estate investments, as was the filling of the Mill Pond. The Mill Dam united a project to benefit by tolls and to utilize the waters of the Back Bay for industrial purposes. The bridges across the Charles and the ferry to East Boston likewise were constructed by men who hoped to make money from tolls, as was the South Boston Bridge, whose projectors counted as well on the rise in value of South Boston land. But these enterprises, though privately conceived and carried out, were built with an eye to the betterment of the city and contributed toward making it a handsomer and more spacious place to live in.[43]

This period saw the extension of the social boundaries of Boston far beyond the political limits of 1790 or even of 1845. During these fifty years six peripheral towns were gradually swept into the vortex of Boston life. In 1790, five — Brighton, Brookline, Cambridge, Dorchester, and Roxbury — were purely agricultural villages, no more connected with Boston than similar communities in Worcester and Berkshire counties. Even Charlestown, in parts of which the beginnings of town life existed, remained primarily rural. In the succeeding decades, however, urban Boston spread beyond the confines of its original narrow peninsula. Since even the reclamation of land from the Bay did not accommodate the city's needs, many Bostonians moved off to the outskirts where house rents were half those in Boston proper, abandoning their homes to the mounting number of hotels, offices, and blocks of stores. As transportation improved and commutation tickets became available at twenty to forty dollars a year, the number of those working in Boston but living elsewhere increased, and the tie between the city and suburbs grew closer.[44]

As a result, Boston absorbed sections of each town socially, whether or not they remained politically intact. South Boston was annexed, and East Boston and the South Cove were developed through the cupidity of real estate speculators.[45] Though attempts at political assimilation by Boston in 1834 failed, the urban portions of Charlestown were soon divorced from Somerville.[46] By 1845 the agricultural areas of Chelsea formed a new township, North Chelsea, leaving the urban districts to the metropolis. In the same way, East Cambridge became distinct from Cambridge, and Roxbury from West Roxbury. Within a decade, Washington Village was torn from Dorchester, and even distant Dedham felt the influence of Boston's proximity. By 1845, Boston had outgrown her

14

charter limits, for its map expanded as rapidly as its face changed.[47]

A geographic redistribution of population accompanied the physical transformation. In 1790 Boston was a small, closely-knit town any part of which was easily reached by foot. The traders lived fairly close to their counting houses and could conveniently return home for the mid-day dinner. There was no great gap between classes, and therefore no desire for sectional distribution. But as the town grew, as the well-to-do became wealthy, and as the outlying districts became more accessible, the people spread out and at the same time were localized in distinctive areas. The filling in of the Mill Pond to form the West End and the levelling of Beacon Hill opened the first two new vicinities. Here and in "New or West Boston" were built the homes of the merchants who gradually abandoned the old North End in the decade or so after the turn of the century. The more numerous middle-class found its outlet in the developing suburbs, first in the South End, where they forced out a small, poorer population, then in South Boston, and finally, in Roxbury and Dorchester. The humbler inhabitants lived in "nigger hill" behind the State House and in the North End, but tended to concentrate particularly about Fort Hill, the cheapest part of the city. By 1845 residential areas were well fixed. The very wealthy either remained on Beacon Hill or moved to the rural suburbs, Roxbury or Cambridge. The middle classes scattered in the South Cove, in South Boston or in the outskirts. Finally, large districts were available at low rents in the North and West Ends.[48]

Accompanying the shift in neighborhoods was a change in

housing. The homes of the upper classes still bore traces of the great flourishing of federal architecture, but the wider use of Quincy granite in the 1830's encouraged a Gothicism imitated from Europe, expressed chiefly in public buildings and churches, but also in pretentious and elaborate residences.[49] The homes of the poor, however, remained unchanged. Small, generally of one story, and built of wood, with inflammable shingle roofs, they possessed few conveniences, but usually held not more than one or two families.[50] Multiple dwellings were slow to develop because of the cheapness of land in less desirable areas. The great tenement house, therefore, was unusual in Boston during this period. There were, of course, no sanitary provisions for the very poor. But, because of the avoidance of overcrowding and diligence in prevention of disease, living was not unhealthy.

Health protection, which enjoyed a tradition of long standing, dating back at least to Cotton Mather's fight for inoculation, acquired a permanent form at the end of the eighteenth century. As a great seaport dealing with many parts of the world, Boston's most immediate need was for a quarantine against the importation of infectious diseases. However, the Board of Health, organized in 1798, acquired not only this authority, but also broad powers for protecting the city internally.[51] And soon the second function absorbed an ever larger share of the Board's attention; throughout the thirty years of its existence, it continued to cope with a host of sanitary problems whose number and complexity increased with the growth of the city. In 1802 it helped spread the results of Jenner's work with smallpox vaccination. It regulated graveyards and the burial of the dead.[52] From rudimentary beginnings in which contractors were hired to cart away rubbish, the Board developed a comprehensive system of garbage collection that served its purpose quite efficiently.[53] It also encouraged the elimination of the old cesspool method of drainage by the substitution of private systems of sewers, though public sewers had to await the inauguration of a new city government.[54]

The problem of supplying the community with a permanent, dependable and pure supply of water was not solved until the new municipal government took charge. Various makeshifts having failed, the authorities finally undertook the ambitious task of connecting a reservoir in Brookline with the waters of Lake Cochituate in Middlesex County, a project which, when completed in 1848, assured the people of their water for the next half century.[55] These precautions reflected the desire of the citizens to make Boston a better and safer place to live in, and helped make it one of the healthiest of the nineteenth-century municipalities.

The expansion of functions necessitated the substitution in 1822 of a more efficient type of administration for the archaic town forms. Until that year, the town meeting determined public policy, theoretically at least. The Board of Selectmen, the only general administrative body, had comparatively little power, and no authority over other municipal agencies, which indeed often competed and quarrelled with one another.[56] Earlier attempts at revision had been defeated by the forces of tradition, by incumbent office-holders, and by fears, persistently expressed, that the cost would be ruinously high. Nevertheless in 1822 the General Court granted a city charter under which Boston's first mayor immediately took office.[57] Under Josiah Quincy, Jr., an efficient police force replaced the old system of watch and constable.[58] But the vested interests in the fire department delayed by several years the introduction of a modernized fire-fighting force. Although a series of disastrous fires, culminating in that of April 7, 1825, on Duane Street, made possible a reorganization, the reform was far from complete, and a volunteer element persisted in the companies until 1873.[59]

The solution of one urban problem — transportation — needed no external stimulation. The city always prided itself upon its well-built and lighted streets,[60] but until the 1820's people either walked or made use of private conveyances. By 1826 traffic had become so heavy that several omnibus lines were established.[61] The first ran every other hour to Roxbury and charged a fare of nine cents each way. Its success encouraged two others from Boston to Charlestown and South Boston, and by 1845 some twenty lines carried the Bostonian about his business quickly and expeditiously.[62] At the same time, railroads developed considerable local business, hackney coaches began to flourish, and a good ferry connected East Boston with the mainland. By 1847 more than 20,000 passengers were carried in and out of the city daily.[63]

Bostonians were also awake to their responsibilities in solving the social problems which beset the modern metropolis. Poverty and pauperism, later the most pressing of these disorders, were of no great importance during this period. Despite the limited opportunities for employment, few depended upon public or private benevolence. The population was small enough and the possibility of leaving broad enough for almost anyone to find work or depart. Consequently, pauperism was nearly unknown, and was declining relative to the total population.[64]

What necessity there was for relief was met generously and competently by the municipality and private agencies. Since the state reimbursed the city for the support of those without legal residence, the city was not anxious to stint on expenditures for much of which it did not pay.[65] The Board of Overseers — a survival of the old town government — administered partial outdoor relief while the city controlled a system of institutions including a House of Industry, a House of Juvenile Reformation (1826), and a municipal lunatic asylum (1839) that took care of those completely dependent. In addition, numerous religious and charitable societies whose objectives included not only the "improvement" of the "moral state of the poor and irreligious" but also the provision of aid and work for the unemployed, supplemented public assistance.[66] In either form relief was always ample enough to justify Miss Martineau's conclusion, "I know no large city where there is so much mutual helpfulness, so little neglect and ignorance of the concerns of other classes." [67]

Comparative freedom from poverty brought comparative freedom from lawlessness. The total number of crimes was small, and increased no faster than the population, a fact attested alike by casual travelers and the research of a trained penologist.[68] Proportionally fewer persons were accused of wrong-doing than in either London or Paris, and the number sentenced for serious transgressions was about half that of Berlin during the same period. Only one Bostonian in sixty-four was brought before a police court in each year, and only one of 107 was convicted.[69] Most of the crimes were not of a grave nature, more than half being misdemeanors arising out of drunkenness, a rather disturbing problem.[70] Bostonians, like other Americans, were not sparing in their use of hard liquors, and though many were able to hold their drinks, by the 1830's drunkenness was widespread enough to beget a thriving temperance movement and numerous abstinence societies.[71]

Prostitution was the only other social problem of any importance. Its frequency seems surprising in view of the relative absence of pauperism and the strict contemporary sexual code. But this was the period in which hundreds of New England farm girls were seeking work in the city. Many, failing to find places soon enough, drifted into the readiest alternative. Thus, a social worker pointed out "the State of Maine, in this manner, furnishes a large proportion of the abandoned females in our city." [72]

On the whole, however, social conditions were exceedingly favorable. Though its sons and daughters might leave it, though its commerce might languish and its industry remain at the handicraft level, Boston was a comfortable and well-to-do city in which the people managed to lead contented and healthy lives.[73] With the utmost confidence in himself, the Bostonian could look out upon the world with an unjaundiced and optimistic eye.

This optimism was the result of more than mere personal well-being. It derived from the fundamental ideas and basic assumptions permeating the social and economic structure of the society. The self-assurance of the merchant-prince in his world suffused the community, engendering a sublime faith in "the perfection of the creation" and of man's role in it. Essentially this confidence was grounded in a complete reliance upon the efficacy of the human will and its power to transform nature and the world. "Nature is thoroughly mediate . . . ," said Emerson, "It offers all its kingdom to man as the raw material which he may mould into what is useful. Man is never weary of working it up . . . until the world becomes at last only a realized will, — the double of man." [74]

In the world of nineteenth-century Bostonians one corollary followed automatically from this assumption: man not only could, but actually was, daily raising the world to an ever-loftier level. Where a few years before there had been only a series of mud flats, there was now a thriving, bustling city. By 1845, the docks sheltered steamers that had crossed the Atlantic, and news of far-flung investments began to arrive through the new medium of the telegraph. Every aspect of daily existence confirmed an already deep-rooted conviction of progress. And this conviction was not merely one of passive acceptance. Rather, it was intensely dynamic and aggressive, driving Bostonians into "the bright and beautiful sisterhood" of reform movements — temperance, prison discipline, women's rights, and other philanthropies, all rungs in the ladder leading to the ultimate, though imminent, perfectibility.[75] Bostonians heard "the Gospel of To-Day" sound "the . . . *assured hope* of Perfect Society" [76] and

lived to the glory of God, with the definite public spirit which belongs to such life. They had . . . absolute faith that God's Kingdom was to come, and . . . saw no reason why it should not come soon.[77]

Naturally, they were democrats.[78] They gloried in the Constitution, valued its blessings, and hoped its principles would spread to all the peoples of the earth. They sympathized with the revolutionary struggles of the French, Greeks, Poles, Magyars, Italians, and Irish and, when they could, aided materially and generously.[79] Nor did they find this attitude at all incompatible with the hegemony exercised by the propertied merchant class over politics within the city,[80] for they believed that "property . . . is the surface action of internal machinery, like the index on the face of a clock," [81] an external indication of worth and ability in a community where trade was "the pendulum" regulating "all the common and authorized machinery of the place." [82] Accordingly, while Bostonians were interested in politics, they were content to leave its actual management to those who had the leisure and ability to devote to it. Indeed, an observer found,

The people here are a little aristocratical but . . . they dont trouble thereselves much about politics as money & business is their aim.[83]

To this democracy, education was a vital necessity. No visitor failed to notice the free school system of Massachusetts and the zeal with which learning was pursued throughout life.[84] The popularity of lectures, evening schools, libraries, and, most striking of all, newspapers and periodicals, bore witness to this intellectual activity. In 1826 Boston boasted twenty-eight periodicals.[85] By 1848 the number had mounted to more than 120 with an aggregate circulation of more than a half-million.[86]

Currents from Europe perpetually expanded the educational process. An increasing number of Bostonians traveled abroad and brought back with them the new ideas that were upsetting the equilibrium of Metternich's continent. With

Ticknor and Bancroft came a wave of thrilling concepts from Germany, while French and English contacts of long standing exercised continuous influence, so that the young men who grew up in the thirties found themselves "married to *Europa*." [87] Few resented these imported ideas. Rather, they agreed with Ezra Gannett that,

Every packet ship . . . brings . . . the thought and feeling which prevail there, to be added to our stock of ideas and sentiments. We welcome each new contribution. We read and reprint foreign literature, we copy foreign manners, we adopt the . . . rules of judgment which obtain abroad. This is natural. It is foolish to complain about it. Imitation is the habit of youth; we are a young people. . . . Hence we shall . . . for a long time . . . receive from Europe a considerable part of our intellectual persuasions and our moral tastes. . . . If I thought it would be of any use, I might suggest the importance of forming a character of our own in spite of the influences . . . across the Atlantic. But it would be a vain undertaking, and perhaps it is not best. All that we can do is, to form a national character *with the help of these influences*.[88]

Indeed cosmopolitan currents had thoroughly transformed the puritan Bostonians whose chief prop, the old orthodoxy, had already been weakened by successive attacks from deism, unitarianism, universalism, and, finally, transcendentalism. Slowly, Bostonians became gentler and more gracious, and developed interests in a wide range of secular diversions. They had early evaded Hancock's interdiction of the theater, first under the guise of "moral lectures" and then openly.[89] The Handel and Haydn Society was formed in 1815, only five years after the Board of Selectmen had prohibited balls as "uncongenial to the habits and manners of the citizens of this place." [90] Through its agency and the aid of pioneer musicians, the taste for music was developed, leading to the flourishing concert life of the thirties.[91]

Bostonians of 1845 had outgrown breeches, satin waist-coats, buckled shoes, and many ideas; they more often drew dividends from Merrimac factories than from India ships. None the less, they were recognizable in their ancestors of 1790. For these changes had unfolded from the Boston of the past. There had been no disruption in the essential continuity of the city's history.

∾ II ∾

The Process of Arrival

1790–1865

Behold the duteous son, the sire decayed,
The modest matron, and the blushing maid,
Forced from their homes, a melancholy train,
To traverse climes beyond the western main,
Where wild Oswego spreads her swamps around,
And Niagara stuns with thundering sound.[1]

CERTAINLY, prospective settlers who could be at all selective would pass Boston by in favor of its younger and relatively more flourishing sisters. For in this community there was no room for strangers; its atmosphere of cultural homogeneity, familiar and comforting to self-contained Bostonians, seemed rigidly forbidding to aliens. And above all, space was lacking. Boston offered few attractions in either agriculture or industry. Its commercial ranks were not broad enough to absorb the sons of its own merchant class, and the fields of retail trading and handicraft artisanry were limited. The constricted social and economic life of the city and the far greater opportunities elsewhere, combined to sweep the currents of migration in other directions.

From time to time isolated individuals did find their way

to Boston, became residents and, being few in number, were readily absorbed by its vigorous culture. Scattered French, English, Scotch, Irish, Scotch-Irish, German, and Italian families appeared throughout the eighteenth and early nineteenth centuries. One could find enough natives of Switzerland, the Azores, Armenia, Poland, Sweden, Spain, China, and Russia to credit the claim that twenty-seven different languages were spoken in Boston.[2] These foreigners, however, were just strays; and the reasons for their coming derived from personal contingencies rather than from great social causes for mass emigration. To their ranks were added, from time to time, deserters from foreign ships in port, for whom American wages and American freedom weighed more heavily than the obligations of contract or the claims of loyalty.[3] More respectable increments came from the merchants and consuls who form a foreign nucleus in any commercial community.[4] Occasionally, too, small groups arrived. Thus when 800 English veterans, out-pensioners of Chelsea Hospital, settled in the eastern United States, some came to Boston.[5] But the great waves of European migration, with one exception, caused scarcely a ripple in the placid stream of the city's life. Only one country directed a dislodged population to a city where no promise dwelled; elsewhere events promoted the departure of those only who could choose their destination more prudently.

Between 1815 and 1865 profound changes in the economic, social and political life of many communities uprooted some 5,000,000 people from the continent of Europe. The most direct cause of this migration from western and central Europe was the dissatisfaction of large groups of people with their political and legal status. Many abandoned their homes because they despaired of improving their circumstances where they were, while others were forced to flee precisely because they sought to alter conditions.

During the French revolutionary period, cautious noblemen, victims of the fighting in La Vendée, disillusioned Feuillant reformers, Girondins, Jacobins, Thermidorians, and, finally, Napoleonic exiles — in all between 150,000 and 200,000 — left their native country.[6] At about the same time, repressive English measures following the abortive insurrection of the Society of United Irishmen under Lord Edward Fitzgerald in 1798, the failure of the uprising of 1803, and the Act of Union which joined the two kingdoms, caused many to leave Ireland.[7] Thereafter, successive upheavals in many lands produced a host of expatriates — German Burschenschaft agitators, Polish and French exiles of the thirties, French-Canadians in 1837, and French, Hungarian, Italian, German, and Irish *émigrés* in 1848.[8]

Many thus became exiles; but few became immigrants. The right of political asylum was universally recognized in western Europe [9] and a revolutionary fugitive could easily find a base close at hand where he might participate in further plots. The first French *émigrés* went to Turin to raise a counter-revolutionary army, while most of their successors concentrated in the Rhineland, on the Austrian frontier, and in England, from which points almost three-quarters eventually returned to France.[10] Similarly the Irish *émigrés* from the beginning looked first to France for asylum. When the United Irishmen decided that "where freedom is, there should our country be," it was "the thoughts of lovely

France" that cheered them.[11] The German radicals tried always to stay as close to home as possible, using nearby territory as a base for attacks against the Metternich system; whole colonies developed in Alsace-Lorraine, Switzerland, and England.[12] And later French, Italian, and Hungarian refugees centered their activities in London where they plotted under Ledru-Rollin, Mazzini, and Kossuth.[13] Those only came to America who gave up active revolutionary projects to start life anew.[14] Nevertheless, enough entered the United States to justify the constant boast of Americans that "the downtrodden . . . Pole . . . the learned . . . German . . . the cultivated and ardent Italian . . . bends hitherward his expatriated steps, as towards a shrine of social and public safety, to contemplate institutions of which he has only read." [15]

Of the 10,000 to 25,000 early French refugees who fled to America, however, few chose to live in Boston.[16] Between 1794 and 1809 occasional groups did arrive from France and from the disturbed districts of the French West Indies. And isolated individuals appeared from time to time. Jean Baptiste Julien, for instance, opened a "Restorator" at the corner of Milk and Congress Streets where he concocted for the first time the *Consommé Julien* and received from Brillat-Savarin a recipe for eggs "brouillés au fromage" which "fit fureur." [17] But most French immigrants of that period either went to Philadelphia or thought of America as the land of the noble savage and went far from Boston in their search for primitivism. In 1848, later French revolutionaries appeared, but on the whole the town was only slightly affected by this emigration.[18]

Fugitives from other political upheavals of the mid-nineteenth century contributed more heavily to Boston's population. The cultural center of America attracted considerable numbers of intellectuals and professionals, though they were continually warned that there was no room for the educated classes in the United States.[19] Thus, the Germans, Karl Beck and Carl Follen, came to Harvard in 1825, and Francis Lieber arrived in Boston in 1827 to teach gymnastics.[20] The fiasco of 1848 drove several large contingents to the city, the most prominent individual being Karl Heinzen.[21] And while most Irish political refugees concentrated in New York — an early center of anti-British activity — many nevertheless settled in Boston. Walter Coxe, an old revolutionary, one of the first, was joined after 1848 by Phelim Lynch and by B. S. Treanor, who became leaders of the Boston Irish community.[22] Among others in this category who struck roots in the city were some Poles in 1831 and in 1834, some Italians, and some Hungarians who came with Kossuth and stayed on.[23]

Much more influential than the political reasons for emigration, however, were the social and economic factors that transformed Europe in the century after 1750. Most fundamental was the fabulous increase in population. Before 1750, years in which births exceeded deaths had alternated with years in which deaths exceeded births, while over long periods of time the number of people remained fairly stationary.[24] After 1750, primarily because of a decrease in mortality among children less than ten, the population mounted steadily, almost doubling in the next century. This expansion, even at the point of redundancy, was itself not enough to provoke emigration, but it was the catalytic agent which converted other economic developments into dynamic causes for mass exodus.[25]

Between 1750 and 1850 the Industrial Revolution destroyed the traditional handicraft industries by creating large-scale factory enterprises, and set loose countless artisans all over western Europe. The change became apparent first in England where a series of inventions after 1785 gradually converted the small-scale, individually-operated, domestic textile industries into large-scale undertakings manned by a proletariat. From England it spread to France and later to Germany. In both England and France the displaced found employment in factories as paid laborers, so that the shift in population was chiefly from rural to urban regions, with little effect upon external migration. The British government, furthermore, discouraged any tendency of skilled laborers to quit the country. The Act of 1782 and the Order in Council of April, 1795, forbade a large variety of workers to leave. Although these restrictions were sometimes circumvented by vessels which cleared for a British port but stopped at New York or Boston instead, they remained fairly effective until repealed in 1824.[26] Even after the removal of legal impediments, emigration was selective in nature and limited in quantity. Not the depressed miner or factory operative, but the independent craftsmen whose standards were steadily lowered by the new industrial system, sought out new lands beyond the sea. Thus, in the 1840's, the London Tailors' Union offered to assist the emigration of 7,000 unemployed tailors, and in Paisley 3,000 combined to secure aid for the same purpose.[27]

In Germany the exodus of displaced artisans was considerably more marked than in England. Throughout this period Germany was industrially dependent upon England and France, producing foodstuffs to supply their industrial cities, and taking in return their finished products. The influx of machine-made goods "when England poured her yarn . . . into the Hanse towns after Waterloo" destroyed German handicrafts and menaced the existence of many artisans.[28] In spite of a steadily increasing population the period between 1835 and 1860 saw a decline in the number of masters in all but a few trades.[29] Because the machines that discharged them were in England, these workers could find no new employment in Germany. They had little choice but to emigrate.[30]

English domination stifled the development of the factory system in Ireland and ruined the industries that had existed before the Union. During the eighteenth century independent craftsmen had, despite British hostility, developed flourishing trades in Cork, Dublin, Limerick, and other Irish cities. But the Act of Union was almost immediately disastrous. With the shift of the capital to London, most of the gentry left Ireland, taking with them the market for Irish manufactures.[31] Thereafter the English parliament persistently retarded the growth of native industry, already handicapped by the depression of the Napoleonic Wars. As a result the Industrial Revolution never reached Ireland, the number of artisans declined steadily, and many manufacturers who had "hitherto been the established employers of numerous workmen" were themselves impoverished "by the stagnation of trade."[32] Faced with pauperization or emigration, 600 of those "who compose the middle ranks of life, and who are the most useful members of society" left in 1797 alone, and the annual number of such emigrants mounted steadily thereafter.[33]

Coterminous with these industrial changes were a whole series of rural changes, generically termed the agricultural revolution, which transformed western European agriculture from a communal activity of peasants on small-scale holdings, to a large-scale capitalist enterprise with a paid proletariat as its labor force. First manifest in the midland and northern counties of England, this conversion derived from the development of new agricultural techniques and the expansion of urban markets. Successive enclosure acts after 1750 implemented the transition by breaking up open fields and replacing them with contiguous holdings. The immediate result was the displacement of innumerable agriculturists who held their land by customary rights but could display no legal title. Furthermore, the position of those who remained on the land was weakened. Large-scale scientific farming, now feasible, put small owners at a disadvantage, and eventually forced many to forfeit their farms.[34] The dispossessed could emigrate to the United States, Canada, or Australia, or they could go to the rapidly expanding cities. England's swelling population, however, set a limit to the number who found employment in urban industries. As early as 1826 a select committee complained that the country was burdened with too much labor, and that the range of industrial opportunities was quickly narrowing.[35] Under these circumstances, those who had managed to salvage anything from the collapse of the old agricultural system, those who still possessed the means for building a new life, chose to migrate. The paupers, the broken in spirit, drifted to the towns.[36]

In southwestern Germany and in Scandinavia similar innovations drove many from their native soil. Unlike the peasants of Prussia and Saxony who in 1800 still retained the servile status acquired after the collapse of the uprisings of the sixteenth century, those of Bavaria, Baden, Württemberg, and the Rhineland were free.[37] In both Norway and Sweden the *bøndar,* the predominant farmers, were also freeholders with extensive, almost aristocratic rights.[38] In all free areas, holdings had shrunk remorselessly through centuries of division and redivision, and tiny plots were a chronic source of discontent among those who found no opportunities at home in a rapidly growing population. Farms had become so small that further division among several heirs was economically impossible. Younger sons could either consent to a reduction in status by becoming day-laborers, or, unhampered by servile obligations, seek fresh opportunties elsewhere.[39]

Decreasing mortality and the consequent rising population between 1800 and 1865 further limited opportunities in the already circumscribed Scandinavian economy. But the situation became critical in the 1840's with the spread of enclosures and the displacement of countless *bøndar.* In that decade the movement advanced rapidly "until the greater part of Sweden south of Norrland and Dalarne had changed village communal ownership to individual farms." This transition inordinately stimulated the volume of emigration which had already started ten years earlier. Thousands of ousted farmers rushed to the seaports to get off to America. Everywhere in Norway and Sweden the fairly well-to-do peasants

33

surrendered their homes and sought elsewhere the opportunities denied them by the change in the system of cultivation.[40]

In Germany increasing pressure on the old agricultural system from new markets for grain and foodstuffs made the situation more acute. The extension of the market was particularly hard upon the southwestern peasant, for it created a tendency toward higher prices and higher rents, made small-scale farming comparatively unprofitable, and stimulated the application of large-scale techniques to agriculture. As a result the next fifty years witnessed a displacement of population similar to that in Sweden.[41] But in Germany as in Scandinavia there were no booming Manchesters or Birminghams into whose factories the peasants could go.[42] Emigration was the only, the inevitable, alternative. After the turn of the century restrictions upon leaving gradually slackened, the prohibition being relaxed as early as 1804 in Bavaria and, after the Wars of Liberation, elsewhere in the southwest. The removal of these restraints and the absence of servile shackles to the land, released a swelling tide, checked only temporarily by the Napoleonic Wars.[43]

Peace in 1815 brought rapid acceleration, and the agricultural depression of 1816–17 carried the movement to abnormally high levels.[44] It developed steadily in the next two decades. In 1846–47 and 1852–55 crop failures in Bavaria and Baden, inevitably accompanied by high prices, further stimulated peasant migration.[45] By that time the web of railroads over southwestern Germany had so increased peasant mobility that the volume of emigration remained consistently high.[46] As a result the number of emigrants, only 1,065 in

1820 and 2,174 in 1830, rose to 32,674 in 1840 and 83,169 in 1850. By 1854 it reached its highest mark, 239,246 and, though it declined thereafter, still numbered 31,360 at its lowest in 1862.[47] Throughout, the desire and ability to leave were confined almost exclusively to the discontented free peasants of southwestern Germany.[48]

Generally then, throughout this period, not the groups without opportunities migrated, but those whose opportunities were narrowing with changes in the economic system. And for a long time the physical difficulties involved in coming to America constituted an additional selective factor. Inland transportation and ocean passage were costly and irregular.[49] Prospective immigrants required more money and information than ordinary peasants or laborers possessed. Indeed, a cautious Scotsman in Boston advised his "countrymen to keep at home if they cannot bring from £500 to £1,000." [50] Above all, newcomers needed ambition and enterprise to carry them through the difficulties of changing worlds. As a result, both the causes and conditions of emigration restricted it to the most prosperous and the most venturesome.

These were not satisfied with what Boston had to offer, for new opportunities were not to be found there. The very conditions which created the impulse to leave directed the emigrants elsewhere. The guidebooks and travel accounts they read spoke clearly enough of what they looked forward to. It was the deep rich soil these books praised most enthusiastically. Cheap land and ideal climatic conditions waiting to be exploited by broad backs and strong arms were the most extolled attractions. For the city they had little but contempt.

35

Equally persistent was the advice to shun the seaboard, to push immediately westward, to settle beyond the Alleghenies at once. Every immigrant was warned, "Go farther west; not until you reach Koshkonong [Wisconsin] will you find America." [51] Hard-working, thrifty agriculturists, whether

Fig. 1. The fortunate pass through Boston to the West

German, English, Norwegian or Swedish, who felt an attachment to the soil and a dislike for confining themselves to the city, did not hesitate to follow this advice. Those able to come could generally well afford to get beyond the seaboard to the west, for they were by no means impoverished when they arrived.[52]

Nor were the artisans more likely to settle in Boston. They had been persons of standing, "not hopelessly and despairingly poor . . . not quite disinherited from the old village economy in which a man did not merely sell his labour but

36

had some kind of holding and independence of his own." [53]
Usually they managed to salvage a bit of capital to bring with
them, and, selective about their destination, sought new
towns from whose rapid growth and fresh opportunities
they might profit. Many landed in Boston, a fairly important
port of entry; but few remained. Some stayed to act as "run-
ners" or to supply the multitudinous needs of immigrants in
transit; others, because they were stranded. But they were not
numerous. Boston derived its immigrants from the ranks of
neither such artisans nor such peasants; they had sufficient
mobility to seek more fertile fields.

Two conditions were essential before a large immigrant
group would stay in Boston. First, the immigrants must be
more interested in escaping from Europe than in what faced
them in America. Secondly, they must have so little mobility
that, once in Boston, they could not go elsewhere because
poverty deprived them of the means, and despondence of the
desire. For a long time this combination of factors did not
apply to any migration that affected Boston. The indentured
servant, the imported contract laborer, and the conditionally
assisted emigrant who lacked mobility were unknown to Boston during this period. [54] Whatever assistance there was, was
directed away from the city. Aid to Germans was either discouraged entirely, as in Baden where only those who could
pay their own passage were permitted to emigrate, or
planned to create consistent, homogeneous groups, first in
eastern Europe, then in South America, and after the 1820's,
in the Balkans and in Texas. [55] Even when these projects
failed, the various *vereine* promoting immigration and ar-
ranging itineraries looked forward to the Germanization of

a single western state. Consequently their routes led directly to the west from New York or New Orleans.[56] Great Britain's assistance was just as persistently directed at strengthening her own colonies, Canada, Australia and New Zealand.[57]

But throughout the early part of the century, across the Irish Sea from England, relentless historic forces steadily neared a culmination which eventually swept thousands of immigrants into a startled and scarcely prepared Boston.

Ever since the treacherous King of Leinster, Dermot Mac-Murrough, fled beyond the sea to call to his aid Henry II, the "Sassenach" King of England, the "dear dark head" of Eire had bent beneath the weight of foreign rulers.[58] But until the seventeenth century the lack of independence had little influence upon the bulk of the people. Subjection began to affect the life of the common Irishman only with the changes in land tenure during the Cromwellian invasions. With Cromwell came a host of land-hungry retainers who had to be satisfied at the expense of the native Irish. The great confiscation created a landlord class of foreign birth and religion while the policy of surrender and regrant destroyed the communal basis of land ownership and concentrated what land was left to the Irish in the hands of a few, reducing the remainder to the position of rent-paying tenants.[59] Ruinous wars decimated the population from 1,300,-000 in 1650 to less than a million in 1660, and confiscations and anti-Catholic penal laws aimed at depriving "the majority of the Irish people of all wealth and ambition," — frankly, "to make them poor and keep them poor." Finally, changes in the land laws destroyed security of tenure, the only safeguard against rapacious absentee landlords.[60]

The dispossessed Irish, forced to rent as tenants at will, had neither fixed tenure nor reasonable freedom from their landlords. Expired leases went always to the highest bidder; the tenant in possession received no preference. The consequent competition for land encouraged a wasteful system of middlemen, and raised rents far above their true value.[61] Normal agriculture proved impossible. The farmers had to concentrate upon rent-paying crops since retention of their precarious hold on the land took precedence over every other consideration. Feeding themselves became a subsidiary matter, solved after a fashion by reliance on the potato. Irish agriculture therefore bore a twofold aspect. Cereal crops and cattle were raised for the market to bring money for rents, while potatoes were grown for food. For this reason grain exports mounted rapidly although very little was available for consumption at home.[62]

Even worse off than the farmers were the cottiers who throughout "remained the fixed substratum of the population." [63] Political changes and changes in land status affected them only remotely, for they had little interest in the former and none in the latter. They were completely landless, neither owning nor having any rights to the soil. From some more fortunate farmer they rented the *use* of enough ground for cabin and potato patch, paying for it by labor for the landlord and by the sale of the ubiquitous pig. The cottiers subsisted on potatoes, to which they occasionally added a bit of milk, these two staples constituting the whole of their diet.[64] Their standard of living was incredibly low. They live, remarked a contemporary, "in such cottages as themselves can make in 3 or 4 days; eat such food . . . as they buy not from others; wear such Cloths as the wool of their own sheep . . . doth make. . . . A hat costs 20d. a pair of stockings 6d. . . . In brief . . . the whole annual expence of such a family . . . of 6 . . . seems to be but about 52s. *per ann.* each head one with another." [65] Their miserable poverty

Fig. 2. Distributing clothing to the cottiers

apathetically perpetuated itself as population grew "disproportionate to the capital and extent of the country," the result "of cheap food and few wants." [66] By the end of the seventeenth century cottiers formed the great bulk of the population, embracing perhaps four-fifths of all families, and their number grew thereafter.

Meanwhile the condition of agriculture continued to degenerate. The growth of population to more than 4,000,000 and the attendant competition for land further raised rents and reduced the size of farms. Infinite subletting and subdivision of land continued until about 1820. Made feasible by the potato diet, it was intensified by the stimulus which Foster's Law of 1784 and the protection provided in the English market after 1806 gave to the production of grain.[67] By 1841, no less than 563,153 of the 691,114 holdings in Ireland consisted of less than fifteen acres.[68] Tiny plots, penal laws, uncertainty of tenure, and the utter hopelessness of deriving more than a bare subsistence, discouraged permanent improvements or replacements, even where the poverty of the farmer did not altogether prohibit them. Irish agriculture seemed doomed to inevitable decay.[69]

By the end of the eighteenth century the great masses of rural Irish accepted the situation as unavoidable. They became reconciled to, if not content with, their inferior status. Since "the labour of one man" could "feed forty," and opportunities for other work were wanting, habits of shiftlessness and laziness developed.[70] By the same token, drunkenness spread among the peasantry and the urban population, particularly when whiskey was cheaper than bread.[71] From time to time hopelessness begot a reckless despair expressed in violent outbreaks which brought swift and merciless reprisals.[72]

The impact of the agricultural revolution upon this economy was bound to differ from that in other countries. The problem facing the landlord — how to adjust the agricultural system to yield a maximum of profit — was immensely complicated by the fact that his land was occupied far beyond its capacity by numerous tenants holding tiny plots on a basis which precluded modernization. To oust the tenants would have undermined the foundations of Tory political power based on the voting rights of the forty-shilling freeholders.[73] And as long as Irish grains had a secure market in England under the provisions of the corn laws and Foster's Law, the landlords willingly suspended action. Relief, they theorized, might come from the extension of the amount of arable land or from the artificial reduction of population. The former they hoped to accomplish by introducing new agricultural techniques and by draining the bogs and swamps; the latter, by encouraging late marriages and continence.[74] Emigration they either resolutely opposed or regarded only as a last resort, an evil to be avoided at all costs.[75]

Nevertheless, there was always some peasant emigration from Ireland, to England at least. Early in the eighteenth century the spalpeen, the itinerant Irishman "going over to reap in harvest," was already a familiar figure there.[76] Every year, the families of hundreds of cottiers whose holdings could not support them "abandoned their dwellings" and went "out to beg through the country" while their men wandered across the Irish Sea, seeking employment as agricultural laborers.[77] By 1820 many walked annually to Dublin, crossed to Liverpool in the steerage at five shillings a head, and after tramping about for months, begging from parish to parish, brought back to Ireland some three pounds.[78] When economic changes created a demand for labor in England many gave up wandering and settled there as industrial proletarians. At the same time Irish farmhands played an increasingly prominent part in England as enclosures created large farms using day laborers. Areas like the West Riding of Yorkshire contained many of these immigrants.[79] By 1841, fully 419,256 persons born in Ireland were permanently domiciled in England and Scotland. London held not less "than one hundred thousand distressed Irish poor" in 1814 and Glasgow, Manchester, and Liverpool contained large colonies.[80] Stimulated by steam navigation across the Irish Channel and by the demand for cheap labor in the construction of the spreading chain of English railroads, the number of migrants continued to grow.[81] Meanwhile a steady movement from southern Ireland to Ulster pushed out many Scotch-Irish farmers who would not "sacrifice . . . comforts which for years they had been accustomed to . . . to pay . . . larger rents." [82] But few of these Irish wanderers reached America; the lack of money was an insuperable obstacle.

The slow siphoning off of Irish population to England brought no relief to those remaining. Throughout the early nineteenth century distress was common. "The country lived in a chronic state approaching famine, and . . . the particular years . . . mentioned . . . as famine years were simply the years in which the chronic symptoms became acute." [83] The slightest failure in any crop brought immediate disaster. A deficiency of potatoes, as in 1822, resulted inevitably in famine.[84]

However, not the impoverishment of the peasants, but the fact that landlords no longer found it politically or economically profitable to keep them on the land, finally caused hordes to flee to America. The precipitate fall in the price of grains after the Peace of 1815, and particularly after 1820, ruined the peasantry and made it difficult for landlords to collect rents.[85] The same drop in prices and competition with other, more efficient agricultural economies convinced the gentry that it would be more profitable to turn land into pasture — a process necessarily involving the consolidation of holdings and the wholesale eviction of tenantry.

Meanwhile, mounting English poor-rates presented an additional threat to Irish landlords. By the 1820's rates in England had reached unprecedented heights.[86] English ratepayers ascribed their difficulties to the Irish paupers in England, and demanded a poor law for Ireland.[87] An act of 1833, permitting English justices of the peace to return Irish dependents to their birthplace, and another, two years later, cutting off aid to nonresidents, aroused bitter resentment in Ireland, for they shifted a heavy burden from English to Irish landlords.[88] Finally, the Irish poor law of 1838 subjected Irish landowners to an incredibly high tax, and at once aroused their eagerness to stimulate emigration.[89] Moreover, they no longer had a political inducement for keeping small tenants on the land since the forty-shilling freeholders had been deprived of their votes in 1829.[90]

To evict prior to 1838 had been dangerous despite a compliant statute of 1816. The ejected had no place to go and, when desperate, constituted a menace to the lives and property of landowners. But the act of 1838 integrated emigration and eviction into a new economic policy. For, one of its leading proponents pointed out, "Emigration would prepare the way for consolidation of farms in Ireland, and for an amended administration of the poor laws in England."[91] The dispossessed could, thereafter, be conveniently and safely lodged in the new workhouses. And since the same law provided for assisted emigration, it was only a step from eviction to workhouse and from workhouse to emigrant ship.[92]

Evictions were inordinately stimulated in 1846 by the repeal of the Corn Laws which destroyed Ireland's protected position in the English market.[93] The climax came with the great famine which struck directly at the basis of the food supply. The potato rot, first appearing in 1845, dragged the hunger-ridden land for five terrible years through a succes-

Fig. 3. An eviction

sion of miseries and left it an economic ruin.[94] Complete chaos caused an upheaval in the system of land tenure, for the gentry were prepared to take advantage of the cottiers' disaster and drove the peasants, unable to pay rent and no longer politically useful, from their holdings. John Mitchel complained, "There is a very prevalent feeling amongst the landlord class . . . that the people of Ireland ought not to be fed . . . upon the grain produced in this country . . . and that it is desirable to get rid of a couple of millions of them . . . taking advantage of the *panic* which is driving the people away. . . ." [95] The number of judgments of eviction mounted from 2,510 in 1847 to 3,385 in 1848 and 3,782 in 1849. The total number of evictions grew from 90,000 in 1849 to 100,000 in 1850. In 1851 it declined to 70,000 with 40,000 in 1852 and 24,000 in 1853. The evictions of 1849, 1850, and 1851

Fig. 4. Searching for potatoes

Fig. 5. The hunger of women and children

alone involved some million persons, and the process of displacement continued until 1870. By 1861 the 491,300 one-room cabins of 1841 had diminished to 89,400.[96]

Those evicted had but one desire — to escape Ireland and English rule as quickly as possible. In the minds of the people the famine ingrained a dread of the hopeless future and a desire to get away at any cost. Even those who loved Ireland best felt there was no hope in remaining. Nothing could reveal the depth of this despair more eloquently than the panic-stricken letters of John O'Donovan, the antiquarian whose love for Ireland and things Irish was an essential part of his being. "I see no hope for Ireland yet," he said, "the potatoes produced too large a population. . . . I see no prospect of relief for two years or more. The number of poor is too great. . . ." "I am sick . . . of Ireland and the Irish and care very little what may happen; for whatever may take place things cannot be worse. . . . I would leave Ireland with a clear conscience!! I would leave it exultingly, retire among the Backwoods of America . . . move into the deserts of the western world there to learn a RUDE but STURDY civilization that knows not slavery or hunger." [97] The intensity of these ideas in the mind of the scholarly librarian threatened by neither hunger nor slavery, was multiplied a thousandfold in the hearts of millions of cottiers who "stood . . . begging for . . . soup which . . . would be refused by well bred pigs . . ." and daily faced the slavery of the workhouse.[98]

From 1835 to 1865 "the stream of emigration" continued to "flow with unabated rapidity," little affected by conditions in America. Though it fell off somewhat in the late fifties, new landlord troubles in the sixties and the reappearance of the potato rot in 1863 stimulated it again.[99] The movement was cumulative in effect. Those who left early did so with the intention of eventually sending for their families, relatives, and friends. Soon large sums of money streamed back to Ireland to aid others across, a course facilitated when Thayer and Warren started the sale of prepaid tickets to Boston.[100] Meanwhile even those only indirectly affected by the upheaval were drawn into the current of migration. Doctors, lawyers, trades people, and artisans moved from deserted villages where they could no longer find a livelihood.[101] To these were added many Irish who, after first emigrating to England or Scotland, decided to go to America.[102] Not until

Fig. 6. Towing out

late in 1864 did any real slackening in the tide occur. By that time some 2,500,000 Irishmen had abandoned their homes.[103]

Changes in ocean navigation after 1840 conditioned the immense volume of this movement and the route it took. The opening by the Cunard Line of regular transatlantic steam communication in 1842 kept rates so low that even the poor could cross. The Line itself did not engage in the immigrant trade until 1863; but by engrossing other passenger business almost at once, it forced the established packet lines to devote themselves to these least desirable customers.[104] By the fifties, one could travel from Liverpool to Boston on a respectable line such as Enoch Train and Company, Page, Richardson, or Wheeler & Armstrong for from $17 to $20, including provisions — rates which made profitable landlord-subsidized emigration.[105]

With the Cunarders came also a significant modification in the direction of traffic. In the old Black Ball days New York had monopolized the transatlantic packet trade.[106] But the Cunard Line was subsidized by the British government which desired, above all, to maintain swift, direct contact with its colonies.[107] When the Post Office Commission of Inquiry reported in 1841 that the best way to get mail from England to Canada was via Boston, the Line was directed in 1842 to establish its terminus there, and before long others regularly followed its route. Within a few years the Enoch Train Line and Harnden and Company, among others, had added considerably to Boston's importance as an immigrant port.[108]

Low as were the rates, the cost of transportation involved for most the expenditure of their last resources. Sailings occurred from Dublin, Cork, and other Irish ports, but the great packet lines, now specialists in the emigrant traffic, invariably started from Liverpool.[109] At the port of embarkation emigrant funds were inevitably depleted by weary weeks of waiting for passage, and any residue was used up during the long crossing.[110] In New York and in Boston the penniless newcomer landed with no alternative but to stay where he was.

Even less fortunate were those who, lacking the money for

passage to New York or Boston, were forced to go to Quebec, Nova Scotia, or the Maritime Provinces in the empty holds of returning timber ships. From Halifax and St. Johns "these debilitated, half starved human-beings" wandered down the coast, drifting aimlessly, sometimes riding on the cheap im-

Fig. 7. Emigrants at dinner

migrant trains of the Eastern Railroad, until they reached a large city — usually Boston — whose charitable institutions would shelter them.[111] As a result the Tenth General Report of the Colonial Land and Emigration Commissioners found that of 253,224 emigrants to Canada and New Brunswick, more than 73,000 went at once to the United States and an overwhelming majority eventually found their way to New England.[112]

That the Irish hegira was unique has been recognized by the more perspicacious students of population.[113] The nature of its distinctiveness may be gathered from the circumstances that produced it. This exodus was not a carefully planned movement from a less desirable to a more desirable home. This was flight, and precise destination mattered little. The *Cork Examiner* noted, "The emigrants of this year are not like those of former ones; they are now actually *running away* from fever and disease and hunger, with money scarcely sufficient to pay passage for and find food for the voyage." [114] No other contemporaneous migration partook so fully of this poverty-stricken helplessness. There was no foundation for the frequent complaints by Boston newspapers and politicians against the export of paupers from England and the continent; [115] even the German famine-scourged "flight from hunger" was "not characterized by the poverty and helplessness that the Irish exhibited. . . ." [116] And in this respect, the Irish migration also contrasted with earlier ones from that country. Until 1835 the north, Ulster and particularly Tyrone, had been the primary source of emigrants, chiefly displaced artisans and fairly well-to-do farmers — in general the wealthiest elements of the population. [117] The new movement concentrated in the south and in the west, especially in Cork, Kerry, Galway, and Clare, and comprised the poorest peasants, assisted in crossing by the bounty of others. From this group, above all, Boston got her immigrant population.

Imperfect as they are, the statistics of immigration by all groups into Boston reflect this situation. [118] Before 1830 the number landing there annually never exceeded 2,000; before 1840 it reached 4,000 only once (1837). Distributed among many nativities, most were transients, westward-bound. The few Irishmen who settled in Boston in this period came primarily from Ulster and Tyrone. [119] Thereafter arrivals increased rapidly from 3,936 in 1840 to 28,917 in 1849. These newcomers were overwhelmingly Irish. Even the large figures for England and the British North American Provinces represented, for the most part, Hibernians who had sojourned in other countries before finally coming to the United States. By 1850, about 35,000 Irish were domiciled in the city; five years later there were more than 50,000 — almost all natives of the southern and western counties. After 1855 the number of Irish in Boston remained fairly constant. For as the famine subsided, the influx declined, except for brief spurts in 1853 and 1854, to a low point in 1862.[120]

The other foreign groups in the city were exceedingly small. The number of Germans has always been exaggerated.[121] The 2,000 in the city proper in 1850 increased gradually to 3,790 in 1865; and not more than 6,500 dwelt in the entire metropolitan area.[122] The English and British North Americans, as has already been pointed out, were largely of Irish descent. The Scots totalled less than 2,000, while the French, Italians, and Scandinavians were even fewer.[123]

Two groups, the Negroes and the Jews, cannot be numbered by their nativity. For the latter one must rely upon guesses. As far back as the eighteenth century some Spanish and Portuguese Jews lived in Boston. These ceased immigrating after 1800, and by 1840 few remained.[124] A slow infiltration of German and even of Polish Jews in the next ten years brought some 200 families to the city, but they failed to increase noticeably thereafter.[125]

Although the colored man's status was probably better there than elsewhere in the Union, Boston attracted few Negroes. In 1790 there were only 767; in 1820 only 1,690; and in

1850 only 2,085. There were 2,216 in 1855 and 2,348 in 1865, but the census of 1860 disclosed no more than 1,615.[126] Obviously, these figures do not reveal the full number of Negroes because runaway slaves avoided enumeration. But in view of the many circumstances conducive to their settlement in the city, their failure to grow more considerably was surprising. Two conditions were primarily responsible. Boston was not an important station in the underground railway and played only a minor role in the surreptitiously organized scheme of aiding the fugitive slaves from the south to Canada. Furthermore its economic opportunities were so narrow that those who had the courage to risk their lives to escape slavery were hardly content to stay there. In 1830, for instance, a group of fifty already in Boston, led by their Methodist preacher, moved on to Canada.[127] Like all other non-Irish groups the Negroes chose to pass Boston by. Only among the Irish did the motives and circumstance of emigration necessitate settlement under the unfavorable conditions dictated by Boston's economic and social structure.

❧ III ❧

The Economic Adjustment

*It was sailing by dead reckoning to them, and they saw
not clearly how to-make their port so; therefore I sup-
pose they still take life bravely, after their fashion, face
to face, giving it tooth and nail, not having skill to
split its massive columns with any fine entering wedge.
. . . But they fight at an overwhelming disadvantage,
— living . . . alas! without arithmetic, and failing so.*[1]

T HE elements conditioning the emigration of the foreigners, together with the social structure of Boston as they found
it, determined their position in the community. These factors
limited the whole orbit of the immigrants' lives in their new
homes. Their work, their health and longevity, their housing, their relations with the government, with their neighbors, and with one another, all were implicit in these two
forces. What drove the Europeans to Boston and what they
found there together produced a new society, far different
from its antecedents, yet unmistakably their heir.

The course of adjustment created a fundamental difference
between two categories of immigrants. Those who quickly
resumed familiar routines easily merged in interests and activities with native Americans. But those whose memories

54

held no trace of recognition for any feature of the new land, made room for themselves, if at all, only with the utmost difficulty. Many faltered, hesitated, were overwhelmed and lost, because in the whole span of their previous existence they found no parallel to guide them in their new life.

The most pressing concern of all newcomers on landing was to obtain employment. Those whose background had equipped them with an industrial skill or mercantile trade had little difficulty in adjusting to the economic conditions of their new world. Most, however, had escaped into a way of life completely foreign and completely unfavorable to them. Thousands of poverty-stricken peasants, rudely transposed to an urban commercial center, could not readily become merchants or clerks; they had neither the training nor the capital to set up as shopkeepers or artisans. The absence of other opportunities forced the vast majority into the ranks of an unemployed resourceless proletariat, whose cheap labor and abundant numbers ultimately created a new industrialism in Boston. But for a long time they were fated to remain a massive lump in the community, undigested, undigestible.

Since at the beginning, at least, the immigrants did not form an integral part of Boston's economy, it is difficult to know precisely how they managed to exist. They played no role in the usual accounts of her commercial and industrial life. Their contemporaries were aware that Europeans were there, of course, but completely neglected them in describing the business of the city. Save for occasional cursory notices of the number of arrivals, trade papers and journals throughout the forties and fifties consistently ignored the newcomers, and travelers' accounts which did mention them frequently misled, as they often do, by emphasizing the curious rather than the commonplace.[2]

For an accurate analysis of what happened to the immigrant in the maze of Boston's business life one must turn to the cold statistics of DeBow's federal census of 1850, the first to enumerate both nativity and occupations. In Boston it revealed a total of 136,881 inhabitants, of whom 37,465 were adult males; and it listed the vocations of 43,567 persons.[3] From the marshals' schedules of this census, the raw data have been classified in Tables XIII and XIV to determine the incidence of various employments in the city and their distribution within each nativity group.[4]

The 43,567 persons for whom material was available were engaged in over 992 distinct pursuits — an average of no more than forty-four persons per occupation in the entire city.[5] This widespread diversity emanated directly from Boston's complete orientation towards small-scale skilled enterprises and away from large-scale unskilled ones. As the nucleus of an important economic area, the town contained a multitude of retail trades. The center of a prosperous urban life, it encouraged the growth of highly skilled handicrafts to satisfy the demands for consumers' goods. Commercial rather than industrial in character, it possessed no large-scale establishments and therefore no great accumulations of labor in any industry or trade.[6] Broad occupational diversification was normal and inevitable in this society.

Viewed according to the nativity of those employed, this heterogeneity was particularly significant, for it reflected the economic health of any group within the city. A high degree of dispersion denoted the presence of considerable numbers of trained workmen, retailers, and merchants who conformed closely to the city's economic pattern. A low degree indicated a deficiency of such elements and presaged a period of difficulty in adjustment.

Table XIV, which gives the number of employed persons in 1850 with the number of occupations and the average number of persons per occupation of each nationality, proves that a general average for the entire city actually understates the extent of diversification. All nativities but one had far fewer persons per occupation than the city as a whole. The average varied almost directly with the number employed. Massachusetts with 13,553 had an average of 20.53; the rest of New England with 7,986 had an average of 14.16; British North America with 1,381 had an average of 7.31; and Germany with 929 had an average of 6.07. As the group grew smaller, its miscellaneous character progressively increased.[7]

The Irish formed the one exception. Their average, twice as high as any other group's, alone approached that of the entire city. While the 13,553 persons of Massachusetts birth worked at over 660 different occupations and New England's 7,986 at 564, Ireland's 14,595 were confined to only 362.[8]

The unusual degree of Irish concentration in an economic organization where dispersion was the rule arose from their convergence in two unskilled employments. A single occupation accounted for 48 per cent of the total Irish laboring force, another for almost 15 per cent more, and a third for 7 per cent.[9] In each of the other nativity groups represented in Charts A and B, no single vocation busied more than 20 per cent of the total working population. In each, the three most popular occupations employed between 24 and 50 per cent of

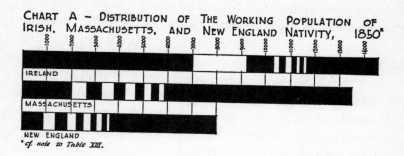

CHART A — DISTRIBUTION OF THE WORKING POPULATION OF IRISH, MASSACHUSETTS, AND NEW ENGLAND NATIVITY, 1850*

IRELAND

MASSACHUSETTS

NEW ENGLAND
* cf. note to Table XIII.

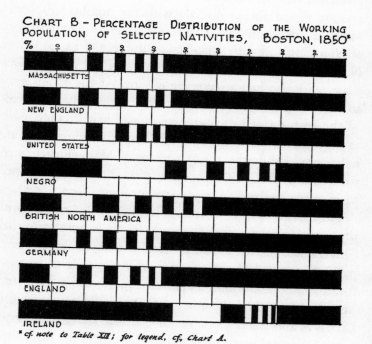

CHART B — PERCENTAGE DISTRIBUTION OF THE WORKING POPULATION OF SELECTED NATIVITIES, BOSTON, 1850*

%

MASSACHUSETTS

NEW ENGLAND

UNITED STATES

NEGRO

BRITISH NORTH AMERICA

GERMANY

ENGLAND

IRELAND
* cf. note to Table XIII; for legend, cf. Chart A.

58

the total, with the remainder of the workers engaged in from forty-three (in the case of the Negroes) to 657 (in the case of Massachusetts) different employments. By contrast, the three most popular occupations among the Irish included more than 70 per cent of the whole, and the ten most popular accounted for more than 80 per cent, leaving only 20 per cent divided among the residual 352.[10]

The concentration of nearly 65 per cent of the Irish working population in two occupations was an anomaly forced upon them by the conditions of their arrival. The vast majority left their ships in East Boston without the slightest conception of how they would earn a livelihood and with only enough money to keep them fed and sheltered for a week or two. "Unable to find employment or transportation elsewhere, . . . without one penny in store, the question, how they should live, was more easily put than solved." [11] Some had the way partly cleared by relatives or friends who assisted them; others managed to go west or to more prosperous eastern cities; and not a few, immediately discouraged by the "overstocked labor market," turned back to Ireland.[12] But most were completely immobilized; the circumstances that brought them to Boston compelled them to remain there, to struggle on as best they could.

They faced exhausting difficulties in making a place for themselves in the city's economic life. There was no one to help them; the hard-pressed Catholic priest and the overburdened benevolent and immigrant-aid societies could assist only a few.[13] Many fell into the clutches of the "Intelligence Bureaus" and the "Swindling Shops," traders in human misery which fleeced the guileless strangers.[14] More generally, the Irish relied upon their own simple ingenuity in finding employment. Tramping the crooked streets from shop to shop, they might, if they were fortunate, find someone to use their heavy labor. Frequenting the docks, watching the arrival of ships from across the water, they sometimes met a short-handed stevedore boss or wharfinger.[15] They procured casual employment on the streets or in the public works that were transforming the physical aspects of the city. But every element of selectivity was denied them. The pressing need for immediate earnings destroyed the possibility of choosing a job or preparing for a trade. Want swept them into the ranks of those 7,007 unskilled, insecure day laborers who informed the census takers that they were just laborers — a classification descriptive not of their function, but of their lack of function.[16] Well might the good Irish priest, Dr. Cahill, lament that "the emigrants from Ireland . . . to escape the horrors . . . of the emaciating poorhouse fly to this country with barely the passage money; and they have often landed . . . [without] a single penny! . . . It is a clear case that these poor friendless strangers, having no money, must have recourse to their only means of subsistence — namely, street or yard laborers or house servants."[17]

No other nationality depended so heavily upon unskilled work. There were 1,545 laborers in the city other than Irish, but in no group did they form a significant proportion. Among the natives no more than 5 per cent were so employed, and only the Negroes and the Germans had as much as 10 per cent. But even in these cases the actual number was small: 115 Negroes and 107 Germans.[18]

An employed laborer could not earn enough to maintain a

family of four. And as long as the head of the Irish household obtained nothing but sporadic employment, his dependents lived in jeopardy of exchanging poverty for starvation.[19] Supplementary earnings — no matter how small — became crucial for subsistence. The sons were first pressed into service, though youngsters had to compete with adults willing to work for boys' wages. To keep the family fed, clothed, and sheltered the women also were recruited. In Ireland they had occupied a clearly defined and important position in the cottiers' economy. That place being gone, they went off to serve at the table of strangers and bring home the bitter bread of banishment.

There was room in the comfortable households of Boston's middle classes for the Irish daughter or sister who wished to lighten her family's load by supporting herself and perhaps contributing a little something besides. There had long been an acute shortage of domestics in New England. Generation after generation of housewives had either done their own work or paid relatively high wages to natives who insisted on being "help," not servants. The supply of such labor had been extremely unsatisfactory and transitory in character. Most Americans "would rather want bread than *serve* to gain it," and farm girls in service for a few years while waiting to be married usually lacked the essential attributes of servility and loyalty.[20] Under these circumstances the "Irish help" were triply welcome for their good spirits, their loyalty, and their cheap wages. In all hotels and in thousands of native homes Bridget became a familiar, indispensable figure.[21] By 1850, at a conservative estimate, 2,227 Irish girls worked as domestic servants in Boston.[22]

For all other groups, the percentage in service was uniformly low.[23] None numbered more than 10 per cent, and of these, many were governesses and housekeepers rather than menial servants.[24] To some extent this preponderance of Irish domestics sprang from the greater percentage of females among the immigrants from Ireland; but above all, it derived from the pressing need to send women out to help support the family.

The tenuous character of their status drove the Irish into a constant search for better jobs and more secure employment. All aspired to skilled positions that would enable them to support their families alone. But the reluctance to employ Irishmen in any but the lowest capacities, added to their lack of capital and of training — itself an insuperable obstacle — rigorously excluded them from such occupations. Early attempts to ban foreigners from certain professions by law had failed,[25] but by 1845 the caption "None need apply but Americans" was familiar in Boston newspaper advertisements.[26] Prejudice became more intense as competition for jobs grew keener, though it proved no formidable barrier to those who had a trade to ply or a skill to offer. But while other groups filtered into the city and were accepted, the Irish remained unneeded and unabsorbed. The few who arrived with professions, or rose from the ranks of the unskilled by a gradual process of recruitment, did not leaven the mass.

The degree of their penetration into any trade varied inversely with its desirability. Employments involving an element of personal service and therefore repugnant and degrading to Americans, quickly fell to the lot of the Irish. Many found work in the care and service of horses, the city's chief transport agent. As these trades called for menial labor of a rather low sort, few competed with the Irish for them. By 1850, more than 300 of the 877 smiths, more than those of any other nativity group, were Irish. The hostlers and stablers were also predominantly Irish, although the stablekeepers, who needed capital, were not.[27]

The same divergence prevailed in services to men as well as to beasts. Everywhere the waiters were Irish, while the skilled cooks were not.[28] Barbers, also skilled workers, were traditionally Negroes, and the elegant and fashionable hairdressers and *coiffeurs* were Frenchmen or Italians.[29] With these exceptions the Irish had the service occupations almost entirely to themselves.

In the truly skilled employments, however, their percentage was low indeed. Only in the building trades did they have any opportunity at all, and that because Boston, like most American cities, was passing through a construction boom. The wealthy merchants were building grand residences down Beacon Hill and on toward the newer Back Bay. The middle classes, moving out to East and South Boston, were erecting hundreds of new dwellings. By their very presence even the Irish created a demand for more housing. They preëmpted the slums and the low rental sections of the city, pushing out the former inhabitants and stimulating the demand for new abodes. In 1843, more than 1,118 new structures were reared, and the annual number grew thereafter.[30] As a result labor was in demand. The various building trades embraced some 5 per cent (775) of the total Irish working population. This compared unfavorably with the 11 per cent (1,594) of Massachusetts birth and with that of the other nativities.[31] But it represented skilled employment for a significant section of the Irish community by which some actually acquired enough influence and capital to become contractors and construction bosses.[32]

In the other skilled occupations and handicrafts, most of which had been well developed before 1845 and did not expand thereafter, the Irish were, in the main, unimportant. They numbered only twenty-eight of the total of 450 employees in the maritime industries, and made no headway in furniture building or cabinet making, where highly trained workmen were needed. Nor did they progress very far in the crafts dealing with precious metals or with the manufacture of musical instruments.[33] Among the ordinary mechanics and machinists their proportion was smaller than any other group's, and relatively few became transport workers, truckmen, coachmen, or even sailors.[34]

They were more poorly represented in the commercial occupations than in the handicrafts. Though many fancied the dignity and independence of the traders' status, few attained it. Among the Irish immigrants were some shopkeepers and merchants who had followed their customers to the New World. A handful of others had accumulated a modicum of capital and longed to join the large and prosperous group of retail distributors of all sorts who supplied the necessities of life to Boston and its hinterland. In most branches of retailing, however, they competed directly against the superior skill and resources of other groups and were doomed to failure from the start.[35]

In some spheres immigrants had an advantage over their native competitors. Where they relied on the patronage of their compatriots they prospered. Food dealers — butchers, fruiterers, and, above all, grocers — dealt directly and intimately with immigrant women who preferred to purchase from those who spoke their own language, carried familiar foodstuffs, and served them as a friend, confidant, and adviser. Each national group, therefore, supported a comparatively large number of grocers and food dealers. With the exception of the Irish and Negroes, newcomers did not suffer by comparison with the native whites.[36] Among the Irish, as among the Negroes, deficiencies of capital and skill weighed more heavily in the balance, and their percentage of such retailers was lower than in any other group.[37]

For the humble immigrant the easiest ingress to commerce was through its least elegant form, peddling. Peddlers needed no permanent place of business. They required only a small capital investment and but passing acquaintance with trading methods. With their stock upon their backs they could move among their countrymen, deal with them on terms of confident familiarity, and earn a respectable livelihood. These inducements were attractive enough to draw approximately 2 per cent of the Irish, and even larger contingents from other groups into itinerant trading.[38]

In other forms of minor retailing involving close personal contacts, each nativity group created a demand for the services of its own members. Inevitably, a circle of saloons, restaurants, boarding houses, and a few hotels catered to foreigners. Germans would never think of residing or dining where they might have difficulty in securing their lager. It comforted the Irish to hear the old country brogue and feel the security of being with their own kind. Like the McGinnis in

Mrs. Dorsey's novel, most immigrants added to their income by keeping a few lodgers of their own nationality.[39] To meet the needs of the unmarried, of sailors, and of those who had either not yet settled down in the city or were on their way west, every group — particularly the Irish and Germans — provided a large number of boarding houses.[40] There were also German lunchrooms, restaurants, and *lager-bier* saloons, Irish bars and dance halls, and even some English coffee houses. From these enterprises many foreign-born saloon-keepers and bartenders earned their livings.[41]

The abundance of boarding houses and saloons was encouraged by, and in turn caused, a paucity of hotels. Hotel-keeping was a substantial business managed and owned by Americans, and none of the foreign establishments in Boston ever gained as high a reputation as the Revere or Tremont House. There were, no doubt, a few Frenchmen and Italians who became prominent as purveyors of food in the genteel tradition of Continental cookery. Although a place always remained for the puddings and *bombes* of the *confiseurs,* even the high esteem in which that tradition was held and memories of the great Julien did not sustain Nicholas Ouvre, Gallieni, and the other *pensionaires* and *restaurateurs* very long.[42] Only those supported by an adequate foreign clientele survived. By the forties the French and Italian places declined visibly. In 1846 Antoine Vigne gave up the Perkins House, a "tremendous establishment" in Pearl Street, and moved to New York where he opened the *Hotel de Paris* on Broadway.[43] No Irish hotel existed in the city until Henry Dooley, a jovial host from the British American Provinces, took over the Merchants Exchange on State Street.[44]

Prospering from the favor of the Irish societies which met there, it remained the only important foreign public house in the city.[45]

If the Irish progressed only slowly in the handicraft and retail trades, they made no impression at all on the financial occupations central to the city's commercial life. Merchants and bankers constituted the keystone of Boston's prosperity. Linked with them were the salesmen and agents, and at a yet lower level, the store clerks and bookkeepers, indispensable cogs in the functioning of the business machine. These classes, despite the differences among them, were all high in respectability and economic position. Theirs was the most favored place in Boston life. The foreigners such as the Frenchman, P. P. F. Degrand, and the Spanish Jew, Abraham Touro, who entered into these ranks, were conspicuous chiefly for their singularity.[46]

Generally, the only opportunity for aliens to figure in commerce or finance grew out of the patronage of their own communities. Foreign ship agents frequently saved enough from the profitable business of remitting funds to Ireland to engage in banking operations for their compatriots. The Tri-Mountain Insurance Company was directed by and at the Irish, and the Germania Life and Germania Fire Insurance Companies, by and at the Germans.[47] The New England Land Company united the prominent Irishman, Patrick Donahoe, with several well-known Bostonians (among them the Know-Nothing mayor, J. V. C. Smith), in a scheme to move the Irish to the west, and a number of other immigrant-controlled real estate agencies prospered.[48] But the commercial community was overwhelmingly American. Almost 90 per cent of all the merchants — 3.4 per cent of the total native working population — were native born. In no foreign group were the merchants proportionately or numerically significant. They ranged from .5 per cent of the group in the case of the Germans to 1.4 per cent in the case of the English. The Irish, as usual, lagged far behind, with only .1 per cent. In the lower categories the non-American groups played as small a role. More than 86 per cent of the agents and 88.2 per cent of the clerks were Americans, while only 4.2 per cent and 3.6 per cent, respectively, were Irish.[49]

The fact that Americans had somewhat recently entered the professions complicated the same basic pattern in that field. At one time Europeans had played a fairly prominent part in the city's professional life. In 1794 the number of qualified Americans was so limited that the builders of the Middlesex Canal advertised for a supervising engineer in French.[50] By 1850, however, the native professionals outnumbered the foreign born in every field, though in all but the government services, where Americans always predominated, the non-Irish immigrants were proportionately as important. These classes amounted to between 3 and 5 per cent of the total of each nativity group, except the Irish, which had only .2 per cent.[51]

In some spheres foreigners usually retained an advantage. They dominated the plastic arts and monopolized the dance, both as performers and teachers. Boston ladies insisted upon taking lessons from Mr. Williams of London, M. Duruissel of Paris or, most of all, from the glamorous Lorenzo Papanti of Leghorn.[52] They liked to study foreign languages either with Frenchmen or Italians, particularly when combined with "tuition on the Piano Forte." [53] There were many prominent foreign musicians. The Englishman Hayter and the German Zeuner, the Frenchman Du Lang and the redoubtable Irishman, Patrick Gilmore, established firm reputations. But the rank and file of professional musicians and music teachers were American-born, as were instructors in most other branches of education. [54]

A small number of professionals served their own co-nationals. A few taught in evening and commercial schools, catering to the special needs of immigrants. [55] All groups demanded priests familiar with their ways and using their own language. Likewise, they preferred lawyers of their own kind, friends they could understand and trust when it was necessary to cope with the law or the government. [56] It comforted the Germans to learn that their doctor was a relative of the oculist to the King of Saxony, and the Irish to believe that their apothecary or physician had practiced for twenty-seven years in County Kerry. [57]

The exceptional Irishman who found satisfactory employment failed to mitigate the abject circumstances of the group as a whole. With no adequate outlets in the handicrafts, in commerce, or in the professions, the rank and file remained totally or partially unemployed. In this respect they differed from every other element. Unabsorbed laborers in other groups were more than counterbalanced by their skilled co-nationals already integrated in the scheme of Boston life. Even the Negroes, who stood closest to the Irish in occupational experience, fared better than they. Emancipation before 1790 did not wipe away the stigmata and disabilities of slave status. It was always difficult to acquire education, skill, or capital, and the prejudices of the classes immediately above confined the Negroes to unpopular tasks.[58] Yet, though their employments were not particularly desirable or well paid, they had specific functions. Negroes were acquainted with the by-ways of Boston's economic organization, and, as time went on, adapted themselves to it. They did not remain simple unskilled laborers to the same extent as the Irish. Despite the risk of being sold as slaves on long voyages, many became seamen; others were barbers, chimney sweeps, and traders.[59] Some, like Robert Morris, a prominent lawyer, even rose to the professional ranks. By the time Walt Whitman visited Boston in 1860 the Negroes were better off there than elsewhere in the United States.[60] While their position shone chiefly by comparison with less fortunate members of their race, it was clearly closer to that of the natives than the Irish.[61] The latter unquestionably were lowest in the occupational hierarchy.

But unless it contained a reliable and constant productive element, no group could continue to subsist by employment in the service trades and by dealing with one another. As it was, the large body of casual, unskilled Irish labor created tremendous social problems and called for more adaptations than either the individual or his family could make for long. Though only a temporary escape was possible, the temptation to try it was great.

Paradoxically, the same immobility that rooted the Irish immigrants in Boston also drove them out to work in all parts of the United States. Surplus labor was an unthinkable anachronism in the body of American economic life. In so many places cheap labor was essential, yet lacking, that it was inevitable the Irish should be used for more productive purposes. In the west, in the south, and in Canada vitally important projects awaited the application of their brawn. From every part of the United States construction bosses in embankments and water projects, tunnels, canals, and railroads called on Boston for the cheap man-power they knew was always available there. Thus the city's role as labor reservoir assumed national proportions; often the Boston Irish newspapers, in single issues, printed advertisements for more than 2,000 men wanted in widely scattered places.[62]

Sooner or later the immigrant in search of employment discovered the labor contractor in search of men. In the columns of their weekly newspapers they saw, or heard read to them, the incredible, tempting advertisements detailing the blandishments of good wages, fine food, and excellent lodgings. The attractions of steady employment were hard to resist. True, railroading meant living a riotous camp life and the absence for a year from women, family and friends, and from the ministrations of the priest. But these partings were not novel to Irish life, for many sons and daughters had already left the family to earn a living. Moreover, before coming to America, the men had been accustomed to this type of migration; each fall the spalpeens had left their plots on the "ould sod" and crossed the Irish Sea to work for English landlords. In Boston as in Ireland, the wives and children remained behind to shift as best they could, sometimes assisted with occasional remittances, often becoming a burden upon the community. In any case, within a year the laborers were back, usually no better off than before.[63]

Unscrupulous exploitation was the theme of the construction camp; and dirt, disorder, and unremitting toil were its invariable accompaniments. Wages ranged from $1.00 to $1.25 a day, though skilled stonelayers and masons often got from $2.00 to $2.50.[64] The more prudent contracted for board as part of their pay, or for their upkeep at a flat weekly rate.[65] But most were victimized by rapacious sub-contractors who monopolized supplies in isolated construction camps and took back in exorbitant prices what they paid out in wages.[66] The railroads themselves frequently resorted to equally dishonest practices. The Irish, after traveling several hundred miles, had no recourse when the company decided to pay less than it had advertised. Many roads, by deliberately asking for more men than they needed, built up large labor reserves with which to bludgeon down the wages of those already working for them. With reason enough, the *Boston Pilot* advised "all laborers who can get employment elsewhere to avoid the railroads . . . to . . . do anything . . . in preference to 'railroading.'"[67] But the Irish were the guano of the American communications system. "Ferried over the Atlantic, and carted over America," despised and robbed, downtrodden and poor, they made the railroads grow.[68]

Back in Boston, the quondam railroaders, like those who stayed behind, still faced the problem of securing permanent employment. Some found openings of a sort as sweepers and janitors in the textile factories of neighboring cities. These were the most wearisome jobs in the mills, the least skilled and the lowest paid — the ones the native operatives would not take. Mill owners soon perceived the potentialities of this docile labor supply. The New England girls who had been working in the factories were independent, militant, and impermanent. "Amateur" rather than "professional" proletarians, they left abruptly when marriage set them free for their true careers. Their insistence upon decent working conditions proved burdensome and led to increasing costs, particularly after Sarah Bagley started the Lowell Female Labour Reform Association in 1845.[69] With men available at rates lower than those paid to women, the manufacturers turned to the Irish to run their machines, raising them from the meaner chores to higher ranks, and eventually using them for all tasks. And, as immigrants invaded the textile field, it lost status; native girls became more reluctant to enter it. By 1865, male employees outnumbered females in woolens and were gaining on them in cottons.[70] Foreign labor, for which Boston served as a convenient recruiting ground, manned both.[71]

Almost as important as textiles was the shoe industry. Before 1850 it had been loosely organized on a handicraft household basis as a supplement to fishing and farming.[72] When the first practical shoe machinery was invented, cheap labor in nearby Boston facilitated the transition to the factory system in towns like Quincy and Lynn. "Green hands," anxious to be exploited, replaced skilled artisans, enabling the "garret bosses" to reap tremendous profits and become large-scale manufacturers.[73] Throughout the fifties and the Civil War the presence of a labor surplus in Boston stimulated infant industries and accelerated the process of industrialization in New England.

This transformation of New England followed the general shift from craftsmanship towards mechanization in all phases

73

of American economy. Emphasizing cheapness and mass production rather than skill, it required an abundant supply of labor. Wherever this essential condition existed, the trend left its impact; without it the change could not be effected. The process was particularly significant in Boston where a consistent deficiency af labor had seriously hampered the growth of industry until the forties. Between 1837, when the first business census was taken, and 1845, the total number of employees in the city's major industries (all those which at any time between 1837 and 1865 employed 100 persons) probably did not increase at all.[74] Few grew significantly, and many actually declined. The prospective manufacturer desiring a site for a new establishment, or the capitalist with an "abundance of money seeking an outlet," found little encouragement. And even those already established who wished to expand were inhibited by the apparently inflexible labor supply.[75]

But in the two decades after 1845 the Irish energized all aspects of industrial development in Boston by holding out to investors magnificent opportunities for profits from cheap labor costs. The total of industrial employees doubled between 1845 and 1855, and again between 1855 and 1865. Between 1837 and 1865, the number of workers in the older industries rose from 9,930 to 33,011, and, in addition, 6,272 appeared in new ones.[76] Meanwhile the stream of immigration through the early fifties replenished the supply of workers already drawn off into factories, and their presence guaranteed a continuance of low prices. Because it possessed this labor reserve after 1845 Boston could take advantage of every opportunity. Within little more than two decades it became the nation's fourth manufacturing city.

There was the ready-made clothing industry, for instance, which had grown appreciably in Boston since its inception by John Simmons in the early thirties. At first an adjunct to the trade in secondhand apparel, then a part of the ship store business which supplied "slops" to sailors on shore leave, it eventually turned to producing cheap garments for southern slaves, for western frontiersmen, and for California miners to whom considerations of style and fit meant little.[77] Until the mid-century, however, Boston was at a disadvantage with New York. Her rival on the Hudson was as accessible to supplies and, as a greater seaport, catered to more sailors and enjoyed more intimate connections with both the south and the west. Wages were also lower in New York, at least to 1845, and the cost of labor was the most important as well as the most variable factor in production, since the industry always "tended to concentrate at the points of cheapest labor." [78] As a result Boston remained behind, unable to compete on equal terms with New York.

Yet it was an exceedingly tempting industry promising high profits if only a way could be found of producing clothes good enough to command a wide market at a price lower than those made in New York. But cheap clothes depended upon cheap wages; and until 1845 the labor force consisted entirely of the ordinary journeyman tailors who worked primarily on custom clothes. The "ready-made" clothiers, unable to pay the same wages as the custom tailors, were compelled to produce only during the twenty-eight

75

weeks or less each year when the journeymen were not busy at their usual work. On this basis the industry could never develop to significant proportions. No matter what degree of standardization the technical process of manufacturing reached, the absence of a cheap labor supply precluded conversion to factory methods. Machines alone could not create a factory system in Boston when only the 473 tailors employed in 1845 were available to man them.[79]

The situation changed, however, with the influx after 1845 of thousands of Irishmen ready to work for any wages. The manufacturers fully realized how important these immigrants were; and on the occasion of a journeymen's strike in 1849 they pointed out to Mayor John P. Bigelow that they had no need of his services as arbitrator, for an abundance of other labor sources was available to them.[80] Henceforth they expanded their business, firm in the assurance that profits would not be menaced by labor costs or strikes. Erstwhile peasants were unskilled, of course, and knew nothing of tailoring. But the simpler parts of the trade were not difficult to learn and it was profitable to press the raw immigrant into service at wages which no true tailor would consider. The invention of Howe's sewing machine in 1846 in Cambridge came just in time to facilitate the training of the Irish by mechanizing and simplifying the sewing operations.[81] By 1850 the 473 tailors of 1845 had grown to 1,547, of whom more than a thousand were Irish.[82] The Civil War brought rush orders for thousands of uniforms and capped the process of expansion.[83] By 1865, these circumstances had produced a distinctive method of factory production known in the trade as the "Boston System." Achieving an ultimate exploitation of cheap hands, it combined machinery with an infinite division of labor "which completely eliminated the skilled tailor." [84]

The factory failed to emerge during this period in New York primarily because of the absence of the labor surplus that made it possible in Boston. Instead, the pressure for cheaper costs led to the growth of the outside shop where the efforts of the entire family were utilized.[85] As a result Boston manufacturers gained an advantage, for the factory system permitted them to reduce wages while producing more *per capita*. The average value of the goods turned out there by a single worker in 1860 was $1,137 as compared with $788 in New York.[86] Moreover the New York employers paid from $8.00 to $10.00 a week for labor, and the Bostonians only from $4.50 to $5.50.[87] These differentials more than offset New York's other advantages. On this basis George Simmons' "Oak Hall," employing 3,000 tailors, became a national institution by 1860 and the whole industry in Boston quadrupled the value of its products between that year and 1870.[88] By then the city had become the center of the factory manufacture of ready-made clothing in the United States, a position it retained as long as cheap labor was available.

Precisely the same development revolutionized other industries. Because of the relative importance of transportation costs, Boston, like New York and Philadelphia, had early become a sugar refining center.[89] In the first four decades of the nineteenth century sugar boiling was a highly skilled but small occupation, carried on in Boston largely by German artisans. Before 1845 the industry employed only about a hundred persons.[90] In the forties, however, a series of mechanical inventions necessitated a complete change in plant and process. All over the country refineries, unable to make the adjustments, closed their doors.[91] In Boston, those surviving put more money into expanded factories, and hired additional hands. The number of employees, many of them Irish, tripled between 1845 and 1855; and the industry grew rapidly after 1858 when the Adams Sugar Refinery built the country's second largest plant in the city.[92] The manufacture of paper hangings experienced a similar transformation. When J. R. Bigelow entered the business in 1841, it was organized on an individual handicraft basis. By 1853 it became completely mechanized and Bigelow's factory itself employed 200 workers.[93]

Many old industries forced out of business by high costs before 1850 resumed on the basis of cheap immigrant labor, and many which suffered no radical change expanded because the surplus of wage-earners was available. In 1848, Jonas Chickering boasted that he employed one hundred men in his piano manufactory; when his sons opened a new plant in 1853 they required 400. Meanwhile the Mason & Hamlin Organ Company opened a mammoth factory in the West End and the total number of workers in the industry rose from 368 in 1845 to 1,248 in 1855. A shortage of hands would have thwarted growth indefinitely.[94]

The creation of new industries most clearly exemplified the importance of cheap labor. The expansion of Boston after 1845 was truly remarkable, particularly in the heavy industries where strong muscles counted most. Scores of new factories, drawing upon the services of hundreds of Irishmen, sprang up in East and South Boston. In 1837 only 776 persons were employed in casting furnaces, in copper and brass foundries, and in making machinery; by 1845 this number had grown to only 859. But in the next decade it almost tripled. By 1855 2,412 persons worked in these industries and an additional 1,097 in new rolling mills, forges, and rail factories.[95]

Fig. 8. Casting room, Alger's Iron Works, East Boston

In this decade, at least seven important iron works began operations in Boston. The Hinckley and Drury Locomotive Works, one of the earliest, expanded steadily after 1848 until it employed four hundred men regularly. Between 1846 and 1848, John Souther launched the Globe iron works, manufacturing locomotives, the first steam shovels, and dredging and sugar mill machinery, an enterprise which alone eventually employed four hundred laborers. In 1847, Harrison Loring built the City Point Iron Works to make engines, machinery, and iron ships. During the same year the Bay State Iron Company was founded in South Boston, and within the next few years, Hawes and Hersey, the Gray and Woods Machine Company, and Chubbuck and Sons established plants in Boston. Meanwhile the older Alger works broadened its own activities rapidly.[96]

In 1845 Donald McKay moved his shipyards to East Boston where he started the most active works in the country.[97] This marked the beginning of a resurgence of shipbuilding in the city. Only eighty-six persons worked in shipyards in 1837, and but fifty-five in 1845. But ten years later the number had increased to 922 and the business flourished thereafter.[98] And this growth characterized all types of industry. Felton and Sons developed their distilleries in South Boston; and James J. Walworth brought his steam fitting and foundry shops from New York, setting up plants in Boston and Cambridge. In these years, too, the Boston Rubber Shoe Company, Robert Bishop and Company, and the Shales and May Furniture Company opened important factories in the city. Upon the discovery of oil and the development of kerosene, the Downer Kerosene Oil Company and the Jenney Manufacturing Company established prominent refineries in Boston. The invention of the sewing machine created an industry which employed 168 persons in 1855 and 245 in 1865. The manufacture of glass found a place in the city in the fifties when machinery made possible the employment of unskilled labor, while the shoe industry and the cognate tanning business drifted in from suburban regions in response to cheap labor costs founded on the presence of the Irish.[99]

In the development of the new Boston the Irish woman was almost as important as the Irish man. When other forms of employment failed her, she turned to the ultimate expedient of women who needed money, sewing at home. The labor of women was used in the domestic manufacture of men's shirts, of women's dresses, and of millinery, where the "making" operations were simple enough to be carried on without supervision.[100] Wages were abysmally low; by constant toil a good seamstress might earn as much as $3.00 a week, but most received as little as $1.50 — just enough for a single woman to pay her rent.[101] For this pittance hundreds of women toiled under miserable conditions through all hours of the day

> Sewing at once with a double thread
> A shroud as well as a shirt.

Home sewing had always existed, but after 1845 an increasing number of women found it their only support.[102] By 1856 more were seeking such work than could find it, though a single large firm such as Whiting, Kehoe and Galouppe sent material out to more than 8,000 women in the city and through all parts of New England.[103] Many German, English, and native women participated, but most were Irish.

To find employment outside the home was a refreshing release from such conditions. After 1846 occurred a gradual but emphatic shift by Irish women to the factory manufacture of women's garments.[104] By 1860 there were at least ten large establishments in Boston, some of which employed as many as one hundred girls to produce cloaks, mantuas, and dresses.[105] After 1850 the number of immigrant women in all

81

types of industry increased steadily until by the time the War broke out they were prepared to step into whatever places men left vacant. In 1865 fully 24,101 women of native and foreign birth were employed in Boston as compared with 19,025 men. Apart from the 19,268 women workers in the clothing trade, there was a significant number in other occupations, many even in heavy industry.[106] The majority of the workers were Irish who, like their men, were contributing an element of fluidity to Boston's economy.

Therein lay the significance of the Irish in the city's economic life. Before their arrival the rigid labor supply had made industrialization impossible. It was the vital function of the Irish to thaw out the rigidity of the system. Their labor achieved the transition from the earlier commercial to the later industrial organization of the city. Without it "the new and larger establishments could not have been operated." [107] Capitalists readily admitted that they could not "obtain good interest for their money, were they deprived of this constant influx of foreign labour." [108]

Those who benefited most from the transition were native Americans. Very few foreigners were manufacturers.[109] English merchants, like Boott and Lodge, did invest in industrial enterprises, and some Irish and Germans figured prominently in fields where they could readily exploit the labor of their own countrymen. Thus, the Irish firms of Carney and Sleeper and of Mahony and Kenna, and the German, Leopold Morse, were among the leading clothing makers.[110] Contrary to the rule, a few other businesses remained in the hands of the immigrants who founded them: John Donnelly, "city bill poster," who helped establish modern outdoor advertising, William S. Pendleton, an Englishman who introduced lithography into the United States, and two highly skilled German silversmiths maintained their positions.[111] But generally Americans gained control even of the piano industry, the manufacture of glass, brewing, and other industries established in Boston by alien newcomers.[112]

Immigration advanced other classes in the community as well as the manufacturers. Since the Irish could not satisfy their own needs, others had to. Irishmen needed doctors and teachers; they consumed dry goods and food, thereby quickening the city's commercial life. The demand for professional and commercial services directly aided the merchants and clerks, the traders and artisans, — the bulk of the American population of the city. A rise in the prevailing occupational level of the native Bostonians resulted from the general decline in labor costs and the increased value of their own services.

The only Americans who suffered permanently from the Irish invasion were the unskilled laborers and domestics, few in number, who competed directly with the newcomers. More important, although they eventually adjusted to the new conditions on favorable terms, was the injury to the artisans displaced by the combination of machinery and cheap labor.[113] They were a large group, eminently respectable, hitherto prosperous, and always influential in the community. Their protest against the use of green hands was one of the significant factors complicating the social orientation of the Irish in Boston.[114]

But though the industrial workers as a class lost ground throughout the period,[115] and though most of the individuals within that class suffered immediately by the transition, in the end they gained. The flexibility of the economic organization of the United States enabled the displaced artisans to set up as manufacturers, to enter other trades, or to move west. Edward Everett Hale pointed out:

We are here, well organized, and well trained, masters of the soil. . . . It must be, that when they come in among us, they come to lift us up. As sure as water and oil each finds its level they will find theirs. So far as they are mere hand-workers they must sustain the head-workers, or those who have any element of intellectual ability. Their inferiority . . . compels them to go to the bottom; and the consequence is that we are, all of us, the higher lifted because they are here. . . . If into the civilized community made up of hand-workers, and workers in higher grades, you pour in an infusion of a population competent at first only to the simplest hand-work, they take the lowest place, and lift the others into higher places. . . . Factory . . . and farm work comes into the hands of Irishmen. . . . Natives . . . are simply pushed up, into foremen . . . , superintendents . . . , railway agents, machinists, inventors, teachers, artists &c. . . .[116]

And the experience of all other groups, even of the Negroes, was similar to that of the native whites. With the minor exceptions occasionally noted above, there was little to distinguish them occupationally. Only the Irish stood apart.

The lads who left Skibbereen and Mallow and Macroom where daily wages ranged from sixpence for common laborers to one shilling sixpence for carpenters, the spalpeens who fled from Cork and the west where cash was scarce, received higher pay in Boston.[117] Of that there was no doubt. They came expecting better wages and got them. Those who once measured their income in terms of potatoes found dollars, no matter how few, a fair return indeed. But mercilessly linked to these fine dollars was the price system, a ruthless monster which devoured the fruits of Irishmen's labor before they could gather them. The "pratties" and milk were gone from their garden; the garden itself was gone; and there was no room for the pig in Dock Square. Faced for the first time with the necessity of purchasing their own food and clothing, the peasants found costs high beyond anything they could have conceived, and rising rapidly throughout this period.[118] By contrast, the much more leisurely increase in

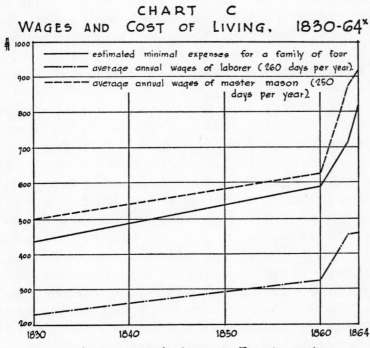

CHART C
WAGES AND COST OF LIVING. 1830-64[x]

———— estimated minimal expenses for a family of four
———·— average annual wages of laborer (260 days per year).
———— average annual wages of master mason (250 days per year).

[x] *Derived from Third Annual Report of the Bureau of Statistics of Labor.... 1872, pp. 517-520.*

wages counted for little.[119] The British consul noted that in spite of the rise in wages "it may be doubted if more food and raiment can be purchased by the workman than previously." [120] As a result, the Irish found the value of their labor low, often too low to support them and their families.[121]

The conditions of work were as bad as its price was low. The laborers and their employers spoke a different language. Their work week in Ireland had not included Sundays, but in Boston they must toil the full seven days.[122] Their day at home had not excluded time off to chat, to smoke, or just to rest; now they had to accept the rigid discipline of the factory or the contract boss. The leisurely independent peasant life was ended — replaced in a fifteen-hour working day by a feverish struggle for bread under the commands of an alien master.

But no matter — if only that struggle were consistently successful. It never was. From the day they landed, the immigrants competed for jobs that were fewer than men. Through all these years unemployment was endemic to the economic system. Even the Civil War brought no surcease; the condition of labor deteriorated steadily. The depression of the first year threw great masses of men out of work, particularly in industrial South Boston, where they starved in their hideous slums.[123] Not until the war had drawn thousands of men into the army and stimulated new manufacturing developments did the demand for labor approximate the supply. By that time employers were making hurried efforts to attract new immigrants — new workers to restore the labor surplus.[124]

Tossed in the swell of impersonal economic currents, the

Irish remained but shabbily equipped to meet the multifarious problems imposed upon them by urban life. Rising prices, ruthless factory exploitation, and unemployment caused "the wreck and ruin that came upon the Irish race in the foreign land!" In the new society "one in a hundred may live and prosper, and stand to be looked at as a living monument of . . . prosperity, but ninety-nine in a hundred are lost, never to be heard of." [125]

❧ IV ❧

The Physical Adjustment

How shall your houseless heads and unfed sides,
Your loop'd and window'd raggedness, defend you
From seasons such as these?

BOSTON'S economic transformation set apart one whole section of society — the unskilled, resourceless, perennially unemployed Irish proletariat, whose only prospect was absorption into industry at starvation wages. In every phase of their reaction to the new environment, economic maladjustment complicated a process relatively simple for other groups. This factor far overshadowed other aspects of Boston's ecological development. By their immobility the Irish crammed the city, recasting its boundaries and disfiguring its physical appearance; by their poverty they introduced new problems of disease, vice, and crime, with which neither they nor the community were ready to cope.

Up to 1840 Boston had easily accommodated the gradual increase in residents, of whatever nationality, for it was well on the way toward a solution of its urban problems. Slowly and often laboriously it had surmounted the original limitations constricting its area. By 1845 the peninsula on which it perched was no longer isolated from the mainland. The Mill

88

Dam obviated complete reliance on the sandy neck, at one time subject to frequent floods; and bridges tied the city to Cambridgeport, Charlestown, and South Boston, while a ferry linked it to East Boston. With the extension of transit facilities, it was no longer necessary for those who worked in the metropolis to live within walking distance of " 'change." Filling operations in the flats created new land and precluded the possibility of an acute shortage of space. Widespread building prevented overcrowding and led to a notable scarcity of slums. The rise in the number of persons per dwelling was probably "more than overcome by a larger and better class of houses," for facilities kept pace with the demand.[1]

After 1840, however, growth by immigration — completely unexpected and at a rate higher than ever before — violently upset the process of physical adjustment.[2] In 1845 the foremost authority on demography in Boston confidently asserted that there could be no further increase in inhabitants.[3] Yet the next decade witnessed the injection from abroad of more than 230,000 souls, of whom enough remained to raise the population more than a third and to convert a densely-settled into an overcrowded city.[4]

Those who were able to break away from the most congested portions of the town's center continued to have no difficulty in securing adequate and comfortable lodgings in many neighborhoods. The rustic villages surrounding Boston eagerly awaited the realtor who might turn abundant farm lands into metropolitan avenues, and welcomed alike foreigners and natives, financially able to escape from the teeming peninsula.

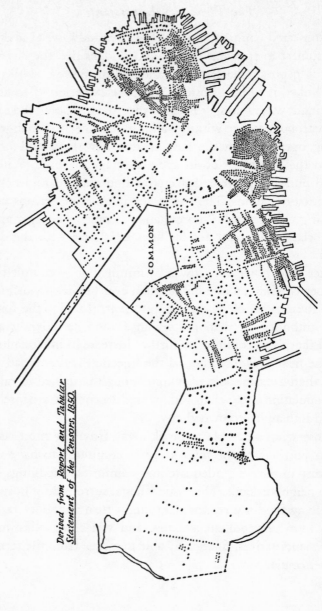

COMMON

Derived from *Report and Tabular Statement of the Censors, 1850.*

MAP I. DISTRIBUTION OF THE IRISH IN BOSTON, 1850, BY STREETS

Primarily, this centrifugal movement winnowed the well-to-do from the impoverished, and consequently segregated the great mass of Irish within the narrow limits of old Boston. There was no such isolation in the distribution of other newcomers throughout the city. Once having secured employment, which their backgrounds enabled them to do more readily than the Irish, they easily adjusted the routines of their old lives to new homes. In some instances, several German, French, or English families resided on the same street, but generally there were no French, German, or English districts.[5] For heterogeneous pursuits scattered these aliens everywhere and limited numbers permitted them to slip at will into almost any section without altering its essential characteristics.

Although some Irish joined the exodus, the overwhelming number remained where they were. Their poverty, combined with Boston's geography, assured that. Unlike every other American city, Boston was completely waterlocked, with no direction in which its people could move without the payment of tolls or fares. Those who could not afford to pay twenty cents per day to go back and forth to the environs, necessarily sought accommodations within short walking distance of their daily fifteen-hour drudgery in the mill or at the wharf.[6] Even those who occasionally worked elsewhere felt compelled to keep close to the source of new assignments.[7] The peaceful suburbs of Roxbury and Dorchester, the quiet streets and roomy houses, were not for them.

Instead, they clustered about the commercial heart of Boston — the narrow peripheral strip of piers and the small area on the peninsula proper pivoting about State Street and ex-

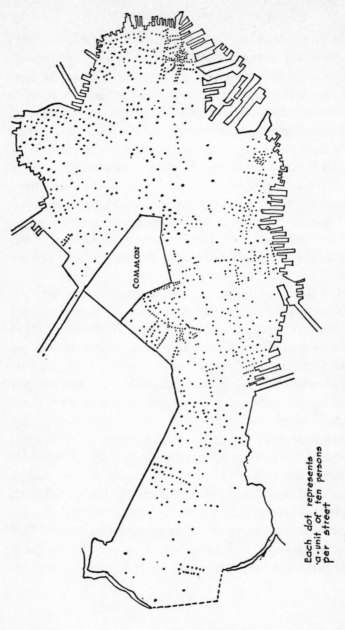

Each dot represents
·a·unit of ten persons
per street

MAP II. DISTRIBUTION OF NON-IRISH FOREIGNERS IN BOSTON, 1850, BY STREETS

COMMON

tending from the water front westward to Washington Street and from Water Street north to Ann. Here were the city's most important enterprises, its docks and markets, offices and counting houses, stores and work-shops. Intertwined with this section, in a long line down Washington Street and its extension, Ann Street, was the garment district, for the merchant was still the manufacturer and his shop the factory.[8] In this region tailors and unskilled laborers were most apt to find work.

Within easy reach of these crucial districts were two centers whose development made them the logical receiving points for the Irish proletariat. Above Ann Street, stretching from Commercial to Causeway Streets, was the North End, always the most congested part of the city. South of Water Street was a similar neighborhood encompassing Fort Hill and Pearl Street and extending to include the South Cove, made land created by filling operations in the 1830's.[9] Both the North End, which in its more prosperous days had contained many fine mansions, and the less elegant but eminently respectable Fort Hill, had once been purely residential, but the encroachment of trade impaired their fashionableness, draining off many old dwellers.[10] Nevertheless, the very proximity of business gave real estate a highly speculative value. Because it was unprofitable to make or maintain improvements where there was a "marked discrepancy between the value placed on the property by the owner and its value for any uses" to which it could immediately be put, landlords permitted their buildings to deteriorate.[11] Their prime object was to avoid expense and to rent at a price sufficient for mere upkeep while waiting to sell.

In this transition originated the Boston slums — precisely the housing the Irish needed. Near the wharves and cheap in rent, these localities became the first home of such immigrants in Boston. Newcoming Irishmen, nostalgic for the Emerald Isle, gravitated towards these vicinities, augmenting the number of Irish already there, and making their countrymen reluctant to leave the home-like community even when they could. As a result, there were few natives in the North End and Fort Hill and even fewer non-Irish aliens, for these groups fled, sacrificing other interests in order to avoid the decline in social status that resulted from remaining.[12]

Several towns convenient to these two primary Irish settlements received those who, "leaving the low and reclaimed land to foreign laborers, plant themselves in the suburbs . . . availing of the frequent omnibuses, or of special trains" to reach the city.[13] Each of these districts experienced approximately the same evolution. At first penetrated only by the very rich, and then by other natives, and English, Scots, and Germans, they gradually attracted some of the more affluent Irishmen after 1845. When industries existed in these places the employees sought homes nearby; but as long as the cost of transportation continued high, the Irish poor who worked in Boston were prevented from commuting. They surmounted this last obstacle only in the 1850's when the horse-railroad stretched from Scollay Square throughout the whole metropolitan region and threw open sections which theretofore had preserved their exclusiveness by steep rates. The laws which chartered these lines limited fares to five cents and provided for round-trip tickets at six and eight cents,

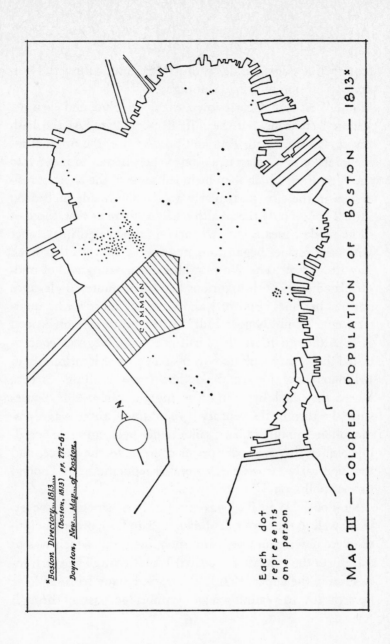

MAP III — COLORED POPULATION OF BOSTON — 1813*

*Boston Directory... 1813...
(Boston, 1813) pp. 272–6;
Boynton, New... Map... of Boston.

COMMON

Each dot represents one person

loosing a floodgate and, by the 1860's, inundating the outskirts of Boston with Irish immigrants.[14]

The West End, Charlestown, the South End, and even the remotest environs, felt the shift in population. As the Irish preëmpted the North End and South Cove, the original inhabitants of every class abandoned their homes to move into the West End, which then included some of the choicest residences in the city, particularly on the south side of Beacon Hill. Though only the wealthiest lived there at first, those of more modest means entered early and increased in number when the former began to drift into the newly filled Back Bay after 1857.[15] The West End became a stronghold of middle-class homes with luxurious fringes of moneyed elegance and shadier ones of poverty and vice. The more sordid quarters centered in "Nigger Hill" on the north side of Beacon Hill. Although more than half the city's Negroes concentrated there, they took up only a small part of it, primarily in Belknap (now Joy) and Southac (now Phillips) Streets, where they had lived in their highly combustible houses since the turn of the century.[16] In addition, there was a cosmopolitan mixture of bars, sailor dance halls, and low boarding houses that were of special concern to the police, and that had early earned a disagreeable reputation as a "horrid sink of pollution."[17]

Most of the West End was respectably American, however. Until well in the 1850's, Irishmen and, indeed, other foreigners were few in number.[18] But soon, the trend which was to transform the area after the Civil War, began. The small industries in the upper West End attracted many Irish; and the horsecar line to Watertown and Cambridge, passing through

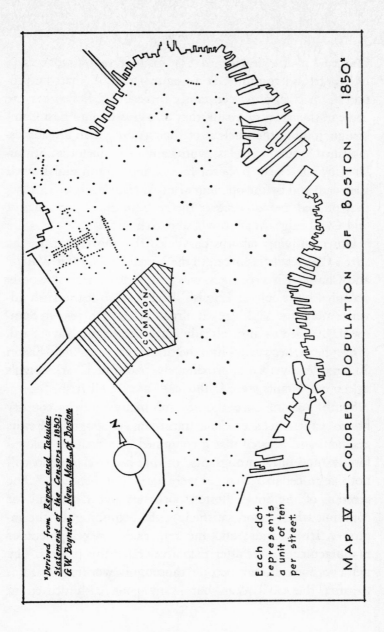

COMMON

N

* Derived from *Report and Tabular Statement of the Censors ... 1850*; G.W. Boynton, *New ... Map ... of Boston.*

Each dot represents a unit of ten per street.

MAP IV — COLORED POPULATION OF BOSTON — 1850*

the heart of the district in 1858, enabled many workers to live there and commute at a nominal rate, so that the proportion of Irish grew constantly thereafter.[19] Following the route of the street railroads, they also crossed into East Cambridge, joining the nucleus of their countrymen already established around the glass works and other factories. Stimulated by the cheap five-cent fare of the Boston and Lowell Railroad, and by the opening of rapid transit service in 1856, they pushed the natives ever further into the dim reaches of Old Cambridge, Watertown, and Arlington.[20]

Other outlying suburbs paralleled this movement. In the 1830's Charlestown, linked to the North End by the Warren and Charles River Bridges, was still "a place almost wholly occupied by people of English descent." [21] But the Irish advance along the Middlesex Railroad (chartered 1854 to Somerville), added to those already employed in the Navy Yard, drove the earlier settlers into the rural wastes of Anglo-Saxon Somerville. By 1860 approximately 10,000 of Charlestown's 25,000 inhabitants were Catholics — almost all Irish.[22]

South Boston, once the seat of many opulent country homes, experienced a similar transition. Although in 1847 its residents still boasted that it contained "not a single colored family" and only immigrants "of that better class who will not live in cellars," changes were already impending.[23] The erection of the South Boston docks created a demand for common wharf labor, satisfied, at the beginning, by the influx of Irish hands; and the remarkable development of manufacturing there after 1840 accelerated this process. The neighborhood did not become thoroughly working-class until after the Civil War, but many poor Irish drifted in throughout the period, particularly after the Dorchester Railroad in 1857 and the Broadway Railroad a few years later made it accessible to those employed elsewhere.[24]

The newcomers edged the natives and even some Irish just beyond South Boston into Dorchester. This town was still thoroughly rural in 1855. But by then the Irish had already so far penetrated into Washington Village, the sector nearest Boston, that it seceded and joined South Boston.[25]

Somewhat more gradual, but ultimately as conclusive, was the development of the Neck or the South End. Its settlement had proceeded slowly, for, as an investigating committee discovered in 1845, none would live there unless they worked there.[26] After the extension of Washington, Harrison, and Suffolk (later Shawmut) Streets, and the introduction of horsecars (1856) through the South End to Roxbury, the Irish trickled into the area.[27] Their representation nevertheless was limited, composed largely of intelligent tradespeople and mechanics, and confined north of Dover Street in a minority among their neighbors. For throughout this period the South End, still a desolate marsh and less desirable than other suburbs, was yet too expensive and inconvenient for the slum dwellers of the North End and Fort Hill.[28]

Its extension, Roxbury, was even more isolated by high fares. Although by 1850, fully 40 per cent of Roxbury's population were foreigners or children of foreigners, these were primarily prosperous groups and included many non-Irish.[29] Only the opening of the street railroads in 1858 exposed Roxbury to the masses who thereafter moved in, forcing their predecessors back into West Roxbury and Dedham.[30]

Noodle's Island, East Boston, eventually the most important outskirt, lay across a narrow arm of Boston Bay. The East Boston Company, founded in 1833 to exploit its real estate, met with slight success until 1840, when the Cunard Line assured the future of the Island by fixing its western terminus there. The construction of piers and the subsequent necessity for stevedores attracted many Irish. In 1850 the introduction of Cochituate water ended the dependence upon wells and increased the capacity of the island. By then, a steam ferry shuttled across the Bay every five minutes transporting as many as 14,000 passengers each day for a two-cent fare and facilitating the migration of many North-Enders.[31] The isolation of Chelsea, the town beyond East Boston, persisted until the Winnisemet Ferry, closed before 1830, was replaced. But after the establishment of the Boston and Chelsea Railroad through Charlestown and the Winthrop Railroad through East Boston, even this remote community added to its population from the continuous drift out of peninsular Boston, and only such towns as Malden, Brighton, and Brookline, without direct connections, were unaffected.[32]

This process consolidated the lines drawn between the Irish and other groups by the city's economic evolution. Almost all the non-Irish, free to take advantage of the rise of contiguous towns, dispersed everywhere, never concentrating in a single section. But although rapid transit permitted some Irish to move out of the densest areas, most remained in the hideous slums of Fort Hill and the North End, subject to all their rotting evils.

Wherever the Irish proletariat resided, distinctive accommodations appeared to meet their extensive demands and limited ability to pay. Upon their arrival they could not hope to find truly permanent homes, for few had any notion of where to live or work. Coming without funds, they shifted about until they found a situation and earned enough to pay the initial costs of establishment. But even employment did not solve their problem, for their jobs were invariably low-paid and transitory. Their every-day expenses, subtracted from their wages, left only privation in the balance. It took years to accumulate even meager reserves, and many never managed to save enough to furnish a flat, much less to buy a home. Unable to afford domiciles of their own, they lodged awhile with friends, relatives, or countrymen; no matter how cramped the quarters of those already settled, there was always more room for the sake of rent, charity, or kinship. Such makeshifts were unsatisfactory, however, and a durable solution awaited the development of the only quarters thousands of Irishmen could afford.

The ultimate housing of the Irish required an extensive process of adaptation on the part of Boston real estate. The simplest form was conversion of old mansions and disused warehouses into tenements. In many cases, boardinghouse keepers, wishing to profit by the new demand, took over properties which, after a few alterations, emerged as multiple dwellings. In other cases, a sub-lease system developed, whereby a contractor, usually Irish himself and frequently a neighborhood tradesman, leased an old building at an annual rental, subdivided it into immigrant flats, and sub-rented it at weekly rates. Sometimes the structure passed through the hands of several agents, completely severing control from ownership.[38] Solely interested in immediate income, having the welfare of neither the building nor the tenants at heart, sub-landlords encouraged a host of evils, while the occupants suffered from their "merciless inflictions." [34] By this metamorphosis "houses . . . long inhabited by the well-to-do class of people, are vacated by them for others in more fashionable quarters . . . and then a less fortunate class of folk occupy for a while, — they, in their turn,

Fig. 9. View of tenements in Stillman Street

to make room for another class on the descending scale . . . till houses, once fashionable . . . become neglected, dreary tenement houses into which the families of the low-paid and poverty smitten . . . crowd by the dozens. . . ." [35]

Despite its lack of conveniences or sanitation, and its general inflammability, the remodeled type was far superior to any other available to the Irish. While those adapted from factories, as was Chickering's old Franklin Square plant, were unrivaled in their perniciousness, even the barracks in Stillman Street in the North End had some benefits of light, air, and privacy (Fig. 9).[36] Whatever the intention of proprietor or lessee, transformed buildings could not utilize space as carefully as those created specifically for immigrants.

New dwellings, completely free of restrictions, displayed every stratagem for economy at the expense of the most hum-

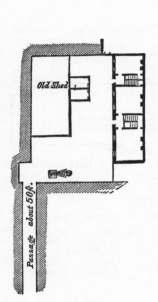

Fig. 10. Plan of place in rear of 136 Hanover Street

Fig. 11. House in rear of 136 Hanover Street

ble amenities. The prevailing architecture on hitherto unused space in the peripheral Irish areas such as the West End, South Boston, and East Boston, was characterized by many flats along a narrow passageway. In 1857, for instance, Samuel Hooper reared two four-story wooden edifices with brick ends in Friends Street Court, each holding thirty-two one-room apartments to which the sun never penetrated. A narrow path, fourteen feet wide, half obstructed by a row of privies and water hydrants, separated the two blocks. In Institute Avenue a similar development centering in an alley of only ten feet, exploited the available plot even more thoroughly.[37]

Within the focal points of Irish concentration, however,

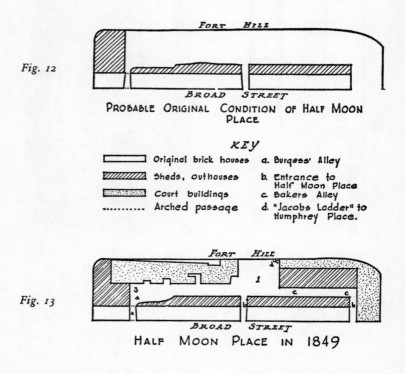

Fig. 12

FORT HILL

BROAD STREET

PROBABLE ORIGINAL CONDITION OF HALF MOON
PLACE

KEY

☐ Original brick houses   a. Burgess' Alley
▨ Sheds, outhouses   b. Entrance to
         Half Moon Place
▨ Court buildings   c. Bakers Alley
⋯⋯ Arched passage   d. "Jacobs Ladder" to
         Humphrey Place.

Fig. 13

FORT HILL

BROAD STREET

HALF MOON PLACE IN 1849

the price of real estate was too high to permit like constructions. Instead, enterprising landowners utilized unremunerative yards, gardens, and courts to yield the maximum number of hovels that might pass as homes. The abundant

Fig. 14. View of Half Moon Place

grounds surrounding well-built early Boston residences, and the hitherto unusable sites created by the city's irregular streets, once guarantees of commodious living, now fostered the most vicious Boston slums. Every vacant spot, behind, beside, or within an old structure, yielded room for still another.[38] And eventually, to correct the oversight of the first

Fig. 15. Burgess' Alley. North view.

builders who had failed to exhaust the ultimate inch, their
more perspicacious successors squeezed house within house,
exploiting the last iota of space. This resulted in so tangled
a swarm that the compiler of the first Boston atlas gave up
the attempt to map such areas, simply dismissing them as
"full of sheds and shanties." [39]

Fig. 16. Burgess' Alley. South view.

The whole brood of evils typical of this development materialized in Half Moon Place (represented by no. 1 in Fig. 13 and pictured in Fig. 14) and the two alleys leading off it. This pest hole consisted of a very limited tract, originally vacant, between the rear of the Broad Street tenements and Fort Hill (Fig. 4). A rise in the value of land led to the excavation of additional portions of the hill, and the erection of tottering rookeries with their backs flush upon it.[40] Not one of these melancholy warrens, moldering at their very conception, opened directly upon a street. The inhabitants of the

107

central court (no. 1, Fig. 13; Fig. 14) and Bakers Alley (c in Fig. 13) emerged to the main thoroughfare through two gaps between the Broad Street buildings (b, Fig. 13), but the less fortunate denizens of Burgess Alley (a, Fig. 13, Figs. 15, 16) made their way through an arched crevice in the house in front of them (Figs. 13, 17). From Half Moon Place there was, as well, a battered staircase, "Jacob's Ladder," which led to the comparative heaven of Humphrey Place above.[41]

Fig. 17. Entrance to Burgess' Alley

Remodeled or new, these dwellings promoted a steady succession of evils, constant factors in the deterioration of the physical aspects of Irish life in Boston. No standards of decency and comfort were too low for erstwhile occupants in Ireland of crammed "hovels . . . without floors, without furniture and with patches of dirty straw." [42] The one evil of which Boston houses were free was excessive height, for most had only two or three stories — a blessing not to be underestimated.[43]

Immigrant rents were everywhere high beyond all reason because of the system whereby middlemen demanded dual and sometimes triple profits, and secured returns greater than on any other real estate in the city. In the Fort Hill district in 1845, the meanest accommodations commanded

$1.00 or $1.50 per week per room; an attic could not be gotten for less than $1.50, and a cellar, for $2.00, all paid weekly in advance.[44]

The failure of building to keep up with the increase of population and the steep cost of apartments bred overcrowding. In 1845 Shattuck warned that the area north of Beach Street could never hold more than 80,000 people with safety.[45] Yet ten years later more than 90,000 resided there.[46]

The Irish sections were the most congested in the city and immigrant homes felt a consequent strain upon living resources.[47] They were "not occupied by a single family or even by two or three families; but each room, from garret to cellar [was] . . . filled with a family . . . of several persons, and sometimes with two or more. . . ." [48] Every nook was in demand. Attics, often no more than three feet high, were popular. And basements were even more coveted, particularly in the Fort Hill area; by 1850 the 586 inhabited in Boston contained from five to fifteen persons in each, with at least one holding thirty-nine every night.[49]

Underground dwellings enjoyed refreshing coolness in the hot summer months and coal-saving warmth in the winter — important advantages in resisting the vicissitudes of Boston's climate. But with these benefits went many drawbacks. Built entirely beneath the street level, they enjoyed no light or air save that which dribbled in through the door leading down, by rickety steps, from the sidewalk above. Innocent of the most rudimentary plumbing, some normally held two or three feet of water, and all were subject to periodic floods and frequent inundations by the backwater of drains at high tide. Above all, there was little space. Some windowless

vaults no more than eighteen feet square and five feet high
held fourteen humans. That marked "A" in Figure 18, for
instance, was no more than six feet in any dimension, with
no ventilation except through bedroom "B" (Fig. 19). In
some, two or more bedrooms huddled next to a parlor-

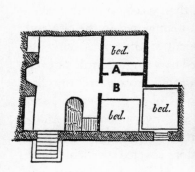

*Fig. 18. Plan of Cellar in Bread
Street*

*Fig. 19. Subterranean bedroom in Bread
Street*

kitchen which often served as bar or grocery as well. These
were by no means exceptional. A committee of philanthro-
pists reported in 1849 that cellars generally contained a "grocery and vegetable shop; and not infrequently, a groggery
and dancing hall . . . ," and mournfully concluded, "As
might be expected, intemperance, lewdness, riot . . . enter
in and dwell there." [50] Despite a suggestion in the following
year that such holes be outlawed, their number increased and
they continued to draw high prices.[51] Indeed, the Irish population could not have been housed without them.

The most serious danger inherent in immigrant quarters

was the complete neglect of sewerage equipment and sanitation of any kind. In many cases, especially in houses "originally designed for warehouses and . . . converted . . . as economically as possible," the absolute lack of facilities obliged the occupants "to supply their necessities as best they" could.[52] Where drainage systems existed, they were inefficient and insufficient. The roads near Fort Hill were ungraded and in vicinities such as the South Cove and the Mill Pond the marshy ground had settled so that "the imperfect sewerage . . . originally provided" had become "altogether useless." [53] Usually residents relied on yard hydrants and water-closets "exposed to the transient custom of tenants or outsiders" alike.[54] Many houses had "but one sink, opening into a contracted and ill-constructed drain, or . . . into a passageway or street, and but one privy, usually a mass of pollution, for all the inhabitants, sometimes amounting to a hundred." [55] No one was responsible for the care of these communal instruments, and as a result they were normally out of repair. Abominably foul and feculent, perpetually gushing over into the surrounding yards, they were mighty carriers of disease. To make matters worse, lack of direct access to the streets in court dwellings made the disposal of rubbish a burdensome problem, most easily solved by permitting it to decay at its leisure in the tiny yards, a process which converted the few feet between adjoining buildings into storehouses of accumulated filth.[56]

The description of Half Moon Place by the Cholera Committee (1849) shows the result such conditions produced. "A large part of the area is occupied by . . . twelve or fourteen privies, constantly overflowing, and by ill constructed and worn out sinks and drains, into which are hourly thrown solid substances, of all sorts, which choke them up and cause the liquid . . . to run over. Into the area . . . a steep . . . staircase affords a passage to Humphrey place, some fifty feet above. Side by side with the staircase, and fully exposed, a large, square, plank drain makes a precipitous descent, conducting, half hidden, half revealed, not only the waste waters of the houses in Humphrey place, but also, the contents of its privies to the area below; which, as may be supposed, is redolent of the fact." [57]

Tenants relied on their own resources in securing heat, and therefore few succeeded in warming their rooms to any degree of comfort. Coal and wood were expensive, particularly since, "being too poor to be economical" and "obliged to buy in small quantities" they had to "pay . . . at least double . . . for wood and coal . . . [by] the bundle and the basket . . . there being neither money . . . , nor place for storage of articles bought in larger bulk." [58] For many the only means of outwitting the cold was to remain in bed throughout the day.[59] Under the circumstances small rooms were an advantage. But rooms were not only small; they were also low, dingy, and suffocating. In the Fort Hill buildings, air and light were complete strangers; either the hill behind or the Broad Street houses in front excluded them. Ventilation shafts were often no more than two feet square. Windows, where they existed, were always closed to keep out the stench of the yards in summer, and the bitterness of the wind in winter. In passage structures, of course, only the top floor saw the sun at all.[60]

In the absence of care and of proper facilities remarkable exertions were required to maintain a minimal standard of tidiness. Rooms were unpainted; closets were rare; furniture, inadequate. Want of any equipment beyond the rudimentary bed and table, a few chairs, and the ubiquitous washtub, necessitated scattering clothing and other articles wherever they might fall or, at best, hanging them on pegs. Baths were unheard of; inside water was uncommon, and the apartments with their own water supply few indeed. Walls were damp, roofs leaked. Stairs were generally dilapidated, windows were often broken, and many buildings had not felt the hand of the repair man in ten or more years. Decay and slothfulness led directly to the prevalence of fires which involved great loss of life and much suffering.[61]

Slovenliness and disorder were inevitable in the squalor of such conditions. "In such a state of things, there can be no cleanliness, privacy, or proper ventilation . . . ; and, with the ignorance, carelessness, and generally loose and dirty habits which prevail among the occupants, the necessary evils are greatly increased both in amount and intensity. In Broad Street and all the surrounding neighborhood . . . the situation of the Irish . . . is particularly wretched. . . . This whole district is a perfect hive of human beings, without comforts and mostly without common necessaries; in many cases, huddled together like brutes, without regard to sex, or age, or sense of decency; grown men and women sleeping together in the same apartment, and sometimes wife and husband, brothers and sisters, in the same bed. Under such circumstances, self-respect, forethought, all high and noble virtues soon die out, and sullen indifference and despair, or disorder, intemperance and utter degradation reign supreme." [62]

Inadequate housing, debarment from the healing sun, and inescapable filth took their toll in sickness and lives. Boston had been a healthy city before the 1840's, a city in which the life-span was long and disease rare. Smallpox, for instance, no longer existed by 1845. Although an unusually large number of cases had cropped up in 1839 and 1840 because of the relaxation of regulations in 1838, there had been no major epidemic since 1792.[63] But after 1845 the pestilence flourished, particularly among the Irish.[64] Nor was this the only scourge miserable living conditions bred to plague the city. Year after year endemic or contagious maladies returned to haunt the depressed areas.[65] In 1849 the cholera spread from Philadelphia and New York to Boston. Despite feverish efforts to halt it, the epidemic swept through the congested courts in the hot summer months, reaping a full harvest of victims with a severity "fully accounted for by the deplorable conditions of the emigrants from Europe." [66] It thrived best in places "least perfect in drainage, the worst ventilated and the most crowded," that is, in Irish districts.[67] The distribution of 611 fatal cases and ninety-six other identifiable ones coincided to a remarkable degree with Irish slum sections. The worst outbreaks occurred in the rear of 136 Hanover Street, Burgess Alley (200 cases), Mechanics Court, and the rear of Batterymarch Street, especially prominent points of Irish concentration.[68] Most of the patients in East Boston likewise resided in neighborhoods like Liverpool Street and "in every instance . . . the houses were without proper *drains*. . . ." In all, more than 500 of the 700 fatalities were Irish, or the children of Irishmen.[69]

More vicious in the long run than the spectacular ills were those which, conceived in squalor, quietly ate away resistance before delivering their final blow. Most important was tuberculosis. This disease had declined in Boston until 1845, but thereafter revived in the hovels of the Irish on whom it fattened year after year, reaching the unprecedented peak of 4.57 deaths per thousand living in 1855.[70] The impact of miserable environment was even more pernicious upon the children of the slums than upon their parents. This period witnessed a rise in infant mortality, attributable primarily to three products of foul surroundings — intestinal disorders, pneumonia, and bronchitis.[71] All three appeared overwhelmingly among the Irish, and, in the opinion of Dr. Howard Damon, superintendent of the Boston Dispensary, the first, including "diarrhœa, cholera infantum, and dysentery," certainly depended "upon two very distinct causes of insalubrity, — overcrowding and imperfect drainage."[72]

Irish longevity, low enough in the homeland, dwindled because of the debilitating crossing and the disheartening conditions in America. So many died soon after arrival that it was said the Irish lived an average of only fourteen years after reaching Boston.[73] Their coming consequently raised the death rate unexpectedly after 1845. Before then it had increased from 2.04 per cent for the ten year period ending 1830 to 2.20 per cent for the decade ending 1840, and to 2.53 per cent for the five years ending 1845, a rise due almost exclusively to the ever larger proportion of elderly people.[74] Far from lowering the mortality, as the injection of a young and medium-aged group should have, the immediate effect of immigration and of the diseases and hardships attending settlement in Boston, was to boost it even further to 2.94 per cent for the five-year period ending 1850. This was twice as high as for the rest of Massachusetts, and higher even than the English slums. After 1850 when the initial shock of transplantation wore off, the rate tended to revert to the level of 1845, with 2.74 per cent for 1850–55, 2.39 per cent for 1855–60, and 2.42 per cent for 1860–65. But though immigration had decreased the proportion of aged people in the city, the death rate still remained above that of most comparable communities.[75]

Mortality was actually not uniform in all groups. In sections inhabited by Americans and other non-Irish it was as low as outside the city, particularly before 1850 when the Irish had not yet spread, carrying disease with them. In that year the death rate was only 1.3 per cent in the Beacon Hill district, where there were but 561 foreigners, chiefly servants, in a total population of 2,615, and only 1.92 per cent in the Back Bay area, where there were 1,348 aliens in a population of 5,121, and these chiefly German; but in Broad Street and Fort Hill where 2,738 out of 2,813 were not natives, and almost all Irish, it was fully 5.65 per cent.[76] One out of every seventeen Broad Street Irishmen died in 1850. As the population scattered, the proportion of deaths in the various regions evened out somewhat; the disparity in 1855 was not as radical as in 1850, and in 1865, even less so. But distinctions did not completely disappear. In 1865 there was still a differential of 1.39 per cent between the North End and Beacon Hill.[77] On the basis of nativity, disregarding geographical variations, this inequality was almost as pronounced. While the rate for the whole city was 2.64 per cent in 1850, that for native Americans was 2.23, for non-Irish foreigners, 2.66, for Germans only 1.31, and for the Irish, fully 3.29.[78] From either perspective, Irishmen, although "not possessing, and scarcely thinking of the luxuries of life" and devoid of "the more debilitating and fatal effects of mental anxiety and luxurious enjoyment," hastened in the midst of life to death.[79]

Nevertheless, the city's foreign population multiplied, partly from continued immigration, but essentially from the fertility of immigrants — a particularly fortunate phenomenon because it came just in time to compensate for decreasing native births. In 1845, when the rate was 1:30 for Boston, it was twice as high (1:15) for the Broad Street section. By 1850 the native ratio was one birth for every forty living, but for the Irish it was one for every nineteen and for the Germans, a very youthful group, slightly larger — one for every seventeen. Although the incidence of births was high among the Germans, their meager number had little effect upon the general trend. Only 2.80 per cent of the total births were German, 35.27 per cent were native, and fully 52.87 per cent were Irish in 1850. The frequency of births among immigrants reflected a high proportion of marriages. One Irishman in fifty and one German in twenty-seven wed in 1850 — a rate higher than the native one in sixty-five, and attributable to the large number of young and middle-aged people.[80]

Fecundity was the only contribution of the Irish toward a solution of the community's social problems. Otherwise, their abject status spawned a brood of evils that burdened civic progress for many decades. Of these misfortunes, pauperism was the most important and the most pervasive, for thousands of Irish were constantly "idle and inactive, when there was an earnest craving for occupation. . . ."[81] Living on the brink of starvation even when at work, they necessarily called upon charity when discarded by the overstocked labor market, joining the ranks of the unemployables who could under no circumstances support themselves and of the aged for whom there was no security in an improvident economy.

Feeding idle mouths, particularly idle foreign mouths, was a difficulty complicated by the wasteful division of functions between Massachusetts' central government and its subdivisions. Although the care of the poor was essentially a municipal matter, the Commonwealth had early assumed the obligation of maintaining those without legal residence. The towns felt no incentive to economize where others paid the bill; instead, they rather welcomed, or at least did not vigorously oppose, the incursion of impoverished strangers who merely lowered the per-capita cost of assisting residents and provided free work-house labor as well.[82] Between 1845 and 1854, therefore, local officials did little to halt the hundreds of beggars who made their way to the Massachusetts almshouses. In that period Irish transient paupers outnumbered the sum of all others, of whatever status or nationality.[83]

But soon enough, Boston, like other municipalities, succumbed to the process which naturally and quietly transferred many to its care. Inevitably, state dependents acquired legal residence, and looked to the city for support. Accentuating the increasing burden even further was "the great influx of Foreign Diseased Paupers" requiring immediate medical attention, who forced Boston in 1847 to establish, at considerable cost, two hospitals on Deer Island, almost all of whose inmates were Irish.[84]

CHART   D
STATE PAUPERS IN MASSACHUSETTS, 1837–1858[x]

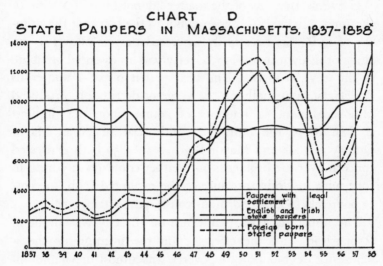

[x] *Derived from "Report of the Special Joint Committee Appointed to Investigate Public Charitable Institutions of Massachusetts....1858," Massachusetts Senate Documents, 1858, no. 2, pp. 131, 143.*

Meanwhile, attempts to reduce the state's expense both by excluding unbonded aliens and by devolving part of the financial responsibility upon localities, failed.[85] Successive committees of the legislature only suggested minor reforms and palliatives to deal with the added load to the budget. The Commonwealth finally cut the Gordian knot by taking the administration into its own hands. In accordance with the recommendation of the Committee of 1851, it provided four workhouses where its wards could be at least partially self-sustaining, and, in addition, it imposed a commutation tax by which immigrants paid for the support of their unfortunate countrymen who became public charges.[86]

However, the crux of the matter lay not in the question of the agency to bear the expense, but in the fact that the number of indigents necessarily increased despite efforts to exclude or disown them. For poverty was an essential attribute of the city's economy. The system that begot a numerous proletariat perpetually on the verge of destitution, produced impoverishment as a matter of course upon the slightest slackening of the human or industrial machine. Mayor Quincy in 1848 and Mayor Bigelow in 1850 both expressed concern over the problem; but neither could do anything to cope with it. Under pressure of the exploited Irish, the cost of poor relief expanded monstrously year after year.[87]

The impact of Irish pauperism on the city was slight in comparison with the effects upon the immigrants themselves; for degradation by poverty was almost inevitable under the circumstances of Irish life in Boston. New conditions dissolved the old ties, habits, and traditions with which they were incompatible. The mores of the peasant farm could not readily be adapted to the tenement and the old adjustments that for many years had limited the social consequences of destitution in Ireland were inadequate in urban Boston. In this society want became a malignant and resourceful adversary; it insinuated itself into personal habits, perverting human relations and warping conceptions of right and wrong. Wherever it appeared, it encouraged intemperance, crime, and prostitution.[88]

Nothing the Irish found in Boston altered their tradition of alcoholic indulgence. Instead, crowded conditions drove men out of their homes into bars where they could meet friends, relax, and forget their anguish in the promised land. In 1846 there were 850 liquor dealers in the city, but by 1849 fully 1,200 groggeries were open for the flourishing trade. A survey by the city marshal in November, 1851, showed the great majority of these to be Irish, and almost half to be concentrated in the North End and Fort Hill.[89] In addition, numerous Irish families sold gin as a sideline, without license, to cater to the demands of their countrymen. Frequently drunk and often jailed for inebriety, the Irish "arrested and turned back" the short-lived temperance movement which had made promising progress up to their arrival.[90] Other nationalities, particularly the Germans, were also fond of the glass, but neither their habits nor environment encouraged or even tolerated excessive drinking.

Frequent intoxication led to the Irish reputation for criminality.[91] This impression actually derived from minor misdemeanors generally committed under the influence of drink, — misdemeanors which in many cases might have earned for more affluent offenders only a tolerant reprimand. Comparatively few Irishmen were guilty of more serious felonies. Negroes, whose transgressions frequently consisted of thefts of coal or wood, suffered from the same prejudice.[92] There were, of course, a few notorious cases involving crimes of violence, such as the trial for murder of the Negro, William Roby, but they were no more typical than Dr. Webster was of Harvard professors.[93] In no group was there an inherent predilection for crime, but among the Irish the combination of poverty and intemperance created a maladjustment expressed by petty infractions of the rules of a society strange to them.

Standing "in false relations to nearly everything about them . . . strangers in a strange land [,] surrounded by circumstances novel to them, met by customs to which they [could] . . . not adapt themselves, influenced by motives often extravagant and wild," the Irish necessarily became "involved in harassing doubt and perplexity." Their bewildered position in the city, together with overdrinking and the ill health of the slums, contributed to the rapid increase of insanity among them.[94] In 1764 the Selectmen had rejected Thomas Hancock's bequest for the relief of idiots because they were too few to justify special attention; and although, in the next eighty years, both state and municipality found it necessary to make provisions for the care of the mentally sick, before the coming of the Irish the problem was neither financially nor medically serious. Thereafter the number of patients and the cost of attending them rose rapidly. Massachusetts expanded its facilities by building two new hospitals and Boston erected an asylum of its own, largely to care for Irish laborers, for among other groups the incidence of lunacy was much lower.[95]

Finally, there was some prostitution among Irish immigrant women whose wages from ordinary employment did not "supply them with the necessities . . . of life." [96] Irish girls at one time enjoyed the reputation of comparative freedom from this vice, and indeed very few were guilty of it; but by 1860 illegitimate births were probably more frequent among them than among any other nationality.[97] The exigencies of the new society had driven many into a course completely alien to their background and training.

Indeed, in adjusting to the relentless drive of harsh, uncontrollable forces, the immigrants changed in many ways; and, in the changing, transformed the old Boston. The gap between the quiet suburban life of early South Boston and the bustling industrialism pervading it after 1850 was no greater than that between the Irishmen who turned their backs upon the placid fields of Kerry and those who tended the clamorous Bay State forges. Green meadows and heavy orchards gave way to dark rolling mills, and bronzed peasants turned into pallid hands whose sun shone from out the roaring hearth of the furnace. City and newcomer both felt the workings of the same force, the inevitable adaptation of new tenants to an old society. Each suffered a thoroughgoing physical metamorphosis, eventually reflected in an equally complete change in character and thought, and leaving in its wake the necessity for a radically different cultural orientation.

V

Conflict of Ideas

As long . . . as the traditions of one's national and local group remain unbroken, one remains so attached to its customary ways of thinking that the ways of thinking which are perceived in other groups are regarded as curiosities, errors, ambiguities, or heresies. At this stage one does not doubt either the correctness of one's own traditions of thought or the unity and uniformity of thought in general.[1]

By 1845 Boston's cultural development had reached a point of close contact with the highest aspects of European civilization. Native Bostonians regarded England as the "mother country." They were proud of their British ancestry and remained "solidly and steadily English, settled down into an English mold and hardened into it."[2] But they had also learned to "expect an importation of the opinions and manners of the old countries" and to "receive from Europe a considerable part of [their] intellectual persuasions and moral tastes. . . ."[3] Newcomers, be they English, French or German, originating from similar backgrounds, and facing few problems of physical or economic adjustment, could participate in a cosmopolitan society on terms of direct and simple equality. For these came prepared to share the world of the Boston merchants — their music and literature, their ideas and politics, their rationalism and their all-pervading optimism. Whatever differences exsited were in degree and pace, easily reconcilable.

The Irish who settled in Boston, however, were products of a milieu completely isolated from the intellectual influences of London, Paris, or even Dublin. And every phase of their experience in America heightened the disparity between their heritage and that of their neighbors. The physical barriers segregating them from the dominant cultural currents of the day disappeared in the New World; but the spiritual ones crossed the Atlantic in the hold of every immigrant ship. Reaffirmed and strengthened by the difficulties of the new environment, these restraints ruled Irish thoughts as vigorously in Boston as in Cork.

In Ireland, a circumscribed agrarian economy gave form to their ideas, to the "implicit . . . *assumptions,* or . . . *unconscious mental habits*" dominating their thoughts.[4] In the bitter atmosphere of poverty and persecution, the Irish had found little in life that was not dark and nothing that was hopeful. Their utter helplessness before the most elemental forces fostered an immense sadness, a deep-rooted pessimism about the world and man's role in it, manifested even "on occasions of great joy and merriment . . . in grief and melancholy. . . ."[5]

Nor was this feeling modified in the transit to the New World. Irishmen fled with no hope in their hearts — degraded, humiliated, mourning reluctantly-abandoned and dearly-loved homes. From the rotting immigrant hulks, they nostalgically joined the local poet in plaintive farewell:

Farewell to thee, Erin mavourneen,
   Thy valleys I'll tread never more;
This heart that now bleeds for thy sorrows,
   Will waste on a far distant shore.
Thy green sods lie cold on my parents,
   A cross marks the place of their rest, —
The wind that moans sadly above them,
   Will waft their poor child to the West.[6]

The old homeland grew lush in their memories when compared with the miseries of constricted tenement districts and the hopelessness of the arbitrary factory economy. They found good cause to complain:

I am tired, fatigued, weary,
   Of this never ending strife —
Of the journey, lone and dreary,
   On the darksome path of life.[7]

Filthy homes, wretched working conditions, and constant hunger mocked the merchants' optimism, and bred, instead, the identical pessimism in Boston as in Ireland. On both sides of the Atlantic, Irish experience generated a brooding recognition that human relationships were transient, subject to the ever-threatening intervention of impersonal evils. The essential pessimism of these immigrants was reflected in the prominent role of the devil in their literature and even in the belief in retributive justice at the hands of a *deus ex machina* as compensation in a basically evil world. Both as peasants whose anxious livelihood derived from the capricious soil, and as cogs in an unpredictable industrial machine, they were victims of incalculable influences beyond their control. For those who met it so frequently in their own experience, untimely disaster, even death, was normal, a part of life accepted without complaint, indeed, without even the need for explanation.[8]

Buffeted about in a hostile universe by malevolent forces more powerful than themselves, Irish peasants could turn only to religion for consolation. The drama of salvation unfolded at every mass became a living reality from which emerged dogmas held with a tenacity beyond secular reason. Man's fall through original sin and his deliverance by grace were not theological abstractions but insistent realities reflected in all the features of their everyday existence.

When we luck at him there, we see our blissed Saviour, stripped a'most naked lake ourselves; whin we luck at the crown i'thorns on the head, we see the Jews mockin' him, jist the same as — some people mock ourselves for our religion; whin we luck at his eyes, we see they wor niver dry, like our own; whin we luck at the wound in his side, why we think less of our own wounds an' bruises, we get 'ithin and 'ithout, every day av our lives.[9]

To those who bore more than their share of hardships, religion's most valued assurance was its promise that "the world did not explain itself" and that man met his true destiny not in this constantly frustrating universe, but in the loftier sphere it preceded.[10] At the death of a child in a popular novel, the priest inwardly "rejoiced that another soul was about being housed from life's tempests"; for all earthly affairs, life itself, were insignificant and death was but a release for the tremendous process of redemption.[11] Preparation for that rebirth thoroughly eclipsed the affairs of the immediate present, engendering an attitude of complete ac ceptance toward mundane problems so long as salvation was unthreatened.[12]

Against the immense forces facing men, reason and science counted for nothing. The Irish scorned the independent rationalism basic to the religious feelings of other Bostonians, and discouraged "reading the bible and putting one's own construction upon it" or allowing "every tinker and ploughboy to interpret scripture as he thought proper." [13] The approval of the hierarchy reinforced this attitude. The pastoral letter of the American bishops in 1843 pointed out that "without faith it is impossible to please God" and warned against "preferring in the least point the dictates of your erring reason." [14]

The true guardian of the faith essential to salvation was the Catholic Church. Two centuries of violent attack in Ireland had strengthened and confirmed its position; for national and economic issues had fused with the religious in opposition to landlords who were at once masters, aliens, and representatives of a hostile faith.[15] Beliefs maintained at great personal sacrifice were not lightly held, and among those who came to America the Church gained particular prestige, for it was one of the few familiar institutions that followed them across the Atlantic.

In the New World as in the Old, Catholicism assumed a distinctive cast from the background of its adherents. Universal rather than national in organization, and catholic in essential dogma, it nevertheless partook of the quality of the men who professed it; for the nature of the milieu modified even religious doctrines, particularly in their application to the problems of secular life. Irish priests and theologians rose from the ranks of the people, surrounded by popular influences which inevitably affected their later work. The continuous process of clerical adjustment to the ideas of those they served intensified Irish devoutness in America, because the conclusions Catholicism derived from its theology coincided with the ideas emanating from the inner circumstances of the peasant-laborer's life.

The confidence of the Irish confirmed the Church's paramount position in their own affairs; church doctrine extended this ascendancy over all man-made institutions, including the state, and urged that

Religious liberty means, not religious slavery, not simply the liberty of infidelity, the liberty to deny and blaspheme, but . . . that religion herself is free . . . to be herself, and to discharge her functions in her own way, without let or hindrance from the State. . . . Who asserts the freedom of religion asserts the subjection of the State. Religion represents the Divine Sovereignty . . . in the affairs of men; the State . . . merely . . . human sovereignty. Is the Divine Sovereignty higher than the human . . . ? Then is religion . . . higher than the State . . . . Religion overrides all other sovereigns, and has the supreme authority over all the affairs of the world. . . . This is a terrible doctrine to atheistical politicians, infidels, and anarchists; and hence . . . they are the enemies . . . of religious liberty. . . .[16]

Since the "freedom of religion" was "its sovereignty" and since "to assert its independence of the State" was "to assert its supremacy over the State," secular government had merely to choose between particular measures within the limits of religious precepts, to which it must conform, and in conforming, compel its subjects to conform.[17]

In defense of this position Catholics argued that

Christianity is "part and parcel of the law of the land." . . . We are professedly a *Christian* State, and acknowledge ourselves bound by the law of nature as interpreted and re-enacted by Christianity.[18]

There could be no true tolerance, for, no matter what their professed beliefs, all citizens must ultimately comply with the basic tenets of the "true religion" through its temporal agency, the state. This opinion forced a denial of

the liberty of each man to be of what religion he pleases, or of none . . . a low and an altogether inadequate view . . . merely a political . . . not a religious right at all; for no religion that has any self-respect can acknowledge that one has the right to be of any religion he chooses. No man has or can have a *religious* or a *moral* right to be of any religion but the true religion. . . . Every religion by its very nature is intolerant of every other, and condemns itself, if it is not.[19]

Any deviation from this concept of "religious freedom" earned bitter condemnation as "latitudinarianism of the very worst sort." [20]

The belief that non-Christians were "free to profess no portion of their religion which contravenes Christian morality" certainly contrasted with the native conviction, as set forth by Channing, that formal sectarian boundaries had little significance. While most Bostonians felt, with John Adams, that "every honest, well-disposed, moral man, even if he were an atheist, should be accounted a Christian," Brownson insisted that "a *Christian* Protestant, is to the Catholic mind simply a contradiction in terms." [21] That disparity reflected a broad difference between the basic attitudes and unconscious presumptions of the rational, progressive optimist and of the religious, conservative pessimist.

This dichotomy was most marked when expressed in terms of concrete attitudes toward the pressing social problems of the period. The mental set of tenement or seminary scarcely harmonized with the rational Bostonian's concept of reform as an infallible guide along the straight path of progress to ultimate perfectibility. Indeed the Irish were completely alien to the idea of progress and necessarily antagonistic "to the spirit of the age." [22] Reform was a delusion inflating men's sense of importance, distorting the relative significance of earthly values, and obscuring the true goals of their endeavor — salvation of the eternal soul. Such movements were suspect because they exaggerated the province of reason, exalting it above faith, futile because they relied upon temporal rather than spiritual agencies, and dangerous because they undermined respect for established institutions. [23]

The failure of the Irish to comprehend fully the democratic feeling basic to reform intensified their hostility. Generations of enforced obedience bred a deep respect for class distinctions. Irishmen could scarcely have a firm appreciation of the equality of man when their very school books taught them

> Q. If the poor will not try to be good, what will follow?
> A. That the rich will not help them. [24]

At best, this acquiescence developed into the feudal loyalty of retainer for master, but more frequently it became the complete servility described by Arthur Young:

A landlord . . . can scarcely invent an order which a servant, laborer or cottar dares to refuse to execute. Nothing satisfies him but unlimited submission. . . . A poor man would have his bones broken, if he offered to lift his hand in his own defense. [25]

In America, too, the Irish agreed that everyone should "mate with their equals, high as well as low," and the *Pilot* pointed out that the poor Irish family was "much more happy and contented in its place in life" than the American.[26] But Judith O'Rourke expressed this acceptance of class most clearly when, scoffing at the possibility of educating her children, she hoped that her sons would "grow up honest good men, like them that's gone afore them, not ashamed of their station, or honest toil," while her daughter " 'll be the same lady her mother is . . . an' that's good enough. . . . She'd look purty I'm thinkin' wid her music in one corner an' I wid my wash tub in another." [27]

Thus, the whole galaxy of reforms that absorbed New England in the thirty years after 1835 met the determined opposition of the Irish Catholic population in Boston. Fundamental patterns of thought combined with group interests to turn them against their neighbors who "devoutly believe in any Woolly horse, any Kossuth, any Montes that may chance to come," and among whom "Freesoilerism, Millerism, Spiritual rappings, Mainea all are current." To follow such doctrines which had already "infected our whole society and turned a large portion of our citizens into madmen" was to become "a philanthropist . . . a person who loves everybody generally and hates everybody particularly." [28]

"Leading in majesty and peerless fidelity, the beautiful constellation of reforms," was abolition. Against slavery the finest spirits in Boston united in a movement which, after 1830, gained steadily in adherents until it dominated the city.[29] Yet the Irish concertedly opposed the spread of "Niggerology." They sometimes recognized that slavery was abstractly bad, and sometimes denied it; but in any case, humanitarianism was as powerless to eradicate the institution as to deal with the other evils in which the world abounded.[30] A number of practical objections reinforced the theory that only the influence of the Church could counteract social maladies.[31] The disruption of the Repeal Movement by O'Connell's anti-slavery speech revealed the danger of the issue; Catholic leaders hesitated to antagonize their powerful and influential communicants in Maryland, Louisiana, and throughout the south, dreading a controversy that might divide the Church as it had other religious groups.[32] And beyond immediate interests and ideology lay a deep horror of endangering the social fabric, or disturbing the Union as it existed.[33]

Even more concrete reasons tied the mass of unskilled Irish laborers to the Church in the belief that

> . . . when the negroes shall be free
> To cut the throats of all they see,
> Then this dear land will come to be
> The den of foul rascality.[34]

They feared the competition of the hordes of freed slaves who might invade the North; and valued the security that came from the existence in the country of at least one social class below them.[35] Rivalry for the same jobs as Negroes, elsewhere bondsmen, but in Boston economically and socially more secure than the Irish, strengthened this feeling and led the latter to object to Negro suffrage which aimed at "setting the Niggers high," to complain that colored people did not know their place, and to resent their "impertinence." [36]

Irish Catholics also turned against the other humanitarian reforms; for these used the state as an instrument for strengthening secular as against religious forces. On these grounds the immigrants fought the current temperance movement, although drunkenness was particularly prominent among them. Inspired by Father Mathew's efforts, the Church itself had attempted to cope with the problem. But it actively challenged the right of the state to legislate on the matter; and therein enjoyed the support of laborers who jealously guarded their only form of relaxation.[37]

Even the preponderance of Irish among the city's lawbreakers did not weaken the conviction that society was powerless to effect reforms attainable only through grace. Because Catholics felt that criminals were born evil, they objected to treating them "with maternal kindness," "merely as afflicted patients." "A superabundance of humanity in the public sentiment" and particularly in the Prisoners' Friend Society pampered wrongdoers by permitting them to work, to receive occasional visitors and to hear church services on Sunday. These "sickly sentimentalists," "worse . . . than the prisoners they whine over," were doomed to failure because most prisoners were

deliberate wrongdoers, intentionally at war with society; men who prefer to obtain a precarious livelihood by robbing . . . to the comforts resulting from the unexciting routine of honest industry . . . *men* who have thus become perverted. . . .[38]

Two current crusades seemed to strike at the roots of family life, and thus at Christian society. To those reared within the grooves of a patriarchal society the "domestic reformers" appeared to "have revived pagan orgies in the pitiful farce of 'Women's Rights,' and Bloomerism." [39] But more menacing to public morality were the common schools and the laws for compulsory education:

The general principle upon which these laws are based is radically unsound, untrue, Atheistical. . . . It is, that the education of children is *not* the work of the Church, or of the Family, but that it is the work of the State. . . . Two consequences flow from this principle. . . . In the matter of education, the State is supreme over the Church and the Family. *Hence,* the State can and does exclude from the schools religious instruction. . . . The inevitable consequence is, that . . . the greater number of scholars must turn out to be Atheists, and accordingly the majority of non-Catholics are people of no religion. . . . The other consequence . . . leads the State to *adopt* the child, to weaken the ties which bind it to the parent. So laws are made compelling children to attend the state schools, and forbidding the parents, if they be poor, to withdraw their little ones from the school. . . . The consequence of this policy is . . . universal disobedience on the part of children. . . . Our little boys scoff at their parents, call their fathers by the name of Old Man, Boss, or Governor. The mother is the Old Woman. The little boys smoke, drink, blaspheme, talk about fornication, and so far as they are physically able, commit it. Our little girls read novels . . . quarrel about their beaux, uphold Woman's Rights, and — . . . . We were a Boston school boy, and we speak of what we know.

When "second rate or tenth rate school masters . . . like Horace Mann . . ." were allowed "by the patient people to tinker over the schools until they . . . nearly ruined them," Irish parents hesitated to entrust their children to the common schools, and fought the laws that required them to do so. Persistent and unequivocal hostility to the "kidnapping" system generated sharp conflicts with other Bostonians who regarded Massachusetts public education as the keystone of its liberty and culture.[40]

In the conflict of ideas the Irish found all other foreign groups in the city ranged with the native Bostonians against them. The Germans could be as optimistic, rational and romantic as the natives, for their emigration rested on hope rather than on bare necessity. Unlike the Irish, they went off singing,

> Leb' wohl geliebtes Mädchen,
> Jetzt reis' ich aus den städtchen
> Muss nun, Feinsliebchen, fort
> An einem fremden Ort.[41]

And in America their economic and physical adjustment was relatively simple, so that within a short time they shared the ideas of the natives. Although divisions existed within the German groups, the predominant sentiment held the spirit of free enquiry and intellectual radicalism essential to human progress, measurable in terms of the development of the individual's personality as " a free man." [42] Consequently, they took the same position as the natives on all social questions save temperance, and were far more extreme on the specific issue of slavery.[43] Being few in number, the French did not always assume a position as a group. When they did, they were moderately liberal in politics and on the question of slavery, as were the English, Negroes, Italians, and smaller groups.[44]

About one point only — the revolutions of 1848 — was adjustment in the conflicting position of the Irish and other Bostonians at all possible. Coming when the immigrants had scarcely settled in their new homes, while the instruments of social control were still weak from the effects of transition, the exciting news from the Fatherland sent a tremendous wave of emotion among the Irish. Mobilized in the Repeal Movement, Irish national sentiment in America had grown steadily for several years. It had captured the *Boston Pilot,* originally a clerical paper founded by Bishop Fenwick, and turned it to support the revolutions against the conservative powers of Europe led by Austria.[45] Through the *Boston Catholic Observer,* the clergy at first resisted this metamorphosis. But they capitulated in 1848 when the Young Irelanders, impatient with O'Connellite conservatism, raised the banners of rebellion from Cork to Belfast, enlisting the loyalty of the great majority of Irish Americans. Enthusiasm was so great the hierarchy dared not stand in the way. By August Archbishop Hughes of New York gave his approval, proclaiming that the rush to arms had transformed the revolution from "plot" to "fact," and sanctioned a Directory collecting funds in New York. Bishop Fitzpatrick did not weaken to the extent of backing the insurrection, but did not openly oppose it. His organ, the *Boston Catholic Observer,* edited by Brownson, cautiously reprinted the Archbishop's statement without comment.[46]

The Bishop hesitated because of the uncertainty of Vatican policy. Pius IX had been regarded as a progressive from his accession.[47] His early liberal efforts promised so much that the future editor of the *Boston Pilot,* Father John T. Roddan, a brilliant young American priest educated at the Propaganda, had returned to Boston "almost a Mazzinian . . . quite enamored of the European revolutionary movements."⁴⁸ While the Pope was undecided, Catholic conservatives vacillated on the subject of revolution and permitted the radicals to dominate Irish opinion.⁴⁹

A common stake in revolutionary success drew the Irish closer to other groups. Young Ireland, influenced by continental ideas, was not far different from Young Italy. Though it lacked the broad humanitarianism of the Boston reformers and was openly sympathetic toward slavery, nationalism nevertheless provided a point of contact with other Bostonians.⁵⁰ Collaboration with abolitionists like Quincy and Phillips was a potential wedge that might have split the Irish from their conservatism and opened their minds to the liberal position. Even the collapse of the insurrection did not discredit it, for many of its leaders eventually found their way to the United States. They were still popular; their opinions still carried weight; and for a time they exerted a positive liberalizing influence over their countrymen through lectures and through their newspapers, the *Irish-American* and the *Citizen*.⁵¹

The rapprochement did not last long, however; it finally gave way before the revived and unified opposition of the clergy. The insurgency of the Roman republic alienated the papacy from the cause of revolution; and the victory of Radetsky's Austrian legions facilitated the adoption of a clear-cut, conservative policy. As a result, Archbishop Hughes and the *Freeman's Journal* disowned Young Ireland, and Catholic policy in Boston as elsewhere resolutely opposed the policies of red republicanism which, in retrospect, it linked with an atheistic plot of Protestants to undermine Catholic civilization. These, it charged:

saw the Church gathering America to her bosom. . . . They saw themselves losing ground everywhere, and, as they gnashed their teeth with rage and pined away, the ministers in white choackers formed in England and in America an Alliance, and, resolved to carry the war into Italy, — to revolutionize that country. It would be a great triumph to them, and to their father, the devil, if they could match Catholic progress in Protestant countries with Protestant progress in Catholic countries. . . . They fermented the revolutions of 1848

by forming

a grand conspiracy, with its central government . . . in London, and its ramifications extending even to this country . . . armed not merely against monarchy, but against all legitimate authority, against all religion except an idolatrous worship of . . . the GOD–PEOPLE . . . , against all morality, . . . law, . . . order, and . . . society itself.[52]

The Church conducted a persistent campaign against the "spirit of radical Protestantism" which had "crept into every class of society, into every . . . political order" and which "nought can destroy . . . but the *true Catholic spirit.*" [53] Time after time it inveighed against the "political atheism" growing out of the belief that "the State, if not the sovereign, is at least not the subject of Religion," a belief that gave rise to "the revolutions, crimes, civil wars which have recently been and are coming again. . . ." [54] Led by Brownson, the Catholic press attacked the uprisings in Europe and their supporters in Boston, urging upon a restless people "the necessity of subordination and obedience to lawful rulers." [55] "Good Catholics," they argued, "must accept . . . the constitution of the State, when once established, whatever its form, yet . . . have no right to conspire to change the con-

stitution, or to effect a revolution in the State. Consequently
. . . our sympathies can never be with those who conspire
against the law, or with the mad revolutionists and radicals,
on the Continent of Europe, who are unsettling every
thing." [56]

In the face of this overwhelming propaganda, the influence of the Young Irelanders waned steadily. The success of
the revolution might have furnished a concrete rallying point
for progressive influences against the conservative tendencies
in Irish life. As it was, the movement dissolved in endless
talk. The conservatives easily recaptured the *Boston Pilot*
when its owner, Patrick Donohoe, ignominiously capitulated
to the Bishop and allowed his paper to be edited by an American priest, John T. Roddan, by now a disciple of Brownson.[57] Continual quarrels divided the ranks of the radicals
and desertion further depleted them. T. D. McGee withdrew
first to the clerical party and then to the hated English from
whom he accepted a cabinet post in Canada. Mitchel, disgusted, retired to the rusticity of Tennessee, and Meagher to
a law practice in New York and the career of a Democratic
politician.[58] Although Fenianism revived Irish nationalism in
1859, it had none of the liberal ideas of 1848. By then the opposition to conservatism had disappeared, lingering only in
the minds of a few die-hards.

Flirtation with revolution was a passing interlude with no
effect upon the normal Irish respect for authority. Always,
conservatism segregated them from other Bostonians, who
believed that all revolutions signified the dawn of a new era
that would spread the light of American liberty over a renaissant Europe. Natives, and for that matter, non-Irish foreign-

ers, had taken an active interest in the Polish struggle for liberty, and had hailed the French revolution of 1830 with delight, though Catholics dubbed it the work of "an irreligious and profligate minority." Americans approved of the uprisings of 1848 set off by the abdication of "that great swindle," Louis Philippe, as unanimously as the Irish eventually disapproved. Henry Adams was an ardent admirer of Garibaldi, and Margaret Fuller, among many, adored Mazzini whom the Irish hated. Almost all Bostonians liked the Hungarians and welcomed Kossuth, but Catholics branded him a disappointed manufacturer of humbugs. The Irish attacked the Swiss for sheltering rebels, and condemned the Fenian Brotherhoods in America; while in the Crimean War, which they called a struggle of "Civilized Society against red republican barbarism," they supported Russia against Protestant England and against Turkey, which had protected Kossuth.[59]

Fighting radicalism everywhere, they consistently maintained the principles of conservatism by defending the Catholic powers of Europe — Spain, Austria, and Italy — the nations considered most backward, ignorant, and intolerant by Boston public opinion.[60] Every unfavorable comment on these countries by an American provoked a bitter defense in the Irish press.[61] In the Mediai matter, they upheld religious intolerance in Italy, and left themselves open to charges of having "a different set of principles to suit the market of every country." [62] In the *Black Warrior* affair they championed Spain and in the Koszta case, Austria against the United States.[63] They went to great lengths in vindicating Napoleon III although most Americans condemned the treachery of the coup d'état of 1851.[64] The Irish were equally firm in shielding Catholic Latin America against filibustering Yankees whose "manifest destiny" led to repeated aggressions. They assailed alike the Texan "brigands" who threatened Mexico and those who attacked Cuba, while they supported the established church in Brazil, in a long series of unfortunate disputations which created bitterness by their very heat and which transferred, in the minds of many Bostonians, the qualities defended in these conservative countries to the Irish themselves.[65]

These political differences testified to the strength of the barrier reared between Irish and non-Irish by diametrically opposed ideas, whose literary and cultural expressions reflected and perpetuated the distinction. Resting on basically different premises, developed in entirely different environments, two distinct cultures flourished in Boston with no more contact than if 3,000 miles of ocean rather than a wall of ideas stood between them.

Irish intellectual life had few contacts with that of their neighbors. Education, rare indeed in Ireland, was scarcely more widespread among the Irish in Boston. The ability to read was by no means commonplace,[66] and repeated warnings against secular works narrowed the nature of what little the Irish did read.[67] The few Irishmen conscious of Boston's contemporary literature were shocked and antagonized by its rational romanticism, regarding it as exclusively Protestant, overwhelmingly English, and suspect on both grounds. Completely alien to the city's literary tradition, they branded Shakespeare a barbaric poet whose "monstrous farces" "befoul the stage with every abomination." Milton became a heretic minion of the Drogheda monster Cromwell, and English literature — "the most pernicious" that ever existed — merely a degraded and degenerate justification of the reformation, typified by "that liar and infidel, Hume" and "that hideous atheist, Hobbs." [68] Because this literature was basic to their thinking, the work of men like Emerson was necessarily rejected. C. M. O'Keefe spoke for many in gratitude that "We Irishmen are not yet reduced to that moral nakedness which startles and appals us in Mr. Emerson," whose "historical . . . is only . . . equalled by his philosophical ignorance." [69]

In place of Emerson's "puerilities" the most popular Irish writing of the day was that which glorified Ireland, its historic tradition, and its Catholic past. The dateless conflict with England, in all its phases, furnished an endless source of romantic themes, at once reflecting and stimulating an Anglophobia out of place amidst the Boston veneration of things English.[70] Stories of the Reformation — the root of all Irish misery — were always popular. A life of Mary, Queen of Scots, sold a thousand copies the day it was published in Boston, and the *Pilot* frequently printed romances and articles based upon the struggles of that period justifying the Catholic position.[71] That conflict continued in a long series of literary arguments, forgetting the injunction of a great German controversialist that disputes should be treated "with the utmost charity, conciliation and mildness." [72] On the contrary these theological battles, waged *fortiter in modo* as well as *in re,* wounded susceptibilities and stored up rancorous bitterness on all sides. Whatever the ultimate justice of the matter, defense of the inquisition and Saint Bartholomew's massacre, and continued attacks upon Luther, Calvin, and Henry VIII, the "infernal triumvirate" of Protestantism, and upon other propagators of "monstrous doctrines," scarcely drew the Irish closer to their neighbors who held completely different views.[73]

The sporadic clashes that marked the early years of Irish settlement in Boston stimulated this antagonism. Fitted into a familiar pattern, these conflicts became mere extensions of the old battle against English Protestantism. The Charlestown Convent fire left a heritage of bitterness, never eradicated. Years later Irishmen resented it and declaimed

> Foul midnight deed! I mark with pain
> Yon ruins tapering o'er the plain;
> Contrast them with your Bunker's height,
> And shame will sicken at the sight!
>
> Already thou hast learnt the rule,
> Of Cromwell's bloody English school;
> And far and wide the fame has flown,
> Of crimes which thou must ever own.[74]

Nor did the novels in which the Irish delighted most — tales of ancient Irish grandeur, glorifying Celtic culture at the expense of Saxon England — improve relations with other Bostonians. The common core of all was the inevitable contrast between Gael and Sassenach, decidedly to the disadvantage of the latter.[75] A series of violent articles by Dr. John McElheran furnished a philosophical and pseudo-ethnological basis for this contrast. "The divine spark of genius radiates from the Celtic centre of the world. . . . The Egyptians . . . the pure Pelasgi of Athens . . . the Romans by themselves — and the ancient Irish . . . show us . . . the natural tendency of the pure Celtic race, uncontaminated by Gothic bestiality, or eastern sensuality." The Gothic race, including the Germans, Scandinavians, Russians, Turks and Anglo-Saxons, were completely different, "essentially stupid . . . false, cruel, treacherous, base and bloody . . ." with "little or no faculty for poetry, music, or abstract science." By every criterion of civilization, the latter were far inferior to the former. And the lowest of all were the Saxons, "the very dregs and offal of the white population in America. . . . These flaxen-haired German men and women . . . are lower than the race with black wool. . . . Even when they are well to do they send their children out to beg." [76] Immensely popular, the publication of these articles elicited a steady stream of letters from readers asking for more of the same from the "Saxon-hating Dr." [77]

As opposed to these discordant tendencies only one strain — pride in their contributions to the making of America — drew the Irish nearer their neighbors. Although "the great current of American history" was "overwhelmingly heretic," and Catholic students could "receive no support" for their "faith from reading it," they cherished its Irish episodes.[78] The early Catholic explorers from St. Brandan to Marquette, and Charles Carroll, the Catholic signer, were important figures whose biographies appeared frequently in their reading. Though they distrusted live Orangemen, the Irish made the dead Scotch-Irish their own; they were fond of tales of John Barry and other Celtic military heroes.[79] But even this was pushed to a dangerous extreme when McElheran claimed all great Americans were "Celtic Normans, and French, and Spaniards, and Celtic Britons . . . and Gaels from Wales and Ireland and the north and west of Scotland. Look to the pedigree of your heroes . . . look at their physique, and say, Is it the type of Gothic nations? . . . Is it fat, lumpish, gross Anglo-Saxon?" [80]

While the chasm between Irish and native ideas deepened, cultural contacts furthered the assimilation of other immigrants. The Irish alone diverged from the Boston norm. All others participated readily in the intellectual life of the community. Englishmen were obviously at home there; and Germans were soon familiar in many phases of the city's activities. Admiring its school system and respecting Harvard, they sent their children to common schools as a matter of course. Germans were widely acquainted with western European literature. Their magazines contained sections on "Anglo-Amerikanischer," English, and French as well as German and German-American literature, while their own writing frequently used American themes and expressed the American spirit.[81] The thought and culture of Frenchmen was also broadly cosmopolitan; English and German works found a secure place in their reading.[82] Meanwhile these groups enriched the natives with a new heritage accepted gratefully. Follen and Beck, together with the Americans, Bancroft, Longfellow, and Ticknor, popularized the German language until more than seventy Harvard men were studying it in the fifties.[83] At the same time, the French press helped make the works of Balzac, Lamartine, and other authors and painters accessible to Bostonians.[84]

Ease of adjustment did not reflect a flat uniformity in the non-Irish groups. Each brought with it an intellectual tradition of which it was proud, and which it was anxious to preserve. But though different in detail, all had the same roots, and eventually coalesced without serious conflict. Thus the clash of two vigorous musical cultures that grew out of German immigration actually enriched both. At the beginning of the nineteenth century, Boston enjoyed a living, fruitful, musical tradition based upon the Anglo-Italianate musical life of eighteenth-century London. It first took concrete form in the Philo-harmonic Society (1810), an amateur group predominantly American in nativity, but including some Englishmen and a Russian, and led by an Anglo-German, Gottlieb Graupner, once oboist in Haydn's London Orchestra. From this nucleus grew the Handel and Haydn Society, an organization of some hundred amateurs formed in 1815 to interpret the oratorios of these composers. Later critics belittled its achievements, but its influence upon the mechanics and artisans who formed its rank and file was deep, and was perpetuated for many years in the rural "singing skewls" of all New England. Throughout at least the first thirty years of its existence, it vigorously sustained the music of those after whom it was named.[85]

Nourished by the fruit of Beethoven's revolt, and steeped in romanticism, German music by 1840 had evolved a tradition that was quite different. At first contact native Bostonians rejected it. Centered in a group of music masters who gave periodic concerts, but whose chief income derived from teaching culturally ambitious Bostonians, their normal musical life had little room for strangers. Traveling professionals might stop for an occasional concert; but isolated performances left little impression and there was no incentive for teachers without pupils to remain in the city. Heinrich, for instance, preferred to live there, but was forced by the financial failure of his concert to go to New York, and Charles Zeuner, who did remain, felt he was misunderstood.[86] With no one to play the new music, Bostonians could not become familiar with or like it.[87] Englishmen and a few Italians closely related to them remained the most popular foreign musicians. Such unfamiliar soil doomed the most valiant attempts at playing Beethoven to failure. Even Woodbridge and Mason confessed defeat after an unsuccessful series of concerts in the Boston Academy of Music, a product of their travels in Germany.[88]

The coming of the Germans who wanted German music teachers for their children made room for the new music. As soon as there was a resident basis of such musicians, Bostonians found opportunities to hear and to like it. Very quickly they learned it was not really strange for it synchronized with the romantic tendencies already woven into their culture. In the spread of the new music, Germans like Dresel, Kreissmann, Leonhard, and Heinrich, the Germania Society which came to Boston in 1849, the Mendelssohn Quintet Club, and the itinerant foreign opera companies were influential, but hardly more so than native teachers like Lowell Mason, or *Dwight's Journal of Music,* which voiced the cause of German romanticism consistently after 1852. Once the two cultures met, they found a common basis, fused, and under the vigorous leadership of Carl Zerrahn produced an ever more fruitful growth thereafter. Germans and Americans, they were the same kind of people, their ideas and feelings were rooted in the same social background; there was no occasion for serious conflict.[89]

The common store of ideas that made this adjustment possible was lacking in the intellectual relations of the Irish and non-Irish. The development of the fundamental aspects of their ideas left them so far apart there was no room for compromise. Contact bred conflict rather than conciliation. Irish Catholics could not think like their neighbors without a complete change in way of life.[90] And natives could adopt no aspect of Catholic ideas without passing through a radical intellectual revolution.

One outstanding personality attempted to adapt Irish Catholicism to American thought and failed signally in the attempt. By 1842 Orestes A. Brownson's intellectual development had itself carried him to the acceptance of many Catholic concepts. In philosophy he felt the need for tradition and revelation; in theology, for grace to counteract original sin and man's innate corruptness. In politics he was a conservative Democrat, opposed to abolition and reform, trying to temper the rule of the people by placing "Justice" above the popular will.[91] But the eminently Irish Bishop Fitzpatrick — "the hierarchical exponent of all that was traditional . . . in Catholic public life" — distrusted Brownson's philosophic background though it had brought him to the Church, and insisted upon complete renunciation before conversion.[92] Brownson yielded, and for ten years loyally submitted to the dictates of his Irish religious superiors, handing over every line he wrote to the censorship of the Bishop. Until 1854 Brownson and the *Review* thoroughly expressed the ideas of Irish Catholicism.[93]

In that year, stimulated by the criticisms of the Know-Nothing movement, Brownson reluctantly concluded that the Church in America must be American rather than Irish and thereby provoked a galling conflict with the Irish clergy that painfully grieved him and eventually drove him to New York where he hoped to profit from the less rigorous supervision of Archbishop Hughes.[94] Thereafter, Brownson evolved a new social philosophy based on Gioberti's theology, which enabled him to attack slavery, support the Republican party, and attempt to reconcile the Church with American ideas by liberalizing it.[95]

This endeavor met vigorous, relentless Irish disapproval. The *Pilot,* hitherto his cordial friend and follower, became his bitter foe, attacking his new position in a long series of sharp articles.[96] His influence among the Irish vanished. Too late he recognized what Father Hecker had always known, that "The R. C. Church is not national with us, hence it does not meet our wants, nor does it fully understand and sympathize with the experience and dispositions of our people. It is principally made up of adopted and foreign individuals." Without a common basis of ideas there could be no conciliation.[97]

The compromise too difficult for the acute mind of an intellectual aristocrat was never even attempted by the great mass of laboring Irishmen, completely preoccupied with the far more pressing problems of earning a bare livelihood. Hedged about by economic and physical as well as cultural barriers, they were strangers to the other society beside them. The development of Irish ideas created a further range of differences between themselves and all others in the city that stimulated and developed consciousness of group identity.

✄ VI ✄

The Development of Group Consciousness

*Thinking to live by some derivative old country mode
in this primitive new country, — to catch perch with
shiners. . . . with his horizon all his own, yet he a
poor man, born to be poor, with his inherited Irish
poverty or poor life . . . not to rise in this world, he
nor his posterity, till their wading webbed bog-trotting
feet get talaria to their heels.[1]*

ALL immigrants to Boston brought with them an awareness of group identity already sharpened by cultural contact
with other peoples. Years of conflict with the English had
strengthened this feeling among the Irish. The Germans em-
igrated during a turbulent period of patriotic awakening;
and the English, French, and Italians had felt impassioned
currents stirred up by the Napoleonic disorganization of Europe. Nationalists to begin with, all retained their ties with
the homeland.

As long as it derived from sources external to Boston society, awareness of nationality expressed merely a sentimental
attachment. Thus, Englishmen observed the birthdays of the
royal family; the Swiss collected funds for the village of
Travers, destroyed by fire in 1865; the French celebrated
mass at the Cathedral upon the death of Princess Adelaide;

while German, Polish, and Hungarian emigrés sympathized with, organized for, and assisted the insurrections at home.[2]

Continuous demands from abroad likewise reaffirmed Irish devotion to the "bright gem of the sea." [3] Her needs were so pressing, so apparent, none could refuse assistance. Meager earnings somehow yielded a steady stream of drafts to friends and relatives who remained behind, and great disasters elicited even more remarkable contributions. Stimulated by Bishop Fitzpatrick's pastoral letter, Boston Irishmen remitted more than $200,000 during the scourge of 1847.[4] The less serious famine of 1863 drew £149 from the Montgomery Union Association of Boston alone, while a committee of Irishmen collected $18,000.[5] And Irish parish priests could always rely upon aid from former parishioners when calamity struck their districts.[6]

Love of Ireland enlisted a host of organizations in the perennial struggle against English oppression. These cropped up sporadically through the twenties and thirties, but until the Repeal Movement of the forties, accomplished little.[7] After 1840, however, agitation against Britain absorbed immigrants' attention for almost a decade, although it proved ultimately only a transitory influence upon Irish life in Boston. "The Friends of Ireland Society," founded October 6, 1840, by J. W. James and John C. Tucker, affiliated in 1841 with O'Connell's Dublin Loyal Association, and established agencies in South Boston, Charlestown, East Boston, Roxbury, and West Cambridge. At regular meetings in each locality it collected large sums of money, and its zeal inspired similar societies throughout the United States, which met in 1842 in convention in Philadelphia. A central directory in New

York, formed in 1843, coördinated their activities and established a national fund for Ireland.[8]

Interest waned, however, as Repealers limited their activities to exacting dues. Collections in 1845 were about half those in 1843; and sparsely attended meetings reflected rising dissatisfaction.[9] The Boston Irish had been intensely loyal to O'Connell;[10] but reckless tugging at the lion's tail by Smith O'Brien, Mitchel, and the more active Young Ireland Party, weaned many away, particularly after the old leader's death.[11] Finally, the purge of radicals from the Repeal Society in 1847 alienated many prominent members, and transferred to Young Ireland complete control of Irish opinion in Boston, already inflamed by revolutionary hopes.[12] Implicit approval by the Church in 1848, however, united conservative Repealers and radicals in the Confederation of the United Friends of Ireland, which resumed collections so vigorously as to provoke strenuous protests from the British ambassador at Washington.[13] But failure took the heart out of the movement, and renewed conservative opposition ended it. Nationalist activity thereafter showed life only in sporadic flurries in the radical press, and in momentary excitement over the exile of O'Brien and his followers.[14] In 1857, the last serious hope vanished with the redistribution of the funds collected in 1848 and saved for a new insurrection.[15]

Although residual loyalties rendered immigrants particularly sensitive, appeals from abroad evoked a response from all Bostonians and frequently presented a common denominator for coöperation. Non-Irishmen promptly and generously aided Ireland, loading the *Jamestown* with supplies for the famine stricken land in 1848, and actively participating in relief work in 1863.[16] Political sympathy, although more intense within each group, also existed outside it. Germans, Frenchmen, Italians, and, for a time, the Irish combined for common revolutionary objectives, thinking in terms of a

Fig. 20. Political discontent — arrest of William Smith O'Brien, 1848

general struggle of western peoples against tyranny — national in form, but liberal in substance.[17]

Thus the recollection of common origin was not a conclusive segregative factor. The group discovered its coherent identity, tested its cohesiveness, and apperceived its distinguishing characteristics only by rubbing against the ineluctable realities of existence in Boston. When experience diluted initial differences, newcomers entered smoothly into the flow of life about them. Otherwise, they remained a discordant element in the closely-knit society; reluctant or unable to participate in the normal associational activities of the community, they strove to reweave on alien looms the sundered fabric of familiar social patterns. Since new soil and new homes called for new forms of behavior, they created a wide range of autonomous organizations to care for their needy, provide economic and political protection for their helpless, and minister spiritual comfort and friendship to those who found it nowhere else.

The yearning for familiar pleasures, for the company of understanding men, and the simple sensation of being not alone among strangers, drew immigrants together in tippling shop and *bierhaus,* and in a wide variety of more formally organized social activities. Of these the most prominent was the Charitable Irish Society. By 1845 it had completely lost its original character and had settled down to the business of commemorating St. Patrick's day with a grand dinner which annually grew more magnificent until it attained the dignity of a Parker House setting in 1856.[18] Few Irishmen could join this venerable association, however. The "bone and sinew" concentrated in the Shamrock Society founded in 1844, and celebrated more modestly, but no less enthusiastically, at Dooley's, the Mansion House, or Jameson's.[19] In addition, informal neighborhood groups sprang up wherever the Irish settled.[20]

Canadians gathered in the British Colonial Society while Scotsmen preserved old customs, sported their kilts, danced to the bagpipe, and played familiar games, either in the ancient Scots Charitable Society, the Boston Scottish Society, or the Caledonian Club (1853).[21] Germans, who felt that Americans lacked *Gemüthlichkeit,* established independent fraternal organizations which often affiliated with native ones. Thus Herman Lodge was Branch 133 of the Independent Order of Odd Fellows, and Branch 71 of the Independent Order of Redmen was known as the Independent Order of Rothmänner.[22] Jews, however, formed none of their own, at first participating in American and later in German groups.[23]

No society considered its activities complete without a ball, annual, semiannual, or quarterly. At Hibernian Hall the Irish danced to the familiar music of Gilmore's band, while the Germans waltzed in Spring, Odd Fellow's, Phönix, or Turner halls to the rhythms of the Germania or Mainz's Orchestra.[24] Balls were so successful that Germans organized a *deutschen Ballgesellschaft,* and the Irish, the Erina Association, to sponsor them; and far-sighted entrepreneurs promoted them nightly to bring business to saloons and halls.[25]

Picnics were as popular; everyone arranged them. In Green Mountain Grove, Medford, Highland Grove, Melrose, or Bancroft's Grove, Reading, Germans enjoyed music and dancing, turning and games, absorbed mammoth lunches at ease, and set their children loose to roam in the woods (at half price).[26] For similar amusement, the Irish favored Waverly Grove or Beacon's Grove, Winchester, where even occasional fights and riots did not detract from the pleasure of escape from narrow streets and constricted homes.[27] For other relaxation the Germans turned to indoor gymnastics through the *Turnverein* founded by Heinzen and to shooting, climaxed by the annual *Turkey-schiessen* of the *Schutzenverein Germania.*[28] The Irish preferred rowing and several clubs engaged in vigorous boat-racing, modeled after regattas in Ireland. Run-of-the-mine matches took place in the harbor from Long Wharf to Castle Island, but major contests such as those of the *Maid of Erin* against the *T. F. Meagher,* or the *Superior* of New Brunswick, occurred in the Back Bay while hundreds of Irish spectators watched from along the Mill Dam.[29]

Militia companies were primarily social organizations, less attractive for their martial exploits than for the small bounty, the opportunity to parade in uniform, and the dinner and speeches that followed target practice and parade.[30] Though others joined American companies,[31] the Irish formed their own. Their earliest, the Montgomery Guards, had disbanded in 1839 after a dispute, but the Columbian Artillery, the Bay State Artillery, and the Sarsfield Guards took its place by 1852. Dissolved by the governor in 1853 as a result of Know-Nothing agitation, they continued their activities in new skins. The Columbian Artillery became the Columbian Literary Association, while the Sarsfield Guards became the Sarsfield Union Association, and their balls, picnics, and lectures suffered no loss in popularity.[32]

Saints' days furnished an annual social climax. The Scots Charitable Society celebrated St. Andrew's Day at a dinner at which "many a 'bannock' and dish of 'haggis' was eaten, and some whiskey punch was drank." [33] But the traditional St. Patrick's Day dinners of the Charitable Irish and the Shamrock Societies soon proved utterly inadequate for the Irish. No banquet room was broad enough to comprehend all the sons of Eire, even had they the price of the dinner. Only a spectacular parade could show their full ranks. Led by mu-

Fig. 21. An Irish militia company — Columbian Artillery

sic, 2,000 marched in 1841; and thereafter, the number of loyal Irishmen and flamboyant bands grew. Mass usually followed, for the Church stressed the supranational, religious aspect of the holiday. But though German Catholics occasionally participated, St. Patrick remained essentially Irish.[34]

Immigrant fraternal activities often outlived the needs which originally fostered them, becoming ancillary rather than essential to the lives of the newcomers who did not differ basically from their neighbors. Among some, however, economic status, geographical segregation, and alien culture sustained and reinforced the initial feelings of strangeness, and magnified the importance of organizations in absorbing the shock of contact with foreign society. The Irish were almost alone in founding associations for material betterment, for only they were confined to a single economic class by industrial stratification. They unhappily realized their position in the city was distinct from that of any other group — exploited, indispensable, yet lowly and unwanted. Despairing of the prospects around them, persistently questioned,

> In the valleys of New England,
>   Are you happy, we would know?
> Are you welcome, are you trusted?
>   Are you not? — Then, RISE AND GO! [35]

some sought escape to the frontier. But desirous as they were of leaving, few had the funds to carry them to the freedom of cheap lands.[36] And those wealthy enough to subsidize emigration were unwilling to tamper with an adequate, tractable, and inexpensive supply of labor and votes. Bishop Fenwick's plan for a colony in Maine (1833), the New England Land Company's project for one in Iowa (1851), and the Buffalo Convention's day-dream of a new Ireland in Canada, all came to nought.[37]

Necessarily reconciled to remaining within Boston, the Irish turned to sporadic and largely futile efforts to improve their economic position there. In 1855 more than 200 East Cambridge Irishmen contributed $6.00 each and formed the first consumers' coöperative to avoid "the petty domineering of would-be tyrants. . . ." [38] They turned also to their own countrymen for advice on the protection of their savings, consulting first the Bishop and the English consuls, and ultimately establishing banks of their own.[39] After an unsuccessful strike in 1843, the tailors established a producers' co-operative under B. S. Treanor, the Young Irelander. That organization failed, but it evolved by 1853 into the Journeymen Tailors' Trade and Benevolent Association. Stimulated by the panic of 1857, the society reorganized (1858), and affiliated with a similar group in Philadelphia.[40] Another large sector of unskilled Irishmen formed the Boston Laborers Association (1846) in an attempt to control dock and warehouse employment. Though it lost a serious strike in 1856, it reorganized in 1862 and grew in strength and vitality through the Civil War, remaining distinctly Irish, as did similar societies of waiters and granite cutters.[41]

Among all groups, of course, there were those who lived from hand to mouth in the shadow of an involuntary and remorseless improvidence. When illness, fatigue, or unemployment cut short their labor, these turned not to the cold stranger, but each man to his countryman, each to his old neighbor. Resenting

> The organized charity scrimped and iced,
> In the name of a cautious, statistical Christ,

all were reluctant to rely upon Boston social agencies, even those set up for their special benefit.[42] Nor could they fall back upon the organizations of their precursory compatriots, for both the Scots Charitable Society (1657) and the Charitable Irish Society (1737) had early shed their original functions, becoming primarily wining and dining clubs.[43]

Numerous benevolent enterprises therefore marked the settlement of each new group in the city. But not all flourished. Many societies, hopefully launched, soon met disaster in seas of disinterestedness. The *Società Italiana di Benevolenza,* an early German Charitable Society, a Scandinavian Benevolent Relief Society, and a Swiss group, all failed to survive.[44] A British Charitable Society, founded in 1816, and a German Assistance Society, founded in July, 1847, with sixty members, struggled through the period, but always remained small.[45] The British organization almost disappeared during the Civil War, while apathy kept down the membership of the German Society, which only spent $300 to $400 annually for assistance. Intimate associations with limited functions, like the *Krankenunterstutzungsgesellschaft* — which provided death and illness benefits — were more successful; and religious institutions continued to extend charity. But on the whole the non-Irish immigrants failed to develop autonomous eleemosynary activities.[46]

The Irish, however, segregated in their murky slums, in their lowly occupations, and their dread of losing religion, never ceased to anticipate harsh treatment from strangers or to distrust unknown ways.[47] Centuries of struggles had engendered an acute wariness of Protestants, of Protestant friendship, and of Protestant assistance that too often masked proselytization with the guise of benevolence. "Talk to them of the Poorhouse and they associate with it all the disagreeable features of the prison-like Unions of their native land. Added to which is the horror, if placed there of being exiled, as they fear, from their priests; and *'they will sooner die in the streets'* (such is their language) than go to Deer Island or South Boston. . . ."[48] This misgiving was, of course, not without justification. Despite laws to restrict their influence, Protestant chaplains dominated the spiritual life of public institutions, controlling the inmates' reading material and religious services, while Catholic priests found great difficulty in securing access even after a resolve of the legislature in 1858 admitted them.[49]

The horror of dying in a hospital without the ministrations of a priest was not allayed until 1863 when Andrew Carney gave a South Boston estate to the Sisters of Charity for the institution named after him.[50] Destitute children, in danger of adoption by Protestants or the state, received earlier attention. In 1833, Sister Ann Alexis and the Sisters of Charity founded St. Vincent's Female Orphan Asylum. Accumulating funds from successive fairs and church collections, they finally purchased a building in 1842, and in April, 1858 opened new quarters, donated by Andrew Carney, to house the increasing number of children. The orphanage was exceedingly popular, but at most accommodated only 200.[51] Father Haskins' House of the Angel Guardian, established in 1851 for neglected boys, supplemented the activities of the Asylum.[52] But since the two combined could care for only a small fraction of those who looked to them for aid, the Irish organized a system of adoption by Catholic families.[53] However, when the Home for Destitute Catholic Children opened in 1864, more than one thousand gamins between the ages of eight and twelve were still prosecuted annually for vagrancy.[54]

Financial limitations necessarily relegated the immense problem of pauperism to the government. An early Hibernian Relief Society (c. 1827) was short-lived. The Irish could do little more for the poor than provide much needed clothing through parish societies, and occasional assistance through the Roman Catholic Mutual Relief Society, and, later, through the Society of St. Vincent de Paul.[55] The religious character of these associations drove the small group of Protestant Irish into a separate "Irish Protestant Mutual Relief Society."[56]

Except for the Negroes who in 1860 opened a home for aged women on Myrtle Street, Beacon Hill, the Irish alone established an independent institutional life. Their strength of numbers facilitated but did not cause separation. By 1865, the Germans, more numerous than the Irish in the year St. Vincent's Orphan Asylum opened, had failed to set up a single permanent agency. Social, economic and intellectual development gradually eliminated the necessity for autarchy in non-Irish groups, but ingrained in the Irish the insistence upon independent charities conducted according to Catholic principles.

Beyond the range of material needs, each group organized to preserve a precious cultural heritage, enlisting a wide variety of social instruments — churches, schools, newspapers, and clubs. Each cherished distinctive traditions whose chances of survival varied with the strength of the differences developed by experience in Boston. Language was the weakest barrier. Attempts to preserve German were futile. Pastors preached the necessity of learning English, and despite difficulties English words inevitably crept into German usage.[57] Thrown into continuous contact with neighbors who spoke no German, even purists inevitably "schäkt" hands, referred to "dem feinsten Köntry der Welt" and "unsere City," and used "no, sörri" and "ohl wreit" as liberally as any Yankee. Business taught them "aber Käsch daun," "Dammädsches," "engahdschd," and "indiht?."[58] Some used the two languages interchangeably, and all adapted the forms of one to the other.[59] French and German easily became second languages which could be acquired by the immigrants' children in the public schools. Separate organizations, founded on linguistic differences alone, proved superfluous.[60]

Similarly, the urge to maintain familiar forms of worship was most meaningful when it embodied a vital social difference. Thus although the Portuguese Jews had a synagogue as early as 1816, when Abraham Touro requested "that his religious profession might be recorded on the Town's books — & that he belonged to a Synagogue of the Jews," German Jews erected their own building in 1843 which in turn did not satisfy the Polish Jews who dedicated still another in 1849.[61] On the other hand, though German Protestants organized a congregation as early as 1839, constructing Zion Church (Shawmut Street, South End) in 1846–47, and a Methodist Church in Roxbury in 1852, they often accepted the facilities of natives. A number of German families, stopping in Roxbury for a few months in 1833, were content to attend St. James Episcopal Church and to send sixty children regularly to Sunday School, and the Reverend A. Rumpff, pastor of the Lutheran Church, worked as a missionary for the Unitarian Fraternity of Churches.[62]

Within the Catholic Church three nativity groups insisted upon national forms. When the Abbé de la Poterie read his first mass in 1788 to a congregation of between sixty and a hundred communicants, primarily French by nativity, but including some Irishmen, dispute arose as to the language to be used.[63] As soon as the English-speaking Reverend John Thayer appeared in Boston, the Irish seized the church by force, ousting the French priest whom the Bishop had delegated "to provide a Preacher for the most numerous part of the congregation." [64] Bishop Carroll finally ended the rift in the tiny Catholic community by retiring both Thayer and de Rousselet and installing the French Father Matignon.[65] Although the French had once preferred to be buried with Protestants rather than with Irish Catholics, and had felt bitter enough to remove their furniture from the church, the tact and kindly wisdom of Matignon and of the saintly Bishop Cheverus reconciled and reunited the two groups. Small in number, facing no serious problems until the forties, they remained harmonious in sentiment.[66]

But as immigration increased, the Church acquired a thoroughly Irish cast, marked by the accession to the episcopacy of John Bernard Fitzpatrick, the Boston-born son of Irish parents, who replaced the Maryland aristocrat Fenwick in 1846, and by an ever larger proportion of Irish-born clergymen, many from All-Hallows Missionary College near Dublin.[67] In its first four decades, the Church had scarcely grown at all. In 1816, Boston contained not more than 1,500 Catholics of all nativities, and Bishop Cheverus felt it could well be served as part of the New York diocese.[68] By 1830, only little St. Augustine's Chapel, South Boston (1819), had joined Holy Cross Cathedral, Franklin Square (1801–03). The three churches built in the thirties to provide for the inhabitants of the North End, the South End and Roxbury, and Charlestown could not serve those arriving in the forties. For in 1843, the absolute maximum capacity of all Catholic places of worship, including 2,000 seats reserved for Germans, was still less than 14,000 — clearly inadequate for the Irish.[69]

Active expansion, however, met the demands. In 1843, the Rev. J. B. M'Mahon opened the indispensable Moon Street Free Church in the heart of the North End slums, the first to accommodate the very poorest. In 1848, the Bishop bought the meeting house of the Purchase Street Unitarian Society for the use of the Irish in Fort Hill, naming it St. Vincent's. Finally, in 1855, the dedication of the Church of St. James, prepared to serve a congregation of 10,000, temporarily settled the problem within peninsular Boston, the Irish population of which did not increase sharply thereafter.[70]

As the Irish spread from the heart of the city, the Church followed, frequently purchasing the empty buildings of displaced Yankees. In 1842, they laid the cornerstone of St. John's Church in East Cambridge, and in 1848, opened St. Peter's, Cambridge. In 1844 the Meeting House of the Maverick Congregational Society in East Boston became the Church of St. Nicholas, joined before long by St. Mary's, the Star of the Sea, and Sacred Heart and Assumption. In 1845 a new church dedicated to SS. Peter and Paul replaced old St. Augustine's Chapel in South Boston, supplemented a few years later by the "Gate of Heaven" Church at City Point (1863). In 1855 a church was built in Brighton and in 1858 one in Brookline.[71]

Thoroughly Irish in character, the Church nevertheless profited by its early quarrels and made special provision for worship by each new national group. By 1840 the French element was thoroughly insignificant, but there were enough German Catholics to require attention. Served at first only by pastors who made occasional trips from New York, and by special masses in the Cathedral, the Germans soon demanded a church of their own. In 1841, they organized Trinity Church and erected a building (completed 1846) on Suffolk Street in the South End, which also served those in Roxbury and East Boston. Disturbed by a quarrel with Bishop Fenwick, however, they built their church slowly and with great difficulty, and remained in debt for many years, for Catholicism did not play the intimate role in German it did in Irish life.[72]

While immigrants might possibly transplant the familiar form of their churches as a matter of habit, they established successful independent educational organizations only in response to needs arising in America. Having no Old-World model — schools at home were either nonexistent or state-controlled — they created new institutions to protect a vital cultural difference. A German school system therefore remained a chimerical hope in the minds of isolated individuals. The ambition of intellectuals to establish a great German university in the New World led to fascinating speculations, but to nothing more. German Catholic priests may have given instruction throughout the period, but their attempt to found a formal academy failed; not until 1863 could they even buy a lot.[73] And the classes maintained by non-Catholic Germans in Roxbury and Boston had no more than ninety students by 1860.[74] Jews provided religious training for their children, but otherwise sent them to the public schools although a six-day teaching week made observance of their Sabbath difficult.

But a separate system was essential to the Irish, for compulsory education drew their children into the common schools, endangering their Catholic souls. Thus challenged, the Church attempted to cope with the problem even before the first Provincial Council of Bishops in 1829 urged the establishment of truly Catholic schools in each community.[75] Sunday Schools, the first line of defense, grew slowly; by 1829 not more than 500 Catholic children received instruction in the whole area. But after 1835 the Young Catholics Friend Society, overwhelmingly Irish by nativity, assumed the burden of these schools in Boston, organized branches in the Irish sections of the city, and educated more than a thousand pupils annually. By 1845 there were 4,100 children in Boston Catholic Sunday Schools. And thereafter societies of the same name exercised similar functions in South Boston and Roxbury.[76]

Parochial schools likewise started slowly, but expanded to meet the influx of Irish. The school Father Matignon is traditionally said to have kept in Holy Cross Church at the beginning of the century, probably offered only occasional haphazard instruction.[77] In 1820, the Ursuline nuns, with the aid of John Thayer and Bishop Cheverus, set up the first school for girls in their convent near the Cathedral. Although almost one hundred pupils attended at one time, it lost contact with the Boston Irish after moving in 1826 to Mt. Benedict, Charlestown.[78] There were classes of some sort in the Cathedral in 1826 and 1829, in Craigie's Point, Charlestown, in 1829, and in connection with St. Vincent's Orphan Asylum after 1830, but another permanent formally organized school was not founded until 1849, when the Sisters of Notre Dame de Namur from Cincinnati established one at St. Mary's, North End. The Sisters extended their activities by 1853 to the Church of SS. Peter and Paul, South Boston, opened academies by 1858 in Roxbury and on Lancaster Street, Boston, a convent on Berkeley Street, Back Bay, in 1864, and, after a quarrel over the use of the Bible in public schools, "Father Wiget's" in the North End in 1859.[79]

Higher education, less important to the mass of Irish laborers, came later. Holy Cross College in Worcester, established in 1843, attracted few Massachusetts residents, for its fees — more than $150 a year — were out of the reach of most.[80] But when the Jesuits opened Boston College on Harrison Street in the South End in 1863, the thirty-dollar annual charge and the possibility of living at home enabled more to attend.[81] Bishop Fenwick's hopes of founding a theological seminary were not realized, however, and in this period Boston Irishmen still found it necessary to send their children to France or to Canada for instruction leading to the priesthood.[82]

On all levels, of course, tuition charges limited attendance to those who could pay. Some, perforce, relied upon common schools. But many failed to attend at all, and the insistence upon parochial education often became a shield for truancy, creating a serious problem of child vagrancy.[83] But though the principle of Catholic instruction for every child remained an ideal rather than a reality, the Irish resisted the temptation of free public schools, and at considerable cost sponsored their own.

Among the Irish, educational efforts took special form in the total abstinence societies. Unable to deal with intemperance as other Bostonians did, they formed groups to provide nonalcoholic relaxation and entertainment. The earliest (1836) had been nonsectarian.[84] But after 1841, these organizations affiliated with the Church, their most active sponsor.

Stimulated by the visit of Father Mathew in 1849, these groups grew rapidly. In addition to the Hibernian and Father Mathew Total Abstinence Societies, clubs flourished in each parish and suburb, closely interrelated, but having no contact with non-Catholics. Thus, in 1865, at a procession after the death of President Lincoln, the nineteen non-Irish temperance groups marched together in Division 2, while the Irish paraded in Division 7.[85]

Their distinctive needs also shaped the less formally organized education of the Irish. Though some took advantage of such non-Catholic agencies as the adult evening school and the sewing school of the Benevolent Fraternity of Churches, most turned all their activities into Catholic channels.[86] Thus, the Young Catholics Friend Society early renounced its plan of inviting lecturers without regard to sect; and other groups adopted the same exclusive Catholic policy. The Hibernian Lyceum, the Tom Moore Club, literary institutes, debating societies, and Young Men's Sodalities all applied religious ideas to literature and current events, while the Boston Gregorian Society, formed in 1836 by young Irishmen, applied them to music.[87]

The French and Germans sponsored similar cultural activities. The *Gesangverein Orpheus* and the *Solo-Club* gave popular concerts for many years, and a society founded in 1847 offered numerous lectures and plays. Even earlier, German Jews founded a "Hebrew Literary Society" which met twice weekly for discussions and kept a file of Jewish, German, and English periodicals. In addition, enterprising saloonkeepers found it profitable to keep *Lesezimmer* where nostalgic countrymen could scan the pages of the *Berliner*

National-Zeitung, the *Leipziger Illustrierte,* and the good-natured *Kladderadatsch.*[88]

Periodicals from home were not enough. Each group at one time or another attempted to develop newspapers to express its own needs in the new world. However, though the press was the immigrants' most powerful educational instrument, it flourished in Boston only to the degree that it satisfied a significant social need. Since almost all these journals appeared weekly they competed with the superior resources of those in New York and failed unless supported by a group conscious of its identity. Thus, the French, first in the field with Joseph Nancrede's *Courrier de Boston* and de Rousselet's *Courrier politique de l'univers* (1792–93), were unable to support one in Boston for any length of time because of competition from the splendid *Courrier des États-Unis* of New York.[89] Edited with great care, displaying an unusual regard for taste and accuracy, the latter was the outstanding immigrant newspaper of the period. In turn weekly, bi-weekly, and tri-weekly, it finally became a daily.[90] Vying with it, *Le Littérateur français* (1836), the *Petit Courrier des familles et des pensions* (1846), *Le Bostonien,* the *Gazette Française,* all of Boston, and the *Phare de New York,* could last only a short time.[91] Newspapers in other groups started hopefully, but faded rapidly. Short-lived Spanish and Italian sheets had little influence.[92] After the quick failure of the first British paper, *Old Countryman,* the English depended upon the *New York Albion* until one of its editors moved to Boston in 1855, and started the *Anglo-Saxon.* In the same year the *European* and in 1857 the *Scottish-American* were established in New York. But none succeeded.[93]

The only non-Irish immigrant paper that flourished in Boston was founded upon the personality of a brilliant editor. The *Boston Merkur* (1846–48), and *Der Neu England Demokrat* (a semi-weekly) had already disappeared when Karl Heinzen transplanted *Der Pionier* from Louisville and New York to Boston. A fiery radical, of deep culture and acute intelligence, extreme on every social issue, Heinzen, exiled from Prussia, had participated in the 1848 revolution in Baden, and had led a stormy career on several German-American papers. His personal organ thrived in Boston's friendly atmosphere, scarcely affected by the founding of the somewhat more popular *Bostoner Zeitung* in 1865, and exercised a deep influence both on Germans and on the Americans like Wendell Phillips and Garrison who read it.[94]

The strongest organs naturally developed among the Irish, who turned to them for news of home, for accounts of their own activities and organizations, and, above all, for sympathetic advice, derived from their own ideas, on the strange issues they faced as residents and citizens of a new world. But until the forties, even the Irish had no stable newspapers in Boston and relied on the New York *Shamrock,* the *Western Star and Harp of Erin,* and their successors.[95] Starting with Bishop Fenwick's short-lived children's paper, the *Expostulator,* a succession of very Catholic papers ingloriously collapsed.[96] The first, edited by the Bishop and Father O'Flaherty, and known variously as the *Jesuit or Catholic Sentinel* (1829–31), and the *United States Catholic Intelligencer* (1831–33), failed completely. Its successor, the *Literary and Catholic Sentinel,* edited by the popular poet, George Pepper, and by Dr. J. S. Bartlett, appeared at the opening of 1835. By

the end of the year, to strengthen its appeal to the Irish, it became the *Boston Pilot* "in honor of one of the most popular
and patriotic Journals in Dublin." [97] Subsisting from appeals
to the generosity of its subscribers, it lasted through a second
year, and gave up. Pepper then attempted to issue a secular
paper, *The O'Connellite and Irish Representative,* but neither that nor his other ventures survived. [98]

The second *Boston Pilot,* founded after his death in 1838 to
express the interests of the Irish-Catholic population of New
England, like its less permanent predecessors, did not pay its
way; by the end of the year, it had only 600 subscribers. It
staggered on, however, although a meeting of its friends to
raise funds was only partially successful. At the end of 1839,
it was still in serious difficulties. But the immigration of the
forties brought security. [99]

Prosperity completely reoriented the *Pilot's* policy. In 1842,
Thomas D'Arcy McGee, a green Irishman of seventeen, elec-
trified a Boston audience with a patriotic oration that won
him an editorial position on the *Pilot,* and made him editor-
in-chief in 1844. Set by him on a radical course, the *Pilot*
preached Irish nationalism, even after he returned to Dublin
to edit the *Nation.* Once drawn into the Repeal Movement,
the paper became dependent less upon the support of the
Church than upon that of popular opinion. And with the
aid of that support it could outlive occasional rivals such as
the *New England Reporter and Catholic Diary.* [100]

Repeal under the respectable auspices of O'Connell was
safe, but after 1845, the *Pilot* espoused the program of Young
Ireland and became intolerable to the Church. To counteract
the *Pilot's* influence, the Bishop, through Brownson, spon-

sored the *Boston Catholic Observer,* a religious rival. At the same time a political newspaper, the *Boston Vindicator,* appeared and was hailed as an ally by the *Observer.*[101] Neither the *Vindicator* nor J. R. Fitzgerald's *Nation* which replaced it, lasted long; but for two years the *Observer* and *Pilot* bitterly fought out the issues of Irish conservatism and radicalism.[102] In 1848, however, the *Pilot* acquired still another competitor. In that year, McGee returned from Ireland, established the New York *Nation,* and by the glamor of actual participation in the revolution drew many readers away from the *Pilot.* Weakened further by continued opposition from the clergy, the *Pilot* recanted in 1849 and turned conservative. The cross and dove replaced the red cap of liberty in its masthead, and Father John T. Roddan, an American priest, became its editor. Although many felt that "Donahoe will have a jolly grill in Purgatory for the evil he has done," his paper remained religiously dependable thereafter.[103]

Meanwhile, McGee's radicalism had antagonized Archbishop Hughes of New York, who forced the *Nation* out of business by a vigorous destructive campaign in 1850. Left without a journal, the Massachusetts radicals invited the still unrepentant rebel to come to Boston where he established the *American Celt* in 1850. But McGee failed to prosper. The *Pilot* and the clergy attacked him and he faced the serious competition of Phelim Lynch's *Irish-American,* which had taken his place in New York by 1849. After two years he finally shed his radicalism and made peace with the Church. But since there was no room in Boston for two conservative papers, he left for Buffalo and eventually for Montreal.[104]

No longer strong enough to support a newspaper, the radicals thereafter confined their reading to the New York *Irish-American*. As the former revolutionaries splintered into cliques, each established an organ: John Mitchel's *Citizen,* Doheny's *Honest Truth* and, *Meagher's Irish News*. But neither these nor occasional fugitive papers like William Jackson's *Irish Pictorial Miscellany* or Patrick X. Keating's *Illustrated Irish Nation* menaced the secure hold of the *Pilot* upon the Irish reading public.[105]

Only the Negroes developed a group consciousness comparable to that of the Irish. Although accepted as equals in some sects,[106] sharp color prejudice compelled colored Methodists and Baptists to organize their own churches in the West End.[107] Discrimination kept them out of the common schools and made necessary the organization of a distinct system with the aid of the town and of the Abiel Smith legacy.[108] The refusal of the white Masons to admit Negroes caused the formation of autonomous lodges affiliated not with other Massachusetts lodges, but with the Grand Lodge of England.[109] Similar motives provoked the attempt to organize a Negro military company, while the struggle for equality for themselves and for freedom for their enslaved kinsmen fostered Russworm's *Freedom's Journal* and the New York *Colored American,* and the organization of vigilantes that helped save Shadrach and attempted to rescue Burns.[110] But Negro awareness of race derived not from differences they desired to cherish, but rather from a single difference — color — which they desired to discard. Thus, as soon as a change in law in 1855 admitted Negroes to the common schools, their own closed.[111] Their consciousness was a factor of the prejudice of others, and declined as that subsided. They lacked the cohesiveness and coherence generated in the Irish by their economic, physical, and intellectual development in Boston.

The flourishing growth of Irish institutions was an accurate reflection of their consciousness of group identity. These autonomous activities had no counterpart in the Old World where the community was a unified whole, adequately satisfying all the social desires of its members. Independent societies developed among immigrants only in Boston in response to the inadequacy of the city as it was to fill their needs. Since the non-Irish foreigners felt differences only at occasional particular points, they diverged from native social organizations infrequently, in localized activities of diminishing vitality. But the development of the Irish had broadened original differences so widely that the *Pilot* concluded, "co-operation for any length of time in important matters between *true* Catholics and *real* Protestants is morally impossible." [112] Unable to participate in the normal associational affairs of the community, the Irish felt obliged to erect a society within a society, to act together in their own way. In every contact therefore the group, acting apart from other sections of the community, became intensely aware of its peculiar and exclusive identity.

The degree of intermarriage at once reflected and buttressed the distinction between the Irish and all others. Among the Irish, religious and social considerations reënforced the natural tendency to mate with their own kind. As Catholics, they were repeatedly warned that union with Protestants was tantamount to loss of faith; while the great majority of non-Irish in the city considered marriage with them degrading.[113] As a result, the percentage of Irish intermarriage was lower than that of any other group including the Negroes, 12 per cent of whose marriages were with whites.[114]

Group consciousness in the newcomers provoked a secondary reaction in native Bostonians, almost nonexistent in the eighteenth and early nineteenth centuries, when French Huguenots, Jews, Scots, Scotch-Irish and Irishmen had had no difficulty in assimilating with the older stock.[115] Americans now became more conscious of their own identity. They began to distinguish themselves, the Anglo-Saxons, from the Irish "Kelts." [116] The old society felt a sense of *malaise* because newcomers did not fit into its categories, and resentment, because they threatened its stability. Uneasy, it attempted to avoid contact by withdrawing ever farther into a solid, coherent, and circumscribed group of its own, until in the fifties it evolved the true Brahmin who believed, with Holmes, that a man of family required "four or five generations of gentlemen and gentlewomen" behind him.[117]

Group Conflict

We still drive out of Society the Ishmaels and Esaus. This we do not so much from ill-will as want of thought, but thereby we lose the strength of these outcasts. So much water runs over the dam — wasted and wasting! [1]

CONSCIOUSNESS of identity particularized groups; but mere pluralism evoked no conflict in Boston society. Those coherently welded by circumstances of origin, economic status, cultural variations, or color differences often moved in distinct orbits, but were part of a harmonious system. In some instances, native Bostonians adopted newcomers; in others, they adapted themselves to the existence of aliens in their community. But whatever friction arose out of the necessity for making adjustments produced no conflict, until the old social order and the values upon which it rested were endangered.

Thus, while prejudice against color and servile economic origin confined the Negroes to restricted residential areas, distinct churches, special jobs, separate schools, and undesirable places in theaters until the 1850's, the relationships between Negroes and other Bostonians were stable and peaceful.[2] Social and legal discriminations still limited Negro privileges in the Park Street Church in 1830, and incited protests when Alcott included a Negro child in his infant school.[3] But the stigmata and penalties for being different were slowly vanishing. Those who urged equality for the South were perforce obliged to apply their convictions at home. An attempt in 1822 to restrict the immigration of Negro paupers failed and repeated petitions after 1839 finally secured the repeal of laws against intermarriage, thus legalizing a process already in existence.[4] In 1855 separate schools were abolished and colored children unconditionally admitted to the public schools, so that by 1866 some 150 Negroes attended the primary, 103 the grammar, and five the high schools of Boston — in all, a high percentage of the Negro children of the city.[5] The state actively defended and protected Negroes' rights, even establishing missions for that purpose in Charleston and New Orleans where Boston colored seamen were often seized as fugitive slaves.[6] Public pressure forced the Eastern and New Bedford Railroads to admit colored people to their cars in the forties; and former slaves began to move to the same streets as whites.[7] In 1863, they were permitted to fight in the Union Army when Governor Andrew, with the aid of Lewis Hayden, recruited the Fifty-fourth Massachusetts Regiment, which included 300 fugitive slaves. In the same year, the militia was opened to them, and a colored company in Ward Six received a grant from the city. Negro regiments were segregated, but many prominent Bostonians "taking life and honor in their hands cast in their lot with" them.[8] By 1865, the Negroes, though still a separate part of Boston society, participated in its advantages without conflict. And most Bostonians agreed that "the theory of a natural antagonism and insuperable prejudice on the part of the white man against the black is a pure fiction. Ignorant men are always full of prejudices and antagonisms; and color has nothing to do with it." [9]

Group consciousness based upon religious differences was likewise not conducive to conflict. The Puritan dislike of Catholics had subsided during the eighteenth century,[10] and had disappeared in the early nineteenth as a result of the good feelings produced by revolutionary collaboration with the French and the growth of the latitudinarian belief that "inside of Christianity reason was free." [11] Governor Hancock had early abolished Pope's Day, and the Constitution of 1780 had eliminated the legal restrictions against Catholics. Catholics established a church in the city in 1789 "without the smallest opposition, for persecution in Boston had wholly ceased," and "all violent prejudices against the good bishop of Rome and the Church . . . he governs" had vanished, along with hostility towards hierarchical institutions in general.[12] Bishop Carroll, visiting Boston in 1791, preached before the Governor, pronounced the blessing at the annual election of the Ancient and Honorables, and was amazed at the good treatment accorded him. Bishop Cheverus commanded the respect and affection of all Protestants.

Thereafter the government was no longer hostile. The City Council frequently gave Catholics special privileges to insure freedom of worship, closing the streets near Holy Cross Church to exclude the noise of passing trucks.[13] It never took advantage of the laws that permitted it to tax all residents for sectarian purposes; on the contrary, Boston Protestants often contributed to Catholic churches and institutions. After 1799 no tithes were collected, by 1820 religious tests were abolished, and in 1833 Church and State completely separated.[14] The anti-Catholic activities of the *New York Protestant* and of the New York Protestant Association in the early thirties had no counterpart in Boston where an attempt to found an anti-Catholic paper (*Anti-Jesuit*) in 1829 failed.[15] Accepted as loyal members of the community, Catholics could easily partake of its opportunities.[16] Their right to be different was consistently defended by natives who urged that the particular sect each person chose was a private matter. "In individual instances where our friends and acquaintances join the Romish Church, there may be reason either to be glad of it or to grieve. If they join the Church . . . because they need its peculiar influence for their own good, if never having found peace in Christ elsewhere they do find it there, ought we not to rejoice in such a result? Why should we doubt that some minds are better fitted to find a personal union with God by the methods of the Catholic Church than by any other?"[17]

There were of course differences between the sects, expressed in theological disputations. As early as 1791 Thayer offered to debate any Protestant in a "controversial lecture."[18] Beecher and Bishop Fenwick, assisted by Father O'Flaherty, engaged in a series of debates in 1830–34, the most prominent of the period. And the religious press and sermons occasionally attacked Catholicism, sometimes violently, in the spirit of all contemporary disputes, while Protestant denominations urged their ministers to resist the spread of "Popery." [19]

But the expression of theological differences did not imply intolerance. Thus the Congregationalists urged their ministers to labor "in the spirit of prayer and Christian love . . . ," and even the *Christian Alliance and Family Visitor,* founded "to promote the union of Christians against Popery," failed to print "a single article or paragraph of any description against . . . Catholics." [20] Arguments were aimed against Catholicism, not against Catholics, just as they were against Methodism, or by the Orthodox against Unitarianism and by "Christians" against transcendentalists.[21] When Beecher became too violent, the *Boston Courier* and the Boston Debating Society, both non-Catholic, denounced him. For though some preferred one sect to another, the predominant feeling among Bostonians of this period was that "wherever holiness reigns, whether in the Protestant or Catholic communion . . . wherever there is a pious heart . . . there is a member of the true church." [22] Indeed, such men as Channing cared little for the particular sect in which they ministered. Their "whole concern was with religion, not even with Christianity otherwise than as it was, in . . . [their] estimation, the highest form of religion. . . ." [23]

Those who recognized distinctions between the sects generally felt that more important were "the grand facts of Christianity, which *Calvinists* and *Arminians, Trinitarians* and *Unitarians, Papists* and *Protestants, Churchmen* and *Dissenters* all equally believe. . . . We all equally hold that he came . . . to save us from sin and death, and to publish a covenant of grace, by which all sincere penitents and good

men are assured of favour and complete happiness in his future everlasting kingdom." [24] In that vein, Holmes' "Cheer-
ful Parson" affirmed,

> Not damning a man for a different opinion,
> I'd mix with the Calvinist, Baptist, Arminian,
> Greet each like a man, like a Christian and brother,
> Preach love to our Maker, ourselves and each other.[25]

And even the more conservative Baptists granted that "the
various erring sects which constitute the body of Antichrist,
have among them those who are beloved of God. . . ."
"Wherein we think others err, they claim our pity; wherein
they are right, our affection and concurrence." [26] In this rose-
ate scheme of salvation there was room even for Jews, and
from Bunker Hill, a poet proclaimed:

> Christian and Jew, they carry out one plan,
> For though of different faith, each in heart a man.[27]

Government action reflected the community's attitude towards immigrants. They were still welcome. The state had
no desire to exclude foreigners or to limit their civic rights;
on the contrary, during this period it relaxed some surviving
restrictions.[28] Since the care of aliens was charged to the
Commonwealth, the problem of poor relief aroused less hostility within Boston than outside it.[29] Yet nowhere was pauperism transmuted into a pretext for discrimination against
the Irish. Legislation aimed only at barring the dependent,
the insane, and the unfit, and shifted to newcomers part
of the cost of those who could not support themselves. The
function of the municipal Superintendent of Alien Passengers, under the act of 1837, was merely to prevent the land-

ing of persons incompetent to maintain themselves, unless a bond be given that no such individual become a public charge within ten years, and to collect the sum of two dollars each from all other alien passengers as a commutation for such a bond.[30] All the subsequent changes in the law only modified it to conform with a decision of the Supreme Court.[31] Attempts to extend these restrictive provisions failed, partly because of the pressure of shipping firms which profited by the immigrant traffic, but primarily because successive administrations recognized that, "The evils of foreign pauperism we cannot avoid," and it is "wise to avail ourselves of the advantages of direct emigration which increases the business of the State." [32]

In the two decades after 1830, however, the differences so tolerantly accepted impinged ever more prominently upon the Bostonians' consciousness. The economic, physical, and intellectual development of the town accentuated the division between the Irish and the rest of the population and engendered fear of a foreign group whose appalling slums had already destroyed the beauty of a fine city and whose appalling ideas threatened the fondest conceptions of universal progress, of grand reform, and a regenerated mankind. The vague discomforts and the latent distrusts produced by the problems of these strangers festered in the unconscious mind of the community for many years. Though its overt manifestations were comparatively rare, the social uneasiness was none the less real.

Thus pauperism aroused some resentment among those who saw Massachusetts overwhelmed by a rising tax bill; [33] and indigent artisans continually complained that Irishmen displaced "the honest and respectable laborers of the State; and . . . from their manner of living . . . work for much less per day . . . being satisfied with food to support the animal existence alone . . . while the latter not only labor for the body but for the mind, the soul, and the State." [34] Above all, as the newcomers developed consciousness of group identity and sponsored institutions that were its concrete expression, they drove home upon other Bostonians a mounting awareness of their differences, and provoked complaints that "instead of assimilating at once with the customs of the country of their adoption, our foreign population are too much in the habit of retaining their own national usages, of *associating too exclusively with each other,* and living in groups together. These practices serve no good purpose, and tend merely to alienate those among whom they have chosen to reside. *It would be the part of wisdom, to* ABANDON AT ONCE ALL USAGES AND ASSOCIATIONS WHICH MARK THEM AS FOREIGNERS, *and to become in feeling and custom, as well as in privileges and rights, citizens of the United States."* [35] The inability of the native-born to understand the ideas of their new neighbors perpetuated this gap between them, rousing the vivid fear that the Irish were "a race that will never be infused into our own, but on the contrary will always remain distinct and hostile." [36]

That fear was the more pronounced because the Catholic Church in these years was a church militant, conscious of its mission in the United States, vigorous and active in proselytization and the search for converts. In the strategy of the hierarchy, and in their own minds, immigrants played a clear role in this process of redemption: they had been carried across the waters by a Divine Providence to present an irrefutable example of fortitude and faith to their unbelieving neighbors, to leaven the dull mass of Protestant America and ultimately to bring the United States into the ranks of Catholic powers.[37] No figure was more insistently, clearly, and admiringly drawn in immigrant literature than that of the humble Irishman in every walk of life who succeeded in converting his employer, friend, or patron.[38] Though Bostonians could not do without the Irish servant girl, distrust of her mounted steadily; natives began to regard her as a spy of the Pope who revealed their secrets regularly to priests at confession.[39] The growth of Catholicism in England warned them that a staunchly Protestant country might be subverted. Meanwhile, close at home, the mounting power of the Oxford movement in the Episcopal Church, reflected in the estrangement of Bishop Eastburn and the Church of the Advent (1844 ff.), and a growing list of widely publicized conversions lent reality to the warning of Beecher and Morse that Catholics plotted to assume control of the West.[40]

Before 1850, the potential friction inherent in these fears broke out only infrequently and sporadically. Incepted by irresponsible elements, these spontaneous brawls were always severely criticized by the community. Indeed, they were only occasionally directed against aliens, more often involving neighborhoods or fire companies. The rowdies singled out no special group. In 1814 West Enders rioted against Spanish sailors, in 1829 against Negroes and Irishmen, and in 1846 against some drunken Irishmen in Roxbury; but these were no more significant than the countless feuds between North

Enders and South Enders, or between truckmen and sailors, details of which enlivened many a police dossier.[41]

The Broad Street riot was exceptional only in size. On June 11, 1837, a collision between a volunteer fire company and an Irish funeral procession led to an outbreak, quelled after an hour or so by the militia. Caused by hot-headed, unruly firemen, proverbially a disruptive factor, it in no way reflected the feeling of the community. The firemen were immediately repudiated, and partly as a result of the affair, Mayor Lyman took the first steps towards replacing the volunteer system with a paid fire department.[42] A less permanent result was the establishment by the disbanded firemen of the *American,* the first anti-Catholic paper in Boston which for somewhat less than a year attacked alternately the Irish and the *"paid patriots"* who replaced them.[43]

Because it served for many years as an argument throughout the country in the propaganda for and against Catholics, the Charlestown Convent fire received a greater degree of notoriety than any other riot.[44] This disturbance grew primarily out of the failure of the school and the rural community in which it was located to adjust themselves to each other. To the laborers who lived nearby, the convent was a strange and unfamiliar institution, with which it was difficult to be neighborly or to follow the customary social forms. In addition, Catholicism meant Irishmen and for non-Irish laborers the convent was a symbol of the new competition they daily encountered. Rebecca Reed's lurid stories of life in the convent and the bickering of the Bishop and the Charlestown Selectman over a cemetery on Bunker Hill, provoked a sense of irritation that came to a head with the appearance and disappearance of Elizabeth Harrison, a demented nun.[45] The refusal of the Mother Superior to admit the Charlestown Selectmen to investigate the purported existence of dungeons and torture chambers until the very day of the fire inflamed

Fig. 22. Reminder of intolerance — ruins of the Ursuline Convent

the forty or fifty Charlestown truckmen and New Hampshire Scotch-Irish brickmakers who led the curious mob; and her threat that, unless they withdrew, she would call upon the Bishop for a defense contingent of 20,000 Irishmen precipitated the holocaust.[46]

After the initial excitement, every section of public opinion in Boston greeted the fire with horror and surprise. Bostonians had not disliked the school; many had actually sent their children there. There is no evidence that the residents of the city had any connection with the plot; not a voice was raised in its support. The press condemned the absence of adequate protection, and deplored the "high-handed outrage." Bostonians asserted that "The Catholics . . . are as . . . loyal citizens as their brethren of any other denomination." A mass meeting at Faneuil Hall expressed sympathy with the unfortunate victims of mob action and, resolving "to unite with our Catholic brethren in protecting their persons, their property, and their civil and religious rights," recommended a reward for the capture of the criminals and compensation to the convent, as did similar meetings under John Cotton in Ward Eight, under Everett at Charlestown, and under Story at Cambridge.[47] A reward of $500 offered by Governor Davis resulted in the arrest of thirteen men, the trial of eight, and the conviction of one. The life imprisonment sentence for the one of whose guilt there seemed to be no doubt was far more significant than failure to convict those who might have been innocent.[48]

The convent, reëstablished in Roxbury, failed "because of lack of harmony among the Sisters." [49] But the legislature was petitioned for compensation repeatedly in the next twenty years. Despite persistent reluctance to grant public funds for religious purposes, $10,000 was voted in 1846, but rejected by the Ursulines.[50] The rise of Know-Nothing sentiments thwarted further overtures, while anti-Catholic activities of city rowdies and the circulation of *Six Months in a Convent* somewhat balanced expressions of sympathy. But these antagonisms were more marked outside than within the city. None of the anti-Catholic papers founded after the publication of that scurrilous book were published in Boston.[51]

Occasional manifestations of hostility in the next few years were restricted in scope. The Montgomery Guards, the first Irish military company, were attacked in 1837 by the rank and file of the Boston City Guards who refused to parade with an Irish company to uphold "the broad principle . . . that *in all institutions springing from our own laws, we all mingle in the same undisguised mass, whether native or naturalized.*" Although the native militiamen complained that "the press . . . condemned our conduct with . . . open-mouthed language of wholesale reprehension . . . ," the very next year the same newspapers severely criticized the Irish soldiers who were finally disbanded in 1839.[52] In 1844 the reaction to the school quarrels in New York, to the riots in Philadelphia, and to the defeat of the national Whig ticket by the Irish vote, produced a short-lived nativist branch of the Whig Party. Although the American Republicans under T. A. Davis gained the mayoralty in 1845, it was only on the eighth ballot, in an election fought primarily on the issue of the local water supply.[53] Nativism declined steadily thereafter. An attempt to revive it in 1847 failed so disastrously, that the *Boston Catholic Observer* could triumphantly proclaim nativism dying.[54]

Nativist fears failed to develop more significantly because the Irish before 1845 presented no danger to the stability of the old society. They were in a distinct minority and, above all, were politically impotent. In 1834 the Irish claimed no more than 200 voters in all Suffolk County, and in 1839, no more than 500, while in 1845 less than one-sixth of the adult male foreigners in Boston were citizens.[55] Only a few had secured the right to vote, or took an interest in politics; their opinions were still a matter of private judgment, with no influence upon the policies of the community. The old inhabitants, as individuals, might look down upon their new neighbors as unabsorbable incubi, but the still powerful tradition of tolerance stifled their accumulated resentments. The dominant group took no step to limit social and political rights or privileges until the ideals of the newcomers threatened to replace those of the old society. At that moment the tradition of tolerance was breached and long repressed hostilities found highly inflammable expression.

The crisis came when, after a decade of efforts in that direction, the Irish acquired a position of political importance. After 1840 their press insisted upon the duty "to themselves as well as to their families" of naturalization and a role in the government. Politicians sponsored societies which aided the unknowing and stimulated the indifferent to become citizens, and professional agents drew up papers, filled out forms, and rapidly turned out new voters for the sake of fees and political power.[56] Between 1841 and 1845, the number of qualified voters increased by 50 per cent, then remained stable until 1852, when it grew by almost 15 per cent in two years, while in the five years after 1850, the number of naturalized voters increased from 1,549 to 4,564. In the same period, the number of native voters grew only 14 per cent.[57] Perennial political organizations flourished with every campaign and further mobilized the Irish vote.[58]

The coherence and isolation of Irish ideas facilitated political organization. And Irish leaders, consciously or unconsciously, encouraged group solidarity and the maintenance of a virtual Irish party. Though the Irish vote was not yet used to serve corrupt personal interests,[59] both those who aspired to gain public office in America through the support of a large bloc of voters, and those who hoped to return as liberators to the Emerald Isle, directed their energies toward activizing their countrymen. These efforts were so widespread that one of the most far-sighted Irish leaders complained that Irish political influence was being "fatally misused" and warned that "keeping up an Irish party in America is a fatal mistake, and . . . I will seek to induce them rather to blend and fuse their interests with American parties, than cause jealousy and distrust by acting as an exclusive and independent faction . . . a man has no right to interfere in American politics unless he thinks as an American. . . ."[60] But such views were rare.

With the political mobilization of the Irish in Boston, tolerance finally disappeared. The possibilities of Irish domination were the more startling because the political situation in Massachusetts, 1845–55, permitted a coherent, independent group to exercise inordinate influence. The unity of the old parties was crumbling as dissatisfied elements demanded new policies to meet the problems of reform, particularly those posed by slavery.[61] Although all, including the most conservative Abbott Lawrence, agreed on the ultimate desirability of reform, they were divided as to the methods of attaining it. Within each political party a restless group contended that the forces of good must prevail immediately, even at the expense of failure in national politics. Their insistence upon immediate, unequivocal action destroyed the coherence of the old alignments and yielded to the unified Irish the balance of power. For four years the reformers found these foreigners square in their path, defeating their most valued measures. In the critical year of 1854 this opposition drove them into a violent xenophobic movement that embodied all the hatreds stored up in the previous two decades.

Rantoul and Morton had blasted the stability of the Democrats, but the Whig party was the first torn asunder by the anti-slavery men. In the early forties, some members had already deserted to the Liberty party, but until 1846 most anti-slavery Whigs continued to believe in "reform within the Party." Even in that year the magic personality of Webster nullified the damage done by Southern aggressions and the turbulent Texas and Mexico questions, and held in rein such conscientious rebels as Stephen C. Phillips, Charles Allen, and Sumner. But the Whig nomination of a slaveholder to the presidency and the rejection of the Wilmot Proviso by their National Convention in 1848 opened an unbridgeable gap between the two factions, though the Whigs remained strong enough to win the gubernatorial election that year and again in 1849.[62]

A similar development among the Democrats led a few to support Van Buren, the Free-Soil nominee in 1848, but the party quickly united to profit from the more serious division of its rivals. In addition, hoping for a coalition, it offered the Whig dissidents an anti-slavery plank in 1849. But these overtures failed; Free-Soilers still preferred coöperation with the Whigs to alliance with the Democrats who, nationally, were the most prominent supporters of the South's peculiar institution. But while Webster squinted at the federal scene and dreamed of the White House, the Whigs would have no meddling with reform. Though controlling the legislature of 1849, they failed to pass a single Free-Soil measure. Finally, their support of the Fugitive Slave Law, and particularly Webster's role in its enactment, completed the cleavage and consolidated the Free-Soil party in Massachusetts.[63]

When the gubernatorial election of 1850 gave no candidate a majority, Democratic ambitions, after seven years of famine, approached fulfillment. The constitution provided for the choice of a governor by an absolute majority, in the absence of which the election was thrown into the legislature — a situation susceptible to a great deal of political maneuvering. In this election the Democratic state platform had endorsed the Free-Soil program, though without a formal coalition. A trade between the two parties, which together had a majority in the legislature that convened in January, 1851, was inevitable. The Free-Soilers, anxious to be heard in Washington, were impatient with the Whig demand that the designation of a senator wait eleven months for a new legislature, and threw their votes for a Democratic governor. In return, the Democrats supported a radical policy and handed the United States senatorship and the organization of the legislature to the Free-Soilers. Banks became speaker of the House, and Henry Wilson, president of the Senate; although the former was nominally a Democrat, both were actually Free-Soilers. The reformers got the better of the bargain, passing a series of radical measures, including a general incorporation law to break the power of monopolies, a law for more democratic control of Harvard College, a homestead and mechanics' lien law, and measures ensuring the secret ballot and plurality voting in national elections.[64]

The coalition held through the election of 1851. But though the Free-Soilers managed to push through the Maine Law over Governor Boutwell's veto, they were dissatisfied. They disliked the governor, who had obstructed many reform measures, and they distrusted their Democratic allies, who had bolted in considerable numbers on Sumner's election to the United States Senate and had contrived to defeat a personal liberty law, acts to liberalize divorce, to protect the property rights of women, and to extend the powers of juries. Whittier voiced the apprehension of the Free-Soilers when he wrote, after seeing the governor's first message, "It is . . . monstrous and insulting. May God forgive us for permitting his election." [65]

The Free-Soilers now recognized the need of a reform in government to gain complete control of the State — a reform impossible under the existing conditions of amending the constitution which called for a two-thirds vote in the House of Representatives of two successive legislatures on each clause.[66] With parties divided as they were, a simple majority was difficult enough, two-thirds almost impossible and two-thirds in two successive legislatures, out of the question. One solution was to change the basis of representation to reduce the influence of the conservative elements opposing them in Boston. But an attempt to do so in 1851 failed, leaving the reformers no alternative but a complete revamping of the constitution by a convention.[67]

In 1851 the Free-Soilers forced through the legislature a resolution for a constitutional convention. But when the question was presented to the voters, Democratic support was weak. The Irish, theretofore consistently Democrats, failed to follow their representatives who had indorsed revision. In the election several thousand who had voted for coalition candidates, turned against the constitutional convention.[68] Of these, more than 1,100 were in Boston, and they were predominantly Irish Democrats bolting the party.[69]

When the Democratic State Convention again supported coalition and revision the following year, the Irish, under J. W. James, the Repeal leader, finally seceded from the party. Though opposing the Democrats in the state election of 1852, they supported the national Democratic party which had repudiated Rantoul and coalition and whose presidential candidate, Pierce, was most acceptable as a conservative. Following the advice of Brownson and the *Pilot,* the Boston Irish became national Democrats and state Whigs. As a result of the confusion, the coalition ticket lost, but the project for a convention won.[70]

Impressed with the opportunity the convention presented for strengthening the party and consolidating its position, the Free-Soilers made special exertions in the March election and gained control. Their imprint upon the constitution that resulted was unmistakable. Single unit senatorial districts and plurality elections by secret ballots were proposed. To decrease the power of the executive, many appointive offices, including the Council, became elective; the judiciary was controlled by limiting the term of office and extending the powers of jurors; and the use of public funds for religious education was prohibited. While these measures would render government more responsive to the voice of the people, the proposed constitution was undemocratic in its most important provision. By changing the system of representation to favor country towns at the expense of large cities, bailiwicks of conservatism, the reformers unquestionably compromised their principles.[71]

With one important exception party lines held in the vote on the adoption of the constitution. The opposition of the few conscientious Free-Soilers who would not support the unfair system of representation was trivial compared with the force of conservative Irish Catholic opinion clamoring for defeat.[72] At the Democratic Convention which indorsed the constitution, James again led a seceding group of Boston Irishmen who formed a party of their own. Pressure for recruitment and organization of voters increased. In September the Calvert Naturalization Society in the South End joined the Ward Three Association of the North End. The *Pilot* repeatedly warned that "No Catholic . . . can possibly vote for this . . . Constitution without giving up rights for which he has been all along contending," and Brownson pointed out its revolutionary implications.[73]

In their campaign, the Irish joined the die-hard Whigs under Abbott Lawrence, who led "hundreds of honest men gulled by their sophistry," in opposing a constitution which seriously curtailed the influences of State Street in politics. Lawrence conferred with Bishop Fitzpatrick on the problem, and Whig newspapers appealed particularly to the Irish. Against this alliance the reformers' contention that the *Boston Pilot* was "trying to lead Irishmen into the jaws of a Boston aristocracy as remorseless as the one they had left Ireland to get rid of" counted little. The combination of Irish votes and cotton money in Boston defeated the constitution and elected a Whig ticket.[74]

In this crisis the reformers inveighed against the lords of the counting house and bemoaned the slowness of rank-and-file Whigs to recognize their true interests, but concluded that while the former could never be redeemed, and the latter would have to be educated, the main obstacle to reform was Catholic opposition. And by this time they had learned that differences with the Irish were too deep to be easily eradicated; they could only be fought. Butler, sensitive to every shift in popular opinion, realized that the "performance, which struck down the Constitution, invoked a bitterness among the people against the Catholic religion, such as had never before been, to any considerable degree, either felt or foreshadowed in the State of Massachusetts." [75]

Through the early months of 1854 a series of unconnected events heightened resentment against Catholics and evoked many antipathies developed since 1830. In December, 1853, Father Gavazzi, a rebellious priest, lectured in Boston on the reactionary role of the Church.[76] A few months later, the visit of the papal nuncio Bedini, who had been connected with the massacre of revolutionaries in Bologna, though not provoking the expected riot, did refresh memories of Irish opposition to liberalism.[77] Meanwhile, events at home confirmed that impression. Failure of the enforcement of the prohibition laws was laid at the door of the Irish, and the State Temperance Committee announced it would fight Catholicism as part of its struggle for human freedom.[78] The Burns case clearly linked the immigrants to pro-slavery forces and man-hunters. The *Pilot* supported the rendition of the fugitive slave; and the selection of the Columbian Artillery

and Sarsfield Guards to protect him against indignant mobs
seeking his freedom, incited an inflammatory handbill:

AMERICANS TO THE RESCUE!
AMERICANS! SONS OF THE REVOLUTION!!
A body of seventy-five Irishmen, known as the
"Columbian Artillery"
have volunteered their services to shoot down the
citizens of Boston! and are now under arms to defend
Virginia in kidnapping a Citizen of Massachusetts!
Americans! These Irishmen have called us
"Cowards and Sons of Cowards!"
Shall we submit to have our Citizens shot
down by a set of Vagabond Irishmen?

that turned many reformers against the Irish.[79] Finally, their
defense of the Kansas-Nebraska Act connected them with
the slave power, and drew criticism from such respectable
sources as the *Commonwealth,* the *Worcester Spy* and Theodore Parker.[80]

Distrust of the Irish at once encouraged and was stimulated by attacks upon Catholics. Hatred and violence
marched arm in arm, sustaining and strengthening each
other. Early in 1853, the purported kidnapping of Hannah
Corcoran, a Baptist convert, almost led to a riot. In the same
year the city government entered into a long-drawn-out controversy with the Catholics over their right to build a church
on the "Jail lands." In May, 1854, John S. Orr, the Angel Gabriel, led a mob that carried away a cross from the Catholic
Church in Chelsea, and in July a church was blown up in
Dorchester. *The Wide Awake: and the Spirit of Washington,*
a vituperative sheet, appeared in October, 1854 to combat the

"swarms of lazaroni from abroad;" and a venomous stream of anti-Papist literature reached Boston, particularly in the form of Frothingham's convent novels (1854).[81]

Meanwhile, as slavery absorbed the attention of Congress and the country, excited Free-Soilers found "every indication that the people are awakening from their unaccountable stupor on the . . . question." [82] The Kansas-Nebraska Bill infuriated even Everett and the conservative Webster Whigs. Sumner's correspondents informed him that "all parties seem to be approaching that happy state of . . . dissolution, for which we have sighed so long." [83] A Freedom Party tentatively formed in Boston, a "Republican" convention adopted a radical program, and a host of excited energies eagerly sought an outlet. Precisely where the immense anti-slavery impulse would be exerted was uncertain, however.[84]

But the Boston municipal elections of December, 1853 had already revealed the ultimate outlet. Only one month after their decisive defeat on the constitution, the reformers rallied to resist the reëlection of Nathaniel Seaver, a Whig supported by the liquor interests. As the "Citizens Union Party," they appealed to nativist feelings and drew 2,000 Whig votes, the entire Free-Soil vote, and 500 voters who had not troubled to go to the polls a month earlier.[85] These 500 voters came from a tremendous fund of nonvoting citizens, many of them Whigs disgusted with their party's vacillation.[86] The lesson to the reformers was obvious and was confirmed by simultaneous elections in Charlestown and Roxbury: [87] the Irish stood in the way of reform; reform forces could best be augmented and galvanized on an anti-Irish basis; the dormant voters must be awakened by an anti-alien alarm.

By 1853 the Order of the Star-Spangled Banner, a nativist secret organization popularly known as the Know-Nothings, had emerged in New York State.[88] Early in 1854 it spread into Massachusetts, swiftly, though quietly and unobtrusively, drawing "into its lodges tens of thousand of . . . anti-Nebraska men, ripe for Republicanism. . . ."[89] These recruits, inwardly ashamed of adopting means incompatible with the principles they professed, wrapped themselves in mantles of secrecy which served as a "spiritual fist-law" for gaining ascendancy without the use of force, and pursued their "purposes with the same disregard of the purposes of the structure external to . . . [themselves] which in the case of the individual is called egoism."[90]

In July, Henry Wilson, already a member, began to harness Know-Nothingism to the anti-slavery cause, and Seth Webb, Jr. decided, "Know-Nothingism is to be an important, perhaps the controlling, element in our state election; it will probably take us out of the hands of the Whigs. Into whose hands it will put us, nobody can tell."[91] The Know-Nothings presented the clearest platform in the next election. Without the support of the intellectual fronts of reform — Adams, Phillips and Sumner — who felt no ends justified nativist methods, they elected Henry J. Gardner, formerly president of the Boston Common Council, to the governorship by the unprecedented majority of 33,000, and gained complete control of the legislature in November. Until 1857, they ruled the state.[92]

Everywhere the success of the party rested upon thousands of new men drawn into politics by nativism.[93] The complexion of the new legislators reflected the ranks from which they rose. Among them were no politicians, and few lawyers. They were true representatives of those for whom they spoke. They included a few rascals and self-seekers; but by and large they were honest men, convinced that they were acting in the best interests of the community. Even the Democratic editor of the *Post* had to admit later that "the moral tone of the party was unquestioned. . . ."[94] Many did not even feel a personal antagonism to the Irish; J. V. C. Smith, an amateur sculptor, and Know-Nothing Mayor in 1854, associated with them in business and executed a fine bust of Bishop Fitzpatrick.[95]

Although the Know-Nothings made numerous mistakes, their administration was progressive and fruitful. They relaid the basis for the school system, abolished imprisonment for debt, established the first insurance commission, took the first steps to eliminate danger from railroad crossings, extended the power of juries, strengthened the temperance, homestead and women's rights laws, made vaccination compulsory, and assumed a firm anti-slavery position by passing a personal liberty law and petitioning for the removal of Judge Loring who had presided at the fugitive slave cases. In general, they embodied in their legislation the program of the party of reform. By 1855, they had sent Wilson to the United States Senate, amended the constitution so that a plurality sufficed in the gubernatorial election, and introduced many other innovations vetoed by the more conservative governor.[96]

The party's anti-foreign accomplishments were quite insignificant. To begin with, they disclaimed any intention of excluding immigrants, but stressed the necessity of making them "be as we are."[97] The most prominent achievement was the disbanding of the Irish military companies which annoyed natives particularly because they carried off prizes at drills. They served no useful purpose and in 1853 the *Boston Pilot* had itself suggested their dissolution. A breach of military discipline provided the pretext for the abolition of the Bay State Artillery in September, followed early the next year by the elimination of the remaining companies. Foreigners on the police force and in State agencies were discharged, and a number of cruel deportations displayed an ugly animus against helpless aliens. Finally, the misdeeds of individual members, notably of the Hiss Nunnery Committee, were exploited by the opposition and did much to discredit the party and obscure its constructive achievements.[98]

Ostensibly the party had acquired power to restrict the influence of immigrants in politics. Yet, though it had absolute control of the government, it failed to pass a single measure to that effect. In 1854, a bill to exclude paupers was not considered until the end of the session, and then referred to committee where it died. A literacy amendment to the constitution was rejected, and an amendment requiring a twenty-one year residence for citizenship which passed, was defeated at the second vote by the next Know-Nothing legislature.[99] Once reform, the essential feature of Know-Nothingism in Massachusetts, was assured, the party leaders attempted to jettison the anti-Catholic program. But the intolerance they had evoked could not readily be dispelled. Its influence persisted long after the death of the party it had served.

The Know-Nothings dissolved over the question of slavery, for the national party drew its strength from incompatible sources. In Massachusetts it was anti-slavery; elsewhere in the North it was unionist; in Virginia and throughout the South, it was pro-slavery.[100] Lack of a unified program inevitably split the party. Despite their strategic position in Congress, they could unite on few measures. Finally, when the national convention adopted a pro-slavery plank in June, 1855, the northerners under Henry Wilson bolted and the Massachusetts Council on August 7 adopted an uncompromising liberal position. At the same time a section of the party broke away and met at Worcester in June, called itself the Know-Somethings or American Freemen, and advocated an abolition platform and an end to secrecy.

The nomination of Fillmore, a pro-slavery man in 1856, completed the break between the state and national parties and a *de facto* coalition with the rising Republican party spontaneously formed. The latter nominated no candidate to oppose Gardner for the governorship, and most Know-Nothings voted for Frémont.[101] Thereafter the Know-Nothings in the state were absorbed in the tremendous growth of the new party, and Banks led the remnants to the Republicans in 1857–58 on his election to the governorship.[102]

Produced by the same reform impulse that fathered Know-Nothingism, the Republican party continued to express animosity toward the Irish, "their declared and uncompromising foe." The defeat of Frémont in 1856 was laid at the door of the Irish-Catholics, and confirmed the party's hostility to them. In retaliation, it helped pass an amendment in 1857 making ability to read the state constitution in English and to write, prerequisites to the right to vote; and in 1859, another, preventing foreigners from voting for two years after naturalization.[103]

Though the restrictive legislation affected all foreigners, the venom of intolerance was directed primarily against the Irish. Waning group consciousness among the non-Irish gave promise of quick acculturation, and similarities in economic condition, physical settlement and intellectual outlook had left little room for disagreement. In fact, the Irish found all others united with the natives against them. A Negro was as reluctant to have an Irishman move into his street as any Yankee,[104] and though the Germans distrusted the Know-Nothings and resented the two-year amendment, liberal principles led them into the Republican party.[105]

Indirectly, the Know-Nothing movement revived Irish nationalism. In Boston, nationalist activities first assumed the guise of the Irish Emigrant Aid Society, whose innocuous title concealed a secret revolutionary club, ostensibly aimed at organizing a liberating invasion of Ireland. Though some hotheads spoke of chartering ships to transport an army of Irish-Americans across the Atlantic, most recognized the obvious futility of such efforts. By and large, they hoped to organize politically, to support anti-English parties in America, to prepare for the Anglo-American war that would free Ireland, and to mobilize support against Know-Nothingism.[106] That the last motive, presumably incidental, was in fact primary, was clear from the movement's exclusively American character: it had no counterpart in Ireland. While expanding rapidly throughout 1855, the organization had little ultimate success. The clergy opposed it, cautious prosecution of would-be liberators in Cincinnati checked its growth, and internal quarrels finally dissipated its strength.[107]

But failure did not end the quest for a fatherland. So long

as the Irish were unaccepted in Boston, they looked back across the ocean. There was "always . . . some . . . machination to draw money from the pockets of the deluded lower order of Irish. . . ."[108] The Fenian Brotherhood emerged after 1859 and despite ecclesiastical disapproval grew in secret until it held its first national convention in Chicago in 1863. Its "centres" in Boston were numerous and active.[109]

Moreover, the Irish persisted in their opposition to reform. With Brownson, they believed Know-Nothingism "an imported combination of Irish Orangism, German radicalism, French Socialism and Italian . . . hate" and regarded Republicanism as its pernicious successor.[110] After 1856 they consistently supported the conservative Democratic party, voting for Buchanan and Douglas.[111] Although the violent phase had passed, the bitterness of conflict and antagonism remained. Out of it had grown a confirmed definition of racial particularism: the Irish were a different group, Celtic by origin, as distinguished from the "true" Americans, who were Anglo-Saxon, of course.[112] Once aroused, hatred could not be turned off at the will of those who had provoked it. The *Springfield Republican* sanely pointed out that "the American party, starting upon a basis of truth . . . has gone on, until [it] . . . denies to an Irishman . . . any position but that of a nuisance. . . ."[113] Group conflict left a permanent scar that disfigured the complexion of Boston social life even after the malignant growth producing it had disappeared.

✑ VIII ✑

An Appearance of Stability

The energy of Irish, Germans, Swedes, Poles, and Cos-sacks, and all the European tribes . . . will construct a new race, a new religion, a new state, a new litera-ture, which will be as vigorous as the new Europe which came out of the smelting-pot of the Dark Ages. . . .[1]

THE crucible of civil war defined and clarified the posi-tion of all elements in Boston society. Republicans and Dem-ocrats, Free-Soilers and Whigs, all approved of the objectives of the struggle for union and, after the firing on Fort Sum-ter, turned their energies towards achieving them. Bostoni-ans now wakened to a realization of the importance of for-eigners. The demand for men was enormous. Particularly after the three-month volunteers trickled home, the commu-nity leaders faced the necessity of utilizing the most fertile source of new recruits — the immigrant groups. Soon after the fighting began, Governor John A. Andrew wrote to the Secretary of War:

Will you authorize the enlistment here . . . of Irish, Germans and other tough men . . . ? We have men of such description, eager to be employed, sufficient to make three regiments.[2]

That Germans supported the war and eagerly flocked to the colors was not surprising in view of their attitude towards abolition and their membership in the Republican party.³ Indeed, by 1861 distinctions of national origin had little influence upon the reactions of Germans, Englishmen, Scots, Frenchmen, and Jews. These participated in the community's effort as a matter of course. The four years of struggle merely reaffirmed their secure position in the city; and whatever new problems they faced were not burdened with memories of old conflicts or with unforgotten resentments of social and economic segregation.

But aid from the Irish was less expected. They had opposed Lincoln, favored slavery, fought reform, and upheld the Democratic party and the South. Moreover those who now called for their help were the very men who, for the preceding six years, had sponsored restriction of Irish rights and privileges. "We hear on all sides the sound of disunion . . . ," John C. Tucker had openly warned, "Supposing it should come, and that Massachusetts stood alone, can she . . . expect that these men, who she is now about to proscribe, will rush to her assistance?" ⁴

Yet stronger ties bound the Irish to the Union. The guns that roared across Charleston Harbor roused an echo of contradiction in the Church's social policy. Complete acceptance of lawfully established government was basic to the thinking of all Irish Catholics; that was at the root of their complaint that abolitionists were revolutionaries, and helped to account for their complete conservatism after 1848. But in April, 1861, there was no doubt as to which section was revolutionary. The issue was not slavery, but unity, and the Church in

Boston agreed with Archbishop Hughes that "It is one country and must and shall be one." [5] The very logic of its political theory ensured obedience to the government in power and transferred loyalty to Washington.

As the war unfolded, more practical reasons drew the ranks of common Irishmen along the same path as the Church in

> The grandest cause the human
> Race on earth can ever know.[6]

Lack of sectional feelings among the immigrants focused their devotion upon the national government; and the bounties that surpassed the average annual earnings of the common laborer rendered patriotism exceedingly profitable. In addition, Great Britain's southern sympathies, clear from the start, encouraged Irish hopes of a war with England in which the United States together with a resurgent Ireland would humble both Saxon and slaveholder. To some extent, therefore, enlistment became a Fenian tactic. "Centres" flourished in every Irish regiment and optimistic liberators sought to acquire in action against the Confederacy, skill for a further struggle. A common Anglophobia thus allied Irish nationalists and American unionists.[7]

The government was quick to take advantage of Irish feeling.[8] Group consciousness now proved no barrier, but actually an aid to united action. An Irish brigade was organized and Meagher was advanced to the generalcy on the basis of dubious military qualifications but of undoubted popularity among his countrymen. Boston alone mustered two regiments. The Columbian Artillery, banned by the Know-Nothings seven years earlier, emerged from its disguise as a fraternal organization, and under its old commander Thomas Cass furnished the nucleus of the Ninth Massachusetts Regiment. The Twenty-Eighth Regiment, also almost exclusively Irish, was formed later. In addition, Irish units joined other regiments and Irish leaders like P. Rafferty and B. S. Treanor became agents to recruit their compatriots.[9]

The war quickened understanding and sympathy. Serving with their own kinsmen and their own chaplain under their own green flag, assured of complete religious equality, the Irish lost the sense of inferiority and acquired the sense of belonging.[10] They were no longer unwanted aliens. In the armies of the field, men of all nativities fought a common battle. Living together, they came, for the first time, to know one another, and knowing each other, they insensibly drew closer together. A Boston volunteer noted in 1863 the strange celebration of St. Patrick's Day by Meagher's Brigade, but the following year found him joining the festivities.[11] And a visiting Englishman noted, "You cannot go through the camp and say — 'There is the sedate Yankee — there the rollicking Irishman' — all seem subdued together into the same good behaviour." [12]

At home, too, antagonisms became less bitter. The community needed the Irish and therefore cultivated their favor. The government relaxed its discriminations against them. On the recommendation of the governor, the two-year amendment was repealed and the foreign-born regained their full civic rights, with the result that Irish politicians advanced to municipal office in ever larger numbers.[13] At the same time other institutions became more tolerant. In 1861 Harvard University conferred the degree of Doctor of Divinity upon Bishop Fitzpatrick, the first time a Catholic divine was so honored.[14] By 1862 Bible reading had paled as an issue. The legislature revoked the law making it compulsory, and the Boston School Board declared its "public schools . . . unexceptional to all denominations and to all of every creed, by the liberality, equality, and just regard for the religious faith of all our citizens." [15] It was not long before the City Hospital decided that "Patients may be visited by clergymen of their own selection, and where there is a wish for the performance of any particular religious rite, it shall be indulged when practicable." [16]

Furthermore, the loyalty of the Irish in the crisis drew them more closely into the city's life. Colonel Corcoran was enthusiastically received by the city governments of Boston and Roxbury, while Patrick Gilmore, whose "When Johnny Comes Marching Home" was sung everywhere, became the most prominent parade-leader in the city.[17] The war had provided an issue on which the Irish did not menace, indeed supported, the existing social order and its ideals. Somewhat unexpectedly, therefore, the bitter sectional conflict created an appearance of harmony within the city.

In the next fifteen years the optimistic assumptions of 1865 seemed on the way to fulfillment. The city entered upon a period of relative stability, by grace of which each element of the population seemed able to locate itself quietly. The lines that divided the Yankees from the Irish were as clearly marked as ever; but there were grounds for hope that a complete rapprochement between the contending groups was imminent.

The tide of immigration had definitely slackened in the

1860's; and it mounted only moderately the first few years of the next decade. After the panic of 1873 it fell into a precipitous decline.[18] Boston did not, therefore, face a recurrence of the crisis of the 1850's after the Civil War.

Between 1865 and 1880 the city was most directly affected by movements that originated in the Western Hemisphere rather than in Europe. British America produced a substantial flow of newcomers to the United States. In Nova Scotia and in Prince Edward Island limited opportunities generated discontent; and the revival of the fisheries and of trade with New England gave some of the people of those provinces the opportunity to move south of the border. In 1880 there were well over 25,000 of them in Boston and Cambridge.[19]

Another sizable contingent of newcomers came from the South. When emancipation gave the freed slaves some mobility, Boston, the old center of abolitionism, proved a magnet for some Negroes of the upper South. Although the total numbers involved were not large, that movement was enough to double the colored population of the city between 1865 and 1880.[20]

Supported by friendly public opinion, the colored men continued to improve their status in the city. A law of 1865 forbade discrimination against them in public places; and, despite adverse judicial decisions, the barriers of prejudice were steadily lowered. In 1866, two Negroes were elected to the state legislature; and thereafter there were frequently colored officeholders, often from wards that were overwhelmingly white. While almost all of them engaged in some form of manual labor, a few individuals rose to affluence and many more advanced to the state of moderate competence that enabled them to move out to thriving suburban communities in Cambridge and in the South End.[21] Meanwhile their churches and other institutions flourished.

Finally, there continued a significant drift to the city from the rural countryside of New England. Farm boys from Maine, New Hampshire, Vermont, and New York State still looked to the Hub for their fortunes; they constituted 14.3 per cent of its population in 1880. A trickle of Chinese — 121 of them by 1880 — added an exotic element to the city's population.[22]

But the great migration of Europeans for the moment seemed over. And of the remnants who came few found Boston attractive. The immigrants of these years had far greater resources than the fugitives of the 1850's and could more readily choose their destinations. Boston stood decisively below New York as a port of arrival; and it failed to hold even those who landed there. Only a tiny fraction of the great English and Scandinavian immigration waves of these years passed through this port, so that those movements contributed but slightly to the city's population. Just about a thousand Italian immigrants in 1880 formed the vanguard of a movement that would become more important later in the century.[23]

The Irish supplied the bulk of the new European arrivals in the city; and they were just numerous enough to take the places of the immigrants of an earlier generation who died. Consequently, although the number of foreign-born in Boston rose slowly, their percentage of the total population remained about the same. Those already established therefore had the opportunity to adjust more thoroughly to the life about them.[24]

With the stimulus of foreign immigration gone, the total population grew largely through natural increase. It thus reflected the composition of the population in the 1850's, with the significant exception that among the native-born of 1880 were a substantial number of the children and grandchildren of immigrants. The spread of the city's residents to neighboring communities proceeded at an accelerated pace and the surrounding villages were quickly engulfed as an ever larger number of Bostonians sought living space in the suburbs. Political boundaries were altered to adjust to the shift of population. Roxbury was swallowed up in 1867, Dorchester two years later, and Charlestown, Brighton, and West Roxbury in 1873.[25]

Some of the old problems were more easily resolved than earlier. In these years the advances of the earlier period were consolidated. The city showed its economic health in the ability to survive two great economic crises. The great fire of 1872 leveled 65 acres and wiped out large parts of the business district.[26] The panic of 1873 struck the city a blow from which it had hardly recovered by the end of the decade. Nevertheless, its industrial growth continued, although at a slower pace. By 1880 Boston stood between third and fifth in manufacturing among the cities of the nation, depending upon the method of computation; it now lived by producing clothing, sugar, iron, candy, and meat and printing products — the industries that had appeared since the arrival of the immigrants.[27]

Local manufacturing and the growth of the mill towns in

the interior led to commercial stability as well. Boston marketed the shoes and cloth of its back country and imported the leather, wool, cotton, and sugar the factories needed. It also developed a flourishing export trade of corn, wheat, and meat that was sustained by improved railroad links to the West. The city, at the same time, was also able to establish profitable new contacts with Cuba, Puerto Rico, and the Caribbean through the import of sugar for its refineries.[28]

Other prewar social problems proved less amenable to the remedy of stability. The cost of government rose alarmingly; the municipal debt almost quadrupled in the 15 years after the war.[29] Yet it proved hard to carry forth desirable improvements. Plans for an impressive park system had been agitated since 1869, yet by 1880 nothing had been accomplished.[30] All available funds had to be reserved for essentials like sewerage improvement.[31]

Living conditions in the poor Irish districts remained harsh and, although the incidence of pauperism, insanity, intemperance, and crime declined, the burden of those disorders still evoked complaints. Then, too, the mortality and disease rates in the city remained high, particularly among the Irish.[32] Furthermore, almost 23,000 of the foreign-born were illiterate, most of them concentrated in the Irish wards.[33] The new times had thus not themselves removed the essential causes of the immigrants' difficulty of adjustment.

For, though the Irish acquired a secure place in the community, they remained distinct as a group. Prejudice against them lingered for many years.[34] Not until 1879, for instance, did Catholic chaplains secure the right to officiate in state institutions.[35] They never merged with the other elements in the city and consistently retained the characteristics originally segregating them from other Bostonians. Even while supporting the Union, their opposition to reform, their dislike of Lincoln, and their hatred of the Negroes, abolition, and the emancipation proclamation, shown in the draft riot of 1863, demonstrated that the basic divergence emanating from the nature of their adjustment to Boston society still existed.[36]

The mass of Irishmen continued to occupy the low places in society they had earlier held. Their wives and daughters performed most of the city's domestic service; and men and boys of Irish ancestry constituted the bulk of unskilled workers. The censuses of 1870 and 1880 still found them two-thirds of the laborers and the *Pilot* estimated that 60 per cent of the group in 1877 still occupied that rank.[37] The new immigrants from Ireland, like their predecessors of the 1850's, were bound down by their immobility. Once trapped in the round of unskilled toil, they could never accumulate the resources to escape. Their advisers, as earlier, preached the virtues of western settlement.[38] But such counsel was as futile as ever. "Some critic in next week's *Pilot* may tell me, why don't I 'go West'," complained a wharfman. "They say a man requires money to take him there and then requires something to start with." [39]

There was more mobility in the second generation, members of which found increased opportunities for apprenticeship and training. Many entered upon semiskilled occupations as longshoremen, teamsters, and draymen. Not a few also advanced to the skilled crafts in the building and furniture trades. But it remained difficult for the sons of Irishmen to move upward into clerical and professional occupations. In those spheres, they faced the barriers of prejudice and of lack of capital. They were also handicapped by their limited access to the facilities for education. At the end of the decade some 9,000 of the 43,000 children in Boston between the ages of 5 and 15 were not in school; and most of them were Irish.[40]

A few businessmen fared well. But the decline in real estate values and the failure of many savings banks after the fire and panic hit the Irish entrepreneurs hard. Most of them lacked the reserves of capital and credit that enabled their Yankee counterparts to survive; and they went to the wall. The fall of Patrick Donahoe in the aftermath of the depression was symbolic, for his countrymen had recognized his wealth through his philanthropies and public prominence.[41]

The dawning consciousness that their place in society was fixed led some Irishmen into union activity. The skilled workers had begun to form associations during the war; and by 1870 a Trades Assembly was active. But there was more marked stratification within the group now than earlier; and the strength of the fortunate few was no consolation to the great mass who remained helpless. When the laborers on a construction job in Newton struck, they were simply replaced by a gang of Italians.[42]

As earlier, the sense of exclusion from full participation in the society around them heightened Irish group consciousness. The newcomers by now had become thoroughly intrenched in their own organizations. The church, although still far from adequate to their needs, retained its central role in their lives.[43] It grew quietly under the moderate leadership of Archbishop Williams, who made no particular effort to develop the parochial school system and whose great achievements were the completion of the cathedral in 1875 and the establishment of a seminary under the Sulpicians, with whom he had himself studied in Paris.[44]

With the increase in the size of the group, internal divisions became more important than earlier. As some of the earlier associations acquired prestige and limited their membership selectively, new ones appeared at their side. Often, too, the fresh arrivals felt uncomfortable in existing organizations which seemed to them unfamiliar and almost alien. They therefore founded new ones, such as the county societies. But that did not diminish the sense of identity of the Irish group as a whole.

The Fenian movement was a distraction for a time. The wild national dream of Irish freedom had a special meaning for the immigrants, connected with their own desire for place in American society. "I am all the more American because of this old love — all Irishmen are," wrote John B. O'Reilly.[45] No more than earlier was nationalism itself divisive. The movement to liberate Ireland was regarded with favor even by old-stock Bostonians, particularly since relations with England remained strained after the Civil War.[46]

The failure of the effort to invade Canada from St. Albans in 1866 took the heart out of the Fenian movement. The organization collapsed soon thereafter and the Boston Irishmen turned with some relief from methods which involved the use of force to more peaceful agitation in support of Parnell's Land League. In one guise or another such activities were to remain important; they were a sign of the unity of the group and of the adjustment of its members to the life of the New World.[47]

The concern with status created by the presence of the Irish immigrants and their offspring affected every group in the city. No man now could think of his place in society simply in terms of occupation or income level. It was necessary also ever to consider ethnic affiliation.

Most of the non-Irish foreign-born groups tried with some success to adapt themselves to the ideals and patterns of action of the society around them.[48] They faced relatively little difficulty in doing so. The old Boston community offered them a ready model for emulation. Yet, at the same time, such people as the Germans and the Jews understood that their own separateness was the product of the recency of their arrival and compensated for it through creation of their own social institutions.[49]

But two segments of the city's population occupied a difficult and anomalous situation. They could not identify themselves completely with the old Boston community; nor yet could they afford to establish an identity completely separate from it.

The large group of unattached individuals and families that had drifted in from rural New England faced this problem with particular urgency. Such men indeed as Isaac Rich the fish dealer, Jacob Sleeper the clothing maker, Lee Claflin the tanner, and H. O. Houghton the printer, earned fortunes as wholesalers or manufacturers. But their wealth did not command the esteem attached to that inherited from overseas trade.[50] In any case, most of these people filled more modest roles as shopkeepers, salesmen, clerks, and skilled artisans; and they were ever haunted by the fear of the loss of status that might send them plunging headlong into the ranks of the proletariat. Therefore they were concerned with education to advance their children, with decent behavior to show their quality, and, above all, with maintaining their distance from the Irish below them. The effort to keep the gulf between themselves and the Irish as wide as possible called for continual emphasis upon their Protestantism and their Yankee heritage.[51]

Paradoxically, the Yankees often found themselves associated with the British-Americans. The latter were recent immigrants and poor; but they too wished to avoid identification with the Irish with whom they competed for places as servants, tailors and laborers. That rivalry, enflamed by differences in religion and in attitudes toward England, steadily generated tension and occasionally, as in 1871, led to riots.[52]

Some of the British-Americans clung to their Presbyterian affiliations after their immigration and they occasionally formed their own societies and Orange lodges. But common language and common Protestantism drew them close to the Yankees.[53] Together the two groups helped to swell the ranks of the Baptist and Methodist churches, the evangelical and revivalistic character of which expressed their desire for self-improvement and spiritual as well as material regeneration.[54]

These people looked for leadership to the descendants of the old Boston families who were still economically and socially dominant in the city. Sometimes the Yankees and

British-Americans resented the aloofness and the religious indifference of the Brahmins. But mingled with the distrust was an element of admiration, as for an aristocracy. Above all, the recent arrivals depended upon the old families, association with which established their superiority over the Irish. Therefore, they followed along as loyal members of the Republican party and were partisans of the old traditions. But though their support was useful they did not find among the Brahmins the leadership they sought.[55]

The Brahmins, and especially the generation that matured after 1860, had recoiled in despair from what their nation and their city had become. Surrendering or softening the ideals of their parents, they did not hope to exercise effective leadership.[56] Indeed, disillusioned by the failure of Civil War idealism, which seemed only to lead to the corruption of Reconstruction and of the Grant administration, they now began to question the validity of democracy. Depressed by the ugliness of industrialization and by the vulgarity of its new wealth, the proper Bostonians wished to think of themselves as an aristocratic elite rooted in the country, after the English model. They moved out to the rural suburbs of Brookline and Milton and resisted proposals to annex those towns to Boston. They sent their children to private schools and found self-contained satisfaction in their gentlemen's clubs.[57]

In the reaction, Brahmin Society became more highly organized and more difficult to penetrate than ever before. A few outsiders managed slowly to find acceptance. But, generally, those who took pride in their descent from old families were more concerned with defining their own exclusive position than with identifying with the mass of Yankees who seemed bogged down in mercantile materialism and evangelical superstition. In the Brahmin's strategy for attaining social esteem, the Yankee Silas Lapham was almost as much an outsider as the most recent Denis or Bridget from Ireland.[58]

Since midcentury a significant number of them had become adherents of the Episcopal Church. That communion grew in size through English immigration. But it acquired social strength from a much smaller group of Bostonians who deserted the congregationalism of their ancestors not so much out of doctrinal differences as out of the desire for an affiliation that gave greater emphasis to authority, order, ritual, and to ties with England.[59]

The lack of adequate leadership that left the Yankees adrift also troubled the Irish, who felt altogether alien to the Brahmins and yet could not readily find within their own group men of sufficient distinction to sustain "the duty of guardianship" and to elicit their support. "No people," complained the *Pilot,* have been "more neglectful of its poor than the rich and educated Irish of America. What schools and colleges have they endowed? What efforts for the establishment of industrial schools have been made to take their poor countrymen from the overcrowded unskilled labor class and distribute them among the different remunerative industries. What reading rooms have they established to keep men from liquor stores and for their mental improvement? None whatever. They shun their countrymen except at election time." [60]

Such complaints expressed the discontent of the Irish with

their leadership, but they did not take account of the significant reasons for its slow development. The communal life of other American groups was largely dominated by the businessmen who supplied the funds for their voluntary activities. The inability of all but a few Irishmen in Boston to rise above the laborers' level deprived them of this source of support and guidance; and no other element in the population took their place. The Catholic clergy were busy with immense parochial tasks and, in any case, since Know-Nothing days had been on the defensive and reluctant to intervene in secular affairs. The Irish immigrants could therefore look for leadership only to occasional individuals who attained political or intellectual prominence in the nationalist movement.[61]

The career of Patrick Collins illustrated the limitations of political leadership in this period. As an upholsterer he had become active in his craft union and in the Trades Assembly. As a gregarious young man he had also been a member of such Irish philanthropic and social organizations as the Columbian Association, the Catholic Union, and the Charitable Irish Society; and in addition he had acquired a local following as a Fenian.

These activities prepared him for politics. Naturally he was a Democrat and became involved in his neighborhood party organization. In 1867 he was chosen secretary of the Ward 7 Democratic Club, and later he served on the city and state committees. In 1867, also, and again a year later, he was elected to the legislature. In 1869, he became state senator for the Sixth District, the first Irishman to penetrate into the upper house.

This measure of success revealed that the possibility of still wider achievements lay not in the quest for other offices, but in the quest for fortune. Collins had already been attracted to law as a career and now entered upon its active practice. In 1871 he attended the Harvard Law School and was admitted to the Massachusetts bar. For the next decade, he concentrated mostly on his own affairs. While his following among the Irish retained its importance to him, he had thereafter also always to consider his standing in the general community.[62]

The problems of the intellectual as a communal leader emerged frequently in the career of young John Boyle O'Reilly, who assumed the editorship of the *Pilot* in 1876, at the age of thirty. O'Reilly had earlier been a fiery Fenian nationalist and still retained a violent dislike for England and a fierce pride in his race and his church. Thus far he was representative of his group. He also vigorously opposed attacks upon Negroes, Jews, and immigrants in general. And like other Irishmen he saw a threat in the Chinese and called for their exclusion.[63]

However, O'Reilly was also attracted by the culture of the Brahmin society around him, in some circles of which he came to be accepted. Before long the necessity of taking account of what his Yankee friends might think softened many of his attitudes.[64] He sometimes wrote as if he were in favor of socialism as an abstract ideal. But more generally he expressed ideas that came close to the point of view of the world of Beacon Hill and Cambridge with which he had contact. Like the liberals of that world whom he admired, he read J. S. Mill with approval and espoused a weak government.[65] Originally a believer in free trade, he soon came around to a moderate protectionist position.[66]

These attachments drew him away from his Irish following. Although the editor of the *Pilot* knew that 80 per cent of its readers were "honest horny-fisted sons of toil" and although he realized that laborers were sometimes obliged to strike or "go to the wall," his advice was to "Give up your trade unions to coerce Capital. You can't do it; every strike has proved it in the long run and the wild attempt earns for you the distrust of the lawful." [67] O'Reilly was suspicious of unions and of strikes, especially when they led to violence, as among the Molly Maguires of Pennsylvania or the followers of Denis Kearney in California.[68] On the whole he felt cooperation, colonization, compulsory arbitration, and political agitation were more useful modes of action.[69] These positions reflected a general timidity when it came to American affairs. He was vigorous enough in sustaining the rights of the Irish against England; but he was fearful of the consequences when one of his countrymen, W. R. Grace, ventured to run for mayor in New York City.[70]

Among the leaders, both Brahmin and Irish, the edge of bitterness was gone. They were willing to accept the fact that the two communities would stand at arm's length of one another. They had learned to tolerate each other and to live together. In politics they recognized a stalemate within which divisive issues were evaded or suppressed. Prohibition thus gave way to local licensing; and both the ten-hour law and the greenback movements were defeated. Although most of the Irish were Democrats, that party also had prominent old-stock adherents like Abbott, Gaston, Adams, Prince, and

Woodbury; and the Republicans still had hopes of winning the immigrant voters over.[71]

Above all there was a resolute effort to pretend that the genuine divisions in the city's life did not exist. Thus, in 1876, Collins, explaining why he supported Charles Francis Adams for the governorship, declared, "I . . . denounce any man or any body of men who seek to perpetuate divisions of races or religions in our midst. . . . I love the land of my birth but in American politics I know neither race, color nor creed. Let me say now that there are no Irish voters among us. There are Irish-born citizens like myself and there will be many more of us, but the moment the seal of the court was impressed upon our papers we ceased to be foreigners and became Americans. Americans we are and Americans we will remain." [72]

For motives similar to those which moved Collins, Henry Cabot Lodge, representative of a new generation of native Bostonians, would one day rise in the Senate and declaim: "The Irish spoke the same language as the people of the United States; they had the same traditions of government, and they had for centuries associated and intermarried with the people of Great Britain. . . . They presented no difficulties of assimilation." [73]

That Collins and Lodge were both inaccurate was less significant than that, though they knew it, they nevertheless felt the necessity of speaking as they did. Their generation had grown up in a city which had already outlived its vigorous commercial youth and the leisurely life attending it. These new Bostonians had not experienced the terrific shock produced by an unexpected influx of swarms of impoverished peasants. They had not witnessed the transformation of a neat, well-managed city into a slum- and disease-ridden metropolis. Even the bitterness of the desperate, violent, Know-Nothing assault upon alien ideas and attitudes was outside their ken. Instead, their most formative years witnessed a great social conflict that tried the loyalty of the Irish and found them not wanting. For them, mutual interests overshadowed the old differences and furnished a basis for cooperation, if not for social equality.

But in this regard the leadership could not altogether count on its following. The Yankees and British-Americans remained fearful and insecure. They were not so willing as the Brahmin was to recognize a place in America for Catholicism; nor did they enjoy the defense of aloofness and distance that protected the Brahmin from contact with the immigrants.[74] These anxious people worried often lest their leaders betray them by relaxing standards; and they therefore resented any measure that treated the Irish as their equals. When Mayor Prince, in 1877, appointed a few Irishmen to the police force, he lost his opportunity for reëlection. After 1880, the Yankees would be swept away by a fresh wave of hatred against the foreigners who seemed to threaten their place in society.

Nor were the Boston Irish soothed by the calm assurance that their interests were identical with those of the rest of the community. In 1876 they did not vote for Adams as Collins asked them to.[75] On the ward level and among the aldermen, Jim O'Donovan and Hugh O'Brien — who would soon be Boston's first Irish mayor — were acting as if there was an Irish vote; and General B. F. Butler was preparing to capitalize on it. And over in the West End, young Martin Lomasney had quit his job as a metal spinner. Convinced that politics was the better way to rise, he was developing a type of organization that would be increasingly important in the city's future.[76]

Depressed to the status of helpless proletarians by the conditions of their flight from Ireland and by the city's constricted economic structure, driven into debilitating slums by their position as unskilled laborers, and isolated intellectually by their cultural background and physical seclusion, the Irish saw insuperable barriers between themselves and their neighbors. As social circumstances dictated, these differences lent themselves to either coöperation or conflict; but so long as they persisted, they stimulated and perpetuated group consciousness in both immigrants and natives and left the community divided within itself.

Boston thus moved uneasily into the last two decades of the century. It was divided within itself. But it had learned it could survive through tolerance. Despite all the difficulties of the four decades since 1840, there was still no demand for an end to immigration, although concern was often expressed about the added burdens of pauperism and criminality and the decline of the birth rate of the Yankees due to their "higher civilization or to a more artificial mode of life and the unwholesome state of society." [77]

But it was still uncertain that the adjustment would endure. A great new tide of immigration was soon to open a new period of rapid expansion. Then both the Yankees and the Irish would recoil from the tolerance of the post-Civil War years. The underlying differences between the two groups would come openly to the surface and the community would enter once more upon a long period of bitterness.

Yet in the longer perspective, it is clear, the possibility of coexistence never vanished entirely. There were always some men in every group who recognized the community of interests which transcended the particular divisions in Boston's population. If they were not much heeded in the trying years after 1880, they nevertheless carried forward into the new century the constructive ideals, the roots of which extended back to an older Boston that had not yet been disrupted by immigration.

APPENDIX

Appendix

NOTE ON THE STATISTICS OF IMMIGRATION INTO BOSTON

Both the federal and state governments kept some statements of immigration into Boston. The state records were kept by the successive Commissioners of Alien Immigration. This material, drawn up at first merely according to port of origin, and only for a short time by nativity, is in general less reliable and less complete than the federal records.[1] The latter, drawn up by the Customs House and transmitted annually to Congress by the Secretary of State, have been completely tabulated for each year 1820–65 in Table VII, Dissertation Copy, 421, and are summarized by five year periods in Table V, *supra*.

There were obstacles to the use of even these data. The annual summaries in each statement referred to different yearly periods, at various times including the calendar year, the fiscal year, and the year ending August 31. This difficulty was avoided by referring back to the original quarterly returns and retabulating them all on the basis of the calendar year. A more serious difficulty was the lack of consistency in the listings. Thus "Great Britain" sometimes included England, Ireland, Scotland, and Wales, sometimes excluded Ireland, and sometimes excluded both Ireland and Scotland, a situation which rendered accurate enumeration of the Irish impossi-

[1] Cf. Tables VII a, VII b, Dissertation Copy, 426 ff.

233

ble. Several attempts were made to find a compensating statistical device, but since the difference originated in the caprice of the individual customs official it was deemed best to accept the data as it was given. The listings of minor localities, wherever possible, were combined into larger geographical units, however.[2] A tabulation by the "Joint Special Committee appointed to investigate the Public Charitable Institutions of . . . Massachusetts . . . 1858" offered different figures for 1831, 1833, 1837 and 1841,[3] but those offered in Table V were more accurate.

All these statistics refer of course only to immigration by sea and must be raised from 30 per cent to 50 per cent to account for those who entered by land.

NOTE TO TABLE XIII

Table XIII was derived from the manuscript schedules of the federal marshals who collected the material for the Census of 1850. These were deposited, when used in this study, in the Division of Old Records of the Bureau of the Census, Commerce Building, Washington, D. C. They have since been transferred to the National Archives.

The Census of 1850 was the first to inquire into both the nativity and occupation of the population. Lacking precedent, its directors faced the complex problems it involved without a consistent formula and without a definite conception of objectives. DeBow and his collaborators apparently made no attempt to coördinate or reclassify the results on the

---

[2] For the details, cf. Dissertation Copy, 424.

[3] Cf. "Report . . . ," *Massachusetts Senate Documents, 1859*, no. 2, pp. 142, 143.

basis of any consistent principle; and the enumerators exercised a wide degree of latitude in recording occupations which resulted in an amazing variety of listings and occupational descriptions. The absence of standardized method and procedure and the failure to define a clear set of occupational categories enormously complicated the task of tabulating the results.

The tabulations in Tables XIII–XVI were made under a procedure designed to eliminate errors arising from the lack of uniformity in occupational description. The enumerators noted 1,466 different occupations. Each of these was tabulated separately by nativity and by ward. From this primary tabulation, 474 listings were eliminated as representing nominal differences only. The remaining 992 distinct occupations were again tabulated and then combined in Table XIII into sixty-four categories, drawn up after a careful historical consideration of the precise nature of the work involved in each occupation.

The basis of this classification was necessarily original. Modern classifications are not applicable to the pre-Civil War period and no previous attempt has been made to classify such occupations scientifically. The compilers of the census themselves used extremely arbitrary groupings that frequently destroyed the value of the figures. DeBow was not at all discriminating. He lumped together in one category "commerce, trade, manufactures, mechanic arts, and mining," while his others were as general as "agriculture," "labor not agriculture," "army," "sea and river navigation," "law, medicine and divinity," "other pursuits requiring education," "government civil service," "domestic servants," and "others."[1] These groupings were extremely unsatisfactory. In Boston almost every employed person could be included in the first classification. Emphasizing the type of product rather than the nature of the work performed, such classifications lacked a valid base.

The same fault marred Shattuck's compilation of the local census of 1845. Having specific reference to Boston, this was in some degree more satisfactory than the federal efforts. Shattuck divided the working population into fourteen groups, those contributing to building, clothing, education, food, furniture, health, justice, literature and arts, locomotion, machinery, navigation, religion, unclassified mechanics, and others (which included 40 per cent of the total).[2] Again the nature of the product rather than the type of work was stressed.

The classifications of the State Census of 1855 and of the Federal Census of 1840 and 1860 followed essentially the same principles and therefore had little value. As a result it was necessary to evolve a complete classification of all 992 occupations, based on the actual character of the work involved in each. Careful precautions were taken to ensure uniformity and to make the tables valid for absolute and comparative purposes.

The enumerators cited more than seventy different localities as the place of birth, but these were combined in the original table into twenty simple nativity groups. In Table XIII "Other United States" includes New England (other than

[1] J. D. B. DeBow, *Seventh Census of the United States 1850* . . . (Washington, 1853), lxxx.

[2] Lemuel Shattuck, *Report to the Committee of the City Council* . . . *Census of Boston* . . . *1845* . . . (Boston, 1846), 83.

Massachusetts); "Other British" includes British North America, England, Scotland, and Wales; and "Others" includes Latin America, Switzerland, the Netherlands, France, Italy, Spain and Portugal, Scandinavia, Russia and Poland, and Miscellaneous, all of which are listed separately in Dissertation Copy, 436 ff. "Negroes" includes all colored people regardless of nativity.

TABLE I
BOSTON INDUSTRIES, 1845 *

Average No. of Employees per Establishment	No. of Industries	No. of Establishments	No. of Employees	Value of Products
1–10	98	837	4,764	$ 7,994,356
11–25	21	79	1,453	1,768,197
26–50	10	35	1,228	1,267,475
51 and over	4	11	807	1,741,400
Unclassifiable	11	?	1,866	1,085,954
TOTAL	144	962	10,118	$13,857,382

* This table is derived from statistics in John G. Palfrey, *Statistics of the Condition of Certain Branches of Industry in Massachusetts for the Year Ending April 1, 1845* . . . (Boston, 1846), 1–8, 43–48, 243, 248, 258–261. These statistics give the total number of employees and the total number of establishments in each industry. From this the average number of employees per establishment in each industry was computed. The column headed "No. of Industries" gives the number of industries in Boston, Charlestown, Brighton, Chelsea, Cambridge, Brookline, and Roxbury, in which the average number of employees per establishment falls within the range indicated in the first column. The third and fourth columns give, respectively, the total number of establishments and the total number of employees comprised in these industries, while the last column gives the value of the products they produced. Unclassifiable industries are those in which the number of establishments is not given because, like the shoe industry, they operated by homework.

TABLE II

POPULATION OF BOSTON AND ITS ENVIRONS *

	1790	1810	1820	1830	1840	1845	1850	1855	1860	1865
Boston (proper)	18,038	32,896	43,298	61,392 §	85,475	99,036	113,721	126,296	133,563	141,083
Islands	282	519	...	...	277	292	325	530	1,000	1,300
East Boston	...	18	...	...	1,455	5,018	9,526	15,433	18,356	20,572
South Boston † ...	...	354	...	...	6,176	10,020	13,309	16,912	24,921	29,363
Roxbury	2,226	3,669	4,135	5,259	9,089	...	18,364	18,469	25,137	28,426
Dorchester	1,722	2,930	3,684	4,074	4,875	...	7,969	8,340	9,769	10,717
Brighton ‡	...	608	702	972	1,425	...	2,356	2,895	3,375	3,854
Charlestown	1,583	4,954	6,591	8,783	11,484	...	17,216	21,700	25,065	26,399
Brookline	484	784	900	1,041	1,365	...	2,516	3,737	5,164	5,262
Chelsea	472	594	642	770	2,390	...	6,701	10,151	13,395	14,403
Cambridge	2,115	2,323	3,295	6,073	8,409	...	15,215	20,473	26,060	29,112
West Cambridge ‡ ..	...	...	1,064	1,230	1,363	...	2,202	2,670	2,681	2,760

* Derived from Carroll D. Wright, *Analysis of the Population of the City of Boston as Shown in the ... Census of May, 1885* (Boston, 1885), 8 ff.; *Massachusetts House Documents, 1837*, no. 19, pp. 9, 10; United States. Census, *Aggregate Amount of ... Persons ... According to the Census of 1820* (s.l. n.d. [Washington, 1820]), 7; *Massachusetts House Documents, 1842*, no. 48, pp. 1, 3, 5; *Massachusetts House Documents, 1831*, no. 10, pp. 1–6; *Report and Tabular Statement of the Censors ... May 1, 1850, Boston City Documents*, no. 42, 59; Joseph C. G. Kennedy, *Population of the United States in 1860; Compiled from the Original Returns of ... the Eighth Census ...* (Washington, 1864), xxxi; Francis DeWitt, *Abstract of the Census of ... Massachusetts ... 1855 ...* (Boston, 1857), 32–50.

† Part of Dorchester until 1804.
‡ Part of Cambridge until 1807.
§ This figure includes Boston proper, and the Islands.

TABLE III
EXPENDITURES FOR POOR RELIEF, CITY OF BOSTON, 1815–1866 *

Year Ending April	Board of Overseers	House of Industry	House of Reformation for Juvenile Offenders †	Total
1815–22 §	$28,400	...	...	$ 28,400
1823	25,859	$ 8,475	...	34,334
1825	20,709	8,398	...	29,107
1826	9,500	12,000	...	21,500
1827	12,256	23,500	$ 4,793	40,849
1828	11,386	16,190	5,500	33,076
1829	12,848	17,996	5,966	36,810
1830	12,803	17,977	6,342	37,122
1831	13,685	19,476	6,223	39,384
1832	14,000	19,999	6,498	40,497
1833	14,542	23,048	6,203	43,793
1834	8,929	18,527	6,645	34,101
1835	12,606	17,521	7,444	37,571
1836	12,916	19,495	6,999	39,410
1837	9,708	23,084	10,299	43,091
1838	11,746	21,509	8,668	41,923
1839	10,257	22,321	10,883	43,461
1840	11,831	21,995	9,490	43,316
1841	12,000	23,483	8,993	44,476
1842	13,000	28,007	4,954	45,961
1843	15,000	31,547	...	46,547
1844	15,000	30,752	...	45,752
1845	15,000	29,151	...	43,151
1846	15,700	28,000	...	43,700
1847	16,500	35,748	...	52,248
1848	21,000	41,314	...	62,314
1849	24,500	55,477	...	79,977
1850	24,500	90,955	...	115,455
1851	30,200	89,334	...	119,534
1852	28,200	111,017	...	139,217
1853	27,700	84,338	...	111,038
1854	30,000	102,610	...	132,610
1855	40,000	77,279	...	117,279
1856	45,000	69,104	...	114,104
1857	49,300	69,462	...	118,762
1858	62,800	97,852	...	160,652
1859	58,000	84,624	...	142,624
1860	60,000	108,389	...	168,389
1861	69,400	76,917	...	146,317
1862	70,200	68,905	...	139,105
1863	90,140	57,869	...	148,009
1864	39,000 ‡	85,792	...	124,792
1865	41,000	91,304	...	132,304
1866	44,500	87,202	...	131,702

* Derived from Boston Committee of Finance, *Auditor's Reports, 1815–1867* (for page references, cf. Dissertation Copy, 419). The figures given refer to current expenditures only.
† After 1843, the House of Industry bore the expense of the House of Reformation for Juvenile Offenders and the Deer Island Almshouse.
‡ The drop after 1863 was due to the shift of persons without settlement to state institutions.
§ Annual average.

TABLE IV
Prison Commitments §

Year	Massachusetts State Prison		Boston Jail		Boston House of Correction †	Boston Juvenile Reformatory
	Total *	From Boston	Debtors	Criminals ‡		
1821	....	..	1,652		...	...
1822	....	..	1,257		...	...
1823	....	..	1,166		250	...
1824	....	49	1,257		572	...
1825	....	37	878		589	...
1826	....	35	...		567	...
1827	....	43	...		504	...
1828	 106	31	...		551	...
1829	 79	37	...		290	...
1830	 115	50	...		334	...
1831	 71	22	...		348	...
1832	 76	51	...		228	...
1833	 119	59	678	1,044	182	...
1834	....	..	...	...	562	...
1835	 116	..	...	...	530	...
1836	 97	28	322	739	570	113
1837	 99	..	543	1,263	887	118
1838	 114	..	526	1,606	1,327	279
1839	 105	..	555	1,245	1,280	236
1840	 103	35	...	...	...	...
1841	 131	32	439	1,341	648	...
1842	 85	29	...	...	...	...
1843	 97	28	...	...	...	...
1844	 105	44	...	...	...	...
1845	 96	40	480	1,676	680	...

* The total commitments between 1805 when the institution was founded and 1827, when the reports begin, numbered 2,070 or an average of ninety per year.
† This column refers to the year ending June 30; the others to the year ending December 31.
‡ These included witnesses and those held for examination before trial.
§ Derived from the annual "Reports of the Inspectors of the State Prison . . . , 1830–1846" in the *Massachusetts Senate Documents*, and from the "Abstract of the Returns of Persons Confined in Jails and Houses of Correction . . . ," 1826 ff. (for page references, cf. Dissertation Copy, 420). Cf. also N. H. Julius, *Nordamerikas sittliche Zustände nach eigenen Anschauungen in den Jahren 1834, 1835, und 1836* (Leipzig, 1839), II, Tables 10, 11, 12.
Blanks denote incomplete or unavailable data.

TABLE V

Passengers Entering Boston by Sea, 1821–1865

Place of Origin †	Five-Year Period ‖ Beginning								
	1821	1826	1831	1836	1841	1846	1851	1856	1861
Great Britain and Ireland	.....	.....	.....	6,996	.....	.....	.....	.....	.....
Great Britain	164	3,030	581	58	7,010	3,603	990	19	1,324
England	286	506	1,712	172	4,545	12,513	10,264	9,654	3,931
Wales	16	.....	7	6	24	316	354	748	23
Scotland	90	55	102	24	389	2,249	2,469	1,870	682
Ireland	827	549	2,361	443	10,157	65,556	63,831	22,681	6,973
British North America	525	648	3,943	3,537	5,654	16,816	21,233	18,240	14,542
Germany	58	311	253	449	301	1,385	2,653	1,198	1,287
France	66	167	57	212	239	381	605	529	362
Italy	14	23	40	42	59	137	186	247	89
Spain and Portugal ‡	48	41	48	80	147	176	540	943	1,017
Holland	27	27	80	182	30	484	399	298	292
Switzerland	3	163	137	7	10	45	25	200	63
Scandinavia	9	38	62	244	110	723	4,120	1,317	708
Latin America §	80	83	147	264	172	429	772	300	226
Russia	4	12	23	4	5	66	40	28	28
Asia Minor	7	18	11	21	20	32	58	45	19
Asia and Pacific Islands	1	1	8	9	8	34	17	85	69
Africa	6	1	16	3	13	15	21	112	92
Unknown and Miscellaneous	**2**	54	31	228	671	18	1,018	1,013	760
United States	*1,564*	*1,727*	*2,149*	*3,921*	*7,177*	*7,686*	*7,910*	*10,396*	*10,234*
TOTAL	3,797	7,454	11,768	16,902	36,741	112,664	117,505	69,923	42,721

† Cf. Dissertation Copy, 424.
‡ Includes Azores.
§ Includes Mexico, West Indies, Central America, South America.
‖ 1832 and 1834 are for nine months only; 1842 includes figures for England and Ireland only.

TABLE VI
NATIVITY OF BOSTONIANS, 1850 *

Country of Birth	Number
United States	88,948
England and Wales	3,213
Ireland	35,287
Scotland	897
Germany	1,777
Prussia	39
France	225
Spain	67
Italy	134
Others	5,038
Unknown	1,256
TOTAL	136,881

* Ephraim M. Wright, *Twelfth Registration Report, 1853* (*Documents Prepared and Submitted to the General Court by the Secretary of State,* Boston, 1854), 110. City of Boston only.

TABLE VII

NATIVITY OF BOSTONIANS, 1855 *

Town	United States	British America	Ireland	England, Scotland and Wales	Germany †	France	Italy	Other Foreign	Unknown	Total
Brighton	2,097	21	697	47	22	2	..	9	..	2,895
Cambridge	13,903	832	4,574	733	251	80	8	66	26	20,473
Charlestown	16,530	557	3,833	467	176	23	7	105	2	21,700
Somerville	4,171	160	1,305	128	27	8	2	5	..	5,806
West Cambridge	1,996	56	511	87	20	..	..	..	..	2,670
Brookline	2,411	68	1,142	66	31	5	1	7	6	3,737
Dorchester	6,198	178	1,542	252	141	12	..	17	..	8,340
Roxbury	11,282	298	5,002	705	1,063	59	7	53	..	18,469
West Roxbury	3,189	103	1,275	157	44	9	3	32	..	4,812
Boston	98,018	5,850	46,237	5,241	3,376	372	245	1,032	119	160,400
Chelsea	7,340	536	1,740	429	42	11	3	49	..	10,150
North Chelsea	595	26	155	17	..	..	..	..	..	793
Winthrop	301	11	87	8	..	..	..	..	..	407
TOTAL	168,031	8,696	68,100	8,337	5,193	581	276	1,375	153	260,742

* [Nathaniel B. Shurtleff], *Abstract of the Census of the Commonwealth of Massachusetts Taken with Reference to Facts Existing on the First Day of June, 1855, with Remarks on the Same Prepared under the Direction of Francis DeWitt, Secretary of the Commonwealth* (Boston, 1857), 98–132.
† Includes Holland.

TABLE VIII

Nativity of Residents of the Boston Area, 1860 *

Country of Birth	Middlesex County	Norfolk County	Suffolk County
United States	166,126	83,693	125,439
England	4,273	2,494	4,472
Ireland	38,098	19,138	48,095
Scotland	1,272	607	1,440
Wales	28	34	61
Germany	629	1,159	1,290
France	187	133	397
Spain	39	9	59
Portugal	19	62	38
Belgium	5	6	19
Holland	67	17	177
Turkey	4	1	6
Italy	29	26	258
Austria	24	21	44
Switzerland	28	55	125
Russia	4	4	38
Norway	28	11	68
Denmark	26	18	97
Sweden	98	41	259
Prussia	150	103	744
Sardinia	1	1	64
Greece	3	3	10
China	9	5	4
Asia	19	13	29
Africa	..	2	20
British America	4,784	1,563	7,503
Mexico	6	1	2
South America	24	18	44
West Indies	59	27	149
Sandwich Islands	15	9	10
Atlantic Islands	39	5	260
Bavaria	33	246	250
Baden	73	331	663
Europe †	133	6	165
Hesse	14	32	107
Nassau	..	4	18
Poland	..	2	78
Württemberg	16	38	142
Australia	1	..	10
Pacific Islands	1	7	8
Other Countries	..	5	38
Total Foreign	50,238	26,257	67,261
Total Population	216,354	109,950	192,700

* George Wingate Chase, *Abstract of the Census of Massachusetts 1860 from the Eighth U.S. Census, with Remarks on the Same Prepared under the Direction of Oliver Warner, Secretary of the Commonwealth* (Boston, 1863), Table IV.
† Not specified.

TABLE IX

NATIVITY OF BOSTONIANS, 1865 *

Town	United States	British America	Ireland	England, Scotland and Wales	Germany †	France	Italy	Other Foreign	Unknown	Total
Brighton	2,840	61	820	86	43	..	..	4	..	3,854
Cambridge	21,063	972	5,588	987	347	73	3	79	..	29,112
Charlestown	20,423	619	4,443	522	242	13	4	133	..	26,399
Somerville	7,050	221	1,729	258	41	8	1	32	13	9,353
West Cambridge ...	2,039	53	551	98	13	..	..	3	1	2,758
Brookline	3,542	106	1,457	85	33	6	3	5	25	5,262
Dorchester	8,393	233	1,647	262	125	11	13	33	..	10,717
Roxbury	18,762	612	6,294	1,056	1,511	79	5	107	..	28,426
West Roxbury	5,029	132	1,426	154	133	10	1	27	..	6,912
Boston	126,432	8,060	46,225	5,480	3,790	367	366	1,533	65	192,318
Chelsea	11,551	531	1,655	512	71	6	5	59	13	14,403
North Chelsea	720	26	101	11	..	..	..	..	..	858
Winthrop	465	25	129	10	4	..	..	..	..	633
TOTAL	228,309	11,651	72,065	9,521	6,353	573	401	2,015	117	331,005

* Oliver Warner, *Abstract of the Census of Massachusetts, 1865: with Remarks on the Same and Supplementary Tables . . .* (Boston, 1867), 70–77.
† Includes Holland.

TABLE X

Nativity of Members of the Boston Repeal Association *

County	Boston	Roxbury	East Cambridge	South Boston	Charlestown
Antrim	5	4	..	..	6
Armagh	4	..	1	2	3
Carlow	17	..	..	3	..
Cavan	28	8	3	4	3
Clare	10	1	1	5	..
Cork	121	11	3	19	28
Donegal	35	4	2	5	7
Down	5	1	..	..	4
Dublin	10	..	2	2	1
Fermanagh	52	1	2	2	10
Galway	21	5	..	6	..
Kerry	23	3	..	5	3
Kildare	21	2	3	5	1
Kilkenny	40	2	7	12	7
Kings	1	..	..	..	..
Leitrim	13	1	..	..	..
Limerick	16	..	..	..	1
Londonderry	26	1	4	..	..
Longford	25	1	15	18	12
Louth	2	1	..	..	2
Mayo	..	..	..	..	1
Meath	20	9	3	3	..
Monaghan	25	1	4	2	1
Queens	12	1	1	3	2
Roscommon	10	47	1	1	2
Sligo	14	6	1	..	1
Tipperary	15	6	5	11	3
Tyrone	39	8	34	5	22
Waterford	15	3	6	2	6
Westmeath	6	1	3	4	..
Wexford	33	..	..	21	4
Wicklow	7	..	..	1	..
Unknown	30	9	25	11	..
TOTAL	701	137	126	152	130

* Derived from *Boston Pilot*, 1841–1843. For citations, cf. Dissertation Copy, 435.

TABLE XI

ADVERTISEMENTS BY BOSTONIANS FOR INFORMATION IN THE *Boston Pilot*, 1841–1864 *

County †	\multicolumn{12}{c}{Two-Year Period Beginning}
	1841	1843	1845	1847	1849	1851 ‡	1853	1855	1857	1859	1861	1863
Antrim	..	1	1	1	..	..	..	2	..	..	..	1
Armagh ...	1	1	1	1	2	1	5	1	4	2	1	..
Carlow	1	2	..	2	..	3	3	2	2	..	1	..
Cavan	2	1	5	11	14	7	4	11	3	7	9	3
Clare	1	..	4	8	13	16	11	10	9	1	6	8
Cork	19	11	58	94	112	106	117	97	67	65	29	56
Donegal ...	2	3	7	4	10	6	6	7	2	4	2	5
Down	..	..	1	1	5	2	..	4	3	3	..	..
Dublin	1	..	..	4	6	7	6	4	1	7	..	2
Fermanagh .	3	..	1	2	5	2	1	6	2	1	2	2
Galway ...	2	2	10	33	40	26	33	26	19	21	12	16
Kerry	2	2	9	16	42	37	41	38	23	29	11	21
Kildare	1	..	3	4	6	3	7	3	1	..	1	..
Kilkenny ..	1	3	5	8	17	14	12	12	3	7	5	4
Kings	1	..	3	1	1	3	..	2	1	1	..	..
Leitrim	1	1	4	8	14	8	13	6	4	4	2	6
Limerick ..	3	3	5	5	24	14	19	13	13	7	4	13
Londonderry	..	..	..	3	4	4	2	3	3	2	2	..
Longford ..	5	1	1	4	7	4	4	1	4	5	6	3
Louth	..	1	1	1	3	6	4	3	..	2	2	3
Mayo	2	1	7	20	16	17	9	11	11	5	1	6
Meath	1	..	8	8	13	6	8	5	6	2	1	..
Monaghan .	..	..	6	3	4	6	6	3	2	2	4	6
Queens	2	..	2	5	4	2	5	3	2	2	3	4
Roscommon	7	8	17	14	19	16	15	18	11	16	3	6
Sligo	2	..	8	12	9	7	7	6	2	2	5	3
Tipperary .	1	3	4	7	20	26	17	7	10	10	10	11
Tyrone	2	2	3	11	2	4	7	4	4	4	6	3
Waterford .	5	4	5	8	18	14	17	11	8	4	6	10
Westmeath .	1	..	..	3	2	1	3	8	1	..	1	3
Wexford ...	..	1	..	2	4	2	6	3	2	4	..	2
Wicklow ..	..	1	1	1	1	..	..	3	1	..	1	..
Unknown ..	..	..	..	..	..	3	7	..	..	..	..	..

* This table was derived from the requests for information of the whereabouts of friends and relatives, inserted regularly in the *Boston Pilot* by immigrants newly arrived in Boston. The *Pilot* was the leading vehicle for such advertisements in the United States (cf. Alexander Marjoribanks, *Travels* . . . [London, 1853], 126). This is the only criterion that has been found to measure the distribution of immigration into Boston from the various sections of Ireland. It is weighted, if at all, in favor of the "old" emigrants from north Ireland, more likely to have friends in America. Nevertheless, it shows a clear preponderance of immigrants from the southern and western counties. Annual figures are given, Dissertation Copy, 430.

† Doubtful locations were decided from John Bartholomew, *Philip's Handy Atlas of the Counties of Ireland* . . . (London, 1881).

‡ Twenty-one months only.

TABLE XII

Negro Population of the Boston Area, 1754–1865 *

Town	1754	1765	1790	1800	1810	1820	1830	1840	1850	1855	1860	1865
Brighton	..	..	..	..	2	1	2	1	5	12	4	..
Cambridge	56	90	60	25	38	53	79	77	141	292	354	371
Charlestown	..	136	25	38	61	38	96	129	206	133	202	109
Somerville	..	..	..	..	..	..	..	..	20	19	28	16
West Cambridge	..	..	..	..	5	3	2	2	2	4	2	6
Brookline	17	18	13	15	6	3	1	3	5	..	3	5
Dorchester	31	37	30	35	26	15	13	16	6	11	10	29
Roxbury	53	80	40	71	76	43	27	26	107	50	60	54
West Roxbury	..	..	..	..	..	..	..	..	..	14	24	47
Boston	989	848	766	1,174	1,468	1,690	1,875	2,427	1,999	2,160	2,284	2,348
Chelsea	35	43	21	20	16	36	8	11	37	70	136	151
North Chelsea	..	..	..	..	..	..	..	..	2	..	1	2
Winthrop	..	..	..	..	..	..	..	..	..	..	..	3
TOTAL	1,181	1,252	955	1,378	1,698	1,882	2,103	2,692	2,530	2,765	3,108	3,141

* Oliver Warner, *Abstract of the Census of Massachusetts, 1865: with Remarks on the Same, and Supplementary Tables* (Boston, 1867), 228–231.

TABLE XIII
DISTRIBUTION OF OCCUPATIONS BY NATIVITY, BOSTON, 1850 *

Occupational Category	Massachusetts	Other U.S.	Unknown	Negro	Ireland	Other British	Germany	Others	Total
Government employees	111	47	..	..	6	5	..	3	172
Police and watchmen	107	115	12	..	12	11	1	1	259
Clergymen	57	73	4	4	9	8	5	..	160
Teachers	108	45	2	..	4	9	13	16	197
Physicians	349	178	14	2	32	46	13	13	647
Actors, musicians	69	42	2	3	24	34	33	42	249
Other professions	271	124	16	..	25	30	4	4	474
Financiers	37	17	..	..	1	1	..	..	56
Merchants	668	227	36	..	18	37	5	14	1,005
Agents, salesmen	340	174	13	..	25	27	9	4	592
Clerks	2,170	1,071	108	3	132	151	19	22	3,676
Food dealers	441	361	7	1	184	53	9	5	1,061
Dry goods dealers	87	55	1	..	10	7	6	..	166
Pedlars, traders	462	354	27	25	211	40	41	23	1,183
Other retailers	604	321	24	11	117	46	17	6	1,146
Shop assistants	20	10	..	36	12	7	2	..	87
Manufacturers	164	88	5	..	48	52	11	10	378
Printers	317	199	11	1	81	80	5	1	695
Confectioners, bakers	124	81	5	17	98	59	55	10	449
Workers in heavy industry	203	156	2	..	247	123	79	9	819
Smiths	234	171	6	3	307	112	36	8	877
Builders, contractors	79	46	..	2	22	26	..	3	178
Carpenters	701	634	24	5	356	302	18	13	2,053
Masons	271	234	11	1	203	37	5	2	764
Painters	461	234	15	3	119	114	10	14	970
Plumbers	36	15	2	..	18	23	2	..	96
Sawyers, carvers	111	47	5	..	40	28	4	2	237
Roofers	14	5	..	..	39	12	..	..	70
Maritime industries	131	69	1	3	22	45	8	28	304
Chandlers, caulkers	110	14	2	..	6	6	..	2	140
Cabinet makers, upholsterers	131	84	3	..	56	62	18	15	369
Polishers, varnishers	44	21	2	..	7	17	3	1	95
Musical instrument makers	108	76	6	..	4	40	20	..	254
Coopers	111	44	..	..	79	32	16	7	289

Workers in precious metals	227	81	6	..	13	47	29	8
								411
Machinists, mechanics	406	297	2	..	68	120	22	15
								930
Undertakers	32	4	..	..	1	..	..	..
								37
Wharfingers	23	9	..	..	1	..	..	1
								34
Leather workers	67	47	7	..	105	46	11	3
								286
Shoemakers	145	71	1	4	206	80	49	14
								570
Hatters	107	47	4	..	38	16	8	2
								222
Tailors	166	127	9	9	1,045	119	41	31
								1,547
Miscellaneous apprentices	97	33	3	..	29	7	..	..
								169
Other artisans	401	238	11	5	172	130	80	12
								1,049
Miscellaneous sup'ts	12	24	1	..	3	4	..	..
								44
Express business	24	43	..	..	10	3	..	..
								80
Transportation, railroads	55	57	3	..	13	6	1	1
								136
Drivers and teamsters	67	124	9	..	37	31	2	1
								271
Truckmen and cabmen	244	616	12	4	169	46	2	1
								1,094
Stevedores	30	43	..	5	41	11	3	7
								140
Master mariners	82	31	3	1	5	13	7	3
								145
Boatmen	45	26	..	..	37	10	2	7
								127
Seamen	328	293	544	142	190	215	23	154
								1,889
Hotel keepers	52	56	..	5	10	15	11	15
								164
Restaurant keepers	112	118	5	5	18	10	4	7
								279
Stable keepers	9	17	..	..	4	1	..	..
								31
Stablers	30	53	2	..	70	9	..	..
								164
Waiters	34	68	2	21	222	8	3	3
								361
Barbers	59	40	1	48	6	6	3	23
								186
Domestic servants	227	369	26	48	2,292	237	31	19
								3,249
Laborers	538	466	19	115	7,007	264	107	36
								8,552
Farmers	12	15	..	..	21	4	..	..
								52
None	629	122	15	25	177	59	17	18
								1,062
Unknown	42	16	13	21	11	7	6	3
								119
TOTAL	13,553	8,983	1,064	575	14,595	3,206	929	662
								43,567

* Supra, 234.

TABLE XIV

Average Number of Persons per Occupation of Each Nativity Group in Boston, 1850 *

Nativity	Total in Boston	Total of Employed Persons	Number of Occupations	Average Number per Occupation
Massachusetts	68,687	13,553	660	20.53
New England	17,220	7,986	564	14.16
United States	3,037	997	203	4.91
Unknown	†	1,064	136	7.82
Negro	1,999	575	46	12.50
British North America	†	1,381	189	7.31
Latin America	†	60	23	2.61
England	3,213 ‡	1,369	255	5.37
Ireland	35,287	14,595	362	40.32
Scotland	897	433	117	3.70
Wales	‡	23	16	1.44
Germany	1,816 ‖	929	153	6.07
Switzerland	†	10	9	1.11
Netherlands	†	36	19	1.89
France	225	143	68	2.10
Italy	134	105	33	3.18
Spain & Portugal	67 §	67	26	2.58
Scandinavia	†	172	46	3.74
Russia and Poland	†	46	19	2.42
Miscellaneous	5,038 †	23	15	1.53
All nativities	136,881	43,567	993	43.87

* Derived from the manuscript schedules of the Seventh Census of the United States (B.C.), with the exception of the first column which is given in J. D. B. DeBow, *Statistical View of the United States* . . . (Washington, 1854), 395, 399.

† Included in miscellaneous. Miscellaneous in the first column includes Unknown, British North America, Latin America, Switzerland, the Netherlands, Scandinavia, Portugal, Russia and Poland as well as the other nativities elsewhere included in this category.

‡ In the first column Wales is included in England.

§ In the first column the figure is for Spain alone; Portugal is included in Miscellaneous in this column.

‖ Includes Prussia.

TABLE XV

LABORERS IN BOSTON, BY NATIVITY, 1850 *

Nativity	Total Working Population	Laborers	Percentage of Working Population
Ireland	14,595	7,007	48.01
Negro	575	115	20.00
Germany	929	107	11.52
England	1,369	119	8.70
British No. Amer.	1,381	115	8.33
New England	7,986	419	5.25
United States	997	47	4.71
Massachusetts	13,553	538	3.97
Others	2,182	85	3.90
TOTAL	43,567	8,552	19.63

* Derived from the marshal's schedules of the Seventh Census, cf. *infra*, note to Table XIII.

TABLE XVI

DOMESTIC SERVANTS IN BOSTON, BY NATIVITY, 1850 *

Nativity	Working Population	GENERAL HOUSE SERVANTS Number	Percentage of Working Population	Other Domestics †
Ireland	14,595	2,227	15.3	65
British No. Amer.	1,381	138	10.0	3
Negro	575	39	6.8	9
England	1,369	62	4.5	6
United States	997	41	4.1	4
New England	7,986	304	3.8	20
Germany	929	30	3.2	1
Others	2,182	60	2.6	13
Massachusetts	13,553	206	1.5	21
TOTAL	43,567	3,107	7.1	142

* Derived from the marshal's schedules of the Seventh Census, 1850 (cf. note to Table XIII). The instructions for this census asked the enumerators to list the occupations of all males above the age of sixteen and thus excluded the female domestic servants. Some enumerators went beyond the letter of their instructions and noted such persons in their schedules. By and large they did not. Only 1,375 servants were listed in the entire state in the official tabulation (cf. J. D. B. DeBow, *Seventh Census of the United States 1850* . . . [Washington, 1853], lxxx), an absurdly low figure in view of the fact that a more careful study in 1845 had found 5,706 in Boston alone (Lemuel Shattuck, *Report to the Committee of the City Council . . . Census of Boston . . . 1845 . . .* [Boston, 1846], 84). In many cases however, it was possible to distinguish the servants from the rest of the family, and where there could be no doubt as to status, they were tabulated whether the enumerator listed them or not. The figures given above are therefore minimal and are probably far below the true numbers. But since the same criteria were used in each nativity group, the table is valid for approximate comparisons between groups.

† Includes butlers, cooks, gardeners, housekeepers, and laundresses. These were specifically listed in the schedules.

TABLE XVII

NUMBER OF EMPLOYEES IN BOSTON INDUSTRIES EMPLOYING ONE HUNDRED OR MORE WORKERS IN ANY YEAR BETWEEN 1837 AND 1865 *

Total Industries Existing in	NUMBER OF EMPLOYEES			
	1837	1845 †	1855 †	1865
1837	9,930	4,928	9,084	33,011
1845	....	6,010	11,364	35,095
1855	....	....	13,147	37,268
1865	....	....	....	39,283

* Summarized from Table XIX, Dissertation Copy, 447, which itemizes 46 individual industries and which was derived from the industrial censuses of Massachusetts, 1837–1865.
† The clothing industries were not included in 1845 and 1855.

TABLE XVIII

CORRELATION OF TUBERCULOSIS WITH HOUSING AND NATIVITY, BY WARDS, BOSTON, 1865 *

Ward	Irish per Hundred	Persons per Dwelling	Death Rate per Thousand by Phthisis	Death Rate per Thousand, All Diseases
5	15.0	8.90	4.61	19.8
6	15.2	7.70	1.82	15.5
11	15.6	7.65	3.21	18.5
9	16.9	8.57	2.91	17.8
2	17.5	8.12	3.31	21.7
4	23.6	11.07	2.13	14.6
10	23.7	11.94	3.22	19.6
12	25.6	7.84	4.94	22.5
8	29.7	11.12	3.65	20.4
1	32.8	16.50	4.80	28.5
3	34.2	12.28	4.34	27.9
7	42.9	16.50	6.09	26.3

* Derived from Charles E. Buckingham, et al., *Sanitary Condition of Boston* . . . (Boston, 1875), 159, 126.

TABLE XIX

DISTRIBUTION OF THE POPULATION OF BOSTON BY AGE PERIODS, 1800–1855 *
Number in Every 10,000

Age Period	1800 to 1820 1800	1810	1820
Under 10	2,584.8	2,750	2,574
10–15	1,223.4	1,240	1,297
16–25	2,304.4	2,381	1,951
26–45	2,571.0	2,612	3,199
Over 45	1,318.4	1,017	979

Age Period	1830 to 1855 1830	1840	1855
Under 5	1,329	1,270	1,258
5–10	1,170	1,103	971
10–15	1,127	1,026	878
15–20	1,117	1,063	954
20–30	1,972	2,065	2,465
30–40	1,221	1,394	1,680
40–50	835	868	962
50–60	555	575	472
60–70	385	358	230
Over 70	289	278	104

* Derived from Lemuel Shattuck, *Letter to the Secretary of State on the Registration of Births, Marriages and Deaths* . . . (s.l., n.d. [Boston, 1845]), 6; Francis DeWitt, *Abstract of the Census of . . . Massachusetts . . . 1855* . . . (Boston, 1857), 90 ff.; Lemuel Shattuck, *Essay on the Vital Statistics of Boston* . . . (Boston, 1893), xvi, xviii, xx.

TABLE XX

NATIVITY OF THE PARENTS OF CHILDREN BORN IN BOSTON, 1863–1865 *

	1863	1865
Both American	1,207	1,306
Both English	69	67
Both Irish	2,375	2,287
Both Scots	27	18
Both British North Americans	122	147
Both Germans	184	197
Unmixed Foreign	93	61
Mixed Foreign	498	463
Mixed	634	698
Unknown	46	31
TOTAL	5,255	5,275

* Derived from the reports of the City Registrar, 1864, 1866, *Boston City Documents, 1864,* no. 47, p. 8; *ibid., 1866,* no. 88, p. 6.

TABLE XXI

PAUPERS IN THE METROPOLITAN AREA, 1848–1860 *

Year †	Total	Having Local Settlement	State Paupers	Foreign State Paupers	Irish and English State Paupers
1845	4,810	1,334	3,188	2,154	1,860
1846	5,640	1,375	4,205	2,947	2,543
1847	7,004	1,371	5,619	4,427	4,010
1848	6,664	1,270	5,374	4,339	3,974
1849	10,245	1,438	8,716	6,218	5,574
1850	11,294	1,026	10,200	7,924	7,130
1851	11,899	1,064	10,610	8,223	7,334
1853	12,068	1,117	10,233	8,080	6,951
1858	11,032	1,889	5,678	5,190	4,711
1859	12,346	2,129	6,092	6,247	5,988
1860	12,617	2,192	....	8,414	6,062

* Derived from material on Boston, Roxbury, Charlestown, Cambridge, Chelsea, Dorchester, West Roxbury, Somerville, Brighton, West Cambridge, Brookline, and North Chelsea in Dissertation Copy, Table XXII, 451 ff. Not all towns are complete in all categories each year.
† Year ending September.

TABLE XXII

NATIVITY OF INMATES OF THE DEER ISLAND HOUSE OF INDUSTRY *
REMAINING ON DECEMBER 31 OF EACH YEAR †

	1855 ‡	1856 ‡	1857 ‡	1858	1859	1860
Boston — native parentage ...	65	47	47			
Boston — Irish parentage	24	30	30	64	51	30
Massachusetts	29	32	32			
New England	29	29	29			
Ireland	128	154	154	266	219	179
England and British Provinces	..	..	..	58	34	28
Italy	..	..	..	..	1	1
Other foreigners	40	39	39	4	..	..
TOTAL	315	331	331	392	305	238

* Contained some paupers as well as criminals.
† Boston Committee of Finance, *Auditor's Reports, 1855*, no. 43, p. 174; *ibid., 1856*, no. 44, p. 210; *ibid., 1857*, no. 45, pp. 208–209; *ibid., 1859*, no. 47, p. 219; *ibid., 1860*, no. 48, p. 242; *ibid., 1861*, no. 49, p. 249.
‡ March 31.

TABLE XXIII

Nativity of all the Inmates in the House of Correction during the Year Ending December 31 *

	1858	1859	1860	1861	1862	1863
Massachusetts	235	218	287	177	98	147
Other United States	158	143	104	107	70	103
England	75	54	39	45	30	33
Ireland	574	457	340	472	336	318
Scotland	24	†	18	12	75	10
British Provinces	88	50	48	44	29	22
Italy	..	..	..	2	..	1
Germany	..	..	..	5	..	..
France	..	..	..	1	..	1
Others	29	34	11	5	6	1
Colored	59	45	39	51	39	?
White	1124	911	808	819	543	?
Total	1183	956	847	870	582 ‡	636

* Derived from Boston Finance Committee, *Auditor's Reports, 1859*, no. 47, p. 218; *ibid., 1860*, no. 48, p. 239; *ibid., 1861*, no. 49, p. 262; *ibid., 1862*, no. 50, p. 275; *ibid., 1863*, no. 51, p. 290.
† Included in Others.
‡ Discrepancy, as given, in the figures.

TABLE XXIV

Nativity of Arrests and Detentions by the Boston Police Department, Year Ending December 31, 1864 *

Nativity	Arrests	Lodgers
United States	2,143	4,580
Ireland	9,791	17,293
England	426	1,011
Africa	160	40
Germany	138	198
France	61	143
Scotland	61	203
Italy	30	25
Sweden	30	36
Portugal	25	7
Canada	15	12
Nova Scotia	9	..
Norway	6	51
Spain	4	12
Others	15	27

* "Annual Report of Chief of Police, 1865," *Boston City Documents, 1865*, no. 8, pp. 8, 9.

TABLE XXV

Amount Paid by the State for the Support of Lunatic State Paupers in Suffolk County,* 1838–1859 †

Year	Amount
1838	$ 1,573
1839	2,192
1840	2,793
1841	6,263
1842	6,820
1843	8,357
1844	9,511
1845	9,384
1846	10,170
1847	9,738
1848	9,940
1849	12,954
1850	15,906
1851	15,830
1852	17,295
1853	19,569
1854	19,805
1855	21,059
1856	18,538
1857	17,465
1858	20,183 ‡
1859	‡

* All in Boston.
† Derived from *Massachusetts Senate Documents, 1848*, no. 47; and from the annual reports of the City Auditor and of the Alien Passenger Commissioners (for page references, cf. Dissertation Copy, 468).
‡ The figures for 1858 also include 1859 until November, when all such insane were transferred to State institutions.

TABLE XXVI

Orphans Supported at St. Vincent's Orphan Asylum, Boston *

1843	18
1846	38
1848	38
1849	47
1851	50
1854	79
1855	81
1856	80
1857	79
1858	159 †
1859	191

* Derived from materials in the *Boston Pilot* and *Boston Catholic Observer*. For citations cf. Dissertation Copy, 471.
† New building opened.

TABLE XXVII

BOSTON MARRIAGES BY NATIVITY, THREE-YEAR PERIOD, 1863–1865 *

BIRTHPLACE OF GROOM	BIRTHPLACE OF BRIDE									TOTAL
	Boston	Massachusetts	United States	Great Britain	Ireland	British America	Germany †	Others	Unknown	
Boston	395	142	193	24	87	52	3	5	..	901
Massachusetts	258	319	320	32	50	57	1	5	4	1,046
United States	381	307	818	58	96	148	10	3	6	1,827
Great Britain	52	27	45	78	126	59	2	2	1	392
Ireland	170	37	47	42	1,997	78	2	5	..	2,378
British America	71	30	64	17	114	164	..	1	3	464
Germany †	51	13	31	11	78	15	247	12	1	459
Others	23	9	25	14	48	19	21	119	..	278
Unknown	1	2	1	..	..	1	..	..	35	40
TOTAL	1,402	886	1,544	276	2,596	593	286	152	50	7,785

* Derived from "Report of the City Registrar, 1863–1865," *Boston City Documents, 1866*, II, no. 88, p. 12; *ibid., 1865*, no. 42, p. 8; *ibid., 1864*, no. 47, p. 9. Cf. also Dissertation Copy, Table XXXII, 472.
† Includes Scandinavia.

TABLE XXVIII

BOSTON VOTERS, 1840–1858 *

Year	Legal Voters	Actual Vote Cast †
1840	14,474	11,573
1844	?	13,502
1845	20,351	10,191
1850	21,220	8,952
1851	?	12,314
1852	21,203	11,956
1853	23,792	12,409
1853	23,792	12,948 ‡
1854	24,157	13,410
1855	24,272	14,340
1856	?	16,865
1857	?	13,525
1858	?	14,466

* Derived from Lemuel Shattuck, *Report to . . . the City Council . . . Census of Boston . . . 1845 . . .* (Boston, 1846), 81; Josiah Curtis, *Report . . . Census of Boston . . . 1855* (Boston, 1856), 11; *Boston Semi-Weekly Advertiser*, November 12, 1851; *ibid.*, November 10, 1852; *ibid.*, November 16, 1853; *ibid.*, December 14, 1853; *ibid.*, November 5, 1856; *ibid.*, November 4, 1857; *Boston Atlas*, November 14, 1854; *Boston Daily Courier*, November 3, 1858; "Report and Tabular Statement," *Boston City Documents*, *1850*, no. 42, p. 12.

† In the November gubernatorial election unless otherwise indicated.

‡ December mayoralty election.

TABLE XXIX

POPULATION OF THE BOSTON REGION
1865–1880 *

	1865	1870	1880
Native white.........	225,168	249,179	325,551
Foreign white.........	102,696	122,912	143,844
Total white..........	327,864	372,091	469,395
Colored..............	3,141	4,914	8,287
Total.............	331,005	377,005	477,682

* Towns included in Table IX, except for parts of West Cambridge, Dorchester, and Belmont transferred to Belmont, Hyde Park, and Cambridge. *See* Tables IX, XII; U.S. Ninth Census, *Population* (Washington, 1872), I, 166, 167; U.S. Tenth Census, *Population* (Washington, 1883), I, 208 ff., 416 ff., 450, 451.

TABLE XXX

FOREIGN-BORN POPULATION OF BOSTON AND CAMBRIDGE
BY SELECTED NATIVITIES, 1880 *

	Boston	Cambridge
Irish.......................	64,793	8,366
British-American............	23,156	3,981
English.....................	8,998	1,396
German.....................	7,396	636
Swedish....................	1,450	169
Italian.....................	1,277	36
Other Foreign-Born	7,726	1,084
Total Foreign-Born........	114,796	15,668

* U.S. Tenth Census, *Population* (Washington, 1883), I.

261

TABLE XXXI

SELECTED OCCUPATIONS IN BOSTON BY SELECTED NATIVITIES, 1880*

	Total	U.S.	Ire.	Ger.	G. Br.	Norway, Sweden	Br. Am.	Others
All...............	149,194	88,244	34,745	3,990	6,650	1,121	11,237	3,207
Agriculture............	1,042	518	358	33	52	4	56	21
Servants..............	17,156	6,042	7,172	194	912	258	2,358	220
Laborers.............	15,854	4,037	10,066	280	436	83	623	329
Shop clerks..........	13,636	11,796	535	128	414	9	630	124
Tailors..............	11,246	6,853	1,866	298	504	64	1,384	297
Traders and Dealers..	9,187	6,599	1,407	324	328	24	280	225
Physicians...........	882	758	28	20	29	..	34	13
Lawyers.............	648	604	18	6	8	1	7	4

* U.S. Tenth Census, *Population* (Washington, 1883), I, 864.

TABLE XXXII

CHURCHES IN BOSTON, 1870 [*]

	Number	Sittings
Baptist.................	25	21,500
Christian...............	1	500
Congregational...........	30	23,200
Episcopal...............	24	12,000
Methodist...............	28	15,925
Catholic.................	28	34,500
Unitarian...............	28	20,500
Universalist.............	11	5,500
Presbyterian.............	7	3,425
German Reformed........	1	600
Jewish..................	6	1,800
Lutheran...............	2	400
German Lutheran.........	2	600
Swedish Lutheran.........	1	500
Colored Methodist........	3	2,075
Others..................	10	2,775

[*] U.S. Tenth Census, *Social Statistics of Cities* (Washington, 1886), I, 112; Ninth Census, *Population*, I, 542.

TABLE XXXIII

ENTRIES AT THE PORT OF BOSTON, 1871–1880 *

Origin	Year Ending June 30									
	1871	1872	1873	1874	1875	1876	1877	1878	1879	1880 **
England	7,073	7,425	8,898	6,087	4,637	2,159	1,596	1,164	1,591	3,529
Ireland	9,693	9,378	11,981	9,395	6,615	3,072	2,021	2,212	2,610	9,099
Scotland	732	936	1,140	784	541	351	177	135	203	764
Germany	2,783	2,304	2,709	1,392	876	531	378	151	233	804
Sweden	398	1,030	1,094	798	476	543	363	461	1,091	3,539
British America	4,461	4,184	3,958	3,507	2,367	1,672	2,380	3,685	3,748	8,641
Others	1,884	1,652	1,896	2,262	2,133	1,383	972	948	888	2,441
Total	27,024	26,909	31,676	24,225	17,645	9,711	7,887	8,756	10,364	28,817

* U.S. Tenth Census, *Social Statistics of Cities*, I, 115.
** Eleven months.

NOTE ON SOURCES

ABBREVIATIONS

B.C.	Bureau of the Census, Division of Old Records, Commerce Building, Constitution Avenue, Washington, D. C.
Bi.A.V	Bibliotheca Apostolica Vaticana, Vatican City
B.M.	British Museum Reading Room, Bloomsbury, London, W.C.1
B.P.L.	Boston Public Library, Boston, Massachusetts
H.C.L.	Harvard College Library, Cambridge, Massachusetts
I.A.H.S.	Irish American Historical Society, New York City
Li.C.	Library of Congress, Washington, D. C.
L.U.N.D.	Library of the University of Notre Dame, South Bend, Indiana
M.S.L.	Massachusetts State Library, State House, Boston
N.L.I.	National Library of Ireland, Kildare Street, Dublin
N.N.L.	National Newspaper Library, British Museum, Colindale Road, Colindale (Hendon), London, N.W.9
N.E.H.G.S.	New England Historical and Genealogical Society, 99 Ashburton Street, Boston
N.Y.P.L.	New York Public Library, Fifth Avenue, New York
P.R.O.	Public Record Office, Chancery Lane, London
R.A.d.S.	Reale Archivio di Stato — Napoli, Piazza del Grande Archivio, Naples, Italy
R.I.A.	Royal Irish Academy, Dawson Street, Dublin
S.J.E.S.	Saint John's Boston Ecclesiastical Seminary, Brighton, Massachusetts
T.C.D.	Trinity College, Dublin, Library, College Green, Dublin

NOTE ON SOURCES

THE materials for the understanding of a community are infinite. To limit sources is impossible, for, in a sense, everything that was written, read, said, or thought, in or about Boston between 1790 and 1880, is germane to the subject of this study. And beyond the purely literary materials lies an endless mine of physical survivals — the relics of the old city, and the descendants of those who lived in it — which offers rich perceptions to those willing to see. Yet this very prodigality bars completeness; the historian can only sample the wide variety before him and compensate by the judiciousness of his choices for the inevitable omissions.

The list which follows is thus in no sense an exhaustive bibliography; it does not even include all the works cited in the footnotes.[1] It only attempts to outline the *types* of material used in this study and to criticize the more important of them.

I. NEWSPAPERS AND PERIODICALS

THE IMMIGRANT PRESS [2] most consciously expressed the varied impulses of immigrant society and forms the most important single source for this study. Newspapers play a threefold part in illuminating the story of aliens. They are the most important source of information on the life of the immigrant community; nowhere else is there as complete a chronicle of arrivals and departures, of the meetings of its so-

267

cieties, and of the doings of its prominent men. Furthermore, the newspaper at once reflected and influenced the views of the immigrants on the problems they faced personally and in relation to the society about them. And because the press was not yet a big business, every significant shade of opinion could afford an organ of expression. Most important of all, the newspapers were the most comprehensive repositories of immigrant literature. The Germans had a few literary monthlies (e.g., *Atlantis. Eine Monatschrift für Wissenschaft . . . herausgegeben und redigiert von Christian Esselen* [Buffalo]; *Meyer's Monatshefte* [New York]), but these were restricted in scope, circulation, and influence. And among other groups formal literary journals found no place at all. The newspapers furnished the foreigners' only reading material and the fiction, the poetry, and the history that attracted their readers are the most sensitive mirrors of what went on in immigrant minds.

THE NEWSPAPERS OF IRELAND were disappointing for the purposes of this study. They threw some light on the famine and on the process of emigration but few were really interested in the condition of the peasantry. The most valuable was the *Cork Examiner* (N.N.L.) (1841 ff.), which retained its interest in Corkonians even in their new homes. Its columns contained occasional news of Boston Irishmen and sometimes letters of considerable importance to friends in the old country. Its rival, the *Cork Constitution* (N.N.L.) (1834 ff.), was less valuable; Tory in sympathy, it was impatient with the emigrants and glad to be rid of them. Dublin papers had little room for anything but politics and the pages of journals like the *Armagh Guardian* (N.N.L.) (1844) and the *Leinster Express* (N.N.L.) were devoted to sensational crimes and to similar news of interest to the gentry who read them.

OTHER PERIODICALS were of secondary importance. Boston's press was, on the whole, well above the average of its contemporaries. In the early period the *Massachusetts Centinel* (continued as the *Columbian Centinel*) (N.Y.P.L.) and the *Independent Chronicle* (H.C.L.) were temperate well-balanced sheets, the one Federalist, the other Republican. After 1830, the *Daily Evening Transcript* (H.C.L.) furnished accurate and generally unbiased news, while the tri-weekly *American Traveller* (H.C.L.) catered to a wider range of interests. Later in the period the *Boston Daily Courier* (H.C.L.) and the Whig *Boston Daily Atlas* (H.C.L.) were reliable, while the *Boston Semi-Weekly Advertiser* (H.C.L.), like its daily counterpart, reflected the interests and opinions of State Street and the business community. In addition, the city was the home of innumerable weeklies that spoke for special causes. The most helpful were the precursors of the Know-Nothing papers, the *American* (B.P.L.) and *Wide Awake: And the Spirit of Washington* (B.P.L.). But in general it was necessary only to sample these in periods of special interest since the most significant articles were liberally quoted in the immigrant papers.

II. PUBLIC DOCUMENTS

This period was intensely interested in the preservation of its records. The abundance of documentary materials published by all branches of government facilitated the solution of many problems; while their general reliability compensated for the lack of vision on the part of their compilers who could not always foresee the uses to which historians would put them.

The quality of the statistical material is especially gratifying. The municipal, state and federal governments all compiled CENSUS RECORDS, which after 1845 included a vast amount of social data of considerable significance. Until then, the federal census had followed fairly traditional forms concentrating primarily upon enumeration of the population for purposes of representation. But Lemuel Shattuck's *Report to the Commitee of the City Council . . . Census of Boston for . . . 1845 . . .* (Boston, 1846) broke new ground in pointing out the potential social usefulness of the census. His report included a mass of well-digested material on all phases of the life of Boston and its people and furnished a model for all subsequent censuses.

The most significant enumeration for the purposes of this study was that of 1850, taken at the height of the immigration, while the process of adjustment was most critical. Fortunately, the federal census of that year was directed by the far-sighted J. D. B. DeBow who published its results in *The Seventh Census of the United States: 1850 . . .* (Washington, 1853) and summarized them in his *Statistical View of the United States . . .* (Washington, 1854). DeBow attempted, with some success, to follow the model set by Shattuck. His was the first federal census, for example, to inquire into both the nativity and occupation of the population; and Vols. XXIII–XXVI of the Original Returns of that census formed the basis for much of the discussion in Chapter III of this work (cf. also *supra,* 234).

The same year also witnessed a municipal census, reported in the "Report and Tabular Statement of the Censors Appointed . . . to Obtain the State Census of Boston, May 1, 1850 . . . ," *Boston City Documents, 1850,* no. 42, and discussed in Jesse Chickering's "Report of the Committee . . . and also a Comparative View of the Population of Boston in 1850 . . . ," *ibid., 1851,* no. 60. This census was unusual and valuable for a street by street tabulation of the nativity of the residents.

Thereafter federal and state censuses alternated every five years in providing an enlightening statistical account of the city's development. Nathaniel B. Shurtleff prepared an *Abstract of the Census of . . . Massachusetts Taken . . . the First Day of June, 1855, with Remarks on the Same Prepared under the Direction of Francis DeWitt* . . . (Boston, 1857), that supplemented the more detailed *Report of the Joint Special Committee of the Census of Boston, May, 1855* . . . (Boston, 1856) by Josiah Curtis. The federal census of 1860 was summarized by Joseph C. G. Kennedy in the *Population of the United States in 1860; Compiled from the Original Returns of the Eighth Census* . . . (Washington, 1864); but the data on Massachusetts may be found in greater detail in George Wingate Chase's *Abstract of the Census of Massachusetts 1860 from the Eighth U. S. Census . . . Prepared under . . . Oliver Warner* . . . (Boston, 1863). The last two decades are ably covered on both the state and the federal levels in Oliver Warner's *Abstract of the Census of Massachusetts, 1865* . . . (Boston, 1867); Carroll D. Wright's *Census of Massachusetts, 1875* (Boston, 1876); the U.S. Ninth Census (Washington, 1872); and the U. S. Tenth Census (Washington, 1883–1888), the two last named prepared under the direction of Francis A. Walker.

The economic history of Massachusetts is remarkably clarified by a series of four INDUSTRIAL CENSUSES, 1837–1865. These were compiled carefully from data collected by the Secretaries of State. John P. Bigelow's *Statistical Tables: Exhibiting the Condition . . . of Industry in Massachusetts . . . 1837 . . .* (Boston, 1838), John G. Palfrey's *Statistics of the Condition of . . . Industry in Massachusetts . . . 1845 . . .* (Boston, 1846), Francis DeWitt's *Statistical Information Relating to . . . Industry in Massachusetts . . . 1855 . . .* (Boston, 1856), and Oliver Warner's *Statistical Information Relating to . . . Industry in Massachusetts . . . 1865 . . .* (Boston, 1866) furnish a sturdy framework for the story of the evolution of Massachusetts' economy through its most important phase. Additional material may be found in McLane's *Documents Relative to the Manufactures in the United States* (22 Congress, 1 Session, *House Executive Documents,* no. 308), in the volumes on manufactures of the Eighth, Ninth, and Tenth Censuses, and in the historical introductions of the *Ninth Census, 1870* (Washington, 1872) and the *Twelfth Census, 1900, Manufactures,* IX (Washington, 1902).

Beyond the bare statistics there is a rich store of records of all the agencies which had contact with immigrants in Boston. The MUNICIPAL DOCUMENTS vary in value. The records of the Town of Boston and the minutes of the Selectmen's Meetings down to 1822, published in seven volumes by the Boston Registry Department between 1896 and 1908, cover a period when the immigrant was not yet prominent enough to warrant more than passing attention. Thereafter there is no complete record of the city government, except between 1826 and 1828, when *Bowen's Boston News-Letter and City Record,* edited by J. V. C. Smith, chronicled its affairs. The *Auditor's Reports* (1813–67) contain the financial details of all the municipal institutions, the *Inaugural Addresses of the Mayors of Boston . . . Published by the City Registrar* (Boston, 1894) give a cross section of the city's problems, and the changes in its laws may be traced in Peleg W. Chandler's *Charter and Ordinances of the City of Boston together with the Acts of the Legislature Relating to the City . . .* (Boston, 1850) and in the City Council's compilation of ordinances in 1856 and 1865. The manuscript records of the town Board of Health (1799–1824) are preserved in the Boston Public Library, but the reports of other city departments are scattered and fragmentary until 1839 when they began to be issued serially in the *Boston City Documents.* The annual reports of the agencies there collected became progressively more important as the aliens assumed greater prominence in the city's life.

It was the STATE, however, that was most prominently concerned with immigrants in this period. Its public DOCUMENTS throw welcome light upon the process of settlement, and in addition possess a wealth of data on all aspects of Boston life. The reports of the State departments were thrown haphazardly into either the *Massachusetts House Documents* or the *Massachusetts Senate Documents* between 1826 and 1856 but thereafter were collected in the *Massachusetts Public Documents* while the two older series were confined to purely legislative concerns. The reports of the State Board of Education, of the Alien Passenger Commissioners, of the State charitable institutions, and of the keepers of jails, included in these documents, were of prime importance.

Although the *Acts and Resolves* of the General Court are available in full throughout the period, the proceedings were printed only under special circumstances as in 1856 when interest in the Know-Nothing legislature induced the *Daily Advertiser* to issue a volume of *Debates and Proceedings*. . . . (Boston, 1856).

The only FEDERAL DOCUMENTS directly relevant to the first half of the nineteenth century are the annual *Letter from the Secretary of State Transmitting a Statement of Passengers Arriving in the United States* . . . (1820 ff.) in the Congressional documents (cf. *supra,* 233). The reports of the national Commissioner of Immigration begin in 1865.

In a somewhat special category is the BRITISH CONSULAR CORRESPONDENCE (P.R.O.) in two series (F.O. 4, F.O. 5). The letters of the English consuls in Boston to their government and to the Embassy in Washington (British Embassy Archives [P.R.O., F.O. 115]) are of considerable value particularly after the 1830's when the early placemen were supplanted by Consuls Manners, Grattan, and Lousada. Their reports touched regularly not only upon the condition of the Irishmen, still theoretically British subjects, but also upon the whole range of social conditions in Boston, and offer intelligent and well-informed comments upon them. The reports of Consul Buchanan, at New York, are also worth consulting. He was intensely interested in the problems of emigration and persistently showered his complaining but helpless superiors in London with long, detailed reports which they found irrelevant, but which are mines of serviceable information.

Outside the run of normal government documents are a number of REPORTS OF INVESTIGATIONS into some of the more pressing problems of the period. Perhaps the earliest was Theodore Lyman, Jr.'s brief report to the House of Representatives on *Free Negroes and Mulattoes . . . January 16, 1822 . . .* (s.l.,n.d.). As immigration grew such inquiries became more frequent. In 1846 public spirited citizens, disturbed by the possibilities of a shortage in housing, prepared the *Report of the Committee on the Expediency of Providing Better Tenements for the Poor* (Boston, 1846). Interest in the causes of cholera provoked the exhaustive analysis by Buckingham's Committee of 1849 into all phases of the city's health and the factors conditioning it (detailed in *Report of the Committee of Internal Health on the Asiatic Cholera . . .* , *Boston City Documents, 1849*, no. 66, and discussed in William Read's "Communication . . . on the Asiatic Cholera . . . 1866," *Boston City Documents, 1866*, no. 21). Although these reports and Dr. Howard F. Damon's *Localities of One Thousand Cases of . . . Diseases . . .* (Boston, 1866), contain some illuminating material, the most accurate descriptions of housing conditions are found in the early *Annual Reports* (1870–1880) of the Massachusetts State Labor Statistics Bureau, based on investigations made in 1866–67, but valid for the whole period after 1850. The Massachusetts Sanitary Commissioners under Shattuck issued a *Report of a General Plan for the Promotion of Public and Personal Health. . . .* (Boston, 1850), summarized in "Sanitary Reform," *North American Review,* July, 1851, LXXIII, which contained an excellent statistical section on the health of the city. The *Sanitary Condition of Boston, the Report of a Medical Commission . . . Appointed by the Board of Health of the City of Boston. . . .* (Boston, 1875) by Chas. E. Buckingham and others, had some useful historical data. Finally, the *Annual Reports* of the Executive Committee of the Benevolent Fraternity of Churches (1835–1866) and of the Children's Mission to the Children of the Destitute (1850–1863) described the findings of two organizations in close contact with the immigrants.

III. Other Contemporary Material

The well-known accounts of visitors to Boston were of value in dealing with the background of the city, but threw little light on the condition of the immigrants. Few travelers ventured off the beaten track that led inevitably from the State House to Bunker Hill and Mount Auburn. La Rochefoucauld-Liancourt's *Voyage dans les États-Unis d'Amérique* . . . (Paris, An VII) gives an early description of the town; "Boston as It Appeared to a Foreigner at the Beginning of the Nineteenth Century . . ." (*Bostonian Society Publications,* Series I, IV) pictures it ten years before and W. Faux's *Memorable Days in America* . . . (London, 1823) ten years after the War of 1812. Harriet Martineau's *Society in America* (New York, 1837) has overshadowed other accounts of the 1830's quite unjustly, for that decade also saw the publication of *A Journal of a Residence . . . in the United States of North America* . . . (London, 1835) by the English abolitionist, Edward S. Abdy, of George Combe's *Notes on the United States of North America during a Phrenological Visit in 1838–40* (Philadelphia, 1841), and of a significant criminological study by Nikolaus Heinrich Julius. *Nordamerikas sittliche Zustände nach eigenen Anschauungen in den Jahren 1834, 1835, und 1836* (Leipzig, 1839). Boston welcomed Sir Charles Lyell, the geologist, ten years later and in return was sympathetically described in *A Second Visit to the United States of North America* (London, 1849). *L'Aristocratie en Amérique* (Paris, 1883) by Frederic Gaillardet, editor of the *Courrier des États-Unis* in this period, is disappointingly superficial; but Thomas C. Grattan's *Civilized America* (London, 1859) embodies the results of his intelligent observations as consul in Boston, and Edward Dicey's *Six Months in the Federal States* (London, 1863) is adequate for the Civil War years.

IMMIGRANT GUIDES fall into a special category. Their most eloquent evidence was negative in so far as they failed to mention Boston at all. *America and Her Resources . . .* (London, 1818) by John Bristed, and Martin Doyle's *Hints on Emigration . . .* (Dublin, 1831) were typical of the English and L. von Baumbach's *Neue Briefe aus den Vereinigten Staaten . . .* (Cassel, 1856), of the German. *The German in America, or Advice and Instruction for German Emigrants in the United States . . .* (Boston, 1851) was worth noting because it was written by Frederick W. Bogen, pastor of the Lutheran church in Boston. The discussion of industrial developments and opportunities in *Erwerbszweige, Fabrikwesen und Handel von Nordamerika . . .* (Stuttgart, 1850) by C. L. Fleischmann, an American consul in Germany, is informative, and Franz Löher's *Geschichte und Zustände der Deutschen in Amerika . . .* (Cincinnati, 1847) contains one of the few good accounts of the German community in Boston.

PAMPHLETS proved useful in many phases of this study. They were one of the most important sources of information on the background of emigration from Ireland. This fugitive literature came from the presses of Dublin and the provincial towns with bewildering frequency; everyone who had an opinion expressed it through this medium. The poor-law issue provoked a particularly valuable succession of controversial publications and the famines of 1814 and 1823 were described in considerable detail by investigating committees. Few of these pamphlets were outstanding; rather their value lay in the cumulative weight of their evidence. Several thousand are admirably arranged in the Haliday Collection of the Royal Irish Academy, catalogued by J. T. Gilbert (MS., R.I.A.).

Similar material for Boston is also plentiful. The Harvard College Library has a complete file of *Directories* from 1789 and of *Almanacs* and *Registers* from 1830. There is no lack of guide books and an abundance of pamphlets on all the important issues of the day. In addition low printing costs and prolific preachers combined to produce an outpouring of sermons that dealt with all phases of the city's intellectual life, and sometimes, as in Parker's case, with many broader aspects of its social and economic structure.

IV. IMMIGRATION AND ITS BACKGROUND

There is no satisfactory GENERAL ACCOUNT of American immigration. The *Immigrant in American History* . . . (Cambridge, 1940) contains a series of provocative essays by Marcus Lee Hansen which display insight as well as scholarship. Carl Wittke's *We Who Built America* . . . (New York, 1939) summarizes the results of recent investigations but is marred by a lack of proportion in emphasis. Probably the best general approach to the problem is through the documents collected in Edith Abbott's *Immigration Select Documents* . . . (Chicago, 1924) and *Historical Aspects of the Immigration Problem* . . . (Chicago, 1926), although in both, the legal aspects are given too much weight. Oscar Handlin, *The Uprooted* (Boston, 1951) examines the effects of migration upon the immigrant.

There are a number of worth-while studies of the causes of emigration both in individual countries and for EUROPE AS A WHOLE. The broader trends in population may be traced in A. M. Carr-Saunders, *Population Problem* . . . (Oxford, 1922) and *World Population* . . . (Oxford, 1936). Maurice R. Davie's *World Immigration* . . . (New York, 1936) contains a more comprehensive general account than René Gonnard's *L'Émigration européenne au XIXe siècle* . . . (Paris, 1906). Far more detailed than either, but in some ways less useful, is *International Migrations* (New York, 1929, 1932) edited by Imre Ferenczi and Walter F. Willcox; lack of consistency among the contributors, and the failure to integrate the discussion with the statistics detract seriously from its value. All of these have been superseded, within the field it covers, by Marcus Lee Hansen's *Atlantic Migration, 1607–1860* . . . (Cambridge, 1940), a careful study of all phases of the movement, particularly valuable for its light on emigration from central Europe. In comparison Edwin C. Guillet's *Great Migration* . . . (New York, 1937), which deals primarily with Great Britain, is superficial. In the last decade or so, interest in the subject of economic development has elicited the following studies by economists which, in general, sustain the argument advanced in this book: Julius Isaac, *Economics of Migration* (New York, 1947); Brinley Thomas, *Migration and Economic Growth* (Cambridge, 1954); and Brinley Thomas, ed., *Economics of International Migration* (London, 1958).

The literature for the background of BRITISH emigration is ample. Élie Halévy's *History of the English People in 1815* (Harmondsworth, 1937) gives a sympathetic account of the social structure of the island while J. H. Clapham describes its economic institutions in *Economic History of Modern Britain* . . . (Cambridge, 1932). Industrial and agricultural changes may be followed in the works of J. L. and Barbara Hammond while the *Population Problems of the Age of Malthus* (Cambridge, 1926) are dealt with in a competent but uninspired fashion by G. Talbot Griffith. Sidney and Beatrice Webb have adequately discussed the problems of poor relief in *English Poor Law Policy* (London, 1910) and *English Poor Law History* . . . (London, 1927–29). Clapham's study of "Irish Immigration into Great Britain in the Nineteenth Century" (*Bulletin of the International Committee of Historical Sciences,* V) draws attention to an important subject. On the problem of population movements to the United States, the older works, Stanley C. Johnson's *History of Emigration from the United Kingdom* . . . (London, 1913) and William A. Carrothers' *Emigration from the British Isles with Special Reference to the* . . . *Overseas Dominions* (London, 1929), have now been supplanted by Rowland T. Berthoff, *British Immigrants in Industrial America 1790–1950* (Cambridge, 1953).

Carl Wittke, *The Irish in America* (Baton Rouge, 1956) is a general survey. The number of scholarly studies of this group remains small. *Ireland and Irish Emigration to the New World from 1815 to the Famine* . . . (New Haven, 1932) have been dealt with in detail by William Forbes Adams in a scholarly study which, however, passes lightly over the poor law issue, and, in addition, is unsympathetic to the peasantry. George O'Brien's *Economic History of Ireland in the Eighteenth Century* (Dublin, 1918) and his *Economic History of Ireland from the Union to the Famine* (London, 1921) are useful and may now be supplemented by R. D. Edwards and T. D. Williams, *The Great Famine* (New York, 1957).

Constantina Maxwell's *Country and Town in Ireland under the Georges* (London, 1940) and *Dublin under the Georges, 1714–1830* (London, 1936) deal primarily with the gentry with only occasional reference to the peasantry. There is considerable material on emigration in the Letters and Papers of William Smith O'Brien (MSS., N.L.I.), and Robert Bennet Forbes' *Voyage of the Jamestown on Her Errand of Mercy* (Boston, 1847) contains a graphic account of the famine. Much undigested information on Irish politics at the turn of the nineteenth century is scattered through R. R. Madden's *United Irishmen* . . . (New York, 1916) and the collection of his papers on the subject in Trinity College, Dublin. *Rossa's Recollections, 1858 to 1898.* . . . (Mariner's Harbor, N. Y., 1898) and *Irish Rebels in English Prisons* . . . (New York, 1880) are autobiographies of Jeremiah

O'Donovan-Rossa, a Fenian, with general reflections on the life of the Irish in the United States; and Thomas D'Arcy McGee's *History of the Irish Settlers* . . . (Boston, 1852) and Edward Everett Hale's *Letters on Irish Emigration* . . . (Boston, 1852) are contemporary accounts worth consulting because of the familiarity of their authors with their subjects.

The GERMAN background is compactly discussed in John Harold Clapham's *Economic Development of France and Germany* . . . (Cambridge, 1936); and Marcus Lee Hansen carefully describes the economic causes of the migrations of the Fifties in "Revolutions of 1848 and German Emigration" (*Journal of Economic and Business History,* II). René Le-Conte summarizes the legal aspects of the movement in *La Politique de l'Allemagne en matière d'émigration* (Paris, 1921) but for a more detailed treatment one must still consult the essays in *Auswanderung und Auswanderungspolitik in Deutschland* . . . (Leipzig, 1892) edited by Eugen von Philippovich. Albert B. Faust's *German Element in the United States, with Special Reference to Its Political, Moral, Social and Educational Influence* (New York, 1927) is a reliable though sometimes intemperate account of the Germans in America, with emphasis on the leading personalities. The discussion of politics in Ernest Bruncken's *German Political Refugees in the United States* . . . (s.l., 1904) is valuable; and Franz Löher's *Geschichte und Zustände der Deutschen in Amerika* (Cincinnati, 1847) is a contemporary history of high order. A. E. Zucker, ed., *The Forty-Eighters* (New York, 1950) and Carl Wittke, *Refugees of Revolution* (Philadelphia, 1952) deal with the movement after the failure of the revolutions of 1848.

Although Howard Mumford Jones' excellent *America and French Culture, 1750–1848* (Chapel Hill, 1927) has a broader scope, most studies of the FRENCH have dealt with political refugees of the revolutionary period. The story of later French immigrants is still largely untold. On the eighteenth-century migrations, Frances S. Childs' *French Refugee Life in the United States, 1790–1800* . . . (Baltimore, 1940) supplements J. G. Rosengarten's *French Colonists and Exiles in the United States* (Philadelphia, 1907), but deals primarily with Philadelphia. Leo F. Ruskowski's *French Emigré Priests in the United States (1791–1815)* . . . (Washington, 1940) adds little to earlier works. The best account of this movement, on the whole, is in the relevant sections of Fernand Baldensperger's *Mouvement des idées dans l'émigration française* . . . (Paris, 1924).

The material on ITALIAN immigration is scarce. Robert F. Foerster's *Italian Emigration of Our Times* (Cambridge, 1919) and Lawrence Frank Pisani's *Italian in America* (New York, 1957) hardly deal with the period before 1880. Paulo G. Brenna's *Storia dell'emigrazione italiana* . . . (Roma, 1928) is brief and superficial. Giovanni Schiavo's *Italians in America before the Civil War* . . . (New York, 1934) is an exhaustive compilation but deals primarily with personalities. Details on the movement can be found only in the ill-organized volumes of Leone Carpi's *Delle colonie e dell'emigrazione d'Italiani all'estero* . . . (Milano, 1874).

Florence Edith Janson's *Background of Swedish Immigration, 1840–1930* . . . (Chicago, 1931) is excellent and Theodore C. Blegen's *Norwegian Migration to America, 1825–1860* (Northfield, 1931) is adequate. Marcus Lee Hansen deals with some phases of the movement from Canada in *Mingling of the Canadian and American Peoples* . . . (New Haven, 1940) and in "Second Colonization of New England" (*New England Quarterly,* II); but the *Report of the Select Committee of the Legislative Assembly Appointed to Inquire into the Causes* . . . *of the Emigration* . . . *from Lower Canada to the United States* . . . (Montreal, 1849), though essential, has been too often overlooked.

V. Other Histories

The *Memorial History of Boston* . . . *1630–1880* . . . (Boston, 1880) edited by Justin Winsor is the most valuable of the numerous GENERAL HISTORIES. The articles are uneven in quality and sometimes do not hang together well, but most are competently written and are not yet outdated. By and large, other works in this category deal with social history in the limited sense. Mary Caroline Crawford's *Romantic Days in Old Boston* . . . (Boston, 1910) is more sober than its title. Samuel Adams Drake's *Old Landmarks and Historic Personages of Boston* . . . (Boston, 1873) is almost purely antiquarian as is the *Town of Roxbury* . . . (Boston, 1905) by Francis S. Drake; but both are accurate and interesting. The similar works of Gillespie and Simonds on South Boston and of Hunnewell on Charlestown can also be used with profit.

The evolution of the municipal GOVERNMENT and of its DEPARTMENTS in their first thirty years may be traced in the *Municipal History of* . . . *Boston* . . . (Boston, 1852) by Josiah Quincy, the first mayor. The municipal institutions are conventionally described in James M. Bugbee's *City Govern-*

ment of Boston . . . (Baltimore, 1887). The history of the police receives sprightly treatment in *Police Records and Recollections; or, Boston by Daylight and Gaslight* . . . (Boston, 1873) by Edward H. Savage, himself a constable at one time. The annals of other city departments are given by Arthur Wellington Brayley in *The Complete History of the Boston Fire Department* . . . (Boston, 1889) and *Schools and Schoolboys of Old Boston* . . . (Boston, 1894). The relationships of the metropolis to the communities around it are analyzed in George Herbert McCaffrey's Political Disintegration and Reintegration of Metropolitan Boston (MS., H.C.L.), a carefully prepared doctoral dissertation.

The COMMERCIAL HISTORY of Boston has been ably treated in Samuel Eliot Morison's *Maritime History of Massachusetts, 1783–1860* (Boston, 1921). Contemporary analyses by E. H. Derby (1850) and James H. Lanman (1844) may be found in *Hunt's Merchants' Magazine and Commercial Review,* X, XXIII. E. S. Chesbrough, the City Engineer, prepared a useful *Tabular Representation of the Present Condition of Boston* . . . (Boston, 1851) which covers a wide variety of topics; and John Macgregor's *Progress of America . . . to the Year 1846* (London, 1847) contains a mass of miscellaneous statistics.

There is no satisfactory INDUSTRIAL HISTORY of Boston, Massachusetts, or New England. Victor S. Clark's *History of Manufactures in the United States* (Washington, 1916–1929) and Emerson D. Fite's *Social and Industrial Conditions in the North during the Civil War* (New York, 1910) contain some references to the city's industries, but their generalizations are not always valid for Boston. Edward C. Kirkland's

Men, Cities and Transportation (Cambridge, 1948) is an outstanding study of New England development; and Oscar and Mary F. Handlin, *Commonwealth* (New York, 1947) examines the role of government in the economy of Massachusetts. *The History of Labour in the United States* (New York, 1918–26), edited by John R. Commons, Norman Ware's *Industrial Worker, 1840–1860* . . . (Boston, 1924), Isaac A. Hourwich's *Immigration and Labor* . . . (New York, 1922), and Edith Abbott's *Women in Industry* . . . (New York, 1913) are excellent studies dealing with aspects of industrial labor in this period and have some data relevant to the problems of Boston. Scattered material may also be found in Albert Aftalion's study of the clothing industries, in Raymond McFarland's study of the fisheries, in Blanche E. Hazard on shoes, Caroline F. Ware on cottons, Paul T. Cherrington and Arthur Harrison Cole on woolens, Lura Woodside Watkins on glass, Jesse Eliphalet Pope on clothing, and Paul L. Vogt on sugar. But the most important source of information on the history of individual companies was a series of industrial compendia; C. L. Fleischmann's *Erwerbszweige* . . . (Stuttgart, 1850), Edwin T. Freedley, *United States Mercantile Guide. Leading Pursuits and Leading Men* . . . (Philadelphia, 1856), volume III of J. Leander Bishop's *History of American Manufactures* . . . (Philadelphia, 1868), *Eighty Years Progress of the United States: a Family Record of American Industry* . . . (Hartford, 1869), *Great Industries of the United States* . . . (Hartford, 1872) edited by Horace Greeley, and C. M. Depew's *One Hundred Years of American Commerce* . . . (New York, 1895) contain descriptions of numerous concerns available nowhere else. One can find hostile comments on Boston's wealthy in *"Our First Men:" a Calendar of Wealth* . . . (Boston, 1846), and friendly ones in A. Forbes and J. W. Greene, *Rich Men of Massachusetts* . . . (Boston, 1851) or in *Aristocracy of Boston* . . . (Boston, 1848).

The materials on the INTELLECTUAL DEVELOPMENT of the city are abundant and familiar. The Bostonians who participated in the "flowering" were extremely self-conscious, wrote a good deal about themselves and their ideas, and, in addition, found frequent biographers. Toward the end of the last century when interest in this group reached a peak, it received friendly and sympathetic, if often uncritical, treatment at the hands of the generation which had been its students. Octavius Brooks Frothingham and others produced a succession of biographies which breathed a pious veneration for a bygone golden age, but which often embodied the results of sound scholarship and patient research. More recent biographers have been more detached and have brought broader perspectives to their work. Henry Steele Commager's *Theodore Parker* . . . (Boston, 1936), for example, contains little that is "new" but paints a vivid and appealing portrait through an understanding examination of its subject's social background. Among the useful biographies of the last decade are also: Arthur S. Bolster, Jr., *James Freeman Clarke* (Boston, 1954); Harold Schwartz, *Samuel Gridley Howe* (Cambridge, 1956); and Oscar Sherwin, *Prophet of Liberty: the Life and Times of Wendell Phillips* (New York, 1958). Other phases of Boston's cultural history are touched on in William B. Whiteside, *The Boston Y.M.C.A.* . . . (New York, 1951), Arthur Mann, *Yankee Reformers in the Urban*

Age (Cambridge, 1954), Barbara M. Solomon, *Ancestors and Immigrants* (Cambridge, 1956), and Barbara M. Solomon, *Pioneers in Service* . . . (Boston, 1956).

The POLITICAL history of the city can hardly be separated from that of the state of which it was capital. *The Commonwealth History of Massachusetts* (New York, 1930), edited by A. B. Hart, contains some articles of value and Samuel Eliot Morison's brief *History of the Constitution of Massachusetts* . . . (Boston, 1917) is useful. Two thorough works cover the specific issues of this period. Arthur B. Darling's *Political Changes in Massachusetts, 1824–1848* . . . (New Haven, 1925), and William G. Bean's Party Transformation in Massachusetts with Special Reference to the Antecedents of Republicanism 1848–1860 (MS. doctoral dissertation, H.C.L., summarized in "Puritan versus Celt 1850–1860," *New England Quarterly,* VII, 70 ff.) trace the impact of new issues upon party structure in scholarly detail. Both, however, labor under the handicap of an untenable thesis. Their attempt to impose a sectional pattern upon Massachusetts politics is hardly successful, and is contradicted by much of their own material; other lines of division were much more important than those between east and west. Edith E. Ware's *Political Opinion in Massachusetts during the Civil War and Reconstruction* . . . (New York, 1916) is a conventional work which fails to prove that the State was never antislavery, and contributes little of value.

Three newspapermen have left valuable comments on the political scene in Massachusetts. William S. Robinson's *"Warrington" Pen-Portraits* . . . (Boston, 1877) contains the penetrating observations of one familiar with all the complexities of state politics in the fifties. George S. Merriam's *Life and Times of Samuel Bowles* (New York, 1885) is a biography with copious extracts from the correspondence of the editor of the *Springfield Republican;* and Benjamin P. Shillaber of the Democratic *Post* has recalled his "Experiences During Many Years" for the *New England Magazine,* VIII, IX.

Bostonians of the period left ample stores of papers and memoirs which were turned into biographies. Josiah Quincy's *Figures of the Past from the Leaves of Old Journals* (Boston, 1883) contains a series of charming vignettes in which his most prominent contemporaries are etched with real understanding; it would be difficult, for instance, to find a shrewder appraisal of Edward Everett than that which appears in the story of his meeting with a French prince. *The Life and Letters of Harrison Gray Otis* . . . (Boston, 1913) is a careful study of one mayor of the city by Samuel Eliot Morison; and the Papers and Correspondence of another, John Prescott Bigelow, are in H.C.L. Also in the H.C.L. is the correspondence of Charles Sumner whose pre-war career is most sympathetically treated in Archibald H. Grimké's *Life* . . . (New York, 1892). The campaign *Life of Henry Wilson* . . . (Boston, 1872) by Jonathan B. Mann is the only formal account; but there are large elements of the autobiographical in Wilson's *History of the Rise and Fall of the Slave Power in America* (Boston, 1872). Fred H. Harrington gives a very unsympathetic, though probably not unjust, account of "Nathaniel Prentiss Banks . . ." in the *New England Quarterly,* IX. Ben Butler has received no adequate discussion; one must still consult his *Autobiography* . . . (Boston, 1892). Henry Greenleaf Pearson's *Life of John A.*

Andrew . . . (Boston, 1904) is a thorough account of the Civil War governor.

BOSTON'S IMMIGRANTS have received occasional treatment and some of their prominent men have found biographers. James Bernard Cullen's *Story of the Irish in Boston* . . . (Boston, 1890) is a compilation of ill-assorted data on Irish institutions and personalities, but is the only work of its kind. The best studies refer to a later period. *Americans in Process* . . . (Boston, 1902) and *City Wilderness* . . . (Boston, 1898) are coöperative investigations of the South and West Ends of Boston at the opening of the Twentieth Century, edited by Robert A. Woods. They contain some material on the historical background but are permeated with a settlement house attitude toward their subjects. Frederick A. Bushee's *Ethnic Factors in the Population of Boston* . . . (New York, 1903) deals with the same period but is almost purely statistical and shows remarkably little insight. The life of Thomas D'Arcy McGee is narrated exhaustively but dully by Isabel Skelton (Gardenvale, 1924), and rapturously by Mrs. J. Sadlier in a "Biographical Sketch" that prefaces his *Poems* . . . (New York, 1869). Michael P. Curran's *Life of Patrick A. Collins* (Norwood, 1906) and James J. Roche's *Life of John Boyle O'Reilly* (Boston, 1891, with collected poems and speeches) deal with later immigrants of prominence. Andrew Carney, the only other Irishman to receive formal treatment, is the subject of a sketch by the Rev. G. C. Treacy in the *Historical Records and Studies* of the American Catholic Historical Society, XIII. Among the Germans, Karl Heinzen has written his own biography, *Erlebtes* . . . (Boston, 1874) and has been written about by Carl Wittke (Chicago, 1945).

Solomon Schindler is the subject of an article by Arthur Mann in the *New England Quarterly,* XXIII (1950), 457 ff.; and the physician Maria Zakrzewska gives the story of her life in *A Practical Illustration of "Woman's Right to Labor"* . . . , ed. by C. H. Dall (Boston, 1860). Lorenzo Papanti, the Italian dancing master, is described by Charles F. Reed in the *Proceedings of the Bostonian Society . . . 1928;* and the Negress, Mrs. Chloe Spear, is the subject of a *Memoir* . . . (Boston, 1832) by a "Lady of Boston."

Additional material on the Negroes may be found in George W. Crawford's monograph on *Prince Hall and His Followers* . . . (New York, 1914) and in the publications on Negro Masonry by Lewis Hayden. There is some data on Boston in W. H. Siebert's *Underground Railroad* . . . (New York, 1898), in Volumes Thirteen and Fourteen of the collection of his manuscripts in H.C.L., and in Charles H. Wesley's *Negro Labor in the United States* . . . (New York, 1927). Material on legal status may be found in Volume IV of Helen T. Catterall's *Judicial Cases Concerning American Slavery and the Negro* . . . (Washington, 1936).

For the story of the CATHOLIC CHURCH we now can turn to the splendid *History of the Archdiocese of Boston* (New York, 1944) by Robert H. Lord, John E. Sexton, and Edward T. Harrington. Earlier Catholic histories had been concerned primarily with specific institutions and with personalities, but within those limits had made a good deal of material available. The Rev. James Fitton's *Sketches of the Establishment of the Church in New England* (Boston, 1872) and the more ambitious *History of the Catholic Church in the New England States* (Boston, 1899), edited by the Very Rev.

Note on Sources

William Byrne and others, supplement John Gilmary Shea's detailed chronicle of the *History of the Catholic Church within the . . . United States . . .* (New York, 1886). Thomas D'Arcy McGee's *Catholic History of North America . . .* (Boston, 1855) has more value for light on its author than for its contributions to serious history. Within a narrower field, the Rev. Arthur J. Riley's temperate and scholarly *Catholicism in New England to 1788 . . .* (Washington, 1936) is one of the best works on any phase of the subject. There is material on the early history of the Church in Boston in the "Catholic Recollections" of Samuel Breck, *American Catholic Historical Researches,* XII; but the most careful account is given in E. Percival Merritt's "Sketches of the Three Earliest Roman Catholic Priests in Boston," *Publications of the Colonial Society of Massachusetts,* XXV. Bishop Fenwick is discussed in an article by Robert H. Lord in the *Catholic Historical Review,* XXII; and Bishop Fitzpatrick in one by Isaac T. Hecker in the *Catholic World,* XLV. Father Hecker himself is the subject of a penetrating biography by Vincent F. Holden (Washington, 1939) which gives a good account of the process of conversion. Arthur M. Schlesinger, Jr.'s *Orestes A. Brownson . . .* (Boston, 1939) is excellent for the early years but does not deal adequately with the issues of the Catholic period. For the latter it is still necessary to consult the pious biography by Brownson's son (Detroit, 1898) and the voluminous edition of the *Works of Orestes A. Brownson* (Detroit, 1882).

Few studies of the ANTI-CATHOLIC movement have dealt with it dispassionately. Most have regarded it as an inherent feature of American Protestant society and have zealously chronicled every reference to "Papists" without examining its true characteristics or causes. Sister Mary Augustina (Ray) in *American Opinion of Roman Catholicism in the Eighteenth Century* (New York, 1936), for instance, has patiently compiled a long list of such references without discriminating between those in which there was a real animus, those which were just thoughtless, and those in which the word was used with no more derogatory sense than "Methodist" or "Quaker."

Undoubtedly the best account of all phases of this movement is Ray Allen Billington's *Protestant Crusade, 1800–1860* . . . (New York, 1938), a conscientious and thorough work, although its conclusions are not always applicable to Boston. Billington unfortunately views the Know-Nothing movement purely from its anti-alien aspect and misses the significance of the reform issue which is hinted at in William G. Bean, "An Aspect of Know-Nothingism — the Immigrant and Slavery," *South Atlantic Quarterly,* XXIII, and Harry J. Carman and R. H. Luthin, "Some Aspects of the Know-Nothing Movement Reconsidered," *ibid.,* XXXIX. The material in Humphrey J. Desmond's study of the party (Washington, 1904) and in the four articles of George H. Haynes (*American Historical Review,* III, *New England Magazine,* XV, XVI, *Annual Report of the American Historical Association, 1896,* I) is distorted by the failure to understand the character of the movement in Massachusetts. Later aspects of nativism are treated in John Higham, *Strangers in the Land* (New Brunswick, 1955), and Charlotte Erickson, *American Industry and the European Immigrant* . . . (Cambridge, 1957).

NOTES

Notes

Foreword

[1] From the introduction to a projected epic, *The Emigrants*, by Thomas D'Arcy McGee (cf. *Poems* . . . [New York, 1869], 130).

[2] Charles Elmer Gehlke, *Émil Durkheim's Contributions to Sociological Theory* (Columbia University Studies in History, Economics and Public Law, LXIII, New York, 1915), 70.

Chapter I. Social Boston, 1790–1845

[1] Bronson Alcott in 1828 (Odell Shepard, *Journals of Bronson Alcott* [Boston, 1938], 15).

[2] In 1641. Quoted by Samuel Eliot Morison, *Maritime History of Massachusetts, 1783–1860* (Boston, 1921), 12. On this trade, cf. Arthur Meier Schlesinger, *Colonial Merchants and the American Revolution, 1763–1776* (New York, 1918), 22 ff.

[3] Cf. Robert Noxon Toppan, *Edward Randolph . . . a Memoir* (Publications of the Prince Society, Boston, 1898–1909), I, 78, 134 ff., III, 79; cf. also George Louis Beer, *Old Colonial System, 1660–1754* . . . (New York, 1912), II, 269, 284, 285; Schlesinger, *op. cit.,* 40 ff.

[4] Cf. George Louis Beer, *British Colonial Policy, 1754–1765* (New York, 1907), 220 ff., 277 ff.; Schlesinger, *op. cit.,* 57 ff.

[5] Beer, *British Colonial Policy,* 228 ff.; Schlesinger, *op. cit.,* 592 ff.

[6] For the revolutionary period and the years following, cf. Robert A. East, *Business Enterprise in the American Revolutionary Era* (New York, 1938), 49 ff.; Samuel Flagg Bemis, *Jay's Treaty, a Study in Commerce and Diplomacy* (New York, 1923), 23, 258; Theodore Lyman, Jr., *Diplomacy of the United States* . . . (Boston, 1828), II, 2, 12, 59 ff., 310 ff.; Morison, *op. cit.,* 174, n. 1; John D. Forbes, "Port of Boston, 1783–1815" (Harvard University Dissertation, 1937).

[7] *Dublin Chronicle,* January 12, 1792; cf. also *Brief Examination into the Increase of the Revenue, Commerce, and Navigation of Great Britain since the Conclusion of the Peace in 1783* (Dublin, 1792), 50; Bemis, *op. cit.,* 22, 24, 25; Justin Winsor, *Memorial History of Boston, Including Suffolk County, Massachusetts, 1630–1880* (Boston, 1881), IV, 202.

8 Cf. Morison, *op. cit.*, 30 ff.

9 *Ibid.*, 43 ff., 50–71; Edward G. Porter, "Ship Columbia and the Discovery of Oregon," *New England Magazine*, June, 1892, VI, 472 ff.; Winsor, *op. cit.*, IV, 204 ff.; La Rochefoucauld-Liancourt, *Voyage dans les États-Unis d'Amérique fait en 1795, 1796, et 1797* (Paris, An VII [1799]), III, 17.

10 *Independent Chronicle* (Boston), April 4, May 27, 1811; Morison, *op. cit.*, 154, 155; Winsor, *op. cit.*, IV, 223.

11 Morison, *op. cit.*, 275; R. B. Forbes, *Remarks on China and the China Trade* (Boston, 1844), 27.

12 Forbes, *op. cit.*, 28; Morison, *op. cit.*, 280 ff.; Winsor, *op. cit.*, IV, 221 ff.

13 La Rochefoucauld-Liancourt, *op. cit.*, V, 167.

14 Winsor, *op. cit.*, IV, 121 ff. For the canal and its effects, cf. Robert Greenhalgh Albion, *Rise of New York Port, [1815–1860]* . . . (New York, 1939), 76–94.

15 Winsor, *op. cit.*, IV, 111.

16 Henry Bradshaw Fearon, *Sketches of America, a Narrative of a Journey* . . . (London, 1818), 109; John Robert Godely, *Letters from America* (London, 1844), I, 17; Oscar Handlin, Ph.D. dissertation, 1940, Harvard College Library, Cambridge, Massachusetts, 10, n. 37, hereafter referred to as Dissertation Copy. Albion stresses the importance of geographical position and the establishment of the packet lines in explaining the preëminence of New York (Albion, *op. cit.*, 16–54). But Boston's position was fully as advantageous as that of New York (cf. *ibid.*, 24–37; Edwin J. Clapp, *Port of Boston* . . . [New Haven, 1916], 21 ff.), and the failure of the packets to develop in Boston was itself the result of the lack of hinterland (cf. Albion, *op. cit.*, 46; *infra*, 299, n. 21).

17 Cf. Edward Everett, "The Western Railroad" (1835), *Orations and Speeches on Various Occasions* (Boston, 1850), II, 144 ff.; Edward Everett, "Opening of the Railroad to Springfield" (1839), *ibid.*, II, 367 ff.; Christopher Roberts, *Middlesex Canal, 1793–1860* (Cambridge, 1938), 19 ff.; Winsor, *op. cit.*, IV, 112–116.

18 "Report of the Select Committee of the House of Representatives . . . on the . . . Expediency of Constructing a Railway . . . to . . . Albany," *Massachusetts House Documents, 1826–27*, no. 13, p. 28.

19 Winsor, *op. cit.*, IV, 126, 129, 138 ff.; Morison, *op. cit.*, 230. Hopes that Boston might share in the great western trade when the completion of the Vermont Central Railroad gave her a direct connection with Canada were never realized; Canadian rail traffic failed to grow significantly in this period ([E. S. Chesbrough], *Tabular Representation of the Present Condition of Boston, in Relation to Railroad Facilities* . . . [Boston, 1851], 25, 26; Grattan to Clarendon, July 10, 1853, British Consular Correspond-

ence, F.O. 5/568; [Otis Clapp], *Letter to the Hon. Abbott Lawrence . . . on the Present Condition and Future Growth of Boston* [Boston, 1853], 4). On the development of transportation, *see also* Edward C. Kirkland, *Men, Cities and Transportation* (Cambridge, 1948); Oscar and Mary F. Handlin, *Commonwealth: A Study of the Role of Government in the American Economy, Massachusetts 1774–1861* (New York, 1947), 108 ff., 115 ff., 185 ff.

²⁰ For the growth of the coastwide trade, cf. Dissertation Copy, 12, n. 45; also E. H. Derby, "Commercial Cities and Towns of the United States — no. XXII — . . . Boston," *Hunt's Merchants' Magazine and Commercial Review*, November, 1850, XXIII, 490.

²¹ Morison, *op. cit.*, 299. Transatlantic trade gravitated towards New York, however, particularly after the establishment of the Black Ball Line in 1816. Similar lines failed in Boston in 1818, 1822, and 1827 because of "the difficulty in obtaining return freights of sufficient amounts" (Consul Grattan, enclosure, May 15, 1844, British Consular Correspondence, F.O. 5/411, no. 12; Morison, *op. cit.*, 232 ff.; Albion, *op. cit.*, 46; H. A. Hill, "Boston and Liverpool Packet Lines . . . ," *New England Magazine*, January, 1894, IX, 549 ff.). Only in the Mediterranean trade did Boston hold a commanding position (Morison, *op. cit.*, 287, 292; statistics in Neapolitan Consular Correspondence, Reale Archivio di Stato, Politica, fasc. 2415, package 63).

²² John Macgregor, *Progress of America . . .* (London, 1847), II, 176; Winsor, *op. cit.*, IV, 229; Morison, *op. cit.*, 228; Albion, *op. cit.*, 63, 241 ff.; Robert G. Albion, "Yankee Domination of New York Port, 1820–1865," *New England Quarterly*, October, 1932, V. 665 ff.

²³ For statements of tonnage, cf. Dissertation Copy, 15, 414; Morison, *op. cit.*, 378; Macgregor, *op. cit.*, II, 170 ff.; Chesbrough, *op. cit.*, 16.

²⁴ Consul Manners to Lord Palmerston, June 10, 1832, British Consular Correspondence (F.O. America, II Series), F.O. 5/276, no. 10, p. 2.

²⁵ Winsor, *op. cit.*, IV, 96, 153.

²⁶ Cf. *Boston Directory, 1789*, 50; *Boston Directory, 1800*, 7; Margaret H. Foulds, "Massachusetts Bank, 1784–1865," *Journal of Economic and Business History*, February, 1930, II, 256 ff.; Albert Bushnell Hart, *Commonwealth History of Massachusetts* (New York, 1929), III, 363 ff.

²⁷ Cf. "Report of the List of Incorporations . . . Granted by the Legislature of Massachusetts . . . ," *Massachusetts Senate Documents, 1836*, no. 90, pp. 47–54; *Massachusetts House Documents, 1840*, no. 60, pp. 13–16; and Dissertation Copy, Table II, 415; Macgregor, *op. cit.*, II, 154; Winsor, *op. cit.*, IV, 164; *Massachusetts Senate Documents, 1838*, no. 38, pp. 5 ff.; *Daily Evening Transcript* (Boston), March 2, 1830.

²⁸ *Massachusetts House Documents, 1840*, no. 60, p. 29; cf. also Winsor,

op. cit., IV, 104 ff., 190 ff.; Derby, *loc. cit.*, 488. For complaints by manufacturers against this financial control, cf. E. B. Bigelow, *Remarks on the Depressed Condition of Manufactures in Massachusetts* . . . (Boston, 1858), 18, 19.

[29] Chesbrough, *op. cit.*, 6 ff.

[30] This is indicated by the professional composition of the population of Boston in 1789, an approximate, though of course, not exact conception of which may be derived from the number of listings in the directory of 1789 classifiable into each of the following groups:

Merchants	183	Marine industries	89
Brokers	31	Mariners	49
Professionals	142	Unskilled laborers	16
Shopkeepers, skilled craftsmen	331	Innkeepers	68
Artisans	501	Unknown	66
		TOTAL	1,476

Total number of families in Boston 3,343

(Tabulated from *Boston Directory* . . . [Boston, 1789], passim. For the number of families cf. S. N. D. North, *Heads of Families at the First Census* . . . *1790, Massachusetts* [Washington, 1908], 10.) Contemporary evidence (analyzed in Dissertation Copy, 20 ff., n. 61) supports this point of view; and the occupational distribution of the city's population seems not to have changed substantially in the next half century. The federal census of 1820 showed 2,905 engaged in manufactures, 2,499 in commerce and 192 in agriculture in Suffolk County in a total population of 43,940 (United States Census, *Aggregate Amount of* . . . *Persons in the United States* . . . *1820* [s.l.,n.d. (Washington, 1820)], 7) while that of 1840 showed, in the city of Boston alone, 5,333 employed in manufactures and trade, 2,040 in commerce, 586 in the learned professions and 10,831 in navigation (the last figure undoubtedly too high, cf. *Massachusetts House Documents, 1842*, no. 48, p. 1; *Massachusetts House Documents, 1849*, no. 127, pp. 6 ff.).

[31] Cf. Morison, *op. cit.*, 101, 103, 330.

[32] See Table I, *supra*, 238.

[33] Total of the towns included in this table, *see supra*, Table II, 239. This has always been true.

[34] C. Bancroft Gillespie, *Illustrated History of South Boston* . . . (South Boston, 1900), 110–112; Lura Woodside Watkins, *Cambridge Glass, 1818 to 1888, The Story of the New England Glass Company* (Boston, [1930], 4, 7, 182; [Anne Royall], *Sketches of History* . . . (New Haven, 1826), 341.

[35] Harriet Martineau, *Society in America* (New York, 1837), II, 59.

[36] *Eighty Years Progress of the United States: a Family Record of American Industry* . . . (Hartford, 1869), 324; Winsor, *op. cit.,* IV, 99.

[37] Cf. *Daily Evening Transcript,* September 25, 30, 1830; *Boston Pilot,* August 30, 1856; Benevolent Fraternity of Churches, *Twenty-Second Annual Report of the Executive Committee* . . . (Boston, 1856), 26.

[38] *Address of the American Society for the Encouragement of Domestic Manufactures to the People of the United States* (New York, 1817), 11, 14. Cf. also Arthur Harrison Cole, *American Wool Manufacture* (Cambridge, 1926), I, 86 ff.

[39] Raymond McFarland, *History of the New England Fisheries* . . . (New York, 1911), 129 ff., 187; Morison, *op. cit.,* 31, 150, 375.

[40] Derby, *loc. cit.,* 496.

[41] This by no means implies that the wealth of Boston was declining. On the contrary, the assessed value of its property rose steadily from $42,140,200 in 1822 to $135,948,700 in 1845, while the valuation of its suburbs in 1840 totalled some $15,000,000 (Nathan Matthews, *City Government of Boston* [Boston, 1895], 190, 191; Derby, *loc. cit.,* 485; Chesbrough, *op. cit.,* 20, 21).

[42] Cf. Jesse Chickering, "Report of the Committee . . . 1850," *Boston City Documents, 1851,* no. 60, pp. 24 ff.; *Historical Review and Directory of North America . . . by a Gentleman Immediately Returned from a Tour* . . . (Cork, 1801), II, 63; *infra,* Table II. For the movement away from rural New England, cf. Percy Wells Bidwell, "Rural Economy in New England at the Beginning of the Nineteenth Century," *Transactions of the Connecticut Academy of Arts and Sciences,* April, 1916, XX, 383–391; for the absence of foreign immigration, cf. Josiah Quincy, *Figures of the Past from the Leaves of Old Journals* (Boston, 1883), 112; [James W. Hale], *Old Boston Town . . . by an 1801-er* . . . (New York, 1880), 34; John Stetson Barry, *History of Massachusetts* . . . (Boston, 1857), III, 372; [William Tudor], *Letters on the Eastern States* (New York, 1820), 315; Timothy Dwight, *Travels in New England* . . . (New Haven, 1821), I, 506.

[43] Cf. Francis S. Drake, *Town of Roxbury . . . Its History and Antiquities* . . . (Boston, 1905), 345; Robert A. Woods, *City Wilderness* . . . (Boston, 1898), 23 ff.; State Street Trust Company, *Boston, England and Boston, New England* . . . (Boston, 1930), 12 ff.; Dissertation Copy, 26, 177; George H. McCaffrey, Political Disintegration and Reintegration of Metropolitan Boston (MS., H. C. L.), 189 ff.; Winsor, *op. cit.,* IV, 25–33, 46. For a perspective of the extent of these operations, cf. the maps for 1789, 1800, 1820, and 1848, cited in Boston, Engineering Department, *List*

of Maps of Boston . . . (*Annual Report of the City Engineer, February 1, 1903*, Appendix I, Boston, 1903), 79, 84, 95, 125.

⁴⁴ Derby, *loc. cit.*, 484 ff.; "Report and Tabular Statement of the Censors . . . ," *Boston City Documents, 1850*, no. 42, pp. 13, 39; Josiah Curtis, *Report of the Joint Special Committee* . . . (Boston, 1856), 4; *Courrier des États-Unis* (New York), June 28, 1850. For the difference in rents, cf. Consul Manners to the Undersecretary of State, March 10, 1832, British Consular Correspondence (F.O. America, II Series), F.O. 5/276, no. 6.

⁴⁵ Edward H. Savage, *Boston Events . . . from 1630 to 1880* . . . (Boston, 1884), 7; Thomas C. Simonds, *History of South Boston* . . . (Boston, 1857), 72 ff.; Boston Common Council, "South Boston Memorial . . . April 22, 1847," *Boston City Documents, 1847*, no. 18, p. 5; Samuel Eliot Morison, *Life and Letters of Harrison Gray Otis* . . . (Boston, 1913), I, 243; Dissertation Copy, 28, n. 89; McCaffrey, *op. cit.*, 182 ff.; Winsor, *op. cit.*, IV, 30, 38–40.

⁴⁶ McCaffrey, *op. cit.*, 53 ff., 196 ff.; Winsor, *op. cit.*, III, 284, IV, 25; Hon. Ellis W. Morton, *Annexation of Charlestown . . . a Condensed Report of the Argument* . . . *February 27, 1871* (Boston, 1871), 5.

⁴⁷ For Boston's relationship to these towns, cf. McCaffrey, *op. cit.*, 147 ff., 170 ff.; "Report of Standing Committee on Towns . . . ," *Massachusetts Senate Documents, 1851*, no. 82, pp. 2, 3, 9 ff.; Winsor, *op. cit.*, III, 275, IV, 26, 41; D. Hamilton Hurd, *History of Norfolk County* . . . (Philadelphia, 1884), 72, 73; John Hayward, *Gazeteer of Massachusetts . . . with a Great Variety of Other Useful Information (Revised Edition)* (Boston, 1849), 41; P. Tocque, *Peep at Uncle Sam's Farm, Workshop, Fisheries, &c.* (Boston, 1851), 20. For the population of all these towns, cf. *infra*, Table II.

⁴⁸ [Hale], *op. cit.*, 29; E. Mackenzie, *Historical . . . View of the United States* . . . (Newcastle upon Tyne, 1819), 103; Van Wyck Brooks, *Flowering of New England, 1815–1865* (New York, 1936), 11, n.; *Wide Awake: and the Spirit of Washington* (Boston), October 7, 1854; Benevolent Fraternity of Churches, *Eleventh Annual Report of the Executive Committee* . . . (Boston, 1845), 27; and *Tenth Annual Report of the Executive Committee* . . . (Boston, 1844), 25.

⁴⁹ Cf. Sándor Farkas, *Útazás Észak Amerikában* (KOLOZSVAR, 1834), 91.

⁵⁰ William Priest, *Travels in the United States* . . . (Boston, 1802), 168.

⁵¹ Boston Board of Health, Records, 1799–1824 (MSS., B. P. L.), I.

⁵² *Rules, Regulations and Orders of the Boston Board of Health Relative to the Police of the Town* . . . (s.l., 1821), 5, 6, 8–16; Boston Board of Health, Records, II.

⁵³ Cf. Robert A. Woods, ed., *Americans in Process* . . . (Boston, 1902), 74.

⁵⁴ *Rules, Regulations and Orders* . . . , 2, 5, 6; and Board of Health Records, IV; also Joseph B. Egan, *Citizenship in Boston* . . . (Philadelphia, n.d. [1925]), 264; Woods, *Americans in Process*, 73.

⁵⁵ Cf. [Theodore Lyman, Jr.], *Communication to the City Council on the Subject of Introducing Water into the City* . . . (Boston, 1834), passim; Winsor, *op. cit.*, III, 252.

⁵⁶ Cf., e.g., Boston City Council, *Report of the Committee* . . . *on the Powers* . . . *of the Overseers* . . . (Boston, 1825), 3 ff.; Winsor, *op. cit.*, III, 221.

⁵⁷ Winsor, *op. cit.*, III, 218 ff.; James M. Bugbee, *City Government of Boston* (Baltimore, 1887), 19 ff.

⁵⁸ Edward H. Savage, *Police Records and Recollections; or Boston by Daylight and Gaslight* . . . (Boston, 1873), 84, 94 ff.

⁵⁹ Cf. Josiah Quincy, *Municipal History of* . . . *Boston* . . . (Boston, 1852), 160; Arthur Wellington Brayley, *Complete History of the Boston Fire Department* . . . (Boston, 1889), 144 ff., 149, 150 ff.; *Boston City Documents, 1873*, no. 97.

⁶⁰ In this period, expenditures on streets rose from $30,000 in 1829 to $180,000 in 1847, on the fire department from $14,000 to $57,000, on constables from $1,500 to $55,000, and on lighting from nothing to $31,000 (Boston Common Council, "Annual Appropriations, 1846–47," *Boston City Documents, 1846*, no. 15, pp. 8 ff.; Josiah Quincy, *Report of the Committee of Appropriations, Boston* [Boston, 1828], 4, 5).

⁶¹ For an estimate of the number of vehicles entering and leaving Boston, cf. Dissertation Copy, 36, n. 120; *Bowen's Boston News-Letter and City Record*, October 14, 1826.

⁶² For a list of these lines cf. Peleg W. Chandler, *Charter and Ordinances of* . . . *Boston* . . . *with the Acts of the Legislature Relating to the City* . . . (Boston, 1850), 68 ff.; cf. also Francis S. Drake, *Town of Roxbury* . . . *Its History and Antiquities* . . . (Boston, 1905), 51; *Bowen's Boston News-Letter and City Record*, February 25, April 29, 1826.

⁶³ Cf. the timetables in George Adams, *Brighton and Brookline Business Directory* . . . (Boston, 1850), 20, 22, 24, 28; Chandler, *op. cit.*, 64 ff.; Tocque, *op. cit.*, 14; Nathaniel Dearborn, *Boston Notions* . . . (Boston, 1848), 221.

⁶⁴ Lemuel Shattuck, *Report to the Committee of the City Council* . . . *Census of Boston for* . . . *1845* . . . (Boston, 1846), 113. Cf. also Sir Charles Lyell, *A Second Visit to the United States of North America* (London, 1849), I, 186; and the remarkable failure of expenditures on paupers to rise in Boston over a period of a quarter-century (cf. *infra*, Table III).

⁶⁵ Dissertation Copy, 39 ff.

⁶⁶ Cf. e.g., [John Gallison], *Explanation of the Views of the Society*

. . . (Cambridge, 1825), 3; Leah Hannah Feder, *Unemployment Relief in Periods of Depression* . . . (New York, 1936), 20; Benevolent Fraternity of Churches, *Act of Incorporation and By-Laws* . . . (Boston, 1859), 4.

[67] Martineau, *op. cit.,* II, 290; also the letter of Father Ambrose Manahan, *Boston Pilot,* April 19, 1851; Winsor, *op. cit.,* IV, 647–649, 672 ff.; *infra,* Table III; Dissertation Copy, 39.

[68] Cf. Table IV, *infra;* D. B. Warden, *Statistical, Political, and Historical Account of the United States* . . . (Edinburgh, 1819), I, 304; "Report of the Attorney-General, 1834," *Massachusetts House Documents, 1834,* no. 4, p. 11.

[69] N. H. Julius, *Nordamerikas sittliche Zustände nach eigenen Anschauungen in den Jahren 1834, 1835 und 1836* (Leipzig, 1839), II, 66, and Tables 2, 3, 9, 12.

[70] Cf. Capt. Marryatt, *A Diary in America with Remarks on Its Institutions* (New York, 1839), 168; also Julius, *op. cit.,* II, Table 11.

[71] Cf. "Report of the City Marshal," quoted in Benevolent Fraternity of Churches, *Twelfth Annual Report of the Executive Committee* . . . (Boston, 1846), 15.

[72] Benevolent Fraternity of Churches, *Twelfth Annual Report of the Executive Committee* . . . (Boston, 1846), 30. Cf. also Savage, *Police Records and Recollections,* 182; Boston Female Society for Missionary Purposes, *A Brief Account* . . . *with Extracts from the Reports* . . . (Boston, n.d.), 15, 16 ff.

[73] Disease and epidemics were rare. Between 1811 and 1820 there were only six cases of smallpox, between 1821 and 1830, only seven. Thereafter the number increased but was unusually large only in 1840 (cf. *supra,* 114).

[74] Ralph Waldo Emerson, "Nature," *Complete Works* . . . (Boston, 1903), I, 40. Cf. also Handlin, *Commonwealth,* 202 ff.

[75] W. H. Channing, *Gospel of Today, a Discourse* . . . *at the Ordination of T. W. Higginson* . . . (Boston, 1847), 11. For reforms, cf. Arthur B. Darling, *Political Changes in Massachusetts, 1824–1848* . . . (New Haven, 1925), 157 ff.; *Daily Evening Transcript,* October 2, 1830; A. B. Hart. *Commonwealth History of Massachusetts* (New York, 1929), III, 518, IV, 273 ff.

[76] Channing, *op. cit.,* 26.

[77] Edward Everett Hale, quoted in M. A. DeWolfe Howe, *Holmes of the Breakfast Table* (New York, 1939), 42.

[78] Cf. Farkas, *op. cit.,* 90, 102, 127.

[79] Cf. *Independent Chronicle,* September 6, 1810; Elizabeth Brett White, *American Opinion of France from Lafayette to Poincaré* (New York, 1927), 86, 119; *supra,* 140, 141, 153, 154; Hart, *op. cit.,* IV, 116.

[80] Cf. Morison, *Maritime History,* 24; Nathan Matthews, *City Government of Boston* (Boston, 1895), 171.

[81] Emerson, *op. cit.,* I, 37.

[82] Theodore Parker, *Sermon of the Moral Condition of Boston . . .* (Boston, 1849), 4.

[83] D. R. Burden to Thomas Russell, July 5, 1796, Russell Correspondence (MSS., T. C. D.), II. Cf. also Consul Manners to Lord Palmerston, June 10, 1832, British Consular Correspondence, F.O. 5/276, no. 10, p. 2.

[84] Cf., e.g., Farkas, *op. cit.,* 122.

[85] *Bowen's Boston News-Letter and City Record,* April 15, 1826.

[86] Dearborn, *Boston Notions,* 200, 201.

[87] Archibald H. Grimké, *Life of Charles Sumner . . .* (New York, 1892), 58 ff. Cf. also, Frank Luther Mott, *History of American Magazines, 1850–1865* (Cambridge, 1938), 228, 229; *supra,* 124. For German influences cf. Brooks, *op. cit.,* 191, 192; Darling, *op. cit.,* 31; Henry Steele Commager, *Theodore Parker* (Boston, 1936), 45, 95 ff.; for French, Howe, *op. cit.,* 36; and for English, *Independent Chronicle,* August 29, 1811; Lieut. Col. A. M. Maxwell, *Run Through the United States . . . 1840* (London, 1841), I, 46.

[88] Ezra S. Gannett, *Arrival of the Britannia, a Sermon . . . Federal Street Meeting-House . . . July 19, 1840 . . .* (Boston, 1840), 16, 17.

[89] John Lambert, *Travels through Lower Canada and the United States . . . 1806 . . .* (London, 1810), III, 118 ff.; Priest, *op. cit.,* 157; Morison, *Harrison Gray Otis,* I, 37, 218 ff.

[90] Cf. *Independent Chronicle,* January 4, 1810.

[91] Cf. Winsor, *op. cit.,* IV, 415 ff.; *supra,* 147; and the advertisements in *Daily Evening Transcript,* 1831, and *Boston Musical Gazette . . . ,* May 2, 1838.

Chapter II. The Process of Arrival

[1] "Native Poet [Oliver Goldsmith]," in "Traveller," as quoted in Hibernicus, *Practical Views and Suggestions on the Present Condition . . . of Ireland . . .* (Dublin, 1823), 117.

[2] Benevolent Fraternity of Churches (Boston), *Twenty-Sixth Annual Report of the Executive Committee . . . 1860* (Boston, 1860), 8. For examples of each of the nationalities cited, cf. Dissertation Copy, 51–53, and the references there cited.

[3] Cf. a bundle of correspondence on this subject in Reale Archivio di Stato, Naples, Politica, Fasc. I, package 17. For Norwegian deserters, cf. Theodore C. Blegen, *Norwegian Migration to America, 1825–1860* (Northfield, Minnesota, 1931), 331.

⁴ For a list of merchants, cf., "British Mercantile Houses Established in Boston," Grattan to Bidwell, November 30, 1848, British Consular Correspondence, F.O. 5/488, no. 6, enclosures; also La Rochefoucauld-Liancourt, *Voyage dans les États-Unis d'Amérique* . . . (Paris, An VII [1799]), III, 139. For some Scotch merchants, cf. Ethel S. Bolton, ed., *Topliff's Travels, Letters from Abroad in the Years 1828 and 1829* . . . (Boston, 1906), 15, 16. For the Marquis Niccolo Reggio and other Italian merchants, cf. *Boston Pilot,* July 11, 1846; Giovanni Schiavo, *Italians in America before the Civil War* . . . (New York, 1934), 226; Reale Archivio di Stato, Naples, Politica, Fasc. I, package 15; Leone Carpi, *Delle Colonie e dell' emigrazione d'Italiani all'estero* . . . (Milano, 1874), II, 230 ff.

⁵ Baker to Consul Skinner, January 14, 1817, British Embassy Archives, F.O. 115/27, f. 185; Joseph Jennings to Chargé d'Affaires, August 18, 1832, British Consular Correspondence, F.O. 5/277.

⁶ Cf. Fernand Baldensperger, *Mouvement des idées dans l'émigration française* . . . (Paris, 1924), I, iii; Leo Gershoy, *French Revolution and Napoleon* (New York, 1933), 131; Emmanuel Vingtrinier, *La Contre-Révolution* . . . (Paris, 1924), I, 36, 37, II, 269; Dissertation Copy, 55, 56.

⁷ Cf. R. R. Madden, *United Irishmen, Their Lives and Times, Newly Edited* (New York, 1916), II, 30 ff., 101, 261, III, 10; R. R. Madden, *Connexion between . . . Ireland and England* . . . (Dublin, 1845), 116, 132; Marcus Lee Hansen, *Atlantic Migration, 1607–1860* . . . (Cambridge, 1940), 65, 66; R. R. Madden, *Life and Times of Robert Emmet* (New York, 1856), 59 ff.

⁸ Cf. Ernest Bruncken, *German Political Refugees in the United States* . . . (s.l., 1904), 11, 12; *Report of the Select Committee of the Legislative Assembly Appointed to Inquire into the Causes . . . of the Emigration . . . from Lower Canada to the United States* . . . (Montreal, 1849), 5; Marcus Lee Hansen, *Mingling of the Canadian and American Peoples* . . . (New Haven, 1940), 115 ff.; Hansen, *Atlantic Migration,* 122 ff.

⁹ Cf. Max J. Kohler, "Right of Asylum with Particular Reference to the Alien," *American Law Review,* LI (May, June, 1917), 384, 399–401.

¹⁰ Vingtrinier, *op. cit.,* I, 69; M. F. de Montrol, *Histoire de l'émigration* . . . (Paris, 1827), 45, 104, 273, 283, 305; Le Comte de Sainte-Colombe, *Catalogue des émigrés français à Fribourg* . . . (Lyon, 1884), passim; Charles Robert, "Les Émigrés Bretons . . . ," *Revue de Bretagne, de Vendée & d'Anjou* . . . , Juin, 1898, XIX, 427 ff.

¹¹ Thomas Atkinson, *Hibernian Eclogues* . . . (Dublin, 1791), 14; Madden, *United Irishmen,* III, 295, IV, 151; Thomas Addis Emmet, *Memoir of Thomas Addis and Robert Emmet* (New York, 1915), II, 61–80.

¹² Otto Wiltberger, *Die deutschen politischen Flüchtlinge in Strassburg,*

1830–1849 (Berlin, 1909), 8 ff.; Karl Heinzen, *Erlebtes. zweiter Theil: nach meiner Exilirung* (*Gesammelte Schriften, vierter Band*) (Boston, 1874), 54, 326, 328, 356.

[13] Alvin R. Calman, *Ledru-Rollin après 1848 et les proscrits français en Angleterre* (Paris, 1921), 35, 93, 105.

[14] Cf. e.g., Heinzen, *op. cit.*, 455.

[15] George Ticknor Curtis, *Rights of Conscience* . . . (Boston, 1842), 18.

[16] Baldensperger, *op. cit.*, I, 105, n. 1; Frances S. Childs, *French Refugee Life in the United States* . . . (Baltimore, 1940), passim.

[17] F. B., "Le Séjour de Brillat-Savarin aux États-Unis," *Revue de Littérature Comparée*, II (1922), 95; Howard Mumford Jones, *America and French Culture, 1750–1848* (Chapel Hill, 1927), 304; J. G. Rosengarten, *French Colonists and Exiles in the United States* (Philadelphia, 1907), 103; Samuel Adams Drake, *Old Landmarks . . . of Boston . . .* (Boston, 1873), 270, 271.

[18] Cf. *Boston Selectmen Minutes from 1787 through 1798* (*Report of Record Commissioners of the City of Boston, XXVII*), *Boston City Documents, 1896*, no. 81, pp. 271, 272; Jackson to Canning, November 19, 1809, British Consular Correspondence, F.O. 5/64, no. 20; MacDonough to Grenville, July 24, 1794, *ibid.*, F.O. 5/6; Francis S. Drake, *Town of Roxbury . . . Its History and Antiquities . . .* (Boston, 1905), 123, 124; Baldensperger, *op. cit.*, I, 107 ff.; Edmund Patten, *Glimpse at the United States . . .* (London, 1853), 14; Jones, *op. cit.*, 135, 167.

[19] Cf., e.g., letters to the Mayor of Boston asking for aid from A. A. Dieffenbach, "stud. theolog." of Berlin, September 18, 1850, and from F. Guillerez, December 13, 1849 (John Prescott Bigelow Papers, 1723–1865 [MSS., H. C. L.], Box VI); Henry Steele Commager, *Theodore Parker* (Boston, 1936), 111 ff.

[20] Bruncken, *op. cit.*, 13; A. B. Faust, *German Element in the United States . . .* (New York, 1927), II, 214 ff.

[21] Heinzen, *op. cit.*, 503; Carl Wittke, *Against the Current* (Chicago, 1945).

[22] Walter Coxe to Thomas Finn, December 14, 1816 in Dr. R. Robert Madden, "Collection of Papers on the History of the United Irishmen, 1790–1832" (MSS., T. C. D.), I; *Irish-American* (New York), May 30, 1857, June 11, 1853.

[23] *Daily Evening Transcript*, November 11, 12, 1831; Samuel A. Drake, *op. cit.*, 264; *Boston Pilot*, February 2, 1856, June 12, 1852, December 10, 1853.

[24] Robert R. Kuczynski, *Population Movements* (Oxford, 1936), 23.

[25] A. M. Carr-Saunders, *World Population* . . . (Oxford, 1936), 30; Walter F. Willcox, ed., *International Migrations*, II (New York, 1931),

49, 78; Donald H. Taft, *Human Migration* . . . (New York, 1936), 86; A. M. Carr-Saunders, *Population Problem, a Study in Human Evolution* (Oxford, 1922), 298–300, 308; Oscar Handlin, *The Uprooted* (Boston, 1951).

[26] Cf. Robert Holditch, *Emigrant's Guide to the United States of America* . . . (London, 1818), 40; Grenville to Hammond, April 15, 1795, British Embassy Archives, F.O. 115/4; Manners to Castlereagh, November 27, 1818, British Consular Correspondence, F.O. 5/135; Hansen, *Atlantic Migration,* 97; [John Talbot], *History of North America* . . . *Including* . . . *Information on* . . . *Emigrating to That Country* (Leeds, 1820), II, 316; Carr-Saunders, *World Population,* 182.

[27] *Boston Merkur,* December 26, 1846; A. H. Simpson to W. S. O'Brien, July 17, 1840 (W. S. O'Brien Papers and Letters, 1819–1854, MSS., N. L. I.), VI, no. 749); also letters from Scotch weavers in 1840 and 1841 *(ibid.,* VI, nos. 737, 739, 777); Edwin C. Guillet, *The Great Migration* . . . (New York, 1937), 29.

[28] John Harold Clapham, *Economic Development of France and Germany* . . . (Cambridge, 1928), 87; Gustav Schmoller, *Zur Geschichte der deutschen Kleingewerbe im 19. Jahrhundert* (Halle, 1870), 661, 671; Eugen von Philippovich, ed., *Auswanderung und Auswanderungspolitik in Deutschland* . . . (Liepzig, 1892), 110.

[29] Schmoller, *op. cit.,* 105, 110.

[30] Cf. Marcus L. Hansen, "Revolutions of 1848 and German Emigration," *Journal of Economic and Business History,* II (1930), 656.

[31] Cf. George O'Brien, *Economic History of Ireland in the Seventeenth Century* (Dublin, 1919), 118, 119, 221; George O'Brien, *Economic History of Ireland in the Eighteenth Century* (Dublin, 1918), 269 ff.; George O'Brien, *Economic History of Ireland from the Union to the Famine* (London, 1921), 297 ff., 415 ff.; William Forbes Adams, *Ireland and Irish Emigration to the New World from 1815 to the Famine* . . . (New Haven, 1932), 57; J. Dunsmore Clarkson, *Labour and Nationalism in Ireland* (New York, 1925), 23.

[32] [Rev. Gilbert Austin], *Charity Sermon for the Sick and Indigent Roomkeepers Preached at St. Peter's, Dublin* . . . *February 19, 1797* . . . (Dublin, 1797), 29; cf. also (Rev. William Hickey), *State of the Poor of Ireland* . . . (Carlow, 1820), 20; Clarkson, *op. cit.,* 58, 59, 101, 106. For a list of industries in the neighborhood of Dublin which were ruined and whose "protestant inhabitants fled to America," cf., *A Freeman's Letter to the Right Hon. Robert Peel on the Present State of the City of Dublin* . . . (Dublin, n.d.), 8, 9.

[33] William Warren, *Political and Moral Pamphlet* . . . *Addressed to the* . . . *Lord Lieutenant* . . . (Cork, 1797), 6; *The Causes of Discon-*

tents in Ireland, and Remedies Proposed . . . (s.l., n.d. [Dublin, 1823]),
46; *Statement of the Proceedings of the Western Committee for the Relief
of the Irish Poor* . . . (London, 1831), 37.

³⁴ For the whole problem, cf. Elie Halévy, *History of the English
People* . . . (Harmondsworth, 1937), I, Bk. II, 31 ff., 37 ff., 58 ff., 70 ff.;
J. L. and Barbara Hammond, *Village Labourer, 1760–1832* . . . (London,
1912), 71.

³⁵ Stanley C. Johnson, *History of Emigration from the United Kingdom to North America* . . . (London, 1913), 16; A. M. Carr-Saunders,
Population (London, 1925), 8.

³⁶ Cf. Paul Mantoux, *Industrial Revolution of the Eighteenth Century*
(New York, 1928), 186.

³⁷ Cf. Max Sering, *Deutsche Agrarpolitik* . . . (Leipzig, 1934), 26; also
Clapham, *op. cit.,* 30 and the end map, "German Empire — Agrarian."

³⁸ Cf. Florence Edith Janson, *Background of Swedish Immigration,
1840–1930* (Chicago, 1931), 43 ff.

³⁹ Cf. Willcox, *op. cit.,* II, 315, 341; Hansen, *Atlantic Migration,* 211 ff.;
Blegen, *op. cit.,* 82, 123, 168 ff.; Janson, *op. cit.,* 40, 55 56; Robert R.
Kuczynski, *Balance of Births and Deaths* (New York, 1928), I, 98, 99.

⁴⁰ Janson, *op. cit.,* 49 ff., 14; Blegen, *op. cit.,* 19.

⁴¹ Imre Ferenczi, *International Migrations,* I (New York, 1929), 116;
Willcox, *op. cit.,* II, 342, 347.

⁴² For the slow growth of German industry, cf. Clapham, *op. cit.,* 86 ff.

⁴³ Cf. Philippovich, *op. cit.,* 6, 111; René Le Conte, *La Politique de
l'Allemagne en matière d'émigration* (Paris, 1921), 7, 9 ff.

⁴⁴ Ferenczi, *op. cit.,* I, 114 ff.; Marcus Lee Hansen, Emigration from
Continental Europe, 1815–1850 . . . (MS., H. C. L.), Chapter I, part 2;
Hansen, *Atlantic Migration,* 79 ff.

⁴⁵ For the status of agriculture in these years, cf. Sigmund Fleischmann, *Die Agrarkrisis von 1845–1855* . . . (Heidelberg, 1902), passim;
Philippovich, *op. cit.,* 77; Willcox, *op. cit.,* II, 316; Hansen, *Atlantic Migration,* 252 ff.

⁴⁶ Maurice R. Davie, *World Immigration* . . . (New York, 1936), 69;
for the development of German railways, cf. Clapham, *op. cit.,* 150 ff.

⁴⁷ Willcox, *op. cit.,* II, 333; E. Tonnelat, *L'Expansion allemande hors
d'Europe* . . . (Paris, 1908), 88.

⁴⁸ René Gonnard, *L'Emigration européène au XIXᵉ siècle* . . . (Paris,
1906), 99; Hansen, *loc. cit.,* 632.

⁴⁹ D. F. Donnant, *Statistical Account of the United States of America*
(transl. . . . by William Playfair . . . , London, 1805), 21; O'Brien,
Union to the Famine, 213; Guillet, *op. cit.,* 43 ff.; Hansen, *Atlantic Migration,* 83, 89.

[50] W. Faux, *Memorable Days in America . . . a Journal of a Tour to the United States . . .* (London, 1823), 29.

[51] Blegen, *op. cit.,* 97, 147, 344; cf. also Whitely Stokes, *Projects for Re-establishing the Internal Peace . . . of Ireland . . .* (Dublin, 1799), 12; Charles Norton, *Der treue Führer des Auswanderers nach den Vereinigten Staaten von Nord-Amerika . . .* (Regensburg, 1848), 4, 5; Walter Cox, *Advice to Emigrants or Observations . . . of the American Union* (Dublin, 1802), 6; *Boston Pilot,* October 23, 1841, September 8, 1848; [Johan Ulrich Buechler], *Land und Seereisen eines St. Gallischen Kantonburgers nach Nordamerika . . . 1816, 1817 und 1818 . . .* (St. Gallen, 1820), 212 ff.; Ole Rynning, *True Account of America* (translated by T. C. Blegen, Minneapolis, 1926), 79 ff.

[52] Thus, emigrants from Bavaria, who numbered 256,336 between 1835 and 1865, took out with them 70,450,198 fl. or an average of 275 fl. per individual (computed from tables in Philippovich, *op. cit.,* 76, 90, 91). Emigrants from Germany as a whole took an average of £29-10-0 with them in 1848–52 and £35-0-0 in 1853–54 (Michael G. Mulhall, *Dictionary of Statistics* [London, 1892], 246).

[53] J. L. and Barbara Hammond, *Skilled Labourer, 1760–1832* (London, 1919), 3.

[54] Young immigrants, among them Joseph Pulitzer, imported on contract to be enlisted for the sake of bounty money, formed an exception during the Civil War. Cf. *Boston Pilot,* March 19, 1864; *Cork Examiner,* April 16, 1864; Don C. Seitz, *Joseph Pulitzer . . .* (New York, 1924), 42; *Bostoner Zeitung,* December 23, 1865. The only earlier exceptions were the *catenoni,* Sardinians imported by Italians in America to act as professional beggars. Surprisingly large numbers of them were brought over and exploited for several years before being freed (cf. account in *L'Eco d'Italia* [New York], May 10, 17, 1851).

[55] Philippovich, *op. cit.,* 112; Marcus L. Hansen, "German Schemes of Colonization . . . ," *Smith College Studies in History,* October, 1923, IX, 9, 11 ff., 17, 33, 37 ff.; Hansen, *Atlantic Migration,* 108 ff., 228 ff.

[56] Hansen, *Atlantic Migration,* 123 ff., 166 ff., 188 ff., 238 ff. For the desire to perpetuate Germanism, cf. Tonnelat, *L'Expansion allemande hors d'Europe,* 31.

[57] Cf. *Daily Evening Transcript,* May 4, 1832; Johnson, *op. cit.,* 16, 344; W. A. Carrothers, *Emigration from the British Isles . . .* (London, 1929), 305; Willcox, *op. cit.,* II, 244 ff.; Guillet, *op. cit.,* 20 ff.; Hansen, *Atlantic Migration,* 115 ff., 227. The English consuls in New York and Boston actually had a fund to assist British subjects in Boston to go to Canada (Buchanan, "Report," October 2, 1816, British Consular Correspondence, F.O. 5/119; Manners to Bidwell, January 2, 1834, British Consular Cor-

respondence, F.O. 5/295, no. 1; Hansen, *Mingling of the Canadian and American Peoples,* 100).

[58] Cf. Helen Landreth, *Dear Dark Head, an Intimate Story of Ireland* (New York, 1936), 142 ff.

[59] Cf. O'Brien, *Seventeenth Century,* 2 ff., 15 ff., 101 ff.

[60] *Ibid.,* 12, 122, 123, 135, 215 ff.; John O'Donovan, *Economic History of Livestock in Ireland* (Dublin, 1940), 73 ff.; O'Brien, *Eighteenth Century,* 52 ff.

[61] Cf. *Lachrymae Hibernicae; or the Grievances of the Peasantry of Ireland . . . by a Resident Native . . .* (Dublin, 1822), 8, 10 ff.; John Revans, *Evils, of the State of Ireland . . .* (London, 1837), 10 ff., 23; O'Brien, *Eighteenth Century,* 66 ff.; O'Brien, *Union to the Famine,* 91.

[62] Robert Bell, LL.B., *Description of the Conditions . . . of the Peasantry of Ireland . . . between the Years 1780 & 1790 . . .* (London, 1804), 4; O'Brien, *Eighteenth Century,* 78 ff., 112, 122 ff.; O'Brien, *Union to the Famine,* 25 ff.; *Statement of the Proceedings of the Western Committee . . .* (London, 1831), 3; Frederick Merk, "The British Corn Crisis of 1845–46 . . . ," *Agricultural History,* VIII (1934), 97.

[63] O'Brien, *Seventeenth Century,* 117, 136 ff.; O'Brien, *Eighteenth Century,* 86 ff.; O'Brien, *Union to the Famine,* 10 ff.; Halévy, *op. cit.,* I, Bk. 2, 25 ff.

[64] O'Brien, *Seventeenth Century,* 140; O'Brien, *Union to the Famine,* 21.

[65] Sir William Petty, *Tracts Chiefly Relating to Ireland Containing . . . the Political Anatomy of Ireland* (Dublin, 1799), 351, 352; O'Brien, *Seventeenth Century,* 138; also *Thoughts on the Present State of the Cottiers . . .* (Dublin, 1796), 6; *Right Honorable Henry Grattan's Answer to the Rev. Michael Sandys* (Dublin, 1796), 8–21.

[66] W. Parker, Esq., *A Plea for the Poor and Industrious, Part the First . . .* (Cork, 1819), 54. Robert Bellew, *Thoughts and Suggestions on . . . the Condition of the Irish Peasantry . . . Second Edition* (London, 1808), 8.

[67] Cf. O'Brien, *Eighteenth Century,* 10–12; O'Brien, *Union to the Famine,* 43.

[68] Cf. Petty, *op. cit.,* 305; O'Brien, *Seventeenth Century,* 175; *Irish National Almanack for 1852 . . .* (Dublin, 1851), 31.

[69] For the effect of these factors on agricultural improvements cf. O'Brien, *Eighteenth Century,* 58, 69, 125; Parker, *op. cit.,* 57, 58; O'Brien, *Union to the Famine,* 27 ff., 99 ff.; Revans, *op. cit.,* 73, 75; and in general, R. Dudley Edwards and T. Desmond Williams, *The Great Famine* (Dublin, 1956), 3 ff.

[70] Petty, *op. cit.,* 366, 367; O'Brien, *Seventeenth Century,* 125; Edward

Notes to Chapter 2

MacLysaght, *Irish Life in the Seventeenth Century* . . . (London, 1939), 38; O'Brien, *Eighteenth Century*, 31 ff.

[71] Cf. O'Brien, *Eighteenth Century*, 39 ff.; MacLysaght, *op. cit.*, 72; *Address to the Public on Behalf of the Poor* . . . (Dublin, 1815), 48; *Annual Report of the Managing Committee of the House of Recovery . . . in Cork Street, Dublin . . . 1813* (Dublin, 1813), 5.

[72] O'Brien, *Eighteenth Century*, 81 ff.

[73] Cf. *Lachrymae Hibernicae* . . . , 4 ff.; O'Brien, *Union to the Famine*, 45; Adams, *op. cit.*, 13.

[74] Cf., e.g., Parker, *op. cit.*, 59; Rev. William Hickey, *State of the Poor of Ireland Briefly Considered* . . . (Carlow, 1820), 23. For Irish publications on agricultural improvements, cf. Dissertation Copy, 86, 87; J. T. Gilbert, Catalogue of Haliday 8vo Pamphlets, 1750–1848 (MS., R. I. A.), I, 378, 409, 436, 460, 498, II, 536, 553, 560, 561, 575, 589, 602, 612, 632, 653; also O'Brien, *Union to the Famine,* 129 ff.

[75] For contemporary opinion opposed to emigration, cf. Dissertation Copy, 87–89.

[76] G. C. Duggan, *Stage Irishman* . . . (London, 1937), 156. The only systematic account of this movement is a short article by J. H. Clapham, "Irish Immigration into Great Britain in the Nineteenth Century," *Bulletin of the International Committee of Historical Sciences,* July, 1933, V, 596 ff.

[77] *Report of the Committee for the Relief of the Distressed Districts in Ireland* . . . (London, 1823), 41; O'Brien, *Eighteenth Century,* 98 ff.; Revans, *op. cit.,* 7, 8.

[78] *A Letter to a British Member of Parliament on the State of Ireland in . . . 1825* . . . (Dublin, 1825), 35; *Poor Rates the Panacea for Ireland* (London, 1831), 9; O'Brien, *Union to the Famine,* 15; Sidney and Beatrice Webb, *English Local Government: English Poor Law History: Part I. The Old Poor Law* (London, 1927), 393.

[79] Cf. J. L. and Barbara Hammond, *Town Labourer, 1760–1832* (London, 1920), 13; George Strickland, *Discourse on the Poor Laws of England. . . . Second Edition* . . . (London, 1830), 68, 22; George A. Grierson, *Circumstance of Ireland Considered* . . . (London, 1830), 59; Ralph Waldo Emerson, "English Traits," *Collected Works* (Boston, 1903), V, 17.

[80] Cf. *An Account of the Calmel Building Charity* . . . *the Institution for Ameliorating the Situation of the Irish Poor in the Metropolis* . . . (London, 1814), 5; O'Brien, *Union to the Famine,* 209; Clapham, *loc. cit.,* 598; *Cork Examiner,* September 16, 1844; Frederick Engels, *Condition of the Working Class in England in 1844* . . . (Transl. by F. K. Wischnewetzky) (London, [1926]), 90 ff.

[81] Sir John Walsh, *Poor Laws in Ireland* . . . (London, 1830), 99; *Thoughts on the Poor of Ireland and Means of their Amelioration By a*

Barrister . . . (Dublin, 1831), 23; W. Neilson Hancock, *On the Condition of the Irish Labourer . . . a Paper Read Before the Dublin Statistical Society* . . . (Dublin, 1848), 7.

82 *The Causes of Discontents in Ireland, and Remedies Proposed* (s.l., n.d. [Dublin, 1823]?), 45, 46.

83 O'Brien, *Eighteenth Century*, 102.

84 Cf. *Report of the Committee for the Relief of the Distressed Districts in Ireland* . . . (London, 1823), 47, 70; O'Brien, *Union to the Famine*, 224 ff.; *Statement of the Proceedings of the Western Committee for the Relief of the Irish Poor* . . . (London, 1831), 4, 7; *Daily Evening Transcript*, September 3, 1830, June 15, 1831; *Boston Pilot*, July 9, 1842.

85 Cf. O'Brien, *Eighteenth Century*, 121; O'Brien, *Union to the Famine*, 52; Adams, *op. cit.*, 10.

86 Cf. Sidney and Beatrice Webb, *English Poor Law History: Part II: The Last Hundred Years* (London, 1929), I, 1, 2.

87 George A. Grierson, *The Circumstance of Ireland Considered with Reference to the Question of Poor Laws* (London, 1830), 1; cf. also the works cited in Dissertation Copy, 92.

88 Cf. Sidney and Beatrice Webb, *English Poor Law Policy* (London, 1910), 53; *Cork Examiner*, March 27, 1844.

89 O'Brien, *Union to the Famine*, 186; S. and B. Webb, *English Poor Law History:* Part II, II, 1025–1030.

90 O'Brien, *Union to the Famine*, 55, 161 ff.; Hansen, *Atlantic Migration*, 132 ff.

91 R. Torrens, *Letter to the Right Honorable Lord John Russell on the Ministerial Measure for Establishing Poor Laws in Ireland* . . . (London, 1838).

92 Cf. O'Brien, *Union to the Famine*, 53, 190 ff., 216; William Stewart, *Comments on the Civil Bill Ejectments Act* . . . (Dublin, 1825), 1, 71; William Stewart, *Comments on the Act 1, George IV, cap. 67* . . . (London, 1826).

93 O'Brien, *Union to the Famine*, 59, 201 ff.

94 *Ibid.*, 237 ff.; Hansen, *Atlantic Migration*, 242 ff.; Edwards and Williams, *Great Famine*, 263 ff.; *Courrier des États-Unis*, February 23, 1847.

95 To W. S. O'Brien, April 24, 1847, William Smith O'Brien Papers and Letters (MSS., N. L. I.), XIV, no. 1882. Cf. also G. H. Kerin to W. S. O'Brien, February 6, 1846, *ibid.*, XI, no. 1501.

96 *Irish National Almanack for 1852*, 26; Gonnard, *op. cit.*, 23; Michael G. Mulhall, *Fifty Years of National Progress, 1837–1887* (London, 1887), 115; Mulhall, *Dictionary of Statistics*, 190. The change in the number of holdings of various sizes shows the extent of consolidation:

Notes to Chapter 2

Number	1841	1849
Less than 1 acre	134,314	31,989
1–5 acres	310,436	98,179
5–15 acres	252,799	213,897
15–30 acres	79,342	150,120
Over 30 acres	48,625	156,960

(*Irish National Almanack for 1852*, 31, 33; O'Brien, *Union to the Famine*, 59).

97 O'Donovan to Daniel McCarthy, February 6, 1848, February 14, 1848, and April 1, 1848 (John O'Donovan, Correspondence, 1845–1861 [MSS., N. L. I.], no. 17, p. 4; no. 18, p. 3; no. 19, p. 3).

98 Robert Bennet Forbes, *Voyage of the Jamestown . . .* (Boston, 1847), 22; Edwards and Williams, *Great Famine*, 391 ff.

99 Cf. references to *Cork Examiner* and *Boston Pilot*, cited Dissertation Copy, 96, 97, ns. 212–214.

100 Cf. *Massachusetts House Documents, 1859*, no. 243, p. 6; Edward E. Hale, *Letters on Irish Emigration . . .* (Boston, 1852), 6; *Cork Examiner*, April 2, 1847. For approximate figures, cf. Johnson, *op. cit.*, 352; Willcox, *op. cit.*, II, 250. For an estimate of the total ($78,000,000), cf. *Boston Pilot*, September 22, 1855.

101 Cf. references to *Boston Pilot*, cited Dissertation Copy, 97.

102 Cf. references to *Boston Pilot*, cited in Dissertation Copy, 98.

103 *Cork Examiner*, June 13, 17, 1864; Mulhall, *Fifty Years*, 115.

104 Cf. *Cork Examiner*, May 21, 1863.

105 Cf. e.g., *Boston Pilot*, January 12, 1856, December 4, 1858; Hale, *op. cit.*, 7. At the same time passage from the continent in the Nordeutschen Lloyd or the Vanderbilt Line still cost $35–$40 (cf. e.g., *Der Pionier*, September 26, 1861; *Der Neu England Demokrat*, December 23, 1857).

106 Cf. *supra*, 7, 8; Frank C. Bowen, *Century of Atlantic Travel, 1830–1930* (Boston, 1930), 7 ff.; Dissertation Copy, 100.

107 Cf. British Consular Correspondence, America I Series, F.O. 4/14, fol. 421; Bidwell to Manners, September 27, 1827, British Consular Correspondence, F.O. 5/229.

108 British Consular Correspondence, F.O. 5/350; F. Lawrence Babcock, *Spanning the Atlantic* (New York, 1931), 79 ff. For Boston's proximity to Canada, cf. "Extract from the Report of the Post Office Commission of Inquiry . . ." (British Embassy Archives, F.O. 115/78, fol. 18).

109 Hansen, *Atlantic Migration*, 183 ff. For unsuccessful attempts to establish regular direct communications with Ireland, cf. *Boston Pilot*, September 18, 1858; *Cork Examiner*, February 23, 1842; *Cork Constitution*, May 23, 1835.

314

[110] Cf. Buchanan to Palmerston, January 9, 1837, British Consular Correspondence, F.O. 5/315; Adams, *op. cit.*, 83; John R. Commons, et al., eds., *Documentary History of American Industrial Society* (Cleveland, 1910), VII, 81 ff.; Guillet, *op. cit.*, 66 ff.; "First Report of the Commissioner of Immigration . . . 1866," Thirty-Ninth Congress, First Session, *House Executive Documents*, VIII, no. 65, pp. 3 ff.; Patten, *op. cit.*, 17 ff.; Hale, *op. cit.*, 11 ff.; *Cork Examiner*, April 5, 1847, October 30, 1848; *Courrier des États-Unis* (New York), March 28, April 13, 1848.

[111] *Massachusetts Senate Documents, 1848*, no. 46, p. 5; *ibid., 1847*, no. 109, p. 5.

[112] Cf. "Report and Tabular Statement of the Censors . . . ," *loc. cit.*, 44; *Massachusetts Senate Documents, 1848*, no. 89, p. 2. This movement has been treated only in brief discussions by Marcus L. Hansen in "Second Colonization of New England," *New England Quarterly*, October, 1929, II, 539 ff., and *Atlantic Migration*, 180 ff. There is a contemporary description in the *Irish-American* (New York), January 20, 1850. For individual cases of such migrations, cf. references to *Jesuit or Catholic Sentinel* (Boston), *United States Catholic Intelligencer* (Boston), and *Boston Pilot*, cited Dissertation Copy, 103, n. 234.

[113] Cf., e.g., Hansen, *Atlantic Migration*, 249.

[114] *Cork Examiner*, March 10, 1847.

[115] Cf. Benevolent Fraternity of Churches, *Fourteenth Annual Report of the Executive Committee* . . . (Boston, 1848), 23, 24; Dissertation Copy, 103, 104.

[116] Marcus Lee Hansen, "Revolutions of 1848," *loc. cit.*, 649.

[117] Cf. A. C. Buchanan, Esq., *Emigration Practically Considered: with Detailed Directions to Emigrants* . . . (London, 1828), 36; O'Brien, *Union to the Famine*, 208, 218; Elizabeth Fry and J. J. Gurney, *Report . . . to the Marquess Wellesley* . . . (Dublin, 1827), 74; Hansen, *Atlantic Migration*, 97, 121; Adams, *op. cit.*, 1, 158; *supra*, 31.

[118] The statistics of immigration into Boston are given *infra*, Table V and are discussed in the note thereto. These include temporary visitors and passengers in transit, and are therefore not altogether satisfactory as a measure of the growth of Boston's immigrant population. More reliable in this respect are the census figures (cf. *infra*, Tables VI–IX).

[119] Cf. the nativity of the members of the Boston Repeal Association, the most representative group of Boston Irishmen in 1840 (*infra*, Table X), and the requests for information in the *Literary and Catholic Sentinel* (Boston), 1835–1836, I, II (cf. note to Table XI, *infra*).

[120] Cf. Jesse Chickering, *Report of the Committee . . . Population of Boston in 1850* . . . (Boston, 1851), 9; *infra*, Table XI. Figures for arrivals should be raised from 30 per cent to 50 per cent to account for immigra-

tion by land. For the available statistics of this type of immigration cf. Dissertation Copy, 428, 429; "Report and Tabular Statement of the Censors . . . ," *loc. cit.*, 47; Josiah Curtis, *Report of the Joint Special Committee . . . 1855 . . .* (Boston, 1856), 19.

[121] Thus they were supposed to number 10,000 in 1849 (*Boston Pilot*, January 13, 1849) although the census of 1850 found only 4,400 in the entire state ("Annual Registration Report, 1852," *Massachusetts Public Documents, 1854*, 95).

[122] Chickering, *op. cit.*, 9; Edward Dicey, *Six Months in the Federal States* (London, 1863), II, 179.

[123] Cf. *infra*, Tables VI–IX; Dissertation Copy, 51–53.

[124] Cf. Lee M. Friedman, *Early American Jews* (Cambridge, 1934), 18 ff.

[125] Cf. *Boston Pilot*, September 22, 1849, October 18, 1851.

[126] Cf. *Boston Pilot*, February 9, 1861; *infra*, Table XII; Chickering, "Report," *loc. cit.*, 15; La Rochefoucauld-Liancourt, *op. cit.*, V, 178.

[127] Only one route, and that by sea, passed through the city (Wilbur H. Siebert, "Underground Railroad," *New England Magazine*, XXVII [1903], 566; Wilbur H. Siebert, *Underground Railroad from Slavery to Freedom* [New York, 1898], map opposite 113; Wilbur H. Siebert, "Underground Railroad in Massachusetts," *New England Quarterly*, IX [1936], 447 ff.). Cf. also *Daily Evening Transcript*, September 28, 1830.

Chapter III. The Economic Adjustment

[1] Henry David Thoreau, *Walden or, Life in the Woods* (*Writings of Henry David Thoreau*, II, Boston, 1894), 322.

[2] Cf., e.g., *Hunt's Merchants' Magazine and Commercial Review* (New York) and *Niles' Weekly Register* (Baltimore, New York and Philadelphia), and travelers' accounts listed in Dissertation Copy, 500 ff.

[3] Cf. *infra*, Table XIII; Francis A. Walker, *The Statistics of the Population of the United States . . . Compiled from the Original Returns of the Ninth Census . . . 1870 . . .* (Washington, 1872), I, 167. A municipal tabulation at another date found a total of 138,788 ("Report and Tabular Statement of the Censors . . . ," *Boston City Documents, 1850*, no. 42, p. 30).

[4] Cf. *infra*, Tables XIII, XIV.

[5] Cf. *infra*, Table XIV.

[6] Cf. *supra*, 10 ff.

[7] Cf. *infra*, Table XIV.

[8] *Idem.*

[9] Cf. *infra,* Chart B.

[10] Cf. *infra,* Charts A and B. The comparison would be even more striking if the Negroes were excluded. The maximum for the three leading occupations in any other group was 30 per cent. The reasons why the Negroes come near the Irish in this respect are discussed *supra,* 69, 70.

[11] Benevolent Fraternity of Churches, *Fourteenth Annual Report . . .* (Boston, 1848), 23, 24.

[12] Cf. e.g., *Irish American,* October 21, 1849; *Cork Examiner,* July 11, 1861.

[13] Cf. Edward E[verett] Hale, *Letters on Irish Emigration . . .* (Boston, 1852), 33.

[14] Cf. *Boston Merkur,* June 5, 1847; *Boston Pilot,* September 25, 1841, February 7, 1857.

[15] There is no way of estimating the actual number of dock laborers in the city. The term "stevedore" generally applied to the contractor who hired the labor in behalf of the merchant. Most laborers were recruited as they were needed. They were predominantly foreign by nativity, and their numbers were quite large (cf. Boston Board of Trade, *Third Annual Report of the Government . . . January, 1857 . . .* [Boston, 1857], 7; *Third Annual Report of the Bureau of Statistics of Labor, Massachusetts . . . 1872, Massachusetts Senate Documents, 1872,* no. 180, p. 56).

[16] The total number of laborers in the city in 1850 was 8,552, which represented a significant increase over the 3,240 of 1845. The number continued to rise until 1855 when it equaled 10,402, and thereafter it declined to 9,745 in 1860 and to 9,103 in 1865. Since almost all these laborers were Irish, it is apparent that the number increased steadily with the growth of Irish immigration from 1845 to the early fifties and declined thereafter as the laborers were absorbed in industry (cf. *infra,* Tables XIII, XV; Lemuel Shattuck, *Report to the Committee of the City Council . . . Census of Boston . . . 1845 . . .* [Boston, 1846], Appendix Y, 43; Oliver Warner, *Abstract of the Census of Massachusetts, 1860* [Boston, 1863], 183, 283; Oliver Warner, *Abstract of the Census of Massachusetts, 1865 . . .* [Boston, 1867], 133).

[17] Dr. Cahill, "Seventh Letter from America . . ." (*Boston Pilot,* March 3, 1860).

[18] Cf. *infra,* Table XV.

[19] *Third Annual Report of the Bureau of Statistics of Labor . . . 1872, Massachusetts Senate Documents, 1872,* no. 180, pp. 516 ff.; Chart C.

[20] Alfred Bunn, *Old England and New England in a Series of Views . . .* (London, 1853), I, 61.

[21] Cf. *Boston Pilot,* August 19, 1854.

[22] Cf. *infra,* Tables XIII, XVI. It was impossible to enumerate accurately

the number of domestics employed in Boston because of deficiencies in the census (cf. *infra,* note to Table XVI). The figures given above and in Tables XIII and XVI are approximate and minimal, intended merely to show the relative proportion in each nativity group. An accurate count of domestics in this period appears to have been made only in the state censuses of 1845 and 1865. The former found 5,706 (Shattuck, *op. cit.,* 84); the latter, 11,204 (Warner, *Abstract of the Census of Massachusetts, 1865,* 142). The figure for 1850 is probably closer to that of 1865 than to that of 1845, so that Table XVI should be scaled radically upward.

²³ Cf. *infra,* Table XVI.

²⁴ Cf. references to *Courrier des États-Unis* (New York), cited Dissertation Copy, 123.

²⁵ Cf., e.g., *Minutes of the Selectmen's Meetings 1799 to . . . 1810* (*Volume of Records Relating to the Early History of Boston,* XXXIII), *Boston City Documents,* 1904, no. 93, p. 122.

²⁶ Cf. *Boston Pilot,* June 16, 1838, June 8, 1839, February 17, 1855, September 30, 1854.

²⁷ Cf. *infra,* Table XIII.

²⁸ *Idem;* Bunn, *op. cit.,* I, 61, 62; Alexander Marjoribanks, *Travels in South and North America* (London, 1853), 177.

²⁹ Cf. *infra,* Table XIII; Dissertation Copy, 126.

³⁰ Cf. "Report and Tabular Statement of the Censors . . . 1850," *Boston City Documents, 1850,* no. 42, p. 49; James H. Lanman, "Commerce of Boston," *Hunt's Merchants' Magazine and Commercial Review,* May, 1844, X, 431, 432.

³¹ Dissertation Copy, 445. The 4,190 persons employed in these occupations were fairly equally distributed among the various nativity groups, with the exception of the British North Americans who were abnormally concentrated in carpentry. The explanation for their unusually high percentage may be that the emigrants from Canada and New Brunswick, coming as a result of the decline of the lumber industry there, were accustomed to working with wood and therefore made better carpenters (cf. *Report of the Select Committee of the Legislative Assembly Appointed to Inquire into the Causes . . . of the Emigration . . . from Lower Canada to the United States . . .* [Montreal, 1849], 6, 11; Marcus Lee Hansen, *Mingling of the Canadian and American Peoples . . .* [New Haven, 1940], 121).

³² Cf., e.g., Patrick Gargan (Conrad Reno, *Memoirs of the Judiciary and the Bar of New England . . .* [Boston, 1900], I, 66); also *infra,* Table XIII.

³³ For all these, cf. *infra,* Table XIII. There were a few exceptions, for which cf. *Boston Pilot,* June 19, 1858.

[34] For coachmen, cf. *infra,* Table XIII. The seafaring community, though vital to Boston's prosperity, has not been more fully discussed because it was not an integral part of the city's population. Sailors on the Boston ships after the forties were no longer the New England boys who had formerly come down to wrest a career from the sea. Instead, Boston's merchant marine was manned by "an international proletariat of the sea." Transient foreigners of many races made up the crews of most ships that sailed out of Boston in these years, with only a slight addition of natives (Samuel Eliot Morison, *Maritime History of Massachusetts* . . . [Boston, 1921], 353, 354; Boston Board of Trade, *Report . . . and a Memorial to Congress on the Subject of Seamen and Marine Disasters* [Boston, 1855], 5; *infra,* Table XIII. The only group permanently domiciled in the city that went to sea were the Negroes (cf. *supra,* 69 ff.).

[35] Cf. the "dry goods dealers" and "other retailers," *infra,* Table XIII. The Irish dry goods and clothing stores catered chiefly to their own group (for immigrant stores cf. references to *Jesuit or Catholic Sentinel* [Boston], *Boston Pilot, and Gazette Française* in Dissertation Copy, 129).

[36] In all, food dealers came to between 3 and 4 per cent of the total working population, cf. *infra,* Table XIII.

[37] The Irish had only about 1 per cent (*idem*) though there were some prominent grocers among them (cf. references to the *Boston Pilot* cited in Dissertation Copy, 130, n. 53).

[38] Cf. *infra,* Table XIII.

[39] Anna H. Dorsey, "Nora Brady's Vow," *Boston Pilot,* February 21, 1857.

[40] For Irish boarding houses, cf. references to *United States Catholic Intelligencer, Jesuit or Catholic Sentinel,* and *Boston Pilot* cited Dissertation Copy, 131; for German boarding houses, cf., references to *Der Pionier, Boston Merkur, Bostoner Zeitung,* and *Neu England Demokrat* cited Dissertation Copy, 132.

[41] Cf. *infra,* Table XIII; also references to *Der Pionier, Bostoner Zeitung, Neu England Demokrat, Boston Pilot,* and *Old Countryman* . . . (Boston), cited Dissertation Copy, 132.

[42] Cf., e.g., *Gazette Française,* April 15, 1851.

[43] *Courrier des États-Unis,* April 9, 1846, March 3, 1844, October 31, 1843.

[44] Cf. *Courrier des États-Unis,* March 3, 1846, October 30, November 6, 1847.

[45] For a list of hotels and boarding houses, cf. *Chase's Pocket Almanac . . . 1850* (Boston, n.d. [1850]), 15, 17.

[46] For Degrand, cf. *Boston Pilot,* January 5, 1856; Justin Winsor, *Memorial History of Boston* . . . (Boston, 1880), IV, 135–137. For Touro,

cf. Christopher Roberts, *Middlesex Canal, 1793–1860* (Cambridge, 1938), 131, 200, 227; Lee M. Friedman, *Early American Jews* (Cambridge, 1934), 21. For a few other exceptional cases, cf. Dissertation Copy, 54.

[47] For these companies cf. *Boston Pilot*, October 5, 19, 1861, March 3, 1860; *Der Pionier*, October 26, 1864.

[48] For the New England Company, cf. *Massachusetts Senate Documents, 1852*, no. 112, p. 2; *supra*, 159. For others, cf. *Boston Pilot*, March 24, 1860.

[49] For these occupations, cf. Dissertation Copy, 446.

[50] Roberts, *op. cit.*, 48.

[51] Cf. *infra*, Table XIII. These figures are for clergymen, teachers, physicians, actors, musicians, and "other professions."

[52] Charles F. Read, "Lorenzo Papanti . . . ," *Proceedings of the Bostonian Society* (Boston, 1928), 41 ff.

[53] *Independent Chronicle* (Boston), January 3, 1811.

[54] For totals cf. *infra*, Table XIII. For other prominent foreigners, cf. Dissertation Copy, 137, 138.

[55] Cf. references to *Boston Pilot* cited in Dissertation Copy, 139.

[56] For Irish lawyers cf. references to *Boston Pilot* and *Irish American* (New York), cited in Dissertation Copy, 139, n. 94.

[57] *Boston Pilot*, September 4, 1852. For similar references to *Boston Pilot, United States Catholic Intelligencer, Jesuit or Catholic Sentinel* (Boston), and *Irish American*, cf. Dissertation Copy, 140, n. 96. For French doctors, cf. *Gazette Française*, April 12, 19, 1851.

[58] Cf., e.g., the *Boston Pilot*, April 18, 1863; also John M. Duncan, *Travels through . . . the United States . . . in 1818 . . .* (Glasgow, 1823), I, 67.

[59] Cf. *infra*, Tables XIII, XV; also La Rochefoucauld-Liancourt, *Voyage dans les États-Unis . . .* (Paris, An VII [1799]), V, 178; E. S. Abdy, *Journal of a Residence . . . in the United States . . .* (London, 1835), I, 121; *Minutes of the Selectmen's Meetings . . . 1818 to . . . 1822 (Volume of Records . . . Early History of Boston*, XXXIX), *Boston City Documents*, 1909, no. 61, p. 12.

[60] Cf. Archibald H. Grimké, *Life of Charles Sumner . . .* (New York, 1892), 220; also *Columbian Centinel* (Boston), June 18, 1791; *Boston Pilot*, September 25, 1858; *Der Pionier* (Boston), July 2, 1862; C. J. Furness, "Walt Whitman Looks at Boston," *New England Quarterly*, July, 1928, I, 356.

[61] Cf. also Charles H. Wesley, *Negro Labor in the United States . . .* (New York, 1927), 43 ff.

[62] Cf., e.g., *Boston Pilot*, April 22, 1854. For other advertisements, cf. the citations in Dissertation Copy, 143, n. 110.

[63] Cf., e.g., Benevolent Fraternity of Churches, *Twenty-First Annual Report of the Executive Committee* . . . (Boston, 1855), 12; Consul Grattan to Lord Aberdeen, January 28, 1843, British Consular Correspondence, F.O. 5/394.

[64] Cf. the advertisements in the *Boston Pilot*, cited Dissertation Copy, 144.

[65] Cf., e.g., *Boston Pilot*, November 6, 1852, February 19, 1853.

[66] For these evils cf. *Irish American*, November 1, 1851; for the truck system cf. John R. Commons, et al., eds., *Documentary History of American Industrial Society* (Cleveland, 1910), VII, 50, 51.

[67] Cf. *Boston Pilot*, July 31, September 11, 1852.

[68] Emerson, quoted in *Boston Pilot*, March 2, 1861; Hale, *op. cit.*, 53. Cf. also Thoreau, *Walden*, 146.

[69] Cf. John R. Commons, *History of Labour in the United States* (New York, 1926), I, 539; B. M. Stearns, "Early Factory Magazines in New England," *Journal of Economic and Business History*, II (1930), 693 ff.; Norman Ware, *Industrial Worker, 1840–1860* . . . (Boston, 1924), 149; Allan Macdonald, "Lowell: a Commercial Utopia," *New England Quarterly*, X (1937), 57; Caroline F. Ware, *Early New England Cotton Manufacture* . . . (Boston, 1931), 12, 64 ff., 198 ff.

[70] Arthur Harrison Cole, *American Wool Manufacture* (Cambridge, 1926), I, 274, 369 ff.; United States Census Office, *Eighth Census, 1860, Manufactures* (Washington, n.d. [1864]), xxxv; M. T. Copeland, *Cotton Manufacturing Industry of the United States* (Cambridge, 1917), 13 ff.; Edith Abbott, *Women in Industry* . . . (New York, 1910), 102, 103.

[71] Cf. Emerson David Fite, *Social and Industrial Conditions in the North during the Civil War* (New York, 1910), 187, n. 1; Susan M. Kingsbury, ed., *Labor Laws and Their Enforcement* . . . (New York, 1911), 56 ff.; C. F. Ware, *Early New England Cotton Manufacture*, 228 ff.

[72] Cf. *supra*, 10; Albert Aftalion, *Le Développement de la fabrique* . . . *dans les industries de l'habillement* (Paris, 1906), 21 ff.; Blanche E. Hazard, *Organization of the Boot and Shoe Industry in Massachusetts before 1875* (Cambridge, 1921), 24 ff., 93, 94.

[73] Cf. Fite, *op. cit.*, 90, 91; George C. Houghton, "Boots and Shoes" (United States Census Bureau, *Twelfth Census, 1900, Manufactures*, IX, 755; Aftalion, *op. cit.*, 61 ff.; *Eighty Years Progress of the United States: a Family Record of American Industry* . . . (Hartford, 1869), 324; Commons, *History of Labour*, II, 76–78; Ware, *Industrial Worker*, 38 ff.; John R. Commons, "American Shoemakers," *Quarterly Journal of Economics*, XXIV (1909), 73 ff.

[74] The actual number cited *infra* in Table XVII fell from 9,930 to

6,010, but this excludes approximately 2,900 in the building and clothing trades not listed in 1845. If these were added the figures for both years become roughly equal.

⁷⁵ Cf. Lousada to Russell, February 29, 1864, British Consular Correspondence, F.O. 5/973; *Third Annual Report of the Bureau of Statistics of Labor,* 535.

⁷⁶ Cf. *infra,* Table XVII.

⁷⁷ Cf. Winsor, *op. cit.,* IV, 98; Jesse Eliphalet Pope, *Clothing Industry in New York* (Columbia, Missouri, 1905), 7; Horace Greeley, et al., *Great Industries of the United States* . . . (Hartford, 1872), 588, 589; *Eighth Census, 1860, Manufactures,* lxiii; Edwin T. Freedley, *United States Mercantile Guide* . . . (Philadelphia, 1856), 125; Cole, *op. cit.,* I, 293.

⁷⁸ Cf. *Documents Relative to the Manufactures in the United States* . . . , United States Congress, 22 Congress, 1 Session, *House Executive Documents,* no. 308, I, 465; Victor S. Clark, *History of Manufactures* . . . (Washington, 1928), II, 447; Martin E. Popkin, *Organization, Management, and Technology in the Manufacture of Men's Clothing* (New York, n.d. [1929]), 36.

⁷⁹ Cf. Pope, *op. cit.,* 11; J. M. Budish and George Soule, *New Unionism in the Clothing Industry* (New York, 1920), 17; Axel Josephsson, "Clothing," United States Census Bureau, *Twelfth Census, 1900, Report, Manufactures,* IX, 296 ff.; for the number of tailors, cf. Shattuck, *op. cit.,* Appendix Y, 40.

⁸⁰ Cf. the MS. letter of thirteen master tailors to Mayor Bigelow, August 13, 1849 (John Prescott Bigelow Papers, Box VI [MSS., H. C. L.]).

⁸¹ Cf. J. Leander Bishop, *History of American Manufactures from 1608 to 1860* . . . (Philadelphia, 1864), II, 474, 475.

⁸² Cf. *infra,* Table XIII.

⁸³ Cf. Pope, *op. cit.,* 9; Fite, *op. cit.,* 89; Clark, *op. cit.,* II, 32.

⁸⁴ Cf. Josephsson, *loc. cit.,* 297; Pope, *op. cit.,* 69 ff. Pope's claim that the Boston System originated among English tailors settled in Boston is accepted by Clark (*op. cit.,* II, 448). The only ground for this hypothesis is the similarity of conditions in the English clothing industry, particularly in Leeds, to those in Boston. This similarity is, however, merely the result of the fact that the factory in England grew out of the same cause that produced it in Boston, a cheap labor surplus (cf. J. H. Clapham, *Economic History of Modern Britain* . . . [Cambridge, 1932], II, 92 ff.; Aftalion, *op. cit.,* 88 ff.; Karl Marx, *Capital, a Critique of Political Economy* . . . *Translated* . . . *by Samuel Moore and Edward Aveling* . . . [Chicago, 1909], I, 514 ff.).

⁸⁵ Pope, *op. cit.,* 70, 15 ff., 23 ff.

[86] Men's Clothing Industry in New York and Boston:

		Value of Product	Number of Employees	Average value per Employee
1860	New York	$17,011,370	21,568	$ 788
	Boston	4,567,749	4,017	1,137
1870	New York	34,456,884	17,084	2,017
	Boston	17,578,057	7,033	2,322

(Derived from material in Pope, *op. cit.*, 303.)

[87] Cf. *ibid.*, 31, 32; *Hunt's Merchants' Magazine*, August, 1853, XXIX, 253; Paul T. Cherington, *Wool Industry* . . . (Chicago, n.d. [1916]), 194.

[88] Cf. Pope, *op. cit.*, 303; C. L. Fleischmann, *Erwerbszweige, Fabrikwesen und Handel der Vereinigten Staaten* . . . (*Stuttgart*, 1850), 333; Freedley, *op. cit.*, 135.

[89] Cf. Paul L. Vogt, *Sugar Refining Industry in the United States* (Philadelphia, 1908), 11, 14.

[90] Cf. Marshals' Schedules of the Seventh Census (MSS., B. C.); also *Boston Pilot*, May 17, 1845, January 29, 1853; Franz Löher, *Geschichte und Zustände der Deutschen in Amerika* (Cincinnati, 1847), 297.

[91] Vogt, *op. cit.*, 16; Victor S. Clark, *History of Manufactures in the United States* . . . (Washington, 1916), I, 491. For some of these inventions, cf. *Scientific American* (New York), October 18, 1851, VII, 36.

[92] Bishop, *op. cit.*, III, 303, 305; Dissertation Copy, 448.

[93] Bishop, *op. cit.*, III, 305.

[94] Cf. *Massachusetts House Documents, 1848*, no. 110; Bishop, *op. cit.*, III, 285, 287; Freeman Hunt, *Lives of American Merchants* (New York, 1856), I, 516; Greeley, *op. cit.*, 115; Dissertation Copy, 447.

[95] Cf. Dissertation Copy, 447.

[96] Cf. Dissertation Copy, 447, 470; *Eighty Years Progress*, 246; Freedley, *op. cit.*, 265, 292, 296, 305, 306; Bishop, *op. cit.*, III, 281, 282, 284 ff., 297 ff., 301, 302, 566; Clark, *op. cit.*, II, 93; Chauncey M. Depew, *One Hundred Years of American Commerce* . . . (New York, 1895), II, 339; Gillespie, *op. cit.*, 37, 45, 110–112, 168.

[97] Bishop, *op. cit.*, III, 295; A. B. Hart, *Commonwealth History of Massachusetts* . . . (New York, 1930), IV, 442 ff.

[98] Cf. Dissertation Copy, 470; Boston Board of Trade, *Third Annual Report* . . . *1857*, 84; Boston Board of Trade, *Seventh Annual Report* . . . *1861*, 175.

[99] For all these companies, cf. Gillespie, *op. cit.*, 44, 162, 173, 175 ff., 186; Bishop, *op. cit.*, III, 148, 288 ff., 307, 310 ff.; Depew, *op. cit.*, I, xxvi, II, 367, 541; Edwin M. Bacon, *Book of Boston* . . . (Boston, 1916), 383; *Third*

Annual Report of the Bureau of Statistics of Labor, 147; Alfred Pairpoint, *Uncle Sam and His Country* . . . (London, 1857), 154 ff., 156. For the number of employees, cf. Table XIII, *infra;* Dissertation Copy, 447.

[100] *Boston Pilot,* November 5, 1853; Fleischmann, *Erwerbszweige,* 336 ff.; Virginia Penny, *Employments of Women* . . . (Boston, 1863), 350, 351.

[101] *Hunt's Merchants' Magazine,* August, 1853, XXIX, 253; Isaac A. Hourwich, *Immigration and Labour, the Economic Aspects of European Immigration to the United States* (New York, 1912), 364.

[102] Cf. Ware, *Industrial Worker,* 48 ff.; Abbott, *op. cit.,* 237.

[103] *Boston Pilot,* August 30, 1856; Benevolent Fraternity of Churches, *Twenty-Second Annual Report* . . . *1856,* 26.

[104] L. L. Lorwin, *Women's Garment Workers* . . . (New York, 1924), 5.

[105] *Ibid.,* 10; *Eighth Census, 1860, Manufactures* (Washington, 1861), lxxxiii ff.

[106] Warner, *Abstract of the Census of Massachusetts, 1865,* 164 ff.

[107] *Report of the Bureau of Statistics of Labor* . . . , *Massachusetts Senate Documents, 1870,* no. 120, p. 91.

[108] Sir Charles Lyell, *Second Visit to the United States* . . . (London, 1849), I, 187; Jesse Chickering, "Report of the Committee . . . Boston in 1850 . . . ," *Boston City Documents, 1851,* no. 60, p. 50.

[109] Cf. *infra,* Table XIII.

[110] *Our First Men* . . . (Boston, 1846), 14, 17, 31; Rev. G. C. Treacy, "Andrew Carney, Philanthropist," United States Catholic Historical Society, *Historical Records and Studies,* XIII, 101 ff.; *Irish American,* February 28, 1852; *Boston Pilot,* September 17, 1853; Dissertation Copy, 166; Reno, *op. cit.,* I, 100.

[111] Cf. advertisements in *Irish American,* October 15, 1859; *Boston Pilot,* August 30, 1862; Bishop, *op. cit.,* II, 318, 319; Freedley, *op. cit.,* 236, 395–398.

[112] Cf. Dissertation Copy, 22, 167–169.

[113] Cf. Lyell, *op. cit.,* I, 186; "Report and Tabular Statement," *loc. cit.,* 49.

[114] Cf. *supra,* 184 ff.

[115] Cf. Ware, *Industrial Worker,* xii, 6 ff., 26 ff., 110 ff.

[116] E. E. Hale, *Letters on Irish Emigration,* 54, 55; Isaac A. Hourwich, "Economic Aspects of Immigration," United States Congress, 62 Congress, 2 Session, *Senate Documents,* no. 696, pp. 10 ff.; Hourwich, *Immigration and Labour,* 367; Depew, *op. cit.,* I, 12, 13.

[117] Cf. *First Report of the General Board of Health in the City of Dublin* . . . (Dublin, 1822), 56, 57.

[118] *Boston Pilot,* November 28, 1863; also Walter B. Smith and Arthur H. Cole, *Fluctuations in American Business, 1790–1860* (Cambridge, 1935), xxvii, 94; Ware, *Industrial Worker,* 31. For the period 1860–1865, cf. *Tenth Annual Report of the Bureau of the Statistics of Labor, January, 1879, Massachusetts Public Documents, 1879,* no. 31, pp. 81 ff.

[119] Cf. Clark, *op. cit.,* II, 143; *Tenth Annual Report of the Bureau of Statistics of Labor,* 67 ff., 78, 87; Edith Abbott, "Wages of Unskilled Labor in the United States, 1850–1900," *Journal of Political Economy,* June, 1905, XIII, 321 ff.; Chart C, *infra.*

[120] Lousada to Russell, May 7, 1863, British Consular Correspondence, F.O. 5/910.

[121] The complaints against high costs are most clearly and most poignantly stated in letters from Irish laborers to friends in Ireland, occasionally reprinted in the Irish press. Cf. particularly the letter to his father from James O'Leary, a Killarney immigrant, dated Boston, December 27, 1863 (*Cork Examiner,* January 23, 1864), and the letter from a Cambridgeport immigrant to his former parish priest (*ibid.,* August 19, 1864).

[122] Cf. *Cork Examiner,* August 19, 1864.

[123] Cf. *Cork Examiner,* July 11, 1861; *Boston Pilot,* October 5, September 28, 1861; also Commons, *op. cit.,* II, 13; Fite, *op. cit.,* 199 ff., 212. For prices and wages, cf. Wesley Clair Mitchell, *History of the Greenbacks* . . . (Chicago, 1903), 239 ff., 280 ff.

[124] Cf. *Boston Pilot,* October 18, 1862, January 16, 1864.

[125] Jeremiah O'Donovan-Rossa, *Rossa's Recollections 1838 to 1898* . . . (Mariner's Harbor, New York, 1898), 154.

Chapter IV. The Physical Adjustment

[1] Lemuel Shattuck, *Report to the Committee of the City Council* . . . *Census of Boston* . . . *1845* . . . (Boston, 1846), 55.

[2] The conventionally accepted figures show an increase of 52.11 per cent for the decade 1830–40 and only 46.58 per cent for 1840–50 and 29.92 per cent for 1850–60 (cf., e.g., Adna F. Weber, *Growth of Cities in the Nineteenth Century* . . . [New York, 1899], 37). This is due to an error of almost 10,000 in the federal census of 1840, which raised the rate of increase for the preceding decade and lowered it for the succeeding one (Shattuck, *op. cit.,* 7 ff.). Cf. also Josiah Curtis, *Report of the Joint Special Committee on the Census of Boston* . . . *1855* . . . (Boston, 1856), 3, 23.

[3] Lemuel Shattuck, *Letter* . . . *in Relation to the Introduction of Water into* . . . *Boston* (Boston, 1845), 13 ff.

[4] Cf. *infra,* Tables II, V; for the density of population in peninsular

Boston in 1845, cf. *Report of the Committee on the Expediency of Providing Better Tenements for the Poor* (Boston, 1846), 4.

⁵ Cf., e.g., *infra,* Map II.

⁶ For communications, cf. Dissertation Copy, 180.

⁷ Cf., e.g., *Report of the Bureau of Statistics of Labor . . . 1870 . . . , Massachusetts Senate Documents, 1870,* no. 120, pp. 175, 176.

⁸ Dissertation Copy, Map IV; also Horace Greeley, et al., *Great Industries of the United States . . .* (Hartford, 1872), 592.

⁹ Robert A. Woods, ed., *City Wilderness . . .* (Boston, 1898), 21 ff.; Justin Winsor, ed., *Memorial History of Boston . . .* (Boston, 1880), IV, 40.

¹⁰ Cf. Albert B. Wolfe, *Lodging House Problem in Boston . . .* (Boston, 1906), 11; Henry F. Jenks, "Old School Street," *New England Magazine,* November, 1895, XIII, 259; Robert A. Woods, ed., *Americans in Process . . .* (Boston, 1902), 16 ff.; Freeman Hunt, *Lives of American Merchants* (New York, 1856), I, 143 ff.; *Wide Awake: and the Spirit of Washington* (Boston), October 7, 1854.

¹¹ Cf. Mabel L. Walker, *Urban Blight and Slums . . .* (Cambridge, 1938), 6, 3 ff.; cf. also James Ford, *Slums and Housing . . .* (Cambridge, 1936), I, 5, 6.

¹² Cf. *supra,* Maps I, II. An analysis of the Broad, Cove, and Sea Street district in 1850 found only 75 Americans in a population of 2,813 (Amasa Walker, *Tenth Report to the Legislature . . . Births, Marriages and Deaths . . . 1851, Massachusetts Public Documents, 1853,* 111; "Report and Tabular Statement of the Censors, . . . 1850," *Boston City Documents, 1850,* no. 42, p. 39).

¹³ E. H. Derby, "Commercial Cities . . . Boston," *Hunt's Merchants' Magazine,* November, 1850, XXIII, 484 ff.

¹⁴ For statutory fare provisions, cf. *Charter and Ordinances of the City of Boston . . .* (Boston, 1856), 422, 424, 433; *Ordinances of the City of Boston . . .* (Boston, 1865), 65; for routes, cf. H. A. Brown, *Guide-Book for the City and Vicinity of Boston, 1869* (Boston, 1869), 23; *Irish-American,* May 8, 1858.

¹⁵ Cf. Woods, *Americans in Process . . . ,* 33 ff.; Winsor, *op. cit.,* IV, 35–37.

¹⁶ For the distribution of Negro population, 1813–1850, cf. *infra,* Maps III, IV. Throughout the period the concentration persisted in the same streets of the West End, with a scattering in other parts of the city. Cf. also [James W. Hale], *Old Boston Town . . .* (New York, 1880), 29; *Daily Evening Transcript,* December 22, 1831; and, in general, Alexander Marjoribanks, *Travels in South and North America* (London, 1853), 177.

[17] Boston Female Society for Missionary Purposes, *A . . . Brief Account . . . with Extracts from the Reports of their Missionaries . . .* (Boston, n.d.), 15 ff. Cf. also *Minutes of the Selectmen's Meetings 1811 . . . 1818* (*Volume of Records . . .*, XXXVIII), *Boston City Documents, 1908,* no. 60, pp. 107, 113, 116.

[18] Cf. Dissertation Copy, Map IX; Woods, *Americans in Process,* 36, 37, 42; Walker, *Tenth Report . . . 1851, Massachusetts Public Documents, 1853,* 110.

[19] Cf. Edwin M. Bacon, *Book of Boston . . .* (Boston, 1916), 110.

[20] Cf. Dissertation Copy, Maps X, XI; George Adams, *Brighton and Brookline Business Directory . . .* (Boston, 1850), 20 ff.; Chauncey M. Depew, *1795–1895 — One Hundred Years of American Commerce . . .* (New York, 1895), I, xxvii.

[21] James F. Hunnewell, *Century of Town Life . . .* (Boston, 1888), 36.

[22] Cf. *Charter and Ordinances of the City of Boston . . .* (Boston, 1856), 436; Dissertation Copy, Maps X, XI; *Boston Pilot,* August 25, 1860.

[23] Boston Common Council, *South Boston Memorial, Boston City Documents, 1847,* no. 18, p. 11.

[24] *Ordinances of the City of Boston . . .* (Boston, 1865), 76; State Street Trust Company, *Boston, England and Boston, New England . . .* (Boston, 1930), 10; Dissertation Copy, Map X.

[25] Cf. Alfred Pairpoint, *Uncle Sam and His Country . . .* (London, 1857), 196–201; Dissertation Copy, Map XI; *Boston Pilot,* June 2, 1855; Edward H. Savage, *Boston Events . . .* (Boston, 1884), 7, 8; George H. McCaffrey, Political Disintegration and Reintegration of Metropolitan Boston (MS., H. C. L.), 194.

[26] *Report of the Committee on Expediency,* 14.

[27] Woods, *City Wilderness,* 26, 27; *Charter and Ordinances of the City of Boston . . .* (Boston, 1856), 408 ff.; *Ordinances of the City of Boston* (Boston, 1865), 78, 79; Francis S. Drake, *Town of Roxbury . . .* (Boston, 1905), 51.

[28] Walker, *Tenth Report . . . 1851, Massachusetts Public Documents, 1853,* 111; cf. also Dissertation Copy, Map XI; *Woods, City Wilderness,* 53, 28–30; *Tenth Annual Report of the Benevolent Fraternity of Churches . . .* (Boston, 1844), 25.

[29] Particularly a large representation of Germans (cf. Dissertation Copy, Map XI). Cf. also "Report and Tabular Statement of the Censors . . . 1850," *Boston City Documents, 1850,* no. 42, p. 34; "Report of the Standing Committee on Towns . . . ," *Massachusetts Senate Documents, 1851,* no. 82, passim.

[30] Cf. D. Hamilton Hurd, *History of Norfolk County* . . . (Philadelphia, 1884), 72, 73; Dissertation Copy, Maps IX, XI.

[31] Winsor, *op. cit.,* IV, 39; Dissertation Copy, Map X; "Report . . . on the East Boston Ferry, 1864," *Boston City Documents, 1864,* no. 44, pp. 4 and passim; *Boston Pilot,* June 8, 1850.

[32] *Ordinances of the City of Boston* . . . (Boston, 1865), 75, 82; Dissertation Copy, 192–194.

[33] For instance, a building in Kingston Court, owned by L. M. Sargeant was leased to T. Thompson whose agent was James Connors, who subleased it to a neighborhood grocer, P. Collins (*Report of the Bureau of Statistics of Labor* . . . *1871, Massachusetts Senate Documents, 1871,* no. 150, pp. 524, 526).

[34] John H. Griscom, *Sanitary Condition of the Laboring Population of New York* . . . (New York, 1845), 6; Ford, *op. cit.,* I, 105, 134.

[35] *Third Annual Report of the Bureau of Statistics of Labor* . . . *1872, Massachusetts Senate Documents, 1872,* no. 180, p. 437.

[36] *Boston Pilot,* June 2, 1855.

[37] *Report of the Bureau of Statistics of Labor, 1870,* 169 ff.; 176; Edward H. Savage, *Police Records and Recollections* . . . (Boston, 1873), 268.

[38] Cf., e.g., the plan and the picture of the house in the rear of 136 Hanover Street, Figs. 10 and 11. For others, cf. Woods, *City Wilderness,* 62 ff.

[39] Cf. C. Pinney, *Atlas of the City of Boston* . . . (Boston, 1861), Plate 17, 23; *Report of the Bureau of Statistics of Labor, 1870,* 166.

[40] Represented by the shaded areas in Fig. 13.

[41] Cf. Fig. 14; also Norman J. Ware, *Industrial Worker, 1840–1860* . . . (Boston, 1924), 13.

[42] Cf. Robert B. Forbes, *Voyage of the Jamestown* . . . (Boston, 1847), 22.

[43] A few in Broad Street were six floors high, but these were exceptional (*Report of the Committee of Internal Health on the Asiatic Cholera* . . . [Boston, 1849], 14).

[44] Cf. *Twelfth Report Benevolent Fraternity of Churches* (Boston, 1846), 17; *Report of the Committee on Expediency,* 12, 13; *Report of the Bureau of Statistics of Labor, 1870,* 165 ff., 175; *Report of the Committee of Internal Health,* 14; *Report of the Bureau of Statistics of Labor, 1871,* 521, 526; *Boston Pilot,* November 8, 1856.

[45] Shattuck, *Letter,* 15. In that year the number of persons per house was already at its maximum, and did not decline appreciably in the next ten years.

Year	Persons per House in Boston	Year	Persons per House in Boston
1790	7.97	1845	10.57
1800	8.31	1850	9.16
1810	8.51	1855	10.16
1820	9.84	1860	8.92
1830	9.99	1870	8.46
1840	10.04		

("Report and Tabular Statement of the Censors . . . 1850," *loc. cit.,* 32; Curtis, *op. cit.,* 11; Carroll D. Wright, *Social, Commercial, and Manufacturing Statistics of the City of Boston* . . . [Boston, 1882], 10; Shattuck, *Report . . . Census of Boston . . . 1845,* 54).

[46] Curtis, *op. cit.,* 7.

[47] Compare Wards 6, 9, 11, with 1, 3, 7, 8 in Map IX, Dissertation Copy.

[48] *Report of the Committee of Internal Health,* 12; *Report of the Bureau of Statistics of Labor, 1870,* 167.

[49] *Report of the Bureau of Statistics of Labor, 1870,* 166–168; *Report of the Committee of Internal Health,* 173; *Courrier des États-Unis,* May 6, 1851.

[50] *Report of the Committee of Internal Health,* 15; also Fig. 10.

[51] "Report and Tabular Statement of the Censors . . . 1850," *loc. cit.,* 15; *Report of the Committee of Internal Health,* 172, 173.

[52] *Report of the Committee of Internal Health,* 13, 14.

[53] *Ibid.,* 11.

[54] *Report of the Massachusetts Bureau of Statistics of Labor, 1870,* 176.

[55] *Report of the Committee of Internal Health,* 13.

[56] *Report of the Bureau of Statistics of Labor, 1870,* 165; *Report of the Committee of Internal Health,* 169, 174; *Report of the Bureau of Statistics of Labor, 1871,* 521, 524; Figs. 18, 19.

[57] *Report of the Committee of Internal Health,* 14.

[58] *Report of the Bureau of Statistics of Labor, 1870,* 164.

[59] Benevolent Fraternity of Churches, *Fourth Annual Report of the Executive Committee* . . . (Boston, 1838), 18.

[60] *Report of the Committee of Internal Health,* 14; *Report of the Bureau of Statistics of Labor, 1870,* 176.

[61] *Report of the Bureau of Statistics of Labor, 1870,* 164 ff., 175 ff.; *Report of the Bureau of Statistics of Labor, 1871,* 521, 522, 525; *Boston Pilot,* August 9, 1856.

[62] *Report of the Committee of Internal Health,* 13.

[63] Cf. Lemuel Shattuck, *Letter to the Secretary of State on the Registra-*

tion of Births, Marriages, and Deaths . . . (s.l., n.d. [Boston, 1845]), 23; Massachusetts Sanitary Commissioners, *Report of a General Plan for the Promotion of Public . . . Health* . . . (Boston, 1850), 69 ff.; "Memorial of the Boston Sanitary Association," *Massachusetts House Documents, 1861,* no. 153, p. 13; Shattuck, *Report,* 144.

[64] Deaths from Smallpox in Boston — five year periods, 1811–65:

Years	Deaths	Years	Deaths
1811–15	6	1841–45	185
1816–20	0	1846–50	349
1821–25	2	1851–55	331
1826–30	5	1856–60	401
1831–35	17	1861–65	250
1836–40	197		

(Derived from data in Charles E. Buckingham, et al., *Sanitary Condition of Boston* . . . [Boston, 1875], 84; "Memorial of the Boston Sanitary Association," *loc. cit.,* 5, 15).

[65] Cf. Massachusetts Sanitary Commissioners, *Report,* 90, 92.

[66] Jesse Chickering, *Report of the Committee . . . 1850, Boston City Documents, 1851,* no. 60, p. 29.

[67] *Report of the Committee of Internal Health,* 8, 165.

[68] Cf. *ibid.,* Map, 163–169; Dissertation Copy, Map XII.

[69] Cf. *Report of the Committee of Internal Health,* 9, 57–160, 180.

[70] Shattuck, *Report,* 146; Massachusetts Sanitary Commissioners, *Report,* 91; Buckingham, *op. cit.,* 122 ff.; "Report by the City Registrar . . . 1864," *Boston City Documents, 1865,* no. 42, p. 27. The close correlation of deaths by consumption with the poor housing conditions of the Irish may be seen *infra,* Table XVIII.

[71] Percentage of Total Deaths Due to Infant Mortality:

Ten Year Period	Percentage Deaths Under One Year Old of Total Deaths	Percentage Deaths Under Five Years Old of Total Deaths
1820–29	8.73	25.69
1830–39	12.66	35.17
1840–49	12.76	37.52
1850–59	23.84	46.49

(Buckingham, *op. cit.,* 53; also Shattuck, *Letter on Registration,* 19).

[72] [William Read], *Communication . . . on Asiatic Cholera . . . 1866, Boston City Documents, 1866,* no. 21, p. 37. One thousand cases of children's intestinal diseases, located Dissertation Copy, Map XII, coincide almost exactly with the Irish areas. Cf. also Buckingham, *op. cit.,* 64–69.

[73] Ware, *op. cit.*, 14.

[74] Massachusetts Sanitary Commissioners, *Report*, 82. For the increase in elderly people, cf. *infra*, Table XIX.

[75] Cf. "Sanitary Reform," *North American Review*, July, 1851, LXXIII, 120; Buckingham, *op. cit.*, 47; Chickering, *op. cit.*, 28.

[76] "Sanitary Reform," *loc. cit.*, 121, 122; *Tenth Report to the Legislature . . . Relating to the Registry and Return of Births, Marriages, and Deaths . . . 1851* (Boston, 1852), 110, 111.

[77] Cf. Curtis, *op. cit.*, 56–58; *infra*, Table XVIII.

[78] Chickering, *op. cit.*, 28.

[79] Chickering, *op. cit.*, 53. Their youth as a group kept the Irish death rate from increasing in the following years and led to Chickering's opinion that the American rate was higher than the foreign (*ibid.*, 32). Chickering was also misled by the large and rapidly growing number of deaths among the Boston-born infants of Irish parents (Curtis, *op. cit.*, 44, 46 ff.).

[80] Cf. *infra*, Table XX; Chickering, *op. cit.*, 17, 19, 23, 52; *Report of the Committee on Expediency*, 7; Dissertation Copy, 450.

[81] Benevolent Fraternity of Churches, *Twelfth Annual Report of the Executive Committee . . .* (Boston, 1846), 11.

[82] Cf. *supra*, 18 ff.; *Massachusetts Senate Documents, 1839*, no. 47, pp. 6 ff.

[83] Cf. *Massachusetts House Documents, 1851*, no. 152, pp. 1, 2; Chart D. After 1854 the number of foreign state paupers declined as they acquired legal residence. Cf. also Table XXI, *infra*.

[84] Boston Finance Committee, *Auditor's Report, 1848*, no. 36, p. 3; Massachusetts Sanitary Commissioners, *Report*, 203.

[85] Cf. Massachusetts Commissioners of Alien Passengers and Foreign Paupers, *Report, 1854* (Boston, 1855), 22 ff.; *Massachusetts House Documents, 1851*, no. 152, pp. 4, 5. Cf. also *Massachusetts Senate Documents, 1859*, no. 2; *Massachusetts Senate Documents, 1839*, no. 47, pp. 10, 13 ff.; *Massachusetts Senate Documents, 1844*, no. 44.

[86] Robert W. Kelso, *History of Public Poor Relief in Massachusetts, 1620–1920* (Boston, 1922), 136; *Massachusetts Senate Documents, 1852*, no. 127; Massachusetts Commissioners of Alien Passengers and Foreign Paupers, *Report, 1851* (Boston, 1852), 3, 6. For the nativities of admissions to the workhouses, cf. Dissertation Copy, 467.

[87] Cf. *Inaugural Addresses of the Mayors of Boston . . .* (Boston, 1894), I, 363, 385. Table III, *infra*, shows the rapid increase of the cost of poor relief after 1847 and particularly after 1850 when the city began to take up the burden of the support of former state paupers. Until then the cost had scarcely risen (cf. also, *supra*, 18 ff.). All available indices point to the Irish as the cause of this growth. Outdoor relief was concentrated in

Irish wards. The Irish were the largest components of the state poorhouse population and a great majority of all paupers in the city and its suburbs after 1845 were Irish (cf. *infra,* Table XXI).

[88] Cf. Theodore Parker, *Sermon of the Moral Condition of Boston . . .* (Boston, 1849), 15, 18, 19.

[89] Cf. Benevolent Fraternity of Churches, *Twelfth Annual Report,* 15; Parker, *op. cit.,* 15; Massachusetts Sanitary Commission, *Report,* 203; *Fifteenth Annual Report of the Executive Committee, Benevolent Fraternity of Churches . . .* (Boston, 1849), 6, 33; *Harbor Excursion and Intemperance in Boston* (Boston, 1853), 8.

[90] Benevolent Fraternity of Churches, *Twelfth Annual Report,* 11, 15; Shattuck, *Report . . . Census of Boston . . . 1845,* 126.

[91] For relative statistics of criminality, cf. *infra,* Tables XXII–XXIV.

[92] Cf. *Boston Pilot,* February 2, 1856, March 3, 1855; *Irish American,* September 12, 1857; *African Repository,* July, 1826, II, 152 ff.

[93] For Roby, cf. Dissertation Copy, 224; for Doctor Webster, cf. Marjoribanks, *op. cit.,* 179 ff.; A. B. Hart, *Commonwealth History of Massachusetts* (New York, 1930), IV, 56.

[94] *Twenty-Sixth Annual Report of the Trustees of the State Lunatic Hospital at Worcester, October, 1858, Massachusetts Public Documents, 1858,* no. 27, p. 20.

[95] Cf. William I. Cole, "Boston's Insane Hospital," *New England Magazine,* February, 1899, XIX, 753; Boston Finance Committee, *Report of the City Auditor, 1864,* no. 52, p. 263; "Abstract of the Returns from Overseers of the Poor," *Massachusetts Public Documents, 1848,* 1; Boston Finance Committee, *Auditor's Report, 1856,* no. 44, p. 219; *infra,* Table XXV; Dissertation Copy, 460.

[96] Cf. *Report of the Bureau of Statistics of Labor, 1871,* 207.

[97] Cf. *Daily Evening Transcript,* August 9, 1831; Massachusetts Secretary of State, "Registry and Return of Births, Marriages and Deaths . . . 1858," no. 16, *Massachusetts Public Documents, 1858,* no. 1, pp. 177 ff.; *ibid., 1859,* no. 17, *Massachusetts Public Documents, 1859,* no. 1, p. 23; *ibid., 1860,* no. 18, *Massachusetts Public Documents, 1860,* no. 1, p. 25.

Chapter V. Conflict of Ideas

[1] Karl Mannheim, *Ideology and Utopia . . .* (London, 1936), 6.

[2] Cf. Grattan to Palmerston, June 15, 1850, British Consular Correspondence, F.O. 5/350; *Cork Examiner,* November 7, 1856; Ralph Waldo Emerson, "English Traits," *Collected Works* (Boston, 1903), V; Edward Everett, *Orations and Speeches . . .* (Boston, 1850), II, 429 ff., 462 ff.; Edward Dicey, *Six Months in the Federal States* (London, 1863), II, 180.

Conflict of Ideas

³ Cf. Ezra S. Gannett, *Arrival of the Britannia, a Sermon . . . Federal Street Meeting-House . . . July 19, 1840 . . .* (Boston, 1840), 16, 17; cf. also, *supra*, 22 ff.

⁴ For a definition of ideas in this sense, cf. Arthur O. Lovejoy, *Great Chain of Being, a Study of the History of an Idea . . .* (Cambridge, 1936), 7 and Chapter I.

⁵ Robert Bell, *Description of the Conditions and Manners . . . of the Peasantry of Ireland . . .* (London, 1804), 17.

⁶ "Izzie," "The Emigrant's Farewell," *Boston Pilot*, August 16, 1862.

⁷ P.L., "I Am Tired," *Boston Pilot*, March 26, 1864.

⁸ Cf. the analysis of Irish newspaper literature, Dissertation Copy, 231–233.

⁹ Kathleen Kennedy in "Cross and Beads," *Boston Catholic Observer*, November 8, 15, 1848.

¹⁰ *Boston Pilot*, August 12, 1854. Compare the English industrial background of Methodism in J. L. and Barbara Hammond, *Town Labourer, 1760–1832 . . .* (London, 1920), 276.

¹¹ Mrs. Anna H. Dorsey, "Nora Brady's Vow," *Boston Pilot*, March 7, 1857.

¹² Cf. Arthur M. Schlesinger, Jr., *Orestes A. Brownson, a Pilgrim's Progress* (Boston, 1939), 205.

¹³ Cf. *Boston Pilot*, September 9, 1854; *United States Catholic Intelligencer*, February 24, 1832; *Jesuit or Catholic Sentinel*, July 19, 1834.

¹⁴ *Boston Pilot*, June 10, 1843.

¹⁵ Cf. Edward MacLysaght, *Irish Life in the Seventeenth Century . . .* (London, 1939), 283–285, 288 ff.

¹⁶ *Boston Catholic Observer*, March 29, 1848; cf. also *Boston Pilot*, January 22, 1853.

¹⁷ *Boston Catholic Observer*, April 5, 1848; cf. also Brownson's description of Charlemagne as an ideal Catholic ruler (*Boston Pilot*, December 4, 1852), and the peasant conception of the priest who ruled the Irish village both as priest and lawgiver (Allen H. Clington, "Frank O'Donnell. A Tale of Irish Life," *ibid.*, January 24, 1863).

¹⁸ *Boston Catholic Observer*, March 22, 1848.

¹⁹ *Ibid.*, March 29, 1848.

²⁰ Cf., e.g., Brownson's criticism of the works of Cardinal Newman and of Bishop John England (Brownson to Father J. W. Cummings, Boston, September 5, 1849 [Brownson Papers, MSS., L.U.N.D.]; Henry F. Brownson, *Orestes A. Brownson's Middle Life: from 1845 to 1855* [Detroit, 1899], 105; Schlesinger, *op. cit.*, 199–201).

²¹ Cf. *Boston Catholic Observer*, March 28, 1848; Brownson, *Works of Brownson*, I, 254; Schlesinger, *op. cit.*, 28; James F. Clarke, *The Church*

333

Notes to Chapter 5

. . . *as It Was* . . . (Boston, 1848), 20; Josiah Quincy, *Figures of the Past from the Leaves of Old Journals* (Boston, 1883), 71; *supra*, 181 ff.

[22] Cf., e.g., *Boston Pilot*, September 9, July 29, 1854.

[23] Cf. J. W. Cummings, D. D., *Social Reform, a Lecture* . . . (Boston, 1853), 18.

[24] *Questions and Answers Adapted to the Reading Lessons and the Stories in Mrs. Trimmer's Charity School Spelling Book, Part I* . . . (Dublin, 1814), Lesson fifth, 11.

[25] Quoted in F. Spencer Baldwin, "What Ireland Has Done for America," *New England Magazine*, XXIV (1901), 73. Cf. also the character of Nora Brady, Mrs. Anna H. Dorsey, "Nora Brady's Vow," *Boston Pilot*, January 3, 1857; also Constantia Maxwell, *Country and Town in Ireland under the Georges* (London, 1940), 55.

[26] *Boston Pilot*, January 10, 1857, July 15, 1854.

[27] Cf. Mrs. Anna H. Dorsey, "Old Landlord's Daughter," *Boston Pilot*, January 21, 1854.

[28] Cf. *Boston Pilot*, April 24, October 16, 1852; Brownson, *Brownson's Middle Life*, 296.

[29] Cf. *Voice of Industry*, January 7, 1848; Henry Steele Commager, *Theodore Parker* . . . (Boston, 1936), 151 ff.; A. B. Darling, *Political Changes in Massachusetts* . . . (New Haven, 1925), 153 ff.; A. B. Hart, *Commonwealth History of Massachusetts* . . . (New York, 1930), IV, 324 ff.; Arthur S. Bolster, Jr., *James Freeman Clarke* (Boston, 1954), 229 ff.

[30] Cf. E. S. Abdy, *Journal of a Residence* . . . *in the United States* . . . (London, 1835), I, 159; Dissertation Copy, 242; *Boston Pilot*, January 22, 1853, February 3, March 3, 1855.

[31] Cf. *Boston Pilot*, February 18, 1854, March 3, 1855; Brownson, *Brownson's Middle Life*, 295 ff.

[32] On this score the *Pilot* objected to Brownson's hostility to slavery after the opening of the Civil War (cf. *Boston Pilot*, April 12, 1862). Cf. also *ibid.*, July 8, 1843; *Cork Examiner*, July 21, 1843; British Consular Correspondence, F.O. 5/426, no. 59.

[33] Cf. *United States Catholic Intelligencer*, October 1, 1831; Brownson, *Brownson's Middle Life*, II, 280 ff.

[34] *Boston Pilot*, December 31, 1859.

[35] Cf. John R. Commons et al., eds., *A Documentary History of American Industrial Society* (Cleveland, 1910), VII, 60; John Robert Godely, *Letters from America* (London, 1844), II, 70; William S. Robinson, *"Warrington" Pen-Portraits* . . . *1848 to 1876* . . . (Boston, 1877), 298.

[36] Cf. *Boston Pilot*, October 18, 1856. Cf. also, the treatment of the Negro characters, Dolly in Agnes E. St. John's "Ellie Moore" (*ibid.*, June 30–September 1, 1860), Phillis in Mrs. Anna H. Dorsey, "Nora Brady's

Vow" (*ibid.*, February 21, 1857), and the butler in Mrs. Anna H. Dorsey, "The Heiress of Carrigmona" (*ibid.*, March 3, 1860).

[37] Cf. *Boston Catholic Observer*, April 12, 1848; *Boston Pilot*, April 24, July 24, 1852, November 9, 1839; *Irish-American*, November 4, 1854.

[38] Cf. *Boston Pilot*, March 29, 1851, January 10, 1857.

[39] Cf. Cummings, *Social Reform*, 7; *Jesuit or Catholic Sentinel*, July 19, 1834.

[40] Cf. *Boston Pilot*, April 24, October 9, 1852; *Boston Catholic Observer*, November 15, 1848; *United States Catholic Intelligencer*, May 18, 1832. For the attitude of other Bostonians, cf. "Report of the Board of Education, 1849," *Massachusetts House Documents, 1849*, no. 1, pp. 105 ff.; Everett, *op. cit.*, II, 235 ff., 313 ff.

[41] *Meyer's Monatshefte*, February, 1855, V, 128.

[42] Cf. Karl Heinzen, *Teutscher Radikalismus in Amerika* . . . [s.l., 1867], 5–27, 237–260; *Atlantis*, August, 1857, VII, 81 ff.; A. Siemering, "Die Prinzipien . . . der modernen Erziehung," *Der Pionier*, January 26–February 2, 1860; *ibid.*, January 5, 1860.

[43] Cf., e.g., Address of the "German Republican Association" of Boston (*European* [New York], December 6, 1856; *Der Pionier*, March 30, 1856). A short-lived Democratic paper took a compromising attitude based on the constitutionality of slavery (*Der Neu England Demokrat*, November 21, 1857), but quickly failed. Germans opposed the temperance movement not because they objected to reform, but because they felt drinking was a legitimate pleasure needing no reform (cf. *Meyer's Monatshefte*, February, 1855, V, 128, 147).

[44] Cf. *Courrier des États-Unis*, September 2, 1835, December 5, 1850, September 23, 1847; *Gazette Française* [Boston], June 28, July 5, 1851; *Colored American* [New York], March 4, 1837; *L'Eco d'Italia* [New York], December 6, April 26, 1851.

[45] Cf., e.g., *Boston Pilot*, January 1, 8, July 19, 1848.

[46] Cf. *Boston Catholic Observer*, August 23, 1848.

[47] Cf., e.g., *Voice of Industry* (Boston), November 26, 1847; *Boston Merkur*, October 2, December 25, 1847, January 1, 1848.

[48] Brownson to Montalembert, June 30, 1851 (Brownson, *Brownson's Middle Life*, 326, 327). For Father Roddan, cf. *Boston Pilot*, December 11, 1858.

[49] Thus Brownson's *Boston Catholic Observer* was occasionally hostile to reactionary Austria (cf., e.g., *Boston Catholic Observer*, December 4, 11, 18, 1847, January 8, 1848).

[50] For the attitude of Irish-American radicals towards slavery, cf. *European* [New York], December 6, 1856; *Irish-American*, January 18, 1851.

[51] Cf. Alfred Bunn, *Old England and New England* . . . (London, 1853), II, 12, 13.

[52] Cf. *Boston Pilot*, January 22, 1853; Brownson, *Brownson's Middle Life*, 418 ff.; *Boston Catholic Observer*, September 20, October 11, November 1, 1848.

[53] *Boston Catholic Observer*, February 16, 1848; cf. also O. A. Brownson, "Liberalism and Catholicity," *Works of Brownson*, V, 476 ff.

[54] *Boston Catholic Observer*, March 29, 1848.

[55] *Boston Catholic Observer*, August 2, 1848. Cf. also the attacks on the *Pilot* by the *New York Freeman's Journal and the Propagateur Catholique* (quoted *Boston Pilot*, August 18, 1849).

[56] *Boston Catholic Observer*, December 6, 1848; Brownson, *Brownson's Middle Life*, 358.

[57] Cf. *Boston Pilot*, September 14, 28, June 22, 1850.

[58] Cf. Frederick Driscoll, *Sketch of the Canadian Ministry* (Montreal, 1866), 81; E. M. Coulter, *William Brownlow* . . . (Chapel Hill, 1937), 48, 49, 65.

[59] For the native attitude, cf. George Sumner, *Oration* . . . *before the Municipal Authorities of* . . . *Boston, July 4, 1859* . . . (Boston, 1882), 24–34; *Daily Evening Transcript*, June 10, 13, 1831; Samuel Adams Drake, *Old Landmarks and Historic Personages of Boston* (Boston, 1873), 264; *Massachusetts House Documents, 1848*, no. 147; Elizabeth Brett White, *American Opinion of France, from Lafayette to Poincaré* (New York, 1927), 119–122; *Voice of Industry*, March 31, 1848; *New Era of Industry*, June 2, 1848; Mason Wade, *Margaret Fuller, Whetstone of Genius* (New York, 1940), 185, 243; Giovanni Mori, "Una Mazziniana d'America . . . ," *Rivista d'Italia e d'America*, September, 1924, II, 478 ff.; George S. Boutwell, "Kossuth in New England," *New England Magazine*, X (1894), 525 ff. For the Irish attitude, cf. *Jesuit or Catholic Sentinel*, November 13, October 30, 1830; *United States Catholic Intelligencer*, October 8, 1831; *Boston Pilot*, June 15, 22, August 31, 1850, April 24, 1852; Brownson, *Brownson's Middle Life*, 418 ff.; Schlesinger, *op. cit.*, 207; *Boston Pilot*, February 8, 1851; *Boston Catholic Observer*, February 23, 1848; *Acta Sanctae Sedis* (Romae, 1865), I, 290 ff.; Dissertation Copy, 259.

[60] Cf., e.g., *Daily Evening Transcript*, January 6, 1832; Wade, *op. cit.*, 225.

[61] *Boston Pilot*, February 11, 1854, March 17, 1855; *Jesuit or Catholic Sentinel*, May 28, 1831, October 23, 1830.

[62] Cf. *Boston Pilot*, February 12, 19, January 22, 29, 1853, November 27, December 11, 1858; *Massachusetts House Documents, 1853*, no. 62.

[63] Cf. *Boston Pilot*, May 27, 1854, August 27, September 17, 1853. Brownson was directed to write articles in defense of Spain by Mme.

Calderon, wife of the Spanish ambassador (cf. Brownson, *Brownson's Middle Life,* 311 ff.), and received from her financial aid through Nicholas Reggio, consul of the Papal States in Boston (cf. Nicholas Reggio to Brownson, Boston, April 1, 1852, Brownson Papers [MS., L.U.N.D.]).

64 Cf. Ralph Waldo Emerson, "English Traits," *Collected Works* (Boston, 1903), V, 350; *Boston Pilot,* March 17–November 10, 1855, November 20, 1852; Brownson, *Brownson's Middle Life,* 359. Catholics turned against him only in 1854 when he showed hostility to Austria and allied with England (*Boston Pilot,* March 4, 1854).

65 Cf. Schlesinger, *op. cit.,* 207; *Boston Pilot,* April 16, 1842, May 23, 1846, January 29, 1853; *United States Catholic Intelligencer,* June 8, 1832.

66 *Boston Pilot,* March 10, 1860.

67 Cf., e.g., the fate of Ellen Harcourt in "Neglect of Prayer" (*Boston Catholic Observer,* July 10, 1847); also, that of Margaret in Mrs. J. Sadlier, "Alice Riordan — The Blind Man's Daughter" (*Boston Pilot,* July 4–September 27, 1851); cf. also *Boston Catholic Observer,* September 6, 1848; *Boston Pilot,* June 9, 1860.

68 Cf. *Boston Pilot,* September 2, August 26, 1854, March 21, January 10, 1857; *Boston Catholic Observer,* June 5, 1847.

69 *Boston Pilot,* January 10, 1857, March 2, 1861.

70 Cf. Dissertation Copy, 263, 264; Thomas Colley Grattan, *Civilized America* (London, 1859), II, 40 ff.

71 Cf. *United States Catholic Intelligencer,* October 1, 1831; *Boston Pilot,* November 8, 1856. Cf. also Elizabeth H. Stewart, "Rising in the North," *ibid.,* September 4, 1858 ff.; Walsh, "Jerpoint Abbey," *ibid.,* June 4, 1859.

72 John Adam Moehler, *Symbolism* . . . (New York, 1844), xi.

73 Cf. Brownson, *Works of Brownson,* I, xix; *United States Catholic Intelligencer,* February 24, July 13, 1832; *Boston Catholic Observer,* January 10, 1847, January 26, 1848; *Jesuit or Catholic Sentinel,* July 2, 1831; *Boston Pilot,* October 5, 1839. For the contemporary Boston view of Luther, cf. Camillo von Klenze, "German Literature in the Boston Transcript," *Philological Quarterly,* XI (1932), 11.

74 J. Tighe, "To Massachusetts," *Boston Pilot,* July 4, 1846; cf. also "Lines on the Ruins of a Nunnery," *Literary and Catholic Sentinel,* August 29, 1835.

75 Cf., e.g., the "historical romances" of C. M. O'Keefe, *Boston Pilot,* May 8, 1858; Mrs. Anna H. Dorsey, "Mona: — The Vestal," *ibid.,* January 5, 1856–March 22, 1856; *United States Catholic Intelligencer,* October 1, 1831.

76 John McElheran, "The Condition of Women," *Boston Pilot,* April 5–July 12, 1856.

⁷⁷ Cf., e.g., *Boston Pilot,* July 26, 1856, and the issues following.

⁷⁸ Cf. *Boston Pilot,* October 16, 1858; *Literary and Catholic Sentinel* (Boston), August 22, 1835.

⁷⁹ Cf., e.g., *Boston Pilot,* November 24, 1855–March 8, 1856, November 15, 1856, January 21, 1854–January 20, 1855; Thomas D. McGee, *History of the Irish Settlers in North America . . .* (Boston, 1852), passim.

⁸⁰ *Boston Pilot,* March 22, 1856.

⁸¹ Cf., e.g., *Meyer's Monatshefte,* March, 1855, V, 223; *ibid.,* April, 1855, V, 298, 302, 309, 312; also "Die schöne Literatur Nordamerika's" (*Amerika, wie es ist . . . Serie III der Volkschriften des deutsch-amerikanischen Vereins . . .* [Hamburg, 1854], 20–28); Franz Kielblock's opera, "Miles Standisch" (*Der Pionier,* April 5, 12, 1860).

⁸² Cf., e.g., *Courrier des États-Unis,* March 3, October 17, 1832, October 18, 1834.

⁸³ Cf. A. B. Faust, *German Element . . .* (New York, 1927), II, 215; Karl Quentin, *Reisebilder und Studien aus dem Norden der Vereinigten Staaten von Amerika* (Arnsberg, 1851), I, 80; von Klenze, *loc. cit.,* 1–25.

⁸⁴ Cf. *Courrier des États-Unis,* March 19, May 21, 1836, November 24, 1832.

⁸⁵ Cf. William Treat Upton, *Anthony Phillip Heinrich . . .* (New York, 1939), 71, 87; O. G. Sonneck, *Early Opera in America* (New York, n.d. [1915]), 144, 145, 197, 217; John Tasker Howard, *Our American Music, Three Hundred Years of It* (New York, 1939), 135–138; Justin Winsor, *Memorial History of Boston . . .* (Boston, 1880), IV, 415–419; John Sullivan Dwight, "Handel and Haydn Society," *New England Magazine,* I (1889), 382 ff.; Henry C. Lahee, "Century of Choral Singing in New England," *ibid.,* XXVI (1902), 102, 103.

⁸⁶ Cf. Winsor, *op. cit.,* IV, 421; *Upton,* Heinrich, 76, 199; Howard, *op. cit.,* 155; Francis H. Jenks, "Boston Musical Composers," *New England Magazine,* II (1890), 476.

⁸⁷ Cf., e.g., the confused criticism which greeted Hermann & Co.'s musical soirées in 1832 (*Daily Evening Transcript,* June 22, 1832).

⁸⁸ Cf. Dissertation Copy, 272, 273; Winsor, *op. cit.,* IV, 423, 426.

⁸⁹ Cf. Winsor, *op. cit.,* IV, 429, 433 ff., 437, 441, 442; Howard, *op. cit.,* 217 ff., 220–225, 244; Upton, *Art Song,* 31, 38, 70; Upton, *Heinrich,* 202 ff.; Elson, *loc. cit.,* 236, 237; Faust, *op. cit.,* II, 269; Christine Merrick Ayars, *Contributions to the Art of Music in America . . .* (New York, 1937), 79.

⁹⁰ Cf. a long article on this subject in *Boston Pilot,* May 31, 1851.

⁹¹ For the early phases of Brownson's thought, cf. Schlesinger, *op. cit.,* especially 75–88, 117–120, 136–137, 140–141, 149, 151, 159, 169, 241; Brownson, "The Convert," *Works of Brownson,* V, 120, 121.

[92] Isaac T. Hecker, "Dr. Brownson and Bishop Fitzpatrick," *Catholic World*, XLV (1887), 7; Schlesinger, *op. cit.*, 193, 194; Brownson, *Brownson's Middle Life*, 4, 8; Henry F. Brownson, *Orestes A. Brownson's Early Life: from 1803 to 1844* (Detroit, 1898), 476 ff.

[93] As such, his works in this period have been used in this chapter. Cf. also Brownson, *Brownson's Middle Life*, 98; Schlesinger, *op. cit.*, 195, 210.

[94] Schlesinger, *op. cit.*, 213, 209 ff., 218, 219.

[95] Schlesinger, *op. cit.*, 219, 248 ff. For the difference in his attitude towards Gioberti's liberalism before and after he left Boston, compare the articles written in 1850 and in 1864 (Brownson, *Works*, II, 102, 106, 110 ff., and *ibid.*, II, 211–270).

[96] *Ibid.*, II, 142, 143; references to *Boston Pilot*, 1857–1864, Dissertation Copy, 277.

[97] Rev. Vincent F. Holden, *Early Years of Issaac Thomas Hecker . . .* (Washington, 1939), 202.

Chapter VI. The Development of Group Consciousness

[1] Henry David Thoreau, *Walden or, Life in the Woods* (*Writings of Henry David Thoreau*, II, Boston, 1894), 325, 326.

[2] Cf., e.g., *Boston Pilot*, November 15, 1862; *Bostoner Zeitung*, November 11, 18, 1865; *Courrier des États-Unis*, March 4, 1848.

[3] "The Irish Emigrant's Lament," *Boston Pilot*, March 2, 1839; T. D. McGee, "A Vow and Prayer," *Poems . . .* (New York, 1869), 123.

[4] Cf. *Boston Catholic Observer*, February 13, March 13, 1847; Robert Bennet Forbes, *Voyage of the Jamestown . . .* (Boston, 1847), xxxix, 8.

[5] Cf. *Cork Examiner*, September 2, 1863; *Boston Pilot*, April 11, May 9, 1863.

[6] Cf., e.g., *Boston Pilot*, June 28, 1862; Thomas D'Arcy McGee, *Catholic History of North America . . .* (Boston, 1855), 148.

[7] Cf. Thomas D'Arcy McGee, *History of the Irish Settlers in North America . . .* (Boston, 1852), 131; *Literary and Catholic Sentinel* (Boston), March 21, 1835, March 26, 1836.

[8] Cf. Grattan to Fox, February 17, 1841, British Consular Correspondence, F.O. 5/360, fol. 59; *Boston Pilot*, January 2, 23, 1841, February 26, 1842, July 15, September 30, December 9, 1843; *Cork Examiner*, March 28, 1842; Dissertation Copy, 282.

[9] Cf. *Boston Pilot*, September 30, 1843, January 3, April 25, May 2, 1846.

[10] *Boston Pilot*, May 28, 1842; *Cork Examiner*, December 24, 1841, July 17, 1844; *Boston Catholic Observer*, July 10, 1847.

[11] *Boston Pilot*, June 26, 1847.

[12] Cf. *Boston Pilot*, July 31, 1847.

¹³ *Boston Catholic Observer,* August 23, 1848; *supra,* 137. For English protests, cf. Palmerston to Crampton, July 7, 1848, British Consular Correspondence, F.O. 5/483, no. 37; Palmerston to Crampton, August 4, 1848, *ibid.,* F.O. 5/483, no. 43; Crampton to Palmerston, August 28, 1848, *ibid.,* F.O. 5/486.

¹⁴ Cf. Crampton to Palmerston, October 9, 1848, *ibid.,* F.O. 5/487, no. 122; Bulwer to Palmerston, May 5, 1851, *ibid.,* F.O. 5/528; Crampton to Granville, January 25, 1852, *ibid.,* F.O. 5/544, 112–113; *Cork Examiner,* February 11, 1852.

¹⁵ *Boston Pilot,* November 14, 1857.

¹⁶ Cf. *Bowen's Boston News-Letter and City Record,* February 25, 1826; McGee, *Catholic History,* 147; Forbes, *op. cit.,* passim; Freeman Hunt, *Lives of American Merchants* (New York, 1858), II, 279; Edward Everett, *Orations and Speeches . . .* (Boston, 1850), II, 533 ff.; *Boston Pilot,* April 11, 1863; *Measures Adopted in Boston, Massachusetts for the Relief of the Suffering Scotch and Irish* (Boston, 1847).

¹⁷ Cf., e.g., the annual "democratic banquets" at the International Salon on the anniversary of the February Revolution of 1848 (*Der Pionier,* February 21, 1861). Cf. also Dissertation Copy, 286; McGee, *Irish Settlers,* 133; and Grattan to Fox, February 17, 1841, British Consular Correspondence, F.O. 5/360, f. 59.

¹⁸ Cf. Dissertation Copy, 287; Very Rev. Wm. Byrne et al., *History of the Catholic Church in the New England States* (Boston, 1899), I, 11.

¹⁹ Cf. Dissertation Copy, 288.

²⁰ Cf., e.g., *Boston Pilot,* May 25, 1861.

²¹ Cf. *Boston Directory, 1853,* 379 ff.; *Boston City Documents, 1865,* no. 59, p. 74. For the Scots Charitable, cf. George Combe, *Notes on the United States . . .* (Philadelphia, 1841), II, 199; James Bernard Cullen, *Story of the Irish in Boston . . .* (Boston, 1889), 37.

²² Cf. L. von Baumbach, *Neue Briefe aus den Vereinigten Staaten . . . mit besonderer Rücksicht auf deutsche Auswanderer* (Cassel, 1856), 183; *Der Neu England Demokrat,* December 30, 1857, February 3, 1858; *Bostoner Zeitung,* December 9, 16, 1865.

²³ Moses Hays had been Grand Master of Masons at the turn of the century (cf. *Columbian Centinel* [Boston], June 4, 1791; Lee M. Friedman, *Early American Jews* [Cambridge, 1934], 18, 19; Carl Wittke, *We Who Built America . . .* [New York, 1939], 41).

²⁴ Cf. *Literary and Catholic Sentinel,* January 16, October 8, 1836; *Boston Pilot,* March 8, 1862, May 25, 1861; *Bostoner Zeitung,* December 9, 16, 1865.

²⁵ Cf. *Boston Merkur,* January 16, 1847; Dissertation Copy, 289, 290.

²⁶ Cf. references to *Der Pionier,* Dissertation Copy, 290, n. 50.

The Development of Group Consciousness

[27] Cf. references to *Boston Pilot* and *Boston Catholic Observer*, Dissertation Copy, 290, ns. 51, 52.

[28] Wittke, *op. cit.*, 217–219; *Bostoner Zeitung*, November 11, 1865; *Der Pionier*, March 11, 1863, September 14, 1864, June 28, 1865.

[29] Cf., e.g., *Cork Examiner*, August 12, 1844; Dissertation Copy, 291.

[30] Cf. L. von Baumbach, *Neue Briefe*, 75; *Boston Pilot*, October 21, 1854; Wittke, *op. cit.*, 174.

[31] Cf., e.g., *Der Pionier*, March 12, 1862; Zachariah G. Whitman, *History of the Ancient and Honorable Artillery Company* . . . (Boston, 1842), 345 ff. 351, 371.

[32] Cf. *supra*, 203; *Boston Pilot*, July 22, 1854, February 24, April 7, 1855; *Irish-American*, February 24, 1855.

[33] *Boston Pilot*, December 22, 1855; cf. Combe, *op. cit.*, II, 199.

[34] Cf. *Boston Pilot*, March 20, 1841, March 6, 1858; *Der Pionier*, March 29, 1865.

[35] McGee, *Poems*, 155; Isabel Skelton, *Life of Thomas D'Arcy McGee* (Gardenvale, Canada, 1925), 261. For interest in the frontier, cf. advertisements of western land agents in *Boston Pilot*, April 24, May 1, 1852, April 2, 1853.

[36] Cf. Sister Mary Gilbert Kelly, *Catholic Immigrant Colonization Projects in the United States, 1815–1860* (New York, 1939), 40.

[37] Kelly, *op. cit.*, 37–47, 208, 209, 223–237, 241; Robert H. Lord, "Organizer of the Church in New England . . . ," *Catholic Historical Review*, XXII (1936), 184; John Gilmary Shea, *History of the Catholic Church within the . . . United States* . . . (New York, 1890), III, 472; *Boston Pilot*, June 12, 1852; Mrs. J. Sadlier, *Biographical Sketch* . . . (in McGee, *Poems*), 28; Skelton, *op. cit.*, 270 ff.

[38] Cf. *Boston Pilot*, September 13, 1856.

[39] Cf. *One Hundred Years of Savings Bank Service* . . . (Boston, 1916), 11; British Consular Correspondence, F.O. 5/397, no. 5; the Columbian Mutual in "Fourth Annual Report on Loan Fund Associations . . . ," *Massachusetts Public Documents, 1859*, no. 9, p. 11.

[40] *Boston Pilot*, April 24, 1847, July 3, 1858; Norman J. Ware, *Industrial Worker 1840–1860* . . . (Boston, 1924), 195; John R. Commons et al., eds., *Documentary History of American Industrial Society* (Cleveland, 1910), VIII, 275–285; *Eighth Annual Report of the Bureau of Statistics of Labor . . . 1877, Massachusetts Public Documents, 1877*, no. 31, pp. 85–86; Dissertation Copy, 295. For the strikes, cf. *Third Annual Report of the Commissioner of Labor, 1887* . . . (Washington, 1888), 1038; John R. Commons, *History of Labour in the United States* (New York, 1918), I, 566, 576; *Irish-American*, July 31, September 4, 1858.

[41] Cf. "Procession," *Boston City Documents, 1865*, no. 59, pp. 71, 72. Cf.

also *Third Annual Report of the Commissioner of Labor, 1887* . . . , 1044; Boston Board of Trade, *Third Annual Report of the Government* . . . *1857* (Boston, 1857), 6–13; *Eleventh Annual Report of the Bureau of Statistics of Labor* . . . *1880, Massachusetts Public Documents, 1880,* no. 15, p. 15; *Boston Pilot,* October 24, 1863, February 6, October 22, 1864; *Third Annual Report of the Bureau of Statistics of Labor* . . . *1872, Massachusetts Senate Documents, 1872,* no. 180, p. 57.

42 Cf. Dissertation Copy, 297.

43 Cf. *supra,* 155 ff.; *Boston Pilot,* April 3, 1841. In 1857, a suggestion that the Scots Charitable Society organize an office to aid immigrant Scots came to nothing (cf. Scots Charitable Society, Records and Minutes . . . [MSS., N.E.H.G.S.], October 15, 1857, 25).

44 Cf. *Constituzione della società italiana di benevolenza, residente in Boston, Massacciussets, Stati Uniti di America* (Boston, 1842), passim; *Verfassung des deutschen Wohlthätigkeit-Vereins, in Boston* . . . (Cambridge, 1835), passim; Albert B. Faust, *Guide to the Materials for American History in Swiss and Austrian Archives* (Washington, 1916), 27; *Boston City Documents, 1865,* no. 59, p. 74.

45 *British Charitable Society for the Years 1849 to 1855. Report* . . . (Boston, 1855), 2, 3; *Boston Merkur,* July 10, 24, 31, August 7, 1847; *Der Pionier, January* 16, 1862.

46 Cf. *British Charitable Society for the Years 1849 to 1855,* 3; *Der Neu England Demokrat,* January 23, 1858; Dissertation Copy, 300; *Boston Merkur,* December 5, 1846, May 9, July 24, 1847; *Constitution, By-Laws and Rules of Order of the Hebrew Congregation Ohabei Shalom* . . . (Boston, 1855), 8; *Der Pionier,* January 5, 1860.

47 Cf., e.g., *Boston Pilot,* May 15, 1841.

48 Benevolent Fraternity of Churches, *Annual Report of the Executive Committee* . . . *1851,* no. 17 (Boston, 1851), 21; cf. also *Fifth Annual Report* . . . *Children's Mission to the Children of the Destitute* . . . (Boston, 1854), 3; "Cross and Beads . . . ," *Boston Catholic Observer,* November 8–15, 1848.

49 Cf. *Massachusetts Senate Documents, 1844,* no. 15, 2–4; *ibid.,* no. 79; *Boston Pilot,* December 4, 1858; Bishop John B. Fitzpatrick to J. P. Bigelow, May 29, 1850, Bigelow Papers (MSS., H. C. L.), Box VI.

50 *Boston Pilot,* March 21, 1863; William H. Mahoney, "Benevolent Hospitals in Metropolitan Boston," *Quarterly Publications of the American Statistical Association,* XIII (1913), 420; Rev. G. C. Treacy, "Andrew Carney . . . ," United States Catholic Historical Society, *Historical Records and Studies,* XIII (1919), 103; Shea, *op. cit.,* IV, 516.

51 Cf. Dissertation Copy, 302, 303, Table XXVI; Lord, *loc. cit.,* 183.

52 Cf. Shea, *op. cit.,* IV, 511.

[53] Cf., e.g., *Boston Pilot,* June 3, 1855.

[54] Cullen, *op. cit.,* 156; *Boston Pilot,* June 4, 1864.

[55] Cf. T. A. Emmet, *Memoir of Thomas Addis and Robert Emmet* . . . (New York, 1915), I, 501; *Jesuit or Catholic Sentinel,* January 29, 1831; *Boston Catholic Observer,* April 17, 1847, October 4, 1848; *Constitution of the Boston Roman Catholic Mutual Relief Society . . . 1832 . . .* (Boston, 1837); Dissertation Copy, 304.

[56] Cf. *Boston Pilot,* June 25, 1842.

[57] Cf. F. W. Bogen, *German in America* . . . (Boston, 1851), 11, 13.

[58] For the use of such words, cf. Karl Heinzen, *Luftspiele* (*Zweite Auflage, Gesammelte Schriften,* II, Boston, 1872), 172, 176, 177, 179, 181, 195, 212 and passim; A. Douai, "Der Ueberfall," *Meyer's Monatshefte,* April, 1855, V, 241; *Der Pionier,* January 31, 1861.

[59] Thus the Germans adapted the past prefix "Ge" to English words, viz., "hab' ich denn gesuppos't," "gekillt," "getschähnscht" (cf. Heinzen, *Luftspiele,* 170, 191). For English words in American French, cf. references to *Courrier des États-Unis,* Dissertation Copy, 306.

[60] Cf. "Annual Report of the Boston School Committee, 1864," *Boston City Documents, 1865,* no. 39, p. 164.

[61] Cf. *Minutes of the Selectmen's Meetings, 1811 to 1817 . . .* (*Volume of Records Relating to the Early History of Boston . . . ,* XXXVIII), *Boston City Documents, 1908,* no. 60, p. 171; Abraham G. Daniels, *Memories of Ohabei Shalom, 1843 to 1918 . . .* (s.l., n.d. [Boston, 1918]); *Constitution, By-Laws and Rules of Order of the Hebrew Congregation Ohabei Shalom . . .* (Boston, 1855); *Boston Pilot,* September 23, 1849.

[62] Cf. Lemuel Shattuck, *Report . . . Census of Boston . . . 1845 . . .* (Boston, 1846), 123; *Boston Merkur,* December 19, 1846; Justin Winsor, *Memorial History of Boston . . .* (Boston, 1880), III, 444; cf. *Journal of the Proceedings of the Annual Convention of the Protestant Episcopal Church in . . . Massachusetts . . . 1833* (Boston, 1833), 30; *Journal of the Proceedings . . . 1834* (Boston, 1834), 17; Benevolent Fraternity of Churches, *Twenty-Third Annual Report of the Executive Committee* (Boston, 1857), 3.

[63] E. Percival Merritt, "Sketches of the Three Earliest Roman Catholic Priests in Boston" (*Publications of the Colonial Society of Massachusetts,* XXV), 173 ff. Cf. also Shea, *op. cit.,* II, 315 ff., 387 ff.

[64] Cf. Merritt, *loc. cit.,* 185, 191 ff., 212 ff.

[65] Cullen, *op. cit.,* 125; *Boston Catholic Observer,* April 3, 1847; Leo F. Ruskowski, *French Émigré Priests in the United States . . .* (Washington, 1940), 11 ff.

[66] Cf. Merritt, *loc. cit.,* 198–201; Shea, *op. cit.,* II, 435 ff., 617, 621, III, 107 ff.; *Boston Catholic Observer,* May 29, 1847; McGee, *Catholic History,*

97 ff.; Ruskowski, *op. cit.*, 121; Frances S. Childs, *French Refugee Life in the United States* . . . (Baltimore, 1940), 40, 41.

[67] Cf., e.g., *Annales de la propagation de la foi* . . . *1865*, XXXVII, 485. For Fitzpatrick, cf. Cullen, *op. cit.*, 131, 132. For Fenwick, cf. Lord, *loc. cit.*

[68] Bishop Cheverus to Archbishop Neale, December 19, 1816, quoted in *Boston Pilot*, February 16, 1856.

[69] Cf. *Boston Pilot*, January 28, February 25, 1843; Shattuck, *op. cit.*, 123; *Boston Catholic Observer*, April 17, 1847; *United States Catholic Almanac, 1833*, 46, 47.

[70] Cf. *Boston Catholic Observer*, May 10, 17, 1848; *Boston Pilot*, January 21, 1843, September 29, 1855.

[71] *Boston Pilot*, May 21, 1842, November 10, December 8, 1855, December 13, 1862, March 28, 1863; *Boston Catholic Observer*, July 5, September 13, 1848; *Cambridge Directory, 1865–6*, 185; Cullen *op. cit.*, 136; C. Bancroft Gillespie, *Illustrated History of South Boston* . . . (South Boston, 1900), 67, 73.

[72] Cf. Rev. James Fitton, *Sketches of the Establishment of the Church in New England* (Boston, 1872), 146, 147; Shea, *op. cit.*, III, 486, 488, IV, 145; *Boston Pilot*, June 25, 1842, January 14, February 25, 1843, May 30, 1846.

[73] Cf. *Boston Pilot*, October 31, 1863; *Boston Merkur*, June 12, 1847; *Boston Catholic Observer*, June 5, 1847; Richard J. Quinlan, "Growth and Development of Catholic Education in the Archdiocese of Boston," *Catholic Historical Review*, April, 1936, XXII, 32.

[74] Cf. *Bostoner Zeitung*, September 1, 1865; *Der Pionier*, March 5, 1862.

[75] Cf. *Official Catholic Year Book, 1928*, 407.

[76] Cf. Fitton, *op. cit.*, 134, 135; Dissertation Copy, 316; *Boston Catholic Observer*, October 25, 1848; *Boston Pilot*, November 18, 1854, November 24, 1855; Shattuck, *op. cit.*, 124.

[77] Cf. Quinlan, *loc. cit.*, 28.

[78] Cf. *Boston Catholic Observer*, June 5, 1847; Quinlan, *loc. cit.*, 29; Winsor, *op. cit.*, III, 519; [Charles Greely Loring], *Report of the Committee Relating to the Destruction of the Ursuline Convent* . . . (Boston, 1834), 5.

[79] Cf. Quinlan, *loc. cit.*, 30, 34; Gillespie, *op. cit.*, 67; *Boston Pilot*, July 24, 1858; Cullen, *op. cit.*, 134, 136; Moses King, *Back Bay District* . . . (Boston, 1880), 18.

[80] Cf. *Massachusetts House Documents, 1849*, no. 130, p. 2; Lord, *loc. cit.*, 183.

[81] Cullen, *op. cit.*, 135; Shea, *op. cit.*, IV, 515; *Boston Pilot*, December 24, 1864.

[82] For examples, cf. *Boston Pilot,* January 18, 1862, June 4, 1864; Cullen, *op. cit.,* 132. Cf. also [Report on Dioceses Subject to the College of the Propaganda] (MS., B. A. Vat. no. 9565), fol. 132; Quinlan, *loc. cit.,* 30.

[83] Cf. *Boston City Documents, 1864,* no. 30, p. 42; *Massachusetts Senate Documents, 1850,* no. 55, pp. 1 ff. For fees, cf. *Boston Pilot,* August 28, 1858.

[84] Cf. *Literary and Catholic Sentinel,* April 16, 1836.

[85] Cf. "Proceedings at the Memorial to Abraham Lincoln . . . ," *Boston City Documents, 1865,* no. 59, pp. 69, 73; also Dissertation Copy, 320.

[86] Benevolent Fraternity of Churches, *Twenty-second Annual Report of the Executive Committee . . .* (Boston, 1856), 7, 8; Benevolent Fraternity of Churches, *Twenty-third Annual Report . . .* (Boston, 1857), 13; Benevolent Fraternity of Churches, *Twenty-fifth Annual Report . . .* (Boston, 1859), 23.

[87] Cf. Dissertation Copy, 320–321; *Literary and Catholic Sentinel,* November 26, 1836.

[88] Cf. *Boston Directory, 1853,* 382; *Der Neu England Demokrat,* November 21, 1857; *Bostoner Zeitung,* January 6, 1866; *Boston Merkur,* December 12, 1846, April 24, 1847; *Der Pionier,* March 14, 28, 1861.

[89] Cf. *Courrier de Boston, affiches, annonces et avis . . . ,* April 23–October 15, 1789; Merritt, *loc. cit.,* 210; Howard Mumford Jones, *America and French Culture* (Chapel Hill, 1927), 136; George Parker Winship, "Two or Three Boston Papers," *Papers of the Bibliographical Society of America,* XIV, 57 ff., 76 ff.; Childs, *op. cit.,* 129.

[90] Cf. *Courrier des États-Unis, journal politique et littéraire,* March 1, 1828, November 14, 1829, November 12, 1839, June 10, April 24, 1851.

[91] Cf. *Literary and Catholic Sentinel,* December 10, 1836; *Courrier des États-Unis,* April 16, 1837; *Boston Almanac, 1846,* 145; *Le Bostonien, journal des salons* (Boston), May 12, 1849 ff.; *Gazette Française* (Boston), September 14, 1850–July 19, 1851; *Le Phare de New York, echo . . . des deux mondes,* February 24, 1851 ff.; also Henri Herz, *Mes Voyages en Amérique . . .* (Paris, 1866), 192 ff.

[92] *El Redactor* (New York), March 10, 1828 ff. (apparently founded in 1827); *L'Eco d'Italia, giornale politico populare letterario* (New York), Februray 8, 1850 ff.; *Il Proscritto, giornale politico, artistico e litterario* (New York), August 7, 1851 ff. For others, cf. *Courrier des États-Unis,* August 2, 1849.

[93] Cf. *Old Countryman: and English, Irish, . . . Colonial Mirror,* October 10, 1829; *Anglo-Saxon, European and Colonial Gazette* (Boston), December 22, 1855 ff., September 12, 1856; *Boston Pilot,* December 29, 1855; *European* (New York), November 15, 1856 ff.; *Scottish-American Journal,* January 30, 1864.

345

⁹⁴ Cf. *Boston Merkur, ein Volksblatt für Stadt und Land,* November 21, 1846 ff.; *Der Neu England Demokrat,* October 17, 1857 ff.; Karl Heinzen, *Erlebtes, zweite Theil: nach meiner Exilirung* (*Gesammelte Schriften,* IV, Boston, 1874); *Gedenkbuch, Erinnerung an Karl Heinzen* . . . (Milwaukee, 1887), 8, 32; *Der Pionier,* April 29, 1863, February 28, 1861; *Bostoner Zeitung, ein Organ für die Neu England Staaten* . . . , September 1, 1865 ff.

⁹⁵ Cf. *Western Star and Harp of Erin* (New York), May 16, 1812–May 1, 1813; Louis Dow Scisco, *Political Nativism in New York State* (New York, 1901), 19.

⁹⁶ Lord, *loc. cit.,* 177. Another children's newspaper, *Young Catholics Friend,* edited by H. B. C. Greene, appeared for a short time in March, 1840.

⁹⁷ *Literary and Catholic Sentinel,* January 3, December 19, 1835, January 2, 1836. To avoid confusion with a later paper of the same name, it is referred to throughout this work by its original title.

⁹⁸ *Ibid.,* June 11, October 22, November 12, 19, 1836; McGee, *History of the Irish Settlers,* 132.

⁹⁹ *Boston Pilot,* December 22, 29, 1838, November 16, 1839.

¹⁰⁰ Cf. Mrs. J. Sadlier, *Biographical Sketch,* 17, 18; Robert D. McGibbon, *Thomas D'Arcy McGee* . . . (Montreal, 1884), 7; Skelton, *op. cit.,* 11 ff.; *Boston Pilot,* July 23, 1842, October 11, 1845.

¹⁰¹ Cf. Shea, *op. cit.,* IV, 154; *Boston Catholic Observer,* January 23, 1847, June 21, 1848. The break was not open at first, the *Observer* being printed by P. Donahoe, owner of the *Pilot* (*ibid.,* January 16, 1847).

¹⁰² The *Pilot* was at a tremendous disadvantage, since it could not openly attack the priest who edited the *Observer.* Its criticisms were guarded and apologetic. But its rival had no scruples, attacking it as "avowedly anti-Catholic," "guilty of uttering *heresy*" cf. *Boston Catholic Observer,* June 7, 14, May 24, and especially June 28, 1848).

¹⁰³ Cf. Henry F. Brownson, *Orestes A. Brownson's Middle Life* . . . (Detroit, 1899), 441; Skelton, *op. cit.,* 162 ff.; *Boston Pilot,* January 1, 1848, January 4, 1851.

¹⁰⁴ Cf. Sadlier, *loc. cit.,* 22, 23, 27–30; Skelton, *op. cit.,* 163 ff., 183 ff., 194 ff., 199, 281 ff.; *Irish-American,* August 12, 1849, May 30, 1857.

¹⁰⁵ Cf. *Citizen* (New York), January 7, 1854; *Boston Pilot,* March 24, 1855, April 24, March 27, 1858, April 2, 1859; *European,* December 6, 1856.

¹⁰⁶ Cf., e.g., *Memoir of Mrs. Chloe Spear, a Native of Africa* . . . *by a Lady of Boston* (Boston, 1832), 41, 49, 71 ff.

¹⁰⁷ John Hayward, *Gazetteer of Massachusetts* . . . (Boston, 1849), 88, 90, 97; *Massachusetts House Documents, 1840,* no. 60, p. 22; Winsor, *op.*

cit., III, 424, 425, 441; *Bowen's Picture of Boston* . . . (Boston, 1829), 149, 151, 152; *Boston Directory, 1830*, 31; W. H. Siebert, *Underground Railroad from Slavery to Freedom* (New York, 1898), facing 235.

[108] Cf. Dissertation Copy, 333 ff.; George W. Crawford, *Prince Hall and His Followers* . . . (New York, n.d. [1914]), 13 ff.; *Minutes of the Selectmen's Meetings* . . . *1818* . . . *1822* (*Volume of Records Relating to the Early History of Boston, XXXIX*), *Boston City Documents, 1909*, no. 61, p. 192; *African Repository and Colonial Journal*, May, 1830, VI, 89; *ibid.*, November, 1827, III, 271; Helen T. Catterall, *Judicial Cases Concerning American Slavery and the Negro* . . . (Washington, 1936), IV, 512 ff.

[109] Lewis Hayden, *Grand Lodge Jurisdictional Claim* . . . (Boston, 1868), 30 ff., 84; Charles H. Wesley, *Richard Allen* . . . (Washington, n.d. [1935]), 93; *Boston Almanac, 1866*, 166, 167.

[110] Cf. *Boston Pilot*, September 8, 1855, June 12, 1852, October 5, 1850, February 22, 1851; Catterall, *op. cit.*, IV, 502 ff.; *Colored American* (New York), January 7, 1837 ff.; Vernon Loggins, *Negro Author* . . . (New York, 1931), 53 ff.; William S. Robinson, *"Warrington" Pen-Portraits* . . . *1848 to 1876* . . . (Boston, 1877), 71 ff., 191; Siebert, *Underground Railroad*, 72, 251.

[111] "Report of the State Board of Education," *Massachusetts Public Documents, 1860*, no. 2, p. 134; *Boston Pilot*, September 15, 1855.

[112] *Boston Pilot*, July 29, 1854.

[113] Cf., e.g., *Courrier des États-Unis*, May 15, 1851; Edward Dicey, *Six Months in the Federal States* (London, 1863), II, 179.

[114] "Annual Report by the City Registrar . . . 1865," *Boston City Documents, 1866*, no. 88, p. 15; *Der Pionier*, January 26, 1860. Table XXVII gives figures of intermarriage in 1863–65 when the degree of assimilation should have been at its height. Only German women married more closely into their own group than the Irish, and that because they were so far outnumbered by German men. However, German male intermarriages more than counterbalanced this.

[115] Cf., e.g., Winsor, *op. cit.*, II, 553 ff.; Wittke, *op. cit.*, 24 ff.; Cullen, *op. cit.*, 194, 195.

[116] Cf., e.g., "The Anglo-Saxon Race," *North American Review*, July, 1851, LXXIII, 53, 34 ff.; and Emerson's use of the term in "English Traits," *Collected Works* (Boston, 1903), V.

[117] Cf. M. A. DeWolfe Howe, *Holmes of the Breakfast Table* (New York, 1939), 7, 12.

Notes to Chapter 7

Chapter VII. Group Conflict

[1] Theodore Parker, *A Sermon of the Dangerous Classes in Society* . . . (Boston, 1847), 12.

[2] Cf., e.g., the sober editorial on Negro problems in *Daily Evening Transcript,* September 28, 1830; cf. also Mary Caroline Crawford, *Romantic Days in Old Boston* . . . (Boston, 1910), 249; Helen T. Catterall, *Judicial Cases Concerning American Slavery and the Negro* . . . (Washington, 1936), IV, 524.

[3] Cf. E. S. Abdy, *Journal of a Residence and Tour in the United States* . . . (London, 1835), I, 133 ff.; Odell Shepard, *Journals of Bronson Alcott* (Boston, 1938), 110.

[4] Cf. [Theodore Lyman, Jr.], *Free Negroes and Mulattoes, House of Representatives, January 16, 1822* . . . *Report* . . . (Boston, n.d.); Henry Wilson, *History of the Rise and Fall of the Slave Power in America* (Boston, 1872), I, 489–492.

[5] 316 between the ages of 10 and 15 ("Report of the School Committee, 1866," *Boston City Documents, 1866,* no. 137, p. 188). Cf. also *Boston Pilot,* September 15, October 6, 1855.

[6] Cf. the letters of Edward Everett to John P. Bigelow, dated July 23, 1839, September 30, 1839 (Bigelow Papers [MSS., H. C. L.], Box V, VI); Arthur B. Darling, *Political Changes in Massachusetts* . . . (New Haven, 1925), 320; Catterall, *op. cit.,* IV, 511, 524; Edward Channing, *History of the United States* (New York, 1925), VI, 93 ff.

[7] Cf. Wilson, *op. cit.,* I, 492–495; Lady Emmeline S. Wortley, *Travels in the United States* . . . (New York, 1851), 60; Edward Dicey, *Six Months in the Federal States* (London, 1863), II, 215.

[8] *Exercises at the Dedication of the Monument to Colonel Robert Gould Shaw* . . . *May 31, 1897* . . . (Boston, 1897), 10; Henry Greenleaf Pearson, *Life of John A. Andrew* . . . (Boston, 1904), II, 70 ff.; William S. Robinson, *"Warrington" Pen-Portraits* . . . (Boston, 1877), 107, 274, 406; A. B. Hart, *Commonwealth History of Massachusetts* . . . (New York, 1930), IV, 535; *Boston City Documents, 1863,* no. 100, pp. 11, 18.

[9] Robinson, *op. cit.,* 298; cf. also Dicey, *op. cit.,* I, 70, 74; *Massachusetts Senate Documents, 1841,* no. 51; *Massachusetts House Documents, 1841,* no. 17.

[10] Thus with few exceptions there was a "general absence of anti-Catholic references" in eighteenth-century textbooks, and the Dudleian lectures were founded to counteract "the rapid rise of liberalism" (Rev. Arthur J. Riley, *Catholicism in New England* . . . [Washington, 1936], 307, 23, 31, 225). The only exception was the hostility, primarily political, to Jesuit activities in Maine (*ibid.,* 6, 193 ff.; Channing, *op. cit.,* II, 131 ff.,

531, 545 ff.). Puritan intolerance sprang from the desire to found a "bible commonwealth" and was therefore directed against Baptists, Quakers and Arminians as well (cf. Channing, *op. cit.*, II, 68; Ray Allen Billington, *Protestant Crusade, 1800–1860, A Study of the Origins of American Nativism* [New York, 1938], 7, 15, 18; Riley, *op. cit.*, 45 ff., 217 ff. When priests visited Boston under circumstances that did not endanger the "Standing Order" they "received a cordial welcome befitting the social amenities exchanged between educated persons" (Riley, *op. cit.*, 190, 184 ff., 206, 207).

[11] Octavius B. Frothingham, *Boston Unitarianism, 1820–1850 . . .* (New York, 1890), 23; Archibald H. Grimké, *Life of Charles Sumner . . .* (New York, 1892), 38. For the popularity of the French in Boston, cf. H. M. Jones, *America and French Culture . . .* (Chapel Hill, 1927), 126; for the effect of the revolution, cf. John G. Shea, "Catholic Church in American History," *American Catholic Quarterly Review,* January, 1876, I, 155; Billington, *op. cit.*, 19.

Those who regard anti-Catholicism as inherent in the nature of Protestant society, and define "the Protestant milieu" as "nothing else than opposition to Catholicism" (Riley, *op. cit.*, vii, 1; "Anti-Catholic Movements in the United States," *Catholic World,* XXII [1876], 810; Billington, *op. cit.*, 1) have been hard put to explain the tolerance of the early nineteenth century. The simplest escape has been to mark it a period of subsidence arising from absorption in other problems (cf. Billington, *op. cit.*, 32; Humphrey J. Desmond, *Know-Nothing Party* [Washington, 1904], 12), with the anti-Catholicism of the forties and fifties simply a recrudescence of forces always present, thus missing completely the significance of the special factors that produced it in those two decades.

[12] Samuel Breck, "Catholic Recollections," *American Catholic Historical Researches,* XII (1895), 146, 148; E. Percival Merritt, "Sketches of the Three Earliest Roman Catholic Priests in Boston," *Publications of the Colonial Society of Massachusetts,* XXV, 218 ff.; William Wilson Manross, *Episcopal Church in the United States, 1800–1840, A Study in Church Life* (New York, 1938), 59; Samuel Eliot Morison, *History of the Constitution of Massachusetts . . .* (Boston, 1917), 24.

[13] Cf. Merritt, *loc. cit.*, 205–207; Billington, *op. cit.*, 20; Josiah Quincy, *Figures of the Past from the Leaves of Old Journals* (Boston, 1883), 311, 312; *Minutes of the Selectmen's Meetings, 1811 to 1817 . . .* (*Volume of Records Relating to the Early History of Boston,* XXXVIII), *Boston City Documents, 1908,* no. 60, p. 69; James Bernard Cullen, *Story of the Irish in Boston . . .* (Boston, 1890), 125; Leo F. Ruskowski, *French Emigré Priests in the United States . . .* (Washington, 1940), 85.

[14] Cf. Morison, *op. cit.*, 24, 32; *Boston Catholic Observer,* April 17, 1847;

Rev. James Fitton, *Sketches of the Establishment of the Church in New England* (Boston, 1872), 141; Darling, *op. cit.*, 23; Hart, *op. cit.*, IV, 12.

[15] Cf. Billington, *op. cit.*, 53 ff., 76. The Boston Irish Protestant Association which Billington claimed was anti-Catholic (*ibid.*, 78, n. 48) specifically disavowed such activities (cf. the correspondence in *Boston Pilot*, June 25, July 2, 1842; also *Boston Catholic Observer*, August 2, 1848).

[16] Cf., e.g., *Jesuit or Catholic Sentinel*, July 23, 1831; Marcus Lee Hansen, *Immigrant in American History* . . . (Cambridge, 1940), 107.

[17] James Freeman Clarke, *The Church . . . as It Was, as It Is, as It Ought to Be, a Discourse at the . . . Chapel . . . Church of the Disciples . . . 1848* (Boston, 1848), 13; Arthur M. Schlesinger, Jr., *Orestes A. Brownson* . . . (Boston, 1939), 175.

[18] Cf. *Columbian Centinel* (Boston), January 26, 1791; *ibid.*, February 2, 1791; *American Catholic Historical Researches*, V (1888), 51.

[19] Cf. Dissertation Copy, 347, 348; Billington, *op. cit.*, 43 ff., 69 ff., 79. For the religious press in general, cf. Frank Luther Mott, *History of American Magazines* . . . (Cambridge, 1938), II, 60.

[20] Cf. the complaints on this score in *Boston Catholic Observer*, March 1, 1848; also Billington, *op. cit.*, 177, 86.

[21] Cf., e.g., Darling, *op. cit.*, 29; Clarence Hotson, "Christian Critics and Mr. Emerson," *New England Quarterly*, March, 1938, XI, 29 ff.

[22] R. C. Waterston, *"The Keys of the Kingdom of Heaven," a Sermon* . . . (Boston, 1844), 13; cf. also Frothingham, *op. cit.*, 48; *Jesuit or Catholic Sentinel*, December 29, 1830, *ibid.*, February 26, 1831.

[23] Frothingham, *op. cit.*, 6.

[24] Richard Price, *Sermons on the Christian Doctrine as Received by the Different Denominations of Christians* . . . (Boston, 1815), 8.

[25] Cf. M. A. DeWolfe Howe, *Holmes of the Breakfast Table* . . . (New York, 1939), 17.

[26] *Minutes of the Boston Baptist Association . . . 1821* (Boston, n.d.), 13.

[27] Cf. Morris A. Gutstein, *Aaron Lopez and Judah Touro* . . . (New York, 1939), 98.

[28] Cf. Massachusetts Commissioners of Alien Passengers and Foreign Paupers, *Report . . . 1851* (Boston, 1852), 14; also Edith Abbott, *Historical Aspects of the Immigration Problem* . . . (Chicago, 1926), 622, 739 ff.; *Cork Examiner*, July 6, 1853; *Massachusetts House Documents, 1828-29*, no. 25; *ibid., 1829-30*, no. 8; *Massachusetts Senate Documents, 1852*, no. 11.

[29] Cf. the source of petitions for repeal of the State pauper laws, *Massachusetts Senate Documents, 1847*, no. 109.

[30] *Ordinances of the City of Boston Passed since the Year 1834* . . . (Boston, 1843), 3, 4; Hart, *op. cit.*, IV, 143 ff.; Edith Abbott, *Immigration. Select Documents* . . . (Chicago, 1924), 105 ff., 148.

[31] Cf. Norris v. City of Boston (7 *Howard's U. S. Reports*, 283, XVII, 139 ff.); *Massachusetts Senate Documents, 1847*, no. 109; *ibid., 1848*, no. 46; Peleg W. Chandler, *Charter and Ordinances of the City of Boston together with Acts of the Legislature Relating to the City* . . . (Boston, 1850), 25 ff.; *Charter and Ordinances of the City of Boston together with the Acts of the Legislature* . . . (Boston, 1856), 34 ff.

[32] *Massachusetts Senate Documents, 1852*, no. 7, p. 7. For the influence of shipping firms, cf. *Massachusetts Senate Documents, 1847*, no. 109, p. 5; Boston Board of Trade, *Second Annual Report of the Government* . . . *1856* (Boston, 1856), 3.

[33] For evidence of this complaint, cf. *American Traveller* (Boston), August 5, 1834; *American*, October 21, 1837; Abbott, *Immigration*, 112 ff.; Edith Abbott, *Historical Aspects of the Immigration Problem* . . . (Chicago, 1926), 572 ff., 758 ff.; *Massachusetts House Documents, 1836*, no. 30, pp. 9 ff.

[34] Cf. *Massachusetts Senate Documents, 1847*, no. 109, p. 4.

[35] *American* (Boston), October 21, 1837.

[36] Mayor Lyman (*Inaugural Addresses of the Mayors of Boston* . . . [Boston, 1894], I, 195).

[37] Cf., e.g., *Boston Catholic Observer*, February 16, 1848; Thomas D'Arcy McGee, *History of the Irish Settlers in North America* . . . (Boston, 1852), 71; Billington, *op. cit.*, 291.

[38] Cf., e.g., Ellie in Agnes E. St. John, "Ellie Moore or the Pilgrim's Crown," *Boston Pilot*, June 30–September 1, 1860.

[39] Cf. James O'Connor, "Anti-Catholic Prejudice," *American Catholic Quarterly Review*, I (1876), 13.

[40] Cf. Billington, *op. cit.*, 118 ff., 263; William Wilson Manross, *History of the American Episcopal Church* (New York, 1935), 283 ff.; *Boston Catholic Observer*, July 24, 1847; S. F. B. Morse, *Foreign Conspiracy against the United States* (s.l., n.d. [186–], 26, 3, 29; S. F. B. Morse, *Imminent Dangers to the Free Institutions of the United States* . . . (New York, 1854), passim; Louis Dow Scisco, *Political Nativism in New York State* (New York, 1901), 21.

[41] Cf. "Boston as it Appeared to a Foreigner at the Beginning of the Nineteenth Century," *Bostonian Society Publications*, Series I, IV, 117, 118; Joseph E. Chamberlin, *Boston Transcript* . . . (Boston, 1930), 37 ff.; *Minutes of the Selectmen's Meetings, 1811 to 1817* . . . (*Volume of Records* . . . , XXXVIII), *Boston City Documents, 1908*, no. 60, p. 113;

Boston Pilot, September 12, 1846; Arthur Wellington Brayley, *Complete History of the Boston Fire Department* . . . (Boston, 1889), 185, 186; Edward H. Savage, *Police Records and Recollections* . . . (Boston, 1873), 65, 66, 110, 257.

⁴² Chamberlin, *op. cit.,* 48 ff.; Brayley, *Complete History,* 197 ff.; State Street Trust Company, *Mayors of Boston* . . . (Boston, [1914]), 15.

⁴³ Cf. *American,* October 21, 1837, March 17, 1838.

⁴⁴ There are numerous short accounts of this affair; but the best, though differing in interpretation from that offered here, is in Billington, *op. cit.,* 68 ff.

⁴⁵ Billington, *op. cit.,* 71 ff.; Shea, *op. cit.,* III, 462, 463; Charles Greely Loring, *Report of the Committee Relating to the Destruction of the Ursuline Convent* . . . (Boston, 1834), 8. Miss Harrison's disappearance was probably not important. In 1830 a rumor spread by the *New England Herald* (Vol. I, no. 28) that "a young lady, an orphan has lately been inveigled into the Ursuline Convent . . . after having been cajoled to transfer a large fortune to the Popish massmen" was ridiculed and had no repercussions (cf. *United States Catholic Intelligencer,* April 24, 1830).

⁴⁶ Billington, *op. cit.,* 81, n. 85; Benj. F. Butler, *Autobiography and Personal Reminiscences* . . . (Boston, 1892), 111; Darling, *op. cit.,* 165, n. 79.

⁴⁷ Cf. Billington, *op. cit.,* 69, 81–85, 86, 108; Loring, *op. cit.,* 2, 6, 16; *American Traveller,* August 15, 19, 1834; [H. Ware, Jr.], *An Account of the Conflagration of the Ursuline Convent . . . by a Friend of Religious Toleration* (Boston, 1834), 3; Chamberlin, *op. cit.,* 44 ff.; *Jesuit or Catholic Sentinel,* August 16, 1834; *ibid.,* August 23, 1834; Crawford, *Romantic Days,* 22.

⁴⁸ Cf. Ware, *op. cit.,* 10; *Jesuit or Catholic Sentinel,* August 23, 1834; Billington, *op. cit.,* 86, 87; Loring, *op. cit.,* 4.

⁴⁹ Robert H. Lord, "Organizer of the Church in New England," *Catholic Historical Review,* XXII (1936), 182.

⁵⁰ Cf. Billington, *op. cit.,* 89, 110, n. 27; *Documents Relating to the Ursuline Convent in Charlestown* (Boston, 1842), 21, 22, 31; "Anti-Catholic Movements in the United States," *Catholic World,* XXII (1876), 814; *Boston Pilot,* February 18, 1854.

⁵¹ Cf. *Boston Pilot,* April 16, 1853; Billington, *op. cit.,* 92 ff.

⁵² Cf. *American,* October 21, 1837; *Boston Pilot,* February 3, 17, 1838, October 12, 1839.

⁵³ Cf. State Street Trust Company, *Mayors of Boston,* 17; Darling, *op. cit.,* 327–329; William G. Bean, Party Transformation in Massachusetts . . . (MS. H. C. L.), 228 ff.

[54] *Boston Catholic Observer,* August 28, June 19, July 24, 1847; Bean, *op. cit.,* 232 ff.

[55] Cf. *Jesuit or Catholic Sentinel,* January 18, 1834; *Boston Pilot,* November 9, 1839; George H. Haynes, "Causes of Know-Nothing Success in Massachusetts," *American Historical Review,* III (1897), 74, n. 1.

[56] Cf. *Boston Pilot,* February 19, 1853; Dissertation Copy, 367.

[57] Cf. Josiah Curtis, *Report of the Joint Special Committee . . . 1855 . . .* (Boston, 1856), 11; "Report and Tabular Statement of the Censors," *Boston City Documents, 1850,* no. 42, p. 12; Billington, *op. cit.,* 325, 326.

[58] Cf., e.g., *Boston Pilot,* July 8, 1860.

[59] The only instance of devious Irish politics in this period came in the election of John C. Tucker to the legislature in 1860 (cf. E. P. Loring and C. T. Russell, Jr., *Reports of Controverted Elections . . . 1853 to 1885 . . .* [Boston, 1886], 89 ff.).

[60] Richard O'Gorman to W. S. O'Brien, May 24, 1849, W. S. O'Brien Papers and Letters, 1819–1854 (MSS., N. L. I.), XVIII, no. 2, 547.

[61] Cf. Darling, *op. cit.,* 312 ff.

[62] Cf. Robinson, *op. cit.,* 28–38, 416, 513; Bean, *op. cit.,* 8–38; Darling, *op. cit.,* 245 ff., 317, 334, 290, n. 67, 326; Wilson, *op. cit.,* I, 545 ff., II, 145 ff.; George S. Merriam, *Life and Times of Samuel Bowles* (New York, 1885), I, 45 ff.; *Reunion of the Free-Soilers of 1848–1852 . . . June 28, 1888* (Cambridge, 1888), 15, 17; Hart, *op cit.,* IV, 97; Grimké, *op. cit.,* 182 ff., 190 ff.

[63] Bean, *op. cit.,* 17, 28, 35 ff., 53 ff.; Darling, *op. cit.,* 340, 349–354; Grimké, *op. cit.,* 205; Haynes, *loc. cit.,* 80; Wilson, *op. cit.,* II, 247 ff.

[64] Cf. Bean, *op. cit.,* 54, 57, 64–87; Wilson, *op. cit.,* II, 347 ff.; *Address to the People of Massachusetts* (s.l., n.d., [Boston, 1852]), 3, 6, 7, 10 ff.; Robinson, *op. cit.,* 47, 433; Hart, *op. cit.,* IV, 99, 475.

[65] Alfred S. Roe, "Governors of Massachusetts . . . ," *New England Magazine,* XXV (1902), 547; Bean, *op. cit.,* 90–92, 113–120; Robinson, *op. cit,* 433; *Address,* 5 ff.; Grimké, *op. cit.,* 209.

[66] A simple majority sufficed in the Senate (Bean, *op. cit.,* 116; Morison, *op. cit.,* 38).

[67] Bean, *op. cit.,* 88, 89. Legislators from Boston were elected on a general ticket which usually denied representation to minorities and gave the whole delegation to the Whigs (cf. Morison, *op. cit.,* 41).

[68] The election of 1851:

	GOVERNOR			CONVENTION	
	State	Boston		State	Boston
Winthrop (W)	64,611	7,388	no	65,846	7,135
Boutwell (D)	43,992	3,632			
Palfrey (FS)	28,599	1,294	yes	60,972	3,813

Notes to Chapter 7

(*Boston Semi-Weekly Advertiser*, November 12, 1851; Bean, *op. cit.*, 109, 111). Cf. also Morison, *op. cit.*, 42.

[69] Bean's claim that the Free-Soilers bolted (*op. cit.*, 111) is wholly illogical since they wanted the convention and the Irish did not (for the Free-Soiler's attitude on constitutional change, cf. Robinson, *op. cit.*, 401 ff.

[70] Cf. in general, Bean, *op. cit.*, 127 ff., 217– 220. For the new attempt to revise the constitution, cf. *Massachusetts Senate Documents, 1852*, no. 36, pp. 6 ff.

[71] Cf. J. B. Mann, *Life of Henry Wilson* . . . (Boston, 1872), 36 ff.; Hon. Charles Allen, *Speech* . . . *at Worcester, Nov. 5, 1853* (s.l., n.d.), 1–3; Bean, *op. cit.*, 147–166; Morison, *op. cit.*, 49–60; Henry F. Brownson, *Orestes A. Brownson's Middle Life* . . . (Detroit, 1899), II, 465, 466; Mann, *op. cit.*, 43.

[72] For Free-Soil opposition, cf. Bean, *op. cit.*, 168, 177.

[73] Cf. Brownson, *Brownson's Middle Life*, II, 455 ff.; Dissertation Copy, 377–378; Bean, *op. cit.*, 221.

[74] Robinson, *op. cit.*, 204; Bean, *op. cit.*, 162, 166, 174–179; Butler, *op. cit.*, 119. The analysis of the vote from which Morison concludes that "the wards where most of the Irish-born population then lived did not poll so heavy a negative vote as the fashionable residential districts" (*op. cit.*, 63) is not valid because the wards were gerrymandered in the redistricting of 1850 to split the Irish vote (cf. Dissertation Copy, 383). Even in 1854 votes against the Know-Nothings showed no special concentration in any area (cf. *Boston Atlas*, November 14, 1854). Bean has shown that votes to defeat the constitution came from Boston: the 5,915 negative balance of Suffolk County more than offset the 997 positive balance elsewhere in the state (*op. cit.*, 173).

[75] Butler, *op. cit.*, 120.

[76] Cf. *Boston Semi-Weekly Advertiser*, November 30, December 3, 1853; Billington, *op. cit.*, 301.

[77] *Boston Pilot*, October 8, 1853, February 11, 1854; Billington, *op. cit.*, 300–302; Desmond, *op. cit.*, 72; Shea, *op. cit.*, IV, 360 ff.

[78] *Massachusetts Life Boat*, September 19, 1854; *cf. also Address of the State Temperance Committee to the Citzens of Massachusetts on the Operation of the Anti-Liquor Law* (Boston, 1853), 2; Billington, *op. cit.*, 323.

[79] Cf. *Boston Pilot*, June 3, 1854; *Irish-American*, September 23, 1854; Billington, *op. cit.*, 435, n. 81; Bean, *op. cit.*, 187, 239, 241.

[80] Cf. Bean, *loc. cit.*, 239 ff.; Carl Wittke, *We Who Built America* . . . (New York, 1939), 168.

[81] *Boston Pilot,* April 9, December 10, 1853, May 13, 1854, January 20, 1855; *Wide Awake: and the Spirit of Washington* (Boston), October 7, 1854; Billington, *op. cit.,* 305–313, 348 ff., 368; Bean, *op. cit.,* 207, 209; Shea, *op. cit.,* IV, 509; Charles W. Frothingham, *Six Hours in a Convent: — or — The Stolen Nuns! . . .* (Boston, 1855).

[82] Albert G. Browne to Sumner, July 28, 1854, Sumner Correspondence (MSS., H. C. L.), XXV, no. 109.

[83] Seth Webb, Jr., July 14, 1854, *ibid.,* XXV, no. 72; also Bean, *op. cit.,* 188 ff.

[84] Cf. Amasa Walker to Sumner, Sumner Correspondence, July 2, 1854, XXV, no. 15; Bean, *op. cit.,* 193; Merriam, *op. cit.,* I, 122.

[85] Cf. *Boston Semi-Weekly Advertiser,* December 10, 1853.

BOSTON ELECTIONS, 1853

Governor	(November)	Mayor	(December)
Whig	7,730	Whig	5,651
Free-Soil	1,403	Citizen's Union	4,691
Coalition Democrat	2,455	Young Men's League	2,010
Hunker Democrat	821	Democrat	596
Total	12,409	Total	12,948

(*Boston Semi-Weekly Advertiser,* November 16, December 14, 1853).

[86] Cf. Darling, *op. cit.,* 290; *infra,* Table XXVIII.

[87] Cf. Bean, *op. cit.,* 246.

[88] Cf. Billington, *op. cit.,* 380; Bean, *op. cit.,* 226; Desmond, *op. cit.,* 60; Scisco, *op. cit.,* 63 ff., 71 ff.

[89] Pearson, *op. cit.,* I, 65.

[90] Cf. Georg Simmel, "Sociology of Secrecy and of Secret Societies," *American Journal of Sociology,* XI (1906), 446 ff., 489.

[91] Webb to Sumner, July 14, 1854, Sumner Correspondence, XXV, no. 72; cf. also Wilson to Sumner, July 2, 1854, *ibid.,* XXV, no. 12; Bean, *op. cit.,* 192; Harry J. Carman and R. H. Luthin, "Some Aspects of the Know-Nothing Movement Reconsidered," *South Atlantic Quarterly,* XXXIX (1940), 221.

[92] Roe, *loc. cit.,* 653; Haynes, *loc. cit.,* 68; Bean, *op. cit.,* 259 ff.; George H. Haynes, "Know-Nothing Legislature," *New England Magazine,* XVI (1897), 21, 22.

[93] Robinson, *op. cit.,* 219. In Boston, 1,101 voters who had not gone to the polls in 1853 cast their ballots for the Know-Nothings together with the whole coalition reform vote, and almost half the Whig vote.

GUBERNATORIAL VOTES IN BOSTON

	1853	1854
Whig	7,730	4,196
Know-Nothing	....	7,661
Free-Soil	1,403	401
Democrat	2,455	1,252
Hunker Democrat	821	....
	12,409	13,510

(*Boston Atlas, November* 14, 1854; *Boston Semi-Weekly Advertiser,* November 16, 1853).

⁹⁴ Benjamin P. Shillaber, "Experiences during Many Years," *New England Magazine*, VIII (1893), 722; George H. Haynes, "Know-Nothing Legislature," *Annual Report of the American Historical Association . . . 1896* (Washington, 1897), I, 178 ff.; Roe, *loc. cit.*, 654.

⁹⁵ State Street Trust Company, *Mayors of Boston*, 23.

⁹⁶ Cf. Billington, *op. cit.*, 425; Robinson, *op. cit.*, 62, 209, 210; Bean, *op. cit.*, 166, 268, 272–277, 284, 286–288; Merriam, *op. cit.*, I, 126, 132 ff., 164; Haynes, "Know-Nothing Legislature," *Annual Report of the American Historical Association . . . 1896*, I, 180–184; Bean, *loc. cit.*, 322.

⁹⁷ Bean, *op. cit.*, 261.

⁹⁸ Cf. Dissertation Copy, 389; Desmond, *op. cit.*, 77; *Boston Pilot*, May 13, 1854, April 7. May 12, 1855; Abbott, *Immigration*, 160, 161; Billington, *op. cit.*, 414 ff.; Bean, *op. cit.*, 291 ff.; Shea, *op. cit.*, IV, 510.

⁹⁹ Cf. *Debates and Proceedings in the Massachusetts Legislature . . . 1856, Reported for the Boston Daily Advertiser* (Boston, 1856), 141, 343, 348; Bean, *loc. cit.*, 322; Billington, *op. cit.*, 413. Most of these measures were sponsored by the purely nativist branch of the party, which declined in importance after 1854 and left the reformers in complete control (cf. Bean, *op. cit.*, 248). To those overlooking the concrete accomplishments of the 1854 legislature, the Free-Soilers under Wilson seemed to have "captured" the Know-Nothing organization in 1855 (cf., e.g., Haynes, "Causes of Know-Nothing Success," *loc. cit.*, III, 81). In fact, true nativists like Morse had so little sympathy for Massachusetts Know-Nothingism that they charged it was "a Jesuitical ruse, gotten up for the purpose of creating a sympathy in favor of the church" (Morse, *Foreign Conspiracy*, 31).

¹⁰⁰ Cf. Bean, *loc. cit.*, 324 ff.; E. Merton Coulter, *William Brownlow . . .* (Chapel Hill, 1937), 124 ff.; Scisco, *op. cit.*, 137; Carman and Luthin, *loc cit.*, 223.

¹⁰¹ Cf. Billington, *op. cit.*, 407 ff., 426; James Ford Rhodes, *History of the United States . . .* (New York, 1893), II, 89 ff.; Bean, *op. cit.*, 295–

Group Conflict

322, 339 ff.; Mann, *op. cit.,* 50; Scisco, *op. cit.,* 146 ff.; Wilson, *op. cit.,* II, 423 ff.; Merriam, *op. cit.,* I, 165, 173 ff.; cf. also Fred H. Harrington, "Frémont and the North Americans," *American Historical Review,* XLIV (1939), 842 ff.

VOTE IN BOSTON, 1856

Presidential		Gubernatorial	
Frémont (R)	7,646	Gardner (KN)	7,513
Fillmore (KN)	4,320	Gordon (Fillmore KN)	7,511
Buchanan (D)	5,458	Bell (Whig)	1,449
	17,424	Beach (D)	5,392
			16,865

(*Boston Semi-Weekly Advertiser,* November 5, 1856).

102 Cf. Fred H. Harrington, "Nathaniel Prentiss Banks . . . ," *New England Quarterly,* IX (1936), 645 ff. The "straight" American party nominated candidates in 1857 and 1858 but received a meager vote and then expired (Bean, *op. cit.,* 362–365). Gardner's personal popularity helped them in the former year but in the latter they received less than 2,000 votes.

VOTES FOR GOVERNOR IN BOSTON

	1857	1858
Republicans	4,224	6,298
Know-Nothings	4,130	1,899
Democrats	5,171	6,369
	13,525	14,566

(*Boston Semi-Weekly Advertiser,* November 4, 1857; *Boston Daily Courier,* November 3, 1858).

103 Cf. Bean, *op. cit.,* 367–372; Bean, *loc. cit.,* 323; Charles Theo. Russell, *Disfranchisement of Paupers . . .* (Boston, 1878), 8; *Massachusetts House Documents, 1857,* no. 114; *ibid., 1859,* no. 34.

104 Cf., e.g., the petition of the residents of Elm Street (Bean, *op. cit.,* 206).

105 Cf. Ernest Bruncken, *German Political Refugees in the United States . . .* (s.l., 1904), 45 ff.

106 Cf. the illuminating report of Consul Grattan to Crampton, Boston, November 23, 1855, British Embassy Archives, F.O. 115/160; also Rowcroft to Crampton, November 12, 1855, *ibid.,* F.O. 115/160.

107 Cf. Grattan to Crampton, January 21, 1856, *ibid.,* F.O. 115/172; Grattan to Crampton, March 4, 1856, *ibid.,* F.O. 115/172; Abbott, *Historical Aspects,* 475, 476; *Citizen* (New York), August 25, 1855, February 9, 1856.

357

[108] Lousada to Russell, September 8, 1864, British Consular Correspondence, F. O. 5/973.

[109] Cf. Jeremiah O'Donovan-Rossa, *Rossa's Recollections* . . . (Mariner's Harbor, N. Y., 1898), 271, 272, 381; "Proceedings . . . ," British Consular Correspondence, F.O. 5/973; E. Wells to Lousada, *ibid.*, F.O. 5/973; *Boston Pilot*, November 21, 1863.

[110] Cf. Bean, *op. cit.*, 257.

[111] Cf. references to *Irish-American* and *Boston Pilot*, 1856–1860, Dissertation Copy, 397, ns. 301–303; *Boston Pilot*, November 3, 1860; *Boston Post*, November 7, 1860.

[112] Cf., e.g., "The Anglo-Saxon Race," *North American Review*, LXXIII (1851), 53, 34 ff.

[113] *Springfield Daily Republican*, July 10, 1857.

Chapter VIII. An Appearance of Stability

[1] Quoted from Ralph Waldo Emerson by Ralph Henry Gabriel, *Course of American Democratic Thought* . . . (New York, 1940), 45.

[2] Henry Greenleaf Pearson, *Life of John A. Andrew Governor of Massachusetts 1861–1865* (Boston, 1904), I, 205.

[3] Cf. Dissertation Copy, 400.

[4] Cf. William G. Bean, Party Transformation in Massachusetts with Special Reference to the Antecedents of Republicanism . . . (MS., H. C. L.), 370.

[5] Cf. *Der Pionier*, August 13, 1862.

[6] James Donnelly, "Song to Colonel Corcoran," *Boston Pilot*, July 20, 1861.

[7] Cf. Marcus Lee Hansen, *Immigrant in American History* . . . (Cambridge, 1940), 143.

[8] Cf. Edward Dicey, *Six Months in the Federal States* (London, 1863), II, 280 ff.

[9] Cf. James Bernard Cullen, *Story of the Irish in Boston* . . . (Boston, 1890), 105–107; Daniel George Macnamara, *History of the Ninth Regiment* . . . (Boston, 1899), 4, 5; *Massachusetts Soldiers, Sailors, and Marines in the Civil War, Compiled . . . by the Adjutant General* (Norwood, 1931), I, 616; Dissertation Copy, 403, 404.

[10] Cf. William Schouler, *History of Massachusetts in the Civil War* (Boston, 1868), I, 230; *Massachusetts Soldiers, Sailors, and Marines . . .* , I, 616, 617; F. Spencer Baldwin, "What Ireland . . . ," *New England Magazine*, XXIV (1901), 80, 82.

[11] Cf. Charles William Folsom, Diary, 1861–1864 (MS., B. P. L.), III, March 17, 1863; *ibid.*, IV, March 17, 1864.

[12] Robert Ferguson, *America during and after the War* (London, 1866), 109, 110.

[13] Cf. the lists in *Municipal Register Containing the City Charter . . . 1866* (Boston, 1866), 58 ff., 105 ff., 173–184; also, *Massachusetts Senate Documents, 1861,* no. 2, p. 23; *ibid.,* no. 102; *Der Pionier,* May 23, 1861.

[14] *Boston Pilot,* July 27, 1861.

[15] *Boston Pilot,* February 1, 1862; "Report of the School Committee, 1863," *Boston City Documents, 1864,* no. 50, p. 42.

[16] "Proceedings at the Dedication of the City Hospital," *Boston City Documents, 1865,* no. 55, p. 95.

[17] Cf. *Boston Pilot,* September 6, 1862; John Tasker Howard, *Our American Music . . .* (New York, 1939), 583.

[18] Table XXXIII; Hamilton A. Hill, *Immigration* (Boston, 1875), 3 ff.; Hamilton A. Hill, *The Present Condition and Character of the Immigration Movement* (Boston, 1876), 4 ff.

[19] Table XXX; Carroll D. Wright, *Census of Massachusetts, 1875* (Boston, 1876), I, 302–303; U. S. Tenth Census, *Population* (Washington, 1883), I, 471; Rowland T. Berthoff, *British Immigrants in Industrial America 1790–1950* (Cambridge, 1953), 83.

[20] Table XXIX; U. S. Tenth Census, *Population,* I, 419, 420; John Daniels, *In Freedom's Birthplace* (Boston, 1914), 85 ff., 140 ff., 458.

[21] Daniels, *op. cit.,* 94, 99 ff., 103, 145.

[22] Wright, *Census of Massachusetts, 1875,* I, 279–282; U. S. Tenth Census, *Population,* I, 477–479, 536–537.

[23] Hamilton A. Hill, *An Inquiry into the Relation of Immigration to Pauperism* (Boston, 1876), 12, 13; Hill, *Immigration,* 8 ff.; Table XXXIII; Wright, *Census of Massachusetts, 1875,* I, 293–294.

[24] Table XXIX; Wright, *Census of Massachusetts, 1875,* I, 279–282; U. S. Tenth Census, *Population,* I, 419, 420, 450 ff., 477–479.

[25] Wright, *Census of Massachusetts, 1875,* I, XXIX, XXX; U. S. Tenth Census, *Social Statistics of Cities* (Washington, 1886), I, 113 ff.; Frederick A. Bushee, "Growth of the Population of Boston," American Statistical Association, *Publications,* XLVI (1898–99), 260 ff.

[26] *Boston City Documents, 1879,* no. 73; U.S. Tenth Census, *Social Statistics of Cities,* I, 106–107; Harold Murdock, ed., *Letters from a Gentleman in Boston to His Friend in Paris Describing the Great Fire* (Boston, 1909).

[27] U. S. Ninth Census, *Wealth and Industry* (Washington, 1872), III, 528, 677, 678; Wright, *Census of Massachusetts, 1875,* I, 551–555, II, 85 ff., 136 ff., 142, 350–352, 768, 857; U. S. Tenth Census, *Manufactures* (Washington, 1883), II, xxiv ff., 259–263, 379, 385–386, 390, 438; U. S. Tenth Census, *Social Statistics of Cities,* I, 159 ff.

[28] Wright, *Census of Massachusetts, 1875,* II, 843, 901; U. S. Tenth Census, *Social Statistics of Cities,* I, 150 ff.; E. C. Kirkland, *Men, Cities, and Transportation* (Cambridge, 1948), I, 362 ff.

[29] U. S. Tenth Census, *Social Statistics of Cities,* I, 115.

[30] U. S. Tenth Census, *Social Statistics of Cities,* I, 111.

[31] U. S. Tenth Census, *Social Statistics of Cities,* I, 131 ff.

[32] U. S. Ninth Census, *Population* (Washington, 1872), I, 599; U. S. Ninth Census, *Vital Statistics* (Washington, 1872), II, 483, 502; Wright, *Census of Massachusetts, 1875,* I, xliii, xliv; U. S. Tenth Census, *Mortality and Vital Statistics* (Washington, 1885), XI, xxi, 501 ff., XII, 442–443, 444–445; U. S. Tenth Census, *Social Statistics of Cities,* I, 119; J. S. Potter, *Past, Present and Future of Boston* (Boston, 1873), 42 ff.; Carroll D. Wright, *An Analysis of the Population of the City of Boston* (Boston, 1885), 14, 15; Hill, *Present Condition of Immigration,* 12 ff.; Hill, *Inquiry,* 14 ff.

[33] U. S. Ninth Census, *Population,* I, 415, 440; Wright, *Census of Massachusetts, 1875,* I, liii; U. S. Tenth Census, *Social Statistics of Cities,* I, 137–139.

[34] Cf., for example, *Boston Pilot,* August 10, 1861, June 21, 1862.

[35] Barbara M. Solomon, *Ancestors and Immigrants* (Cambridge, 1956), 46.

[36] Cf. Lewis Hayden, *Grand Lodge Jurisdictional Claim . . .* (Boston, 1868), 50; Dissertation Copy, 408; *Boston City Documents, 1863,* no. 75; *ibid., 1864,* no. 6, pp. 31–34; Edith E. Ware, *Political Opinion in Massachusetts during the Civil War and Reconstruction* (New York, 1916), 103.

[37] Table XXX; U. S. Ninth Census, *Population* (Washington, 1872), I, 778; *Boston Pilot,* October 13, 1877.

[38] *Boston Pilot,* March 23, 1878, September 20, 1879.

[39] *Boston Pilot,* November 29, 1873. Cf. also Wright, *Census of Massachusetts, 1875,* II, 358, 825.

[40] *Boston Pilot,* May 1, 1876, June 23, 1877.

[41] James B. Cullen, *Story of the Irish in Boston* (Boston, 1890), 229 ff.; Joseph V. Donahoe and Michael J. Jordan, "Patrick Donahoe," American Irish Historical Society, *Journal,* XXIII (1924), 127 ff.

[42] *Boston Pilot,* April 28, 1876.

[43] Table XXXII.

[44] Robert H. Lord, John E. Sexton, and Edward T. Harrington, *History of the Archdiocese of Boston* (New York, 1944), III, 6 ff., 53 ff.; John E. Sexton and Arthur J. Riley, *History of Saint John's Seminary Brighton* (Boston, 1945), 51 ff.

[45] O'Reilly to Edward Whipple, March 20, 1878.

[46] *Boston Herald,* June 2, 6, 1866; *Boston Transcript,* June 6, 1866. Cf. in general, *supra,* 209; Henri Le Caron (pseud. of Thomas M. Beach),

Twenty-Five Years in the Secret Service (London, 1892); William D'Arcy, *The Fenian Movement in the United States: 1858–1886* (Washington, 1947).

[47] James Jeffrey Roche, *Life of John Boyle O'Reilly* (New York, 1891), 115 ff., 143; Carl Wittke, *The Irish in America* (Baton Rouge, 1956), 150 ff.

[48] Cf., for example, Arthur Mann, "Solomon Schindler," *New England Quarterly*, XXIII (1950), 457.

[49] Barbara M. Solomon, *Pioneers in Service. The History of the Associated Jewish Philanthropies of Boston* (Boston, 1956), 6 ff.

[50] Daniel L. Marsh, *Founders of Boston University* (Boston, 1932), 9 ff.; H. E. Scudder, *Henry Oscar Houghton* (Cambridge, 1897).

[51] Cf. *infra*, n. 74.

[52] Table XXX; U. S. Tenth Census, *Social Statistics of Cities*, I, 115.

[53] Berthoff, *op. cit.*, 158, 178, 191, 193.

[54] Table XXXII; William B. Whiteside, *The Boston Y.M.C.A. and Community Need; A Century's Evolution, 1851–1951* (New York, 1951), 63 ff.

[55] Cf., for example, Mary B. Claflin, *Under the Old Elms* (New York, 1895), 33–34; Scudder, *op. cit.*, 89–90.

[56] Arthur Mann, *Yankee Reformers in the Urban Age* (Cambridge, 1954), 7 ff.

[57] Solomon, *Ancestors and Immigrants*, 11, 13, 15, 21, 25 ff.; Alfred D. Chandler, *Annexation of Brookline* (Brookline, 1880).

[58] Julia Ward Howe, *Is Polite Society Polite* (Boston, 1895), 12–14; John T. Morse, Jr., *Life and Letters of Oliver Wendell Holmes* (Boston, 1896), II, 169.

[59] Table XXXII. Cf. also Alexander V. G. Allen, *Life and Letters of Phillips Brooks* (New York, 1900), I, 621 ff., II, 9, 26, 92; Morse, *Holmes*, I, 281; Solomon, *Ancestors and Immigrants*, 45; Timothy L. Smith, *Revivalism and Social Reform* (New York, 1957), 100 ff.

[60] *Boston Pilot*, July 7, 1877.

[61] Lord, Sexton, and Harrington, *op. cit.*, II, 719 ff.

[62] M. P. Curran, *Life of Patrick A. Collins* (Norwood, 1906).

[63] *Boston Pilot*, May 20, 1876, June 30, 1877, March 8, 1879; Roche, *op. cit.*, 142.

[64] Roche, *op. cit.*, 101 ff.

[65] Mann, *Yankee Reformers*, 24 ff.

[66] *Boston Pilot*, November 24, 1877, October 26, 1878.

[67] *Boston Pilot*, August 11, 1877, August 17, 1878, February 28, 1880.

[68] *Boston Pilot*, May 3, 1876, February 17, 24, 1877, January 19, 1878, June 29, July 6, 13, August 17, 1878, March 29, 1880; Roche, *op. cit.*, 185.

[69] *Boston Pilot,* August 4, 11, 25, 1877.

[70] *Boston Pilot,* November 7, 1880.

[71] Curran, *Collins,* 37.

[72] Patrick A. Collins, *Speech in support of Charles Francis Adams for Governor of Massachusetts, Delivered at Marlboro, Massachusetts on September 14, 1876* (Boston, 1876); Roche, *op. cit.,* 128, 129.

[73] "Speech of Henry Cabot Lodge on Immigration," 60 Cong., Sess., *Sen. Doc. No. 423,* p. 3.

[74] James Parton, "Our Roman Catholic Brethren," *Atlantic Monthly,* XXI (1868), 433 ff. Rejoinder in *Zion's Herald,* May 28, August 13, September 10, 24, 1868. Lord, *et. al., op. cit.,* III, 66.

[75] *Boston Pilot,* October 7, 1876.

[76] *Boston Herald,* December 5, 6, 1925; Benjamin F. Butler, *Butler's Book* (Boston, 1892), 967 ff.; Cullen, *op. cit.,* 216 ff.; Solomon, *op. cit.,* 47 ff.; Oscar Sherwin, *Prophet of Liberty the Life and Times of Wendell Phillips* (New York, 1958), 586 ff.

[77] Hamilton A. Hill, *et. al., Arguments in Favor of the Freedom of Immigration* (Boston, 1871); Dr. Nathan Allen, "Statement," Massachusetts Board of State Charities, *Third Annual Report* (Boston, 1867), 31; Hamilton A. Hill, "Immigration," National Conference of Charities and Correction, *Proceedings 1875* (Boston, 1875), 92–96; "Report of the Committee on Immigration," National Conference of Charities and Correction, *Proceedings 1881* (Boston, 1881), 218–227; Solomon, *op. cit.,* 43. For differential fertility data, cf. Wright, *Census of Massachusetts, 1875,* I, xlii, xliii, 408–422.

Index

Index

Balls, 23, 156
Balzac, Honoré de, 146
Bancroft, George, 13, 23, 146
Bancroft's Grove, 156
Bank of the United States, 8
Bankers, 67
Banking, 8, 9
Banks, N. P., 194, 204
Banquets, 155, 157, 340
Baptists, 175, 183, 199, 220, 349
Barbers, 63, 70
Barry, John, 145
Bars, 66, 96, 121
Bartenders, 66
Bartlett, J. S., 172–73
Basements. *See* Cellars
Batterymarch Street, 114
Bavaria: emigration from, 34, 310; peasants of, 33
Bay State Artillery, 157, 203
Bay State Iron Company, 80
Beach, E. D., 357
Beach Street, 109
Beacon Hill, 13, 15, 96, 116
Beacon Hill Light, 13
Beacon's Grove, 156
Bean, W. G., 354
Beck, Karl, 29, 146
Bedini, Gaetano, 198
Beecher, Lyman, 181, 182, 186
Beethoven, L. van, 148
Beggars, 118, 310
Belknap Street, 96
Bell, 357
Benevolent Fraternity of Churches, 164, 170
Benevolent societies, 59, 160, 161
Berkeley Street, 169
Berliner National-Zeitung, 170–171
Bible, 128, 169, 211
Bierhaus, 155
Bigelow, J. R., 78
Bigelow, John P., 76, 120
Billington, R. A., 350
Birth rate, 117, 228
Bishop, Robert, and Company, 80
Black Ball Line, 49, 299

Black Warrior case, 141
Blighted areas. *See* Slums
Bloomerism, 135. *See also* Women's rights
Board of Health, 16
Board of Overseers, 19
Board of Selectmen, 17, 23, 122
Boarding houses, 71, 96, 101
Bologna, 198
Bøndar. *See* Peasants
Bookkeepers, 67
Boott, Kirk, 82
Boston Academy of Music, 148
Boston and Chelsea Railroad, 100
Boston and Lowell Railroad, 98
Boston Catholic Observer, 137, 173, 190
Boston City Guards, 190
Boston City Hospital, 211
Boston College, 169
Boston Courier, 182
Boston Debating Society, 182
Boston Dispensary, 115
Boston Gregorian Society, 170
Boston Irish Protestant Association, 350
Boston Laborers Association, 160
Boston Merkur, 172
Boston Pilot, 72, 143, 150, 176, 198, 203; after *1865,* 216, 222, 224, 225; history of, 173, 174, 175; on constitutional reform, 196, 197; on revolution, 137, 140, 141
Boston Post, 202
Boston Repeal Association, 315. *See also* Repeal movement
Boston Rubber Shoe Company, 80
Boston School Board, 211
Boston Scottish Society, 155
"Boston System," 76
Boston Vindicator, 174
Bostoner Zeitung, 172
Bostonien, 171
Bounties, 209, 310
Boutwell, G. S., 195, 353
Brahmins, 177, 220, 221, 222, 224, 227
Brass foundries, 79

364

Index

Brazil, 142
Bread Street, 110
Bread trade, 2
Brewing industry, 83
Brickmakers, 187
Bridges, 13, 89, 98
Brighton, 14, 100, 166; annexed, 214
Brillat-Savarin, J. A., 28
British Charitable Society, 161
British Colonial Society, 155
British North Americans, 52, 57, 155, 212, 220, 227, 318. See also Canada; and by province
Broad Street, 107, 108, 112, 113, 116, 117
Broad Street Riot, 187
Broadway Railroad, 99
Brookline, 14, 100, 166, 221
Brownson, O. A., 130, 173, 206, 333, 334, 336, 337; and the Irish, 149, 150; on constitutional revision, 196, 197; on revolution, 137, 139
Brownson's Quarterly Review, 149
Buchanan, James, 206, 357
Buffalo, 174
Buffalo Convention, 159
Building trades, 63, 318, 322
Bulfinch's Pillar, 13
Bunker Hill, 183, 187
Burgess Alley, 108, 114
Burns, Anthony, 175, 198
Burschenschaft, 27
Business district, 91
Butchers, 65
Butler, Benjamin F., 198, 227

Cabinet making, 64
Cahill, Dr. W., 60
Calderon de la Barca, Mme., 336, 337
Caledonian Club, 156
California, 4, 225
Calvert Naturalization Society, 197
Calvin, John, 144
Cambridge, 14, 15, 80, 96, 98, 166, 189; immigrants in, 212; Negroes in, 213
Cambridgeport, 89

Canada, 38, 159, 169, 212, 218, 298. See also British North Americans; Emigration
Canadian fraternal societies, 155–156
Canals, 6
Canton, 4
Carney, Andrew, 162
Carney and Sleeper, 82
Carpentry. See Building trades
Carroll, Charles, 145
Carroll, John, 165, 180
Cass, Thomas, 210
Casting furnaces, 79
Castle Island, 157
Catenoni, 310
Cathedral, 218
Catholic Church, abstinence societies, 169–170; activities against, 144, 187, 188, 199, 200; and abolition, 133; and Civil War, 208, 209; and common schools, 135, 136; and Irish ideas, 128, 129, 130; and Irish nationalism, 205, 206; and prison reform, 134; and reform, 133, 134, 135; and revolution, 137–141; and temperance, 134; and women's rights, 135; attitude to, in Boston, 180, 181, 182, 185, 186, 199, 215; charities, 161–163; churches in Boston, 164–167, 199, 217, 218, 227; conservatism, 133, 139, 141, 142; colleges, 169; French in, 164, 165, 166; Germans in, 158, 166, 167; in England, 186; Irish in, 128, 129, 130, 164, 165, 166, 223; laws against, 38; literature against, 189, 199, 200; newspapers, 172, 173, 174, 175; newspapers against, 181, 187, 189; on intermarriage, 176; prejudice against, 180–182, 190, 198, 203; schools, 167, 168, 169. See also Irish immigrants; Know-Nothing Party
Catholic Union, 223
Causeway Street, 93
Cellars, 109, 110
Cemetery, 187

365

Index

366

Index

Index

DuLang, 69
Duruissel, 68
Dwight's Journal of Music, 148
Dysentery, 115

East Boston, 10, 13, 14, 18, 99, 100, 114, 152; churches, 166, 167; ferry, 13, 18, 89, 100; industries, 10, 78–80
East Boston Company, 100
East Cambridge, 14, 98, 159, 166
Eastburn, Manton, 186
Eastern Railroad, 50, 179
Education, 22, 135, 136, 142, 167, 168, 169, 175, 196. *See also* Schools
Elections, 196; constitutional convention, 196; gubernatorial, 193, 196, 200–204, 355, 356, 357; municipal, 190, 200; presidential, 204
Ellie, 351
Ellie Moore, 334
Elm Street, 357
Emancipation Proclamation, 216
Emerson, R. W., 21, 22, 143, 207, 358
Emigrants. *See* by nativity
Emigration: assisted, 30, 37, 44, 51; economic, 29 ff.; from Baden, 34, 37; from Bavaria, 34, 310; from Boston, 12, 53; from Canada, 27; from England, 30, 32, 51; from Europe, 26 ff., 51; from France, 27, 28; from Germany, 27, 28, 30, 34, 35–38, 51; from Hungary, 27, 28; from Ireland, 27, 28, 31, 32, 42, 43, 46–51; from Italy, 27, 28; from Poland, 27; from Scandinavia, 33, 34; from West Indies, 28; Negro, 53, 212; of artisans, 30, 31, 32; peasant, 32–36, 46–51; political, 27 ff.; Scotch-Irish, 43; sporadic, 26
Employment, search for, 55, 59, 60
Enclosures, 32
Engineers, 68
England, John, 333
England: agriculture in, 32; and Civil War, 209; Boston attitude to, 124, 220, 222, 224, 225; Catholicism in,

186; clothing industry in, 322; consuls of, in Boston, 159; immigration to, 27, 28, 42, 43; industry in, 30; influence of, 23, 124; Irish hatred of, 143, 152, 153, 205, 209; oppression by, 38, 39, 152; trade laws, 2, 3; trade with, 3, 7. *See also* Emigration
English immigrants, 26, 213; and Civil War, 208; benevolent societies, 161; coffee houses, 66; dancers, 68; distribution of, 91; ideas, 136, 146; merchants, 68, 82; musicians, 69, 147, 148; nationalism, 151; newspapers, 171; number of, 52; seamstresses, 81; tailors, 322
English words, 163, 164
Enoch Train and Company, 49
Episcopal Church, 186, 222
Erie Canal, 6
Erina Association, 156
Europe: influence of, 22, 23; population of, 29. *See also* Emigration
European, 171
Everett, Edward, 189, 200
Evictions, 44, 46
Exclusion laws, 119. *See also* Restrictions
Expostulator, 172

Factory system, 10, 11. *See also* Mechanization of industry
Faith, 128, 131
Fall River, 7, 9
Famine, 43, 45, 152, 153
Faneuil Hall, 189
Farmers, 39. *See also* Peasants
Farmhands, 42. *See also* Peasants
Father Mathew Total Abstinence Society, 170
Father Wiget's, 169
Felton and Sons, 80
Fenian Brotherhood, 140, 141, 206, 209, 218, 223, 224
Fenwick, B. J., 137, 159, 165, 167, 169, 172, 181, 187
Ferguson, Robert, 359

368

Index

Ferries, 13, 18, 89, 100
Fertility, 117
Feuillants, 27
Fifty-Fourth Massachusetts Regiment, 179
Filibusters, 142
Fillmore, Millard, 204
Finance. *See* Banking
Fire, Charlestown Convent, 187, 188, 189; Duane Street, 18; of 1872, 214
Fire companies, 187
Fire Department, 18
Fishing, 2, 11
Fitzgerald, Edward, 27
Fitzgerald, J. R., 174
Fitzpatrick, J. B., and *Boston Catholic Observer*, 173, 174; and *Boston Pilot*, 140; and Brownson, 149; and Catholic churches, 165, 166; bust of, 202; Harvard degree to, 210, 211; letter on Irish famine, 152; on constitutional revision, 197; on revolution, 137
Follen, Carl, 29, 146
Food Dealers, 65
Forges, 79
Fort Hill, 13, 15; churches, 166; death rate, 116; Irish in, 93, 94, 100; saloons, 121; sewerage, 111; tenements, 107, 108, 109, 112
Fort Sumter, 207
Forty-shilling freeholders, 42, 44
Foster's Law, 41, 42
Foundries, 79
France, 22, 23, 27, 169. *See also* Emigration
Franklin Square, 102
Fraternal societies, 155, 156
Fraternity of Churches. *See* Benevolent Fraternity of Churches
Free Soil Party, 193–197, 200, 207, 355, 356
Free Trade, 225
Freedom of religion, 129
Freedom Party, 200
Freedom's Journal, 175
Freeman's Journal, 138

Frémont, J. C., 204
French immigrants, 26, 28; and Civil War, 208; Catholics, 164, 165, 166; cooks, 28, 66; cultural groups, 170; dancers, 68; distribution of, 91; hairdressers, 63; hotels, 66; Huguenots, 177; ideas, 136, 146; merchants, 67; musicians, 69; nationalism, 151; newspapers, 146, 171; number, 52
French language, 164
French Revolution, 22, 27, 141
Friends of Ireland Society, 152
Friends Street Court, 104
Frothingham, C. W., 200
Fruiterers, 65
Fugitive Slave Law, 194
Fugitive slaves, 53, 175, 179, 198, 199, 202
Fuller, Margaret, 141
Funerals, 187
Fur trade. *See* China trade
Furniture building, 64

Gabriel, Angel, 199
Gallieni, 66
Galway, 51
Gannett, Ezra, 23
Garbage collection, 17, 111
Gardner, H. J., 201, 204
Garibaldi, Giuseppe, 141
Garment district, 93
Garret bosses, 73
Garrison, W. L., 172
Gaston, William, 225
Gate of Heaven Church, 166
Gavazzi, Alessandro, 198
Gazette Française, 171
General Court. *See* Legislature
Geography of Boston, 91
German Assistance Society, 161
German Charitable Society, 161
German immigrants, 26, 28; and Civil War, 207, 208; and Irish, 145; and reform, 136; after *1865*, 219; balls, 156; benevolent societies, 161; birth rate, 117; boarding houses, 65, 66;

369

Index

Index

373

Index

Index

Index

Index

Index

Salvation, 127
Sandwich Islands. *See* Hawaii
Sardinia. *See* Italy
Sargeant, L. M., 328
Sarsfield Guards, 157, 199
Sarsfield Union Association, 157
Savings banks, 217
Saxony, 33
Scandinavia, 33. *See also* Emigration
Scandinavian Benevolent Relief Society, 160
Scandinavian immigrants, benevolent societies, 160; number, 52, 213
Schools, 167–169, 170, 175, 178, 179, 190, 202, 211, 217, 221. *See also* Common schools
Schutzenverein Germania, 156
Scollay Square, 94
Scotch immigrants, 26; and Civil War, 208; assimilation, 177; fraternal societies, 155, 156; newspapers, 171; number, 52
Scotch-Irish, 145, 146; emigration, 43
Scotch-Irish immigrants, 26; assimilation, 177; brickmakers, 188
Scotland, immigration, 43
Scots Charitable Society, 155, 157, 160
Scottish-American, 171
Seamen, 64, 70, 186
Seamstresses, 81, 82
Seaver, Nathaniel, 200
Second generation, 216
Secrecy, Know-Nothing, 201, 204
Secret ballots, 196
Selectmen. *See* Board of Selectmen
Selectmen, Charlestown, 187
Seminary, theological, 169, 218
Senate, Massachusetts, 353
Senatorship, U. S., 194, 202
Servants, 61, 62, 83, 186
Service trades, 62, 63
Sewerage, 17, 109–112, 114, 115, 215
Sewing, 81, 82
Sewing machine, 76, 80
Shadrach, 175
Shakespeare, William, 142

Shales and May Furniture Company, 80
Shamrock, 172
Shamrock Society, 155, 157
Shattuck, Lemuel, 89, 109, 325
Shawmut Street, 99, 164, 167
Shillaber, B. P., 356
Shipbuilding, 10, 80
Shipping firms, 184
Shoe industry, 7, 10, 11, 73, 80
Shooting, 156
Shopkeepers. *See* Merchants
Silversmiths, 83
Simmons, George, 77
Simmons, John, 75
Sisters of Charity, 162
Sisters of Notre Dame de Namur, 168
Six Months in a Convent, 189
Slave trade, 3
Slavery, 3. *See also* Abolition
Slaves, fugitive, 53, 175, 179, 198, 202
Sleeper, Jacob, 219
Slops, 75
Slums, 13, 89, 93, 100–114
Smallpox, 16, 114
Smith, Abiel, 175
Smith, J. V. C., 67, 202
Smiths, 63
Smuggling, 2
Socialism, 2
Societa italiana di benevolenza, 160
Societies. *See* Abstinence societies; Benevolent societies; Charitable societies; Fraternal societies; Immigrant aid societies
Society of Jesus, 169, 348
Society of St. Vincent de Paul, 163
Society of United Irishmen, 27
Solo-Club, 170
Somerville, 14, 98
South, Know-Nothings in, 204
South America, 37
South Boston, 13, 14, 15, 89, 98, 99, 161, 162; churches, 165; industries, 78, 80, 86; repeal movement in, 152; schools, 168

Index

Index

Index

Women, employment of, 61; in industry, 11, 72, 73, 81, 82; property rights, 195
Women's clothing industry, 81, 82
Women's rights, 135
Women's rights law, 202
Woodbridge, W. C., 148
Woodbury, C. L., 226
Woolen industry. *See* Textile industry
Worcester, 204
Worcester Spy, 199
Workhouses, 44. *See also* Almshouses
Württemberg, 33

Yankees, 213, 219–222, 227, 228. *See also* New England
Young, Arthur, 131
Young Catholics Friend, 346
Young Catholics Friend Society, 168, 170
Young Ireland, 137, 138, 140, 153, 173
Young Italy, 138
Young Men's League, 355

Zerrahn, Carl, 148
Zeuner, Charles, 69, 148
Zion Church, 164